Great Educators of the World

Great Educators of the World

RAMNATH SHARMA
D.Phil. D.Litt.

First Edition - 2004

ISBN No. : 81-88817-18-X

Published by **SPRING BOOKS**
410, A.K.D. Towers, Sec-14, Gurgaon-122 001. Haryana - India

Printed in India at
EFFICIENT OFFSET PRINTERS
215, Shahzadabagh Indl. Complex, Phase-II, Delhi-110 035.

PREFACE

Selection of great educators for this books has been made both from West and East. Among Western educationists, great thinkers have been drawn not only from European countries but also from U.S.A. Besides, thinkers have been drawn from the ancient, medieval and modern times. Thus, this volume includes educational thought of Plato; Aristotle; Ignatious Loyola; John Amos Comenius; John Locke; John Henrich Pestalozzi; Jean Jacques Rousseau; John Friedrich Herbart; Friedrich August Froebel; Maria Montessori and John Dewey from the West.

Among educators from the East, those thinkers have been selected who were not only deeply ingrained in Indian educational thought but also had first hand knowledge of Western educational thought and system. This has made their educational thought enlightening to educationists all over the world. These include Swami Vivekananda, Sri Aurobindo, Mohandas Karam Chand Gandhi, Rabindranath Tagore, Sarvepalli Radhakrishnan and Manabendra Nath Roy.

In the present days of educational upheaval all over the world, the study of these great educators will undoubtedly help in clearing issues and finding out solutions.

With material drawn from anthentic original works of each of the above mentioned great educationists, arranged under suitable headings, each chapter has been planned to provide a complete and brief picture of the educational philosophy of each great educationist along with its epstemological meta physical and social background. Thus the book is bound to evoke interest in the minds of educationists in all the countries of the world. Incidentally, it lays down the blue print for a universal philosophy of education.

Ram Nath Sharma

CONTENT

CONTENT

1

Plato

"Athens is a looking glass, into which the Western World became conscious of its philosophic problems." —**Dewey**

Ever since knowledge dawned in human mind man has been thinking about problems : ontological, epistemological, eschatological and axiological. The questions of philosophy in the beginning of human knowledge, were everywhere mixed with psychological problems. Thus, psychology, in the beginning, was concerned with the nature of the mind and the processes of consciousness. As men lived in small groups and the society was generally confined to a particular village, the solutions offered were very simple. There were hardly any distinctions between social and political problems as the political institutions were developed as a means to social welfare. Therefore, most of the ancient thinkers did not distinguish between social philosophy and political philosophy. As the life was simple and social stratification and differentiation was not complex the thinkers offered solutions working in more than one field of knowledge. Most of the thinkers were teachers and men of education who used to pass their life completely free from worldy affairs. The state and the society gencrally extended support to these scholars and they were generally respected and followed. The job of instruction and education of younger generation was generally entrusted to these men of letters. The state provided finance but not interfered in the process of education. These great teachers formed their own personal discourses and learning through their lives. In this way, society was generally governed by the teachings of these great scholars, though the administrative machinery was almost everywhere in the hands of the state.

BIOGRAPHICAL SKETCH

Plato was born in 427 B.C. the son of noble parents. According to Trabing he first studied music, poetry, paintint, and philosophy with other maters and became a pupil of Socrates in 407 B.C., remaining with him until the latter's death (399 B.C.) when he accompanied Socrates to Mega. He is said to have travelled in Egypt and Asia Minor, to have visited Italy and the Pythogoreans (388 B.C) and to have lived for a time at the court of Dionysius I, the tyrant of Syiracuse, who became his enemy and sold him into salavery as a prisoner of war: but all of these storeis have been denied. He founded a school in the groves of Academus, the Academy, where he taught mathematics and the different branches of philosophy, by means of connected lectures and the dialogue. The story goes that he interupted his work on two occasions (367 B.C. and 361 B.C.), by further visites to Syracuse, presumably in 7the hope of assisting in the realisation of his ideal State, and that he was disappointed in this hope. His death occurred in 347 B.C.

The life of Plato can be divided into three ages. In the first age he received the education from his great master Socrates besides some other minor teachers. He lived with Socrates for eight years and received intstruction and ideas in different fields of human thought. After the death of Socrates, perturbed as he was Plato went on his journey through Egypt, Cyrene, Italy and Cicley etc. For ten years he was roaming in different countries, observing their ways of life, social and political structures and institutions and discussing with scholars of different countries. It was in this age that he planned his important dialogues. During this period Plato's thinking was generally centred around ideas, the universals. The dialogues written during this period do not exhibit much literary excellence. The important dialogues written during this period were *Gorgias, Theatetus, Sophistes, Statesman and Parmenides.*

After ten years of journey in different countries Plato's mind was almost settled. He now returned to Athens and started third and the most important age of his life. He established an institution known as Academy or Gymnasium. Here he started to live as a teacher, a mathematician and a philosopher. For 40 years he educated hundreds of illustrious disciples and created dozens of dialogues upto his death at the age of 82.

WORKS OF PLATO[1]

It seems unlikely that all of Plato's works have come down to us. Of the writings transmitted under his name (35 Dialogues, 13 letters), most of the Letters and some of the Dialogues are considerd to be spurious, although it seems likely that several of the Letters including the philosophically important seventh letter, are genuine.

Chronological Order of Work

Attempts have been made by many scholars to arrange the dialogues in chronological order. One method of ordering them employs the criterion of relative maturity of philosophical doctrine, but this method has produced very different orderings by different scholars. A method which has in recent year proved very useful is the ordering of the dialogues in acordance with stylometric considerations, adopting as a standard the style and vocabulary of *The Laws*, which is universally accepted as the latest of the dialogues. Sir David Ross, after summarising the results of these stylistic and linguistic investigations suggests the following probable order of the Platonic dialogues :

1. **First Period** (before 389–388B.C.): Charmiders, Laches, Enthyphro, Hippias Major, and Meno.
2. **Second Period** (between 389–388 B.C. and 361–366 BC): Cratylus (date doubtful). Symposium 385 B.C. or later), Phaedo, Republic, Phaedrus, Parmenides, Theaetetus (369 B.C. or later).
3. **Third Period** (between 367–366 B.C. and 361–360 B.C.): Sophistes, Politicus:

---

1. **Taylor, *Plato : The Man and His Work, Chapt. 1.***

4. Fourth Period (after 361–360 B.C.) : Timaeus, Critias, Philebus, Seventh Letter (353–352 B.C.), Laws. (Plato's Theory of Ides, Ch. I.)

This list does not include those of the earlier dialogues which throw little or no light on Plato's Theory of ideas : the Apology, Crito, Lysis, Protagoras, Gorgias and Euthydemus.

Spurious Dialogues

Among the thirty five dialogues the following are now generally rejected as spurious : Alcibiades I and Alcibiades II Epinomis, Anteras, Hippachus, Theages, Minos, Cleitophro, Io, and Menexenus. Many scholars have questioned the genuineness of Hippias Major.

Translation and Commentaries

The following is the list of important translations and commentaries on Plato's dialogues :

1. *The Dialogues of Plato,* trans by B. Jowet, 3rd ed. 5 vols., 1892;
2. Jowett trans. of *The dialogues of Plato* with an Introduction by R. Demos, 2 vols, 1937;
3. *Thirteen Epistles,* trans. by L.A. Post, 1925;
4. A.E. Taylor, *Plato : Timaeus, and Critias,* 1929 and *The Laws of Plato,* 1934;
5. J. Woward, *The Platonic Episteles,* 1932;
6. F.M. Cornford, *Plato and Parmenides* 1939;
7. Plato's Cosmology, 1937; *Plato's Theory of Knowledge* 1935;
8. G.R. Morrow, *Studies in the Platonic Epistles,* 1935;
9. A.E. Taylor, *Commentary on Plato's Times,* 1928;
10. *R. Hackforth Plato's Examination of Pleasure:* A Translation of the Philebus, 1945, and Plato's Phaedrus, 1952;
11. *The Republic, trans.* by F.M. Cornford, 1942;
12. J.B. Skemp, *Plato's Stateman,* 1952;
13. R.S. Bluck, *Plato's Phaedo,* 1955;
14. G. Grote, *Plato,* 1965;

15. E. Zeller, *Plato and the Older Academy,* trans. by S.F. Alleyne and A. Goodwin, 1888;
16. B. Bosanquet, *A Companion to Plato's Republic*, 1895;
17. T.G. Ritchie, Plato, 1902;
18. T. Gomperz, *Greek Thinkers,* vols. II and III, 1905;
19. J.A. Stewart, *The Myths of Plato,* 1905;
20. W. Lutolawski, *Origin and Growth of Plato's Logic,* 1905;
21. E. Baker, *Political Theory of Plato and Aristotle,* 1906;
22. J.A. Stewart, *Plato's Docrtrine of Ideas*, 1909;
23. R.L. Nettleship, Lectures on the *"Republic" of Plato*, 1914;
24. J. Burnet, *The Socratic Doctrine of the Soul,* 1916;
25. P.E. Moore, *Platonism*, 1917, and *The Religion of Plato,* 1921;
26. E. Barker, *Greek Political Theory*: *Plato and His Predecessors*, 1918;
27. E Rohde, *Psyche,* 1894, 1925;
28. A.E. Taylor, Plato: *The Man and His Work*, 1926;
29. A.E. Taylor, *Platonism and Its Influence,* 1927;
30. G. Santayana, *Platonism and the Spiritual Life.* 1927;
31. J. Burnet, *Platonism,* 1928;
32. G.C. Field, *Plato and His Contemporaries.* A Study in Fourth Century Life and Thought. 1930;
33. F.M. Cornford, *Before and after Socrates,* 1932;
34. C. Ritter, *The Essence of Plato's Philosophy*, trans. by A Allan, 1933;
35. P. Shorey. *What Plato Said,* 1933, and *Platonism Ancient and Modern*, 1938;
36. F.H. Anderson, *The Argument of Plato,* 1934;
37. R.L. Nettleship, *Theory of Education in Plato's Republic* 1935;
38. F.M. Cornford, *Plato's Theory of Knowledge,* 1935;
39. G.M.A. Grube, *Plato's Thought,* 1935;
40. L. Robin, *Plato*, 1935;
41. W.A. Hardie, *Study in Plato*, 1936;
42. R. Demos, *The Philosophy of Plato,* 1939;

43. J. Stenzel, *Plato's Method of Dialectic,* 1940;
44. P. Leon, *Plato*, 1940;
45. R. Robinson, *Plato's Early Dialectic,* 1941, 2nd ed. 1953;
46. F. Solmsen, *Plato's Theology;* 1942;
47. W. Jaeger, Paideia Vol. III *The Conflict of Cultural Ideas in the Age of Plato,* 1945;
48. A Koyre, *Discovering Plato,* 1945;
49. H.F. Cherniss, *Aristotle's Criticism of Plato and the Academy,* 1944, and *The Riddle of the Early Academy,* 1945;
50. J. Wild, *Plato's Theory of Man,* 1946;
51. R.S. Bluck, *Plato's Life and Thought,* 1949;
52. W.D. Ross, *Plato's Theory of Ideas*, 1951.

UNIVERSAL UPSURGE OF KNOWLEDGE

Ever since knowledge dawned in human mind, man has been thinking about problems: ontological, epistemological, eschatological and axiological. The questions of philosophy in the beginning of human knowledge were everywhere mixed with psychological problems. Thus philosophy in the beginning was concerned with the nature of the mind and the processes of consciousness. As men lived in small groups and the society was generally confined to a particular village, city or group of villages, the solutions offered were simple. There was hardly any distinction between social and politial problems as the political institutions were developed as a means to social welfare. Therefore, most of the ancient thinkers did not distinguish between social philosophy and political philosophy. As the life was simple and soical stratification and differentiation was not complex, the thinkers offered solutions working in more than one field of knowledge. Most of the thinkers were teachers and men of eduction who used to pass their life completely free from wordly affairs. The state and the socity generally extended support to these scholars and they were generally respected and followed. The job of instruction and education of the younger generation was generally entrusted to these men of letters. The state supported finance but not personal institutions where their disciples collected to hear their learned discourses and learn through their lives. In this way, society was generally govenred by the teachings of these great scholars though the administrative meachinery was almost everywhere in the hands of the state.

The above outline of the early status of knowlege and education is applicable to East and West. It was equally found in the Indo-Gangetic plains the world has developed from similar sources, fulfilled similar needs and evolved similar human thought not geographical conditions. It is hence that one finds a similarity between the Indian philosophy of Upanishads and the ancient wisdom of Socrates, Plato and Aristotle, the great masters of Greek thought. This will be amply clear from the discussions of the various facets of Platonic thought in this chapter. In conclusion we will refer to certain similarities between the thought of Plato and the Indian wisdom, thus pointing out the universal conclusions in human knowledge which are as much relevant today as they were thousands of years ago.

COMPREHENSION OF PLATO'S THOUGHT

Philosophy began in wonder as well as in the urge for the understanding of world enigma. Men everywhere realised that the sensual world is not the only world effective in their life. They, therefore, tried to rise from the sensuous world to reach the height of supra-sensuous. Thus ancient philosohy in India as well as in Greece was essentially an attempt to ise from sensuous impure to non-sensuous pure thought. Plato's philosophy is an example of such an attempt and his attempt, though carried out thousands of years ago, still stands unbeaten. The theory of ideas has been the source of evolution of idealist school in western philosophy. As knowledge in his days was inter-connected and comprehensive Plato has discussed a wide variety of human problems including those of epistemology, metaphysics, psychology, social and political philosophy. In those ancient days even astronomy and physical sciences were very much connected with social sciences and philosophy. Therefore one finds important references to even these in the writings of Plato. Thus philosophy was considerd as the knowledge of the Absolute, known as Brahman in India. It was a knowledge of the essence, the substance, that by knowing which everything else can be known. The philosopher was in search of a key to understand the world enigma. His search was not for the particulars but for the universal behind the particulars. His enquiry was directed to a theory which could explain all the facets of the sensual world. He wanted to know the mystry of creation, its what, how and why? He looked inwards, outwards as well as upwards. He analysed psychological process, wondered at the nature of creator and tried to unterstand the world around him. Thus philosophical practice was a comprehensive process. It included every branch of knowledge, nay the whole of human life. The philosopher therefore was everywhere held in high esteem.

PLATO'S HERITAGE

In Greek thought Plato was not the first philosopher. Long before him illustrious schools of philosophy, including great scholars developed and contributed important ideas in various fields of knowledge. This can be labelled as Pre-Socratic age which started from 6th century B.C., and went on upto the middle of 5th century B.C. The advent of sophists marked the end of this period. Then came the Socratic age in Greek thought. Socrates argued with the sophists and showed the hollowness of their thinking. he condemned negative approach to human knowledge and presented positive ideas. He himself wrote nothing but only used to discuss with various persons. It was his illustrious disciple Plato who gave a literary presentation to the ideas of Socrates in his famous dialogues. These dialogues again, are the sources of Plato's thought. In fact one can hardly distinguish between the though of Socrates and Plato. Plato, as a humble disciple of his master, never claimed the originality,but eulogised Socrates and his thought. After Plato Aristotle was an illustrious philosopher of the Socratic age in Greek thought. His death in 322 B.C. markd the end of Socratic age which can be rightly considered as the source of all western human knowledge.

PLATO'S ORIGINALITY

Thus Plato's philosophy was influenced, besides the ideas of his master Socrates, by the Milesian idea of substance, the infinite of Anaxemander, the number of Pyhagoras, the universal of Heraclitus, the essence of Parmenides, the dialectics of Zeno, the love of Empedocles, the human criteria of Protagoras, and his own experience of contemporary social and political conditions. This, however, does not mean the Plato's thoughts were a mere summary or synthesis ofthe ideas of his predecessors. It is certainly to be credit of this first great cosmopolitan philosopher of the world that he presented a synthetic philosophy which marks the apex of Greek thought. His thought influenced almost all the social sciences particularly sociology and political science. In philosophy it had been the source of almost all great movements of which some followed his principles while other criticised them. Even the German philosopher Immanual Kant who made a Copernican revolution in the field of philosophy, owed much to Platonic thought.

CLASSIFICATIN OF PLATO'S THOUGHT

Plato's philosophy was has been divided into three classes- Dialectic, Physics and Ethics, Of these, Dialectic has been considered to be the most important in the field of philosophy while Ethics has influenced sociology, political science, education, economics and all the fields of humanities. Dialectic includes his theory of ideas and epistemology. Physics includes his conceptions about the physical world and his views concerning psychology. Ethics includes Plato's ideas concerning the individual life, the soical life, the political life, the internatinal relations, peace and war and the realisation of an ideal state.

EPISTEMOLOGICAL BACKGROUND OF EDUCATION

"We are content, then as before", Plato said in *The Repulbic*" to call the first part *science* and the second *understanding* and the third *belief* and the fourth, *conjecture*: these last two together we may call *opinion* and the two exercise of *reason.* Opinion is concerned with becoming, and exercise of reason with being; and what being is to becoming, that exercise of reason is to opinion, that seience is to belief, and understanding to conjecture."[1] The discussion of the philosophy of any thinker should start with a review of his theory of knowledge known as epistemology. Epistemology is the philosophy of knowledge. It enquires into the sources of knowledge, types of knowledge, their limitations and possibilities and inter-relationships. It is a critical evaluation of various methods, techniques and means of knowledge. It is the basis of metaphysics and axiology together with which it forms the subject matter of philosophy. It enquires into the sources of validity to knowledge and therefore prescribes criteria for evaluating knowledge in different fields. Plato has made important contributions in all the above mentioned different fields of epistemology.

Positive and Negative Aspects

Epistemology of Plato can be derived from any one any of his single dialogue. His epistemology was both positive as well as negative. While on the one hand it discussed the nature of knowledge, its sources, limitations and bases of validity, on the other hand it also discussed the nature of untruth, error and fallacies of thought. While on the one hand he tried to explain what is true knowledge, he also pointed out what is false knowledge. He tried to find out as to what are the objects of our sensual as well as rational knowledge and what objects transcend their fields. In his famous work *The Republic* Plato has presented the positive aspect of his epistemology pointing out the nature of knowledge and the nature of truth and reality. The negative aspect of his epistemology has been presented in his dialogue *Theaeteus*. In it he has pointed out objects which cannot be called subject to knowledge and truth. In order to understand Plato's epistemology, one should attend to both of its aspects, positive as well as negative.

Four Types of Knowledge

In his magnum opus *The Republic* Plato has presented his views concerning epistemology in the 6th book. Here he discussed the following four types of knowledge—Conjectural, Practical or Sensuous, Hypothetical and finally Rational.

1. Conjectural Knowledge—Conjectural knowledge is the lowest type of knowledge. In fact it is not knowledge but a mere appearance of it. It includes illusions, hallucinations, dreams and pathological experience etc. Thus the knowledge of a snake in a rope, silver in necre and the double moon in the sky, the mirage in the desert etc., and the words like hare's horn and son of a barren woman come within conjectural knowledge. Thus it deals with illusory experiences and ideas. It is always erroneous. It is never actual but always possible though it influences people.

2. Practical or Sensuous Knowledge—While conjectural knowledge of Plato can be compared to *Pratibhasika* knowledge of Samkara Vedanta, the practical or sensuous knowledge may be compared with Samkara's *Vyavaharika* knowledge. As is clear from its title it is the knowledge of the world, the knowledge received through various sense organs. Thus our knowledge of things is practical knowledge. It includes knowledge received through visual auditory, olfactory, gustatory and tactual receptors. It is the knowledge of colours, tastes, smells, sounds and skin sensations. This knowledge, though considered to be final by man of common sense, has been demonstrated as only a possible knowledge by the philosophers. Things are not as they appear to us. What they are in reality, we do not know we know that our knowledge concerning things is conditioned by our mental mechanism. As Kant pointed out in tradition with Plato's epistemology, man's knowledge is a result of a synthesis between percepts and concepts.

Is Knowledge Perception?

While discussing the idea of Protagoras that knowledge is perception Plato has pointed out that this is an opinion and not knowledge. According to Protagoras and Sophist thinkers, knowledge achieved through sense organs is the true knowledge. Such a view, however, is falsified by our everyday experiences. No reliable predictions can be made on the basis of such a knowledge. As David Hume pointed out, in tradition with Plato's epistemology, the sensory experiences lead to ideas which are possible but not necessary.

Again, our perceptual knowledge at times is self-contradictory. An object near to us appears to be bigger than the same object at a far distance. In comparison to a heavy thing something may appear as lighter but in comparison to a lighter thing the same thing may appear heavier. Thus as Gestalt psychologists later on pointed out, in tradition with Plato, an object is influenced by its field. All perceptions are in a certain background and this backgroung influences our sensory experiences. The same object in a white, red or black background appears to be having different colours. Similar is the case with geometrical and other forms. Now, which of these contradictory experiences may be considerd as representing the actual object? It is clear that none of these experiences represents the object but only a facet of it which is related to space-time. Sensory experiences do not give us universal and eternal knowledge. They are temporary and falliable though useful for practical purposes. However true they may be considered in the field of practical life, the scientists agree with the philosophers that they are possible and not necessary.

If we accept with Protogoras that knowledge is perception it will result in the impossibility of all education, discourse and validity. If all the perceptions are equally true, then there is hardly any distinction between the perception of an untrained and trained persons. The educator therefore will have nothing to teach to the educand. Similarly a discourse generally consists of two opposite sides, both of which are based upon certain experiences. If experiences alone were sufficient to guarantee the validity of a knowledge, both the sides of a discourse may be equally true which leads to the contradictory position that contraries are equally true. Similarly contradictory theories of validity will be equally valid which will make assessment of validity impossible. One will have to accept that while his own perceptions are valid for himself, other's perceptions are valid for others. Using this reasoning known as turning the tables, Democritus has criticised the above mentioned theory advanced by Protagora.

If perceptions were knowledge, one must admit all objects of perception. Man, however, is not the only perceiver. The animals and birds of different varieties have sense organs which perceive in a way different from that of human beings. Protogoras has not explained whether the perceptions of human beings alone are valid or equal validity may be granted to perceptions of the animals. Thus his dictum that knowledge is perception is self contradictory. According to it truth is what appears to be ture. If it is so there is hardly any question of the validity of truth.

The theory advanced by Protagoras will eliminate objectivity from the field of knowledge. It is a against objectivity of truth and fails to distinguish between truth and falsehood. Nothing can be true and uutrue at the same time. It can be true for one and untrue for another, but not both for the same person. It may be admitted that while what I perceive is true for me other's perceptions may be ture for them, but if the same thing is perceived differently by different persons, we must have a criteria of assessing the objectivity of truth.

Besides, there are some phenomena which are not subject to perception. For example, universals are not subject to perception. We may perceive human beings but not humanity, the universal found among human beings. Similarly, words such as equality, liberty, fraternity and all values are not subject to perception and yet they have not been accepted as false. The processes of classification, comparison, imagination and reasoning include a wide variety of phenomenon which are not subject to perception. In the perception of a white piece of paper the perceptions of witheness and paper etc., require classification as well as comparison, which however are not sensory processes.

1. Stace, A Critical History of Greek Philosophy, pp. 178-17

Each sensation, as distinct from another sensation, involves comparison by the human mind. Kant rightly pointed out that without the subsumption of forms of intuition under categories of ideas and finally their synthesis in a unity of apperception knowledge is not possible. All these processes, as Kant rightly pointed out, are A-priori i.e., not subject to perception. All knowledge involves a double cognition. While on the one hand by perception of a piece of paper shows the existence of an object outside me, it also proves the existence of a perceptual mechanism in my mind. Therefore, the dictum that knowledge is perception is oversimplified and unscientific.

3. Hypothetical Knowledge—This knowledge, as is clear by its title, is not final but hypothetical. It is similarly not sensory or practical. It includes the knowledge of numbers and forms as found in different branches of mathematic. As David Hume pointed out, in Platonic traditions, all mathematical knowledge is exact but no actual since whatever is necessary is not factual. In hypothetical knowledge we arrive at certain conclusions through the processes of inductive generalisations and logical deductions. The truth of these generalisations and deductions is hypothetical as it depends upon the validity of sensory knowledge. In mathematics the basic definitions as those of point, line etc., are taken as axioms. They are not derived from such sensory perceptions but defined as such. Deductions made on the basis of these definitions therefore are not real though necessary. In Platonic epistemology hypothetical knowledge is the mediator between the practical sensuous knowledge and the rational insight. In other words, it establishes a relation between the world of things.

4. Rational Insight—In Platonic epistemology rational insight is the highest form of knowledge. Thus Plato can be called the fore runner of rationalist philosophy in the West. The rational insight gives us a knowledge of forms, concepts or ideas. It is achieved through a dialectical process unhindered by sensory perceptions. It is not subject to sensory knowledge. Therefore, it does not give us knowledge of things. It is not a knowledge of particulars but a knowledge of universals, but so far as each object partakes in a certain universal, the knowledge of a universal give some knowledge of the object. This field of knowledge is the basis of Plato's famous theory of ideas which will be discussed in details in sequence.

Knowledge is not Opinion

Besides rejecting the theory of Protagoras that knowledge is perception, Plato has also rejected another current theory of his time that knowledge is the opinion. According to Plato, knowledge is not opinion, neither right opinion nor wrong opinion. now wrong opinion. For example, if a person decleares that the Government will resign next Saturday, this is not knowledge even if it comes out to be true accidentally. Right opinion again, is mostly a blind guess and therefore cannot be called knowledge proper. For example, if our conscience intuitively or instinctively believes in a certain thing and cannot lay-down reasons for such a belief, it cannot be called knowledge even though it may come out to be true. Knowledge, according to Plato, is not only knowledge of the object and its nature but also includes knowledge of the reasons why it is so. Knowledge is not instinctive belief but complete understanding. It is rational comprehension. Thus it is not based on fiath, but on reason. An orator utilising the sentiments of the audience can make them believe in his opinion but he cannot create knowledge. An opinion can be changed by arousing emotions and sentiments and therefore it is unstable and indefinite. Knowledge, on the other hand, cannot be changed like this. One who knows cannot be befooled by verbal jugglery. While knowledge is always true, opniöns, both right and wrong, are always false. Distinguishing between knowledge and right opinion Plato has advanced the argument that instruction can implant knowledge. While this is not true about right opinion, knowledge and true reason are invariably related and found together. right opinion is irrational. It can be changed by stimuli and motivation. It can be divided among participants. This however, is not true about knowledge which can be shared only by rational human beings. Comparing the role of opinion and knowledge in *The*

Republic, Plato has pointed out that while the object of knowledge is Pure Being, Opinion lies in between Being and Non-Being. In other words, Opinion is in between knowledge and ignorance.

Nature of Knowledge

After rejecting the two above mentioned rival theories concerning the nature of knowledge, Plato has advanced his own theory about the nature of knowledge. Accepting the Socratic views Plato has pointed out that knowledge is attained through concepts. It cannot be changed by the personal experiences of the individual. It gives objective knowledge, since it is based upon reason. While opinion is based upon instinct and imagination knowledge is attained through reason. It is the same thing as to say that knowledge is availed through concepts.

Comparison with Socratic Epistemology

In the epistemology of Plato one finds two approaches. Firstly, he explains Socratic theory of ideas in details in his dialogues *Phaedo* etc. Here he writes as a disciple of his master Socrates, who according to him, was the greatest scholar and the best person of his type. Secondly, Plato has modified Socratic theory of ideas, as discussed in his dialogue *Parmenides*. According to some scholars this dialogue includes condemnation of Socratic theory of ideas. This, however, is not so. Plato has not rejected the theory of his master, he has only modified it. While according to Socrates concepts are found in human mind Plato maintains that ideas are supra-sensual and as much real as the real things of the objective world. While Socrates has only mentioned the absolute idea of Good, Plato has elaborately described the nature of good, through various similies. According to Socrates, ideas are indescribale and subject of intuitive experience. This has been accepted by Plato. According to Plato ideas cannot be completely described. Again, Socrates has not pointed out the relationship between ideas, while Plato has classified the ideas is a systematic sequence in which the idea of Good occupies the highest place. All the ideas, according to Plato, are the expressions of the highest idea of Good. Every idea exists because of the idea of Good.

Plato has rejected both the theories advanced by Socrates to explain the relationship of the world of things with the world of idea, participation theory and copy theory. According to participation theory the world of things participates in the world of ideas. According to copy theory things are only copies of ideas. Rejecting both these theories Plato has maintained that the acceptance of participation theory leads us to the wrong conclusion that the world of things, as a part of the world of ideas, is equally real. This will lead to negation of any distinction between the worldly and other woldly. On the other hand, copy theory will result in practical difficulties because it will make the objective world absolutely unreal. According to Plato the world of things is neither a part nor a copy of the world of ideas.

Modification of Socratic Theory

Rejecting Socrates theories about the relationship of the world of things and the world of ideas Plato has modified Socratic theory of ideas. According to Socrates, concepts are rules of thought and they regulate thought. In order to decide about the right and wrong in any thing we compare it with the ideal and draw conclusions. In other words, the concepts is the standard for judging things. Plato, on the other hand, maintained that concepts are real entities and not mental in nature. In fact they are transcendental and exist outside the mind. In order to prove the objectivity of concept, Plato admits the correspondence theory maintained by Parmenides according to which there is a correspondence between the idea and the object. Here Plato can be called the forerunner of the British philosopher John Locke. Again, Plato supports his theory of ideas by everyday experience. In our everyday life we admit an idea to be true corresponding to which a thing is available in the objective world. If there is nothing in the objective world, corresponding an idea the idea is held as false. It has existence only in the human mind and has no connection with the objective reality. Thus an idea can be true only if things corresponding to it are found in actual world, otherwise it is false. Now, knowledge is the knowledge of truth and therefore, knowledge of concepts or ideas. These ideas or concepts, however, are not found in the world outside, as objects are not general entities.

Status of Worldly Knowledge

The conclusion that knowledge is a knowledge of concept leads to the corollary that sensory knowledge is false. While the sense organs provide us experience of many horses, only reason provides us the concept of horseness. A horse is real only so far as it represents the idea of horseness. The idea of horseness is the reality, the horses are not absolutely real. This can be also explained with reference to the concept of beauty. A thing is beautiful only in so far as it represents or shares in the absolute idea of Beauty. Beauty does not mean an object but an idea. It is, however, found the different proportions in the worldly things. Things can be compared according to their beauty. This comparison is based upon the standard of aboulute beauty which is an idea or concept. Nothing in the actual world is a true copy of the idea of beauty. If it is accepted that the idea of beauty is purely mental it should not be found in the worldly things. It is a fact, however, that beauty is found in the worldly things. Therefore, even in order to maintain the reality of the practical world, one must admit the reality of the idea of beauty. Similar arguments can be advanced to prove the reality of other ideas as well. In his book *The Republic* Plato has advanced similar arguments to prove the reality of the idea of justice.

Sense Perception and Reason

Thus, according to Plato, there are two means of knowledge, Sense Perception and Reason. Sense perception is attained through five sence organs. It gives us a knowledge of the things of external world. Reason, however, is the knowledge of ideas. The characteristics of sense perception are contrary to the characteristics of ideas. The ideas have absolute existence. They are pure being and absolute existent. The sensory objects, on the other hand, are non-being and non-exitent. Whatever existence they have is due to the ideas. While, on the one hand, Plato has accepted Absolute Being, he has also accepted Absolute Non-being. The physical world falls in between these two. While concepts are universal, sense perceptions are particular. While concepts is one, sense perceptions are many. While concepts are beyond space-time, sense perceptions are within space-time. While concepts are eternal, immutable and formless the sense perceptions are changing, mutable and formed. Thus Plato has accepted the concept of Absolute Becoming advanced by Heraclitus. The world is the constant process of momentary sense-perception. It is Becoming while concepts are Being. The knowledge of Becoming, according to Plato, is not real knowledge as it is constantly changing. Knowledge according to Plato, as it was according to Indian thinkers of his time, is eternal and immutable. Therefore, the knowledge of concepts alone can be called knowledge.

Critical Evaluation

Platonic epistemology has been bitterly criticised by various scholars. Modern science and the scientist philosophers do not accept Platonic explanation of the objective word. According to modern science, knowledge of the external world is very much possible and the denial of sense perception will lead to denial of all science. Even if worldly things are changing, mutable and impermanent, they are subject to knowledge. For example, one can know the mountains, the rivers, the planets and the stars etc. They may not be as much permanent as the concept and yet they are sufficiently permanent to be known.

This criticism of Plato's epistemology, however, is based upon a misunderstanding of his theory of ideas. He has used the word sense-perception in the sense of pure sensation which has no element of reason in it. Even, according to modern psychology, pure sensation, without a rational element is a myth and non existent. Plato has not maintained that the worldly things are unreal as here's horns and the son of a barren woman. When concepts are involved in the world, how can the world be unreal?

In his dialouge *Sophist,* Plato has pointed out that it is impossible to imagine absolute non-being. Even the illusion, so far as it is an illusion, has some existence. After knowledge we know the unreality of an illustion. Similarly, after the knowledge of the world of ideas one feels that the world of things is not as much real. This however, does not mean that the existence of the physical world has been absolutely denied. In his dialogue *Symposium*, Plato has maintained that the physical world exists between absolute being and the absolute non-being. Thus he provides some sort of reality to the physical world, much more than that of illusion, hallucination or dream. In fact the physical world is real in practice. In his dialogue *Theatetus,* Plato has maintained that the world of sense perception is much more real than the world of dream or the world of sense perception is much more real than the world of dream or the world of imagination. Therefore, it cannot be maintained that Plato denied the reality of the physical world. In his simili of cave, he has elaborated this point in details.

"Now consider, what their release would be like, and their cure from these fetters and their folly; let us imagine whether it might naturally be something like this. One might be relased, and compelled suddenly to standup and turn his neck round and walk and look towards the firelight; all this would hurt him and he would be too much dazzaled to see distinctly those things whose shadows he had seen before."[1]

"Then suppose he were compelled to look towards the real light, it would hurt his eyes, and he would escape by turning them away to things which he was able to look at, and these he would believe to be clearer than what was being shown to him."[2]

"Supose, now, that someone should drag him thence by force, up the rough ascent, the steep way up and never stop until he could drag him out into the light of the sun, would he not be

---

1. **E.H. Warmington and Philip G. Rouse (Ed.) Great Dialogues of Plato, Trans. by W.H.D. Rouse, Mentor, New York, 1956, p. 316.**
2. **Ibid.**

distressed and furious at being dragged; and when he came into the light, the brilliance would fill his eyes and he would not be able to see even one of the things now called real?"[1]

"He would have to get used to its, surely, I think, if he is to see the things above. First, he would most easily look at shadows, after the images of mankind and the rest in water, lastly the things themselves. After this he would find it easier to survey by night the heavens themselves and all that is in them, gazaing at the light of the stars and moon, rather than by day the sun and the sun's lignt."[2]

"Last of all, I suppose, the sun; he could look on the sun itself by itself in its own place and see what is like; not reflections of it in water or as it appears in some alien setting."[3]

"And if there were honours and praises among them and prizes for the one who saw the passing things most sharply and remembered best which of them used to come before and which after and which together, and from these was best able to prophesy accordingly what was going to come—do you believe he would set his desire on that and envy those who were honoured men or potentates among them? Would he not feel as Homer says, and heartily desire rather to be self of some landless man on earth and to endure anything in the world, rather than to opine as they did and to live in that way?"[4]

"Then we must apply this image, my dear Glaucon, to all we have been saying: The world of our sight is like the habitation, in prison, the firelight there to the sunlight here, the ascent and the view of the upper world is the rising of the soul into the world of mind; put it so and you will not be far from my own surmise, since that is what you want to hear; but God knows if it is really true. At least, what appears to me is, that in the world of the know,

---

1. **Ibid.**
2. **Ibid.**
3. **Ibid.**
4. **Ibid, p. 315.**

last of all, is the idea of the good, and with what toil to be seen! And seen, this must be inferred to be the cause of all right and beautiful things for all, which gives birth to light and the king of light in the world of sight and, in the world of mind, herself the queen produces truth and reason; and she must be seen by one who is to act with reason publicly or privately."[1]

Importance of Education

Education was a subject to which Plato attached the greatest importance. In the *Republic* he reckons it with war, the conduct of campaigns and the administration of states as amongst 'the grandest and most beautiful' subjects, and the *Laws* he repeats that it is 'the first and fairest thing that the best of men can ever have.' In the *Laches*, which is professedly a treatise on education, he asks: 'Is this a slight thing about which you and Lysimachus are deliberating? Are you not risking the greatest of your possessions? For children are your riches; and upon their turning out well or ill depends the whole order of their father's house.' Again in the *Crito* he says: 'No man should bring children into the world who is unwilling to perservere to the end in their narture and education.' The extent and elaborateness of the treatment of education in the *Republic* and in the *Laws* likewise testify to the importance of the subject in Plato's mind.

The difficulties which arose from the educational methods of the sophists deeply perplexed Plato. His early dialogues everywhere bear the mark of this perplexity, a perplexity which, it seems, was common to the foremost minds of Greece at that time. From any quarter; the *Euthydemus* ends with an appeal to Socrates by Crito concerning the education of Critobulus his son.

Current Greece Education Systems

The type of education which was then current in Greece can be gathered from several references in the dialogues. In the *Crito* it is asked: "Were not the laws which have the charge of education right in commanding your fahter to train you in Music and

1. **Ibid pp. 315-316.**

Gymnastic?"[1] and the answer of Socrates is: 'Right, I should reply.' In the *Protagoras* it is stated: 'I am of opinion that skill in poetry was the principal part in education and this I conceive to be the power of knowing what compositions of the poets are correct, and what are not, and how they are to be distinguished and of explaning, when asked, the reason of the difference.'[2] In the *Timaeus* Critias says: 'Now the day was that day of the Apaturia which is called the registration of youth, at which, according to custom, our parents gave prizes for recitations, and the poems of several poets were recited by us boys, and many of us sang the poems of Solon, which at that time had not gone out of fashion.'[3]

Education of Greek Youth

The best account of the education of Greek youth is the sketch given in the *Protagoras*.[4] 'Education and admonition commence in the first years of childhood, and last to the very end of life. Mother and nurse and father and tutor are quarrelling about the improvement of the child as soon as ever he is able to understand them; he cannot say or do anything without their setting forth to him that this is just and that is unjust; this is honourable, that is dishonourable; this is holy, that is unholy; do this and abstain from that. And if he obeys, well and good; if not, he is straightened by threats and blows, like a piece of warped wood. At a later stage they send him to teachers, and enjoin them to see his manners even more than to his reading and music; and the teachers do as they are deisred. And when the boy has learned his letters and is beginning to understand what is written, as before he understood only what was spoken, they put into his hands the works of great poets, which he reads at school; in these are contained many admonitions and many tales and praises and encomia of ancient famous men, which he is required to learn by heart, in order that he may imitate or emulate them and desire to

1. **Crito**
2. **Protagoras**
3. **Timaues**
4. **Protagoras**

become like them. Then, again, the teachers of the lyre take similar care that their young disciple is temperate and gets into no mischief; and when they have taught him the use of the lyre, they introduce him to the poems of other excellent poets, who are the lyric poets; and these they set to music, and make their harmonies and rhythms quite familiar to the children's souls, in order that they may learn to be more gentle and harmonious, and rhythmical, and so more fitted for speech and action; for the life when of man in every part has need of harmony and rhythm. They they send them to the master of gymnastic, in order that their bodies may better minister gymnastic, in order that their bodies may better minister to the virtuous mind, and that they may not be compelled through bodily weakness to play the coward in war or any other occasion. This is what is done by those who have the means, and those who have the means are the rich; their children begin education soonest and leave off latest. When they have done with masters, the state again comples them to learn the laws, and live after the pattern which they furnish, and not after their own fancies; and just as in learning to write, the writing-master first draws lines with a style for the use of the young beginner, and gives him the tablet and makes him follow the lines, so the city draws the laws, which were the invention of good law-givers who were of old time; these are given to a young man, in order to guide him in his conduct whether as ruler or ruled; and he who transgresses them is to be corrected, or, in other words, called to account, which is a term used not only in your country, but also in many others.

Education of Greek Maiden

Xenophon's *The Economist* furnishes the complementary education of the Greek maiden. 'Ah, Ischomachus, that is just what I [Socrates] should like particularly to learn from you. Did you yourself educate your wife to be all that a wife should be, or when you received her from her father and mother was she already a proficient well skilled to discharge the duties appropriate to a wife? Well skilled! (he replied). What proficiency was she likely to bring with her, when she was not quite fifteen at the time she wedded me and during the whole prior period of her life and been most carefully brought up to see and hear as little as possible, and to ask the fewest questions? Or do you not think one should be satisfied, if at marriage her whole experience consisted in knowing how to take the wool and make a dress, and seeing how her mother's handmaidens had their daily spinning-tasks assigned them? For (he added) as regards control of appetite and self-indulgence [in reference to culinary matters], she had received the soundest education, and that I take to be the most important matter in the bringing up of man or woman.'[1]

Plato's Own Treatment of Education

Plato's own treatment of education is to be found in the *Republic*. Rousseau has said: 'If you wish to know what is meant by public education, read Plato's *Republic*. Those who merely judge books by their titles take this for a treatise on Politics, but it is the finest treatise on Education ever written.'[2] Likewise Edward Caird has affirmed of the *Republic* that "perhaps it might best be described as a treatise on Education, regarded as the one great business of life from the beginning to the end of it."[3]

The *Republic* is professedly an inquiry into the nature of justice. But justice is essentially a social virtue.

Aristotle said in Politicies (iii, 13) 'Justice has been acknowledged by us to be a social virtue.' Consequently to determine the nature of justice Plato is driven to construct in thought an ideal state wherein he hopes to find justice 'writ large'. Rousseau said in *Emile,* (p. 202) 'It is true....that we have a very imperfect knowledge of the human heart if we do not also examine it in crowds; but it is none the less true that to judge of men we must study the individual man, and that he who had a perfect knowledge of the inclinations of each individual might foresee all their combined effects in the body of the nation.'

---

1. **The Works of Xenophon. Translated by H. G. Dakyns, London: Mcmillian & Co. Ltd., 1897. Vol III, Part I, pp. 226-7.**
2. **Emile, Everyman translation, p. 8.**
3. **Education of Theory in the Greek Philosophers (Glasgow: J. Maclehose & Sons, 1904). i, 140.**

Because of the multiplicity of human wants and of the insufficiency of any one individual to satisfy these by his own efforts, the state, in Plato's view, is necessary. It is likewise advantageous, since by reason of the diversity in the natural endowment of the individuals constituting the state the greatest efficiency can only be attained by the application of the principle of the division of labour and by cooperative effort.[1] These two principles are implied in the oft-quoted statement of Aristole: 'The state comes into existence originating in the bare needs of life, and continuing in existence for the sake of a good life.'[2]

The application of the principle of the division of labour results in the separation of the citizens of the state into two classes—the industrial or artisan and the guardian class, the duty of the former being to provide the necessaries of life, the duty of the latter being to enlarge the boundaries of the state.[3] a proceeding which involves war—that luxuries may be available for the citizens and the state be something more than 'a community of surve.'

AIM OF EDUCATION

Plato says in The *Republic,*

"Then to help these two natures, as it seems, I would say some god has given two arts to mankind, music and gymnastic, for the philosophic and the high spirited parts; not for soul or body particularly, except by the way; but for both together, in order that they may be fitted together in concord, by being strained and slackened to the proper point."

"Then the one who best mingles music and gymnastic, and most proportionably applies them to the soul, would most rightly be called the perfect musician and master of melody, much rather than the one who tunes together the strings of harps; and that is what we say."

---

1. **Politics, i, 2.**
2. **Republic, pp. 369-72.**
3. **Ibid p. 373.**

According to Plato, Man's mind is always active. Man is attracted towards all things, that he sees in his surroundings, and he runs after them. The educator should take advantage of this propensity in the child educate him. He should pay attention to the objects which surround the child. Such objects should be beautiful so that the child is naturally attracted to them and his curiosity is aroused. The process of education advances through this constant interaction between the stimulus by which the mind develops. For this reason the child should be kept in beautiful environment. In fact, the human individual requires such an environment not only in infacy but through his entire life. Because, according to Plato, the process of education is never complete. it continues throught one's life. Plato has laid the greatest stress on mental development in education. He conceives of the state as an advanced mind. Education aims not merely at providing information but at training the individual in his duties and rights as a citizen. Just as the state evolves from the mind, the mind itself passes through all those stages of development through which the state passes. In Plato's opinion, the aim of education is human perfection, and with this end in view, he suggest a curriculum which comprehends all subjects.

CURRICULUM OF EDUCATION

Plato's education has its objective in the realization of truth, a truth which is comprehensive, not limited or narrow. Plato, therefore, believes that development of the mind, body and soul is essential. For this reason he has divided the curriculum into three parts—

1. Bodily Development—Plato's philosophy believes bodily development to be of the utmost importance in education, but this bodily development is achieved not merely through exercise and gymnastic activity, but also through a regulated and controlled diet. The educatior must guide and train the educand to attend to his food. He must be a kind of doctor who advise a particular kind of diet after acquainting himself with weaknesses of the educand's body. This must be done in order to get rid of these debilities and finally to lead to complete development of the body.

2. Educational Impressions—But it must be remembered that bodily development is only a means to mental development, because a healthy mind resides only in a healthy body. Although much importance is attached to bodily development, even greater importance is attached to mental development. Being under the influence of Pythagoras, Plato recommended the teaching of mathematics as of supreme importance. The first step in the teaching of mathematics is the teaching of arithmetic. Geometry and Algebra should then be taught. Plato believed that the teaching of mathematics can remove many mental defects. In addition to mathematics, Plato considered the teaching of Astronomy as of great significance, as part of higher education.

3. Training in Music—In order to achieve balance in education. Plato stressed the value of musical training as a supplement to training in gymnastics. Exercise is the source of bodily development while music helps in the development of the soul. But music and literature taught to the student must be capable of building character. Plato suggested that the child's curriculum should be purged of all literature and musical epics which tended to generate such qualities as cowardice, weakness, selfishness, egoism, etc. He was critical of the epics of Homer and other contemporary poets on this ground. Plato considered balance in human life to be of the greates importance, because in the absence of such a balance, man should neither fulfil his social obligation nor enjoy his own private life to the full.

Scope of Education

For each of the three classes of the community—the producing, the military and the governing—Plato ought to have provided, we should imagine, an appropriate form of training; but although the education of the soldier and that of the ruler or philosopher are treated at considerable length, no mention is made in the *Republic* of the education of the industrial class.[1] The

1. Cf. Aristotle, *Politics*, ii, 5, 23: 'What will be the education, form of government, laws of the lower class Socrates has nowhere determined.'

education of the members of this class, had Plato dealt with it, would doubtless have been of a strictly vocational nature, not, however, a state scheme of vocational training but something resembling rather "the constitution of apprenticeship as it once existed in Modern Europe."[1] There would be no specific training in citizenship, for these members of the community have no voice in the government of the state; their characterstic virtue is obedience, technically 'temperance'—to know their place and to keep it.[2]

The fact that this large element in the community is denied the benefits and privileges of citizenship, the communistic scheme being confined to the guardian class, must be regarded as a serious defect in Plato's ideal state. It has been attributed to Plato's aristocratic prejudices, and to the Greek contempt for the mechanical arts. Aristotle regards the artisans as of even less account than the slaves, and maintains that they can only attain excellence as they become slaves, that is, come under the direction of a master. If, however, a state is to be safe, or be 'a unity', as Plato phrased it, all must share in the government. Contrasting the Greek with the modern ideal of virtue, T.H. Green says: 'It is not the sense of duty to a neighbour, but the practical answer to the question Who is my neighbour? that has varied'. This explains the defect in Plato's scheme, and helps us to appreciate the increased difficulty of our present-day ethical, social and education problem.

PRINCIPLES OF CURRICULUM

1. Improvement of the Soul—Plato's first treatment of education, the training of the guardians including the military and

1. **Lewis Campbell, *Plato's Republic*, p. 65.**
2. **Ibid. p. 54. Plato refers to the workers as 'those whose natural talents were defective from the first, and whose souls have since been so grievously marred and enervated by their life of drudgery as their bodies have been disfigured by their crafts and trades.' Republic, 495.**

ruling classes, is a general education government mainly by the principle of imitation. Its two main divisions are the current forms of Greek education, namely, music[1] and gymnastic, but as Plato again warns us: 'Neither are the two arts of Music ans Gymnastic really designed, as is often supposed, the one of the training of the soul, the other for the training of the body. I believe that the teachers of both have in view chiefly the improvement of the soul.'[2]

2. Mental to Precede Physical Education—Al the outset of his treatment of education he asserts that we should begin education with music and go on to gymnastic afterwards; mental is thus to precede physical education. Aristotles view how was opposed to that of Plato. Aristotle say: 'The care of the body ought to precede that of the soul, and the training of the appetitive part should follow: none the less the care of it must be for the sake of the reason, and our care of the body for the sake of the soul.' The mothers and nurses are to tell their children the authories tales only: 'Let them fashion the mind with such tales, even more fondly than they mould the body with their hands.'

Recognising the importance of first impressions Plato says, "They beginning, is the most important part of any work, especially in the case of a young and tender thing."[3] Consequently consideration of the tales to be told to infants is not beneath the dignity of a philosopher.[4]

3. The Young should be Trained in both True and False—Music includes narratives, and these are of two kinds, the ture and the false.[5] Somewhat paradoxically Plato maintains that the young should be trained in both, and that we should begin with the false; fables, he implies, are best suited to the child mind. He thus

1. **Politics, i, 3.**
2. **Almost equivalent to the term Arts in a university curriculum.**
3. **Republic, 377.**
4. **Cf. Aristotle, Politics, vii, 17.**
5. **Republic, 376.**

recognises the truth of art as well as the truth of fact. But according to Plato not all fables should be taught, 'for a young person cannot judge what is allegorical and what is literla; anything that he receives into his mind at that age is likely to become indelible and unalterable; and therefore it is most important that the tales which the young first hear should be models of virtuous thoughts.'

4. Nothing must be Admitted in Education which does not Conduce to the Promotion of Virtue—For 'true and false' Plato substitutes the standard 'good and evil', He declines to take upon himself the task of composing fables suitable for children. But using as a criterion the principle just enunciated, he assumes a moral censorship over the tales then current. Plato remarks, 'The narrative of Hephaestus binding Here his mother, and how on another occasion Zeus sent him flying for taking her part when she was being beaten, and all the battles of the gods in Homer—these tales must not be admitted into our state, whether they are supposed to have an allegorical meaning or not.'[1]

Plato proceeds to pass in review the stories about the Gods and formulates the following theological canons: 1. 'God is not the author of all things, but of good only'—and the poet is not to be permitted to say that those who are punished are miserable and the God is the author of their misery.[2] 2. 'The Gods are not magicians who transform themselves, neither do they deceive mankind in any way.'[3] The tales to be told to children must conform to these principles, and others are not to be told to the children from their youth upwards, if they are to honour the gods and their parents, and to value friendship.[4]

5. More Fear of Slavery than of Death—After having considered those the fables dealing with the gods, Plato proceeds

1. **Ibid. 378.**
2. **Ibid 380.**
3. **Ibid 383.**
4. **Ibid 386.**

to consider those relating to heroes and the souls of the departed. To make the citizens free men who should fear slavery more than death, the other world must not be reviled in fables but rather commended. All weepings and wailings of heroes must be expunged from fables; likewise all descriptions of violent laughter, for a fit of laughter which has been indulged to excess almost always produces a violent reaction.'[1]

6. High Value Set on Truth—In the tales to be recited to children a high value is to be set upon truth; 'if anyone at all is to have the privilege of lying, the rulers of the state should be the persons; and they, in their dealings either with their enemies or with their own citizens, may be allowed to lie for the public good. But nobody else should meddle with anything of the kind.'[2] Temperance, implying obedience to commanders and self-control in sensual pleasures, is to be commended, while covetousness is to be condemned. The fables concerning heroes and others must accordingy be amended to agree with these principles.

The use is likewise to be forbidden of such language as implies that wicked men are often happy, and the good miserable; and that injustice is profitable when undetected, justice being a man's own loss and another's gain.[3]

Principal Form of Narratives

1. Simple Narration—Having thus discussed the matter of the narratives to be used in education, Plato addresses himself to a consideration of their form.[4] In compositions he distinguishes between direct speech, which he calls 'imitation', and indirect speech, which he calls 'simple narration'. 'Imitation' is only to be allowed of the speech and action of the virtuous man: the speeches of others are to be delivered and their actions described in the form of narration. The reason Plato gives is that 'imitation

1. Ibid. 386-8.
2. Ibid
3. Republic, 392.
4. Ibid. 392-403.

beginning in early youth and continuing far into life, at length grows into habits and becomes a second nature, affecting body, voice and mind.'[1]

2. Discard of Effiminate and Convivial—In respect to music in its limited and modern sense, Plato maintains that all harmonies which are effeminate and convivial are to be discarded and only such retained as will make the citizens temperate and courageous. The rhythm is to be determined by the nature of the words, just as the style of words is determined by the moral disposition of the soul.

3. Art Must be Moral—So must it be with the other arts and crafts, and not only the poets, but the professors of every other craft as well, must impress on their productions the image of the good.[2] Here we have the origin of the old quarrel between poetry and philosophy, or between art and morality. Plato will not entertain the idea of 'art for art's sake'; the only criterion he will recognise is the ethical.

4. Unconscious Assimilation—The reason of Plato's solicitude for a good and simple environment for the children who are to be the future guardians of the state is his belief in the efficacy of unconscious assimilation or imitation in the formation of character. As evidence of this we may cite the following: 'We would not have our guardians grow up amid images of moral deformity, as in some noxious pasture, and there browse and feed upon many a baneful herb and flower, day by day, little by little, until they silently gather a festering mass of corruption in their own soul. Let our artists rather be those who are gifted to discern the true nature of the beautiful and graceful; then will our youth dwell in a land of health, amid fair sights and sounds, and recevie the good in everything; and beauty, the effluence of fair works, shall flow into the eye and ear, like a healthgiving breeze from a purer region, and insensibly draw the soul from earliest years into likeness and sympathy with the bearuty of reason.'[2]

---

1. Ibid. 395.
2. Ibid. 401.

5. Rhythm and Harmony—'And therefore', Plato continues, 'musical training is a more potent instrument than any other, because rhythm and hormony find their way into the inward places of the soul, on which they mightily fasten, imparting grace, and making the soul of him who is rightly educated graceful, or of him who is ill-educated ungraceful.' That the result of a musical education should be the production of harmony and grace in the individual is repeated in the introduction to Plato's treatment of higher education or the education of the philosopher. There, he says, 'music was the counterpart of gymnastic, and trained the guardians by the influences of habit, by harmony making them harmonious, by rhythm rhythmical.'[1] The end throughout was the Greek ideal of manhood, a life which in itself was a work of art.

General Principles of Gymnastic

Plato's treatment of gymnastic in the *Republic* is decidedly brief.[2] The contents himself with indicating no more than the general principles. 'Gymnastic as well as music should begin in early years; the training in it should be careful and should continue through life', he says, adding, however, 'Now my belief is, not that the good body by any bodily excellence improves the soul, but, on the contrary, that the good soul, by her own excellence, improves the body as far as this may be possible.'

(i) *Moderate System*—Plato prescribes a simple moderate system such as would be productive of health and the utmost keenness of both eye ear.[3] On the habit of body cultivated by professional gymnasts he disapproves as unsuitable for men who have to undergo privations in war and variations in food when on a campaign. Abstinence from delicacies is also enjoined. The whole life, however, is not to be given up to gymnastics for anyone who does nothing else ends by becoming uncivilised—'he is like

1. Ibid, 522.
2. Ibid, 403-12
3. Republic, 404.

a wild beast, all violence and fierceness, and knows no other way of dealing; and he lives in all ignorance and evil conditions, and has no sense of propriety and grace.'[1]

Such then is, in outline, Plato's scheme of early training with its training in music and gymnastic. The dances which will be in vogue, the hunting and field exercises and the sports of the gymnasium and the race-course, he adds,[2] must correspond with the foregoing outlines.

(ii) *No Training in Manual Arts*—There is one omission from this early education to which attention ought to be directed, for the omission is intentional on Plato's part; it is the absence of any reference to a training in the manual arts. The reason for the omission is incidentally disclosed by Plato in a later section of *Republic*: All the useful arts were reckoned mean.[3]

(iii) *No Compulsion*—There are other omissions evidently unintentional. The subjects of the higher education, Plato later recognises, must be begun in youth, hence in dealing with the education of the ruler or philosopher we find him stating: 'Calculation and geometry and all the other elements of instruction, which are a preparation for dialectic, should be presented to the mind in childhood; not, however under any notion of forcing our system of education.'[4]

The principle of teaching-method here implied he elaborates by adding: 'Bodily exercise, when compulsory, does no harm to the body; but knowledge which is acquired under compulsion obtains no hold on the mind... Then do not use compulsion, but let early education be a sort of amusement; you will then be better able to find out the natural bent.' In the *Laws* the positive significance of play in education is emphasised. Thus, as has frequently been pointed out, we do not have to come to modern

---

1. **Ibid, 411.**
2. **Ibid, 412.**
3. **Ibid, 522.**
4. **Ibid. 536.**

times, to Herbart, Froebel or Montessori, to find the child's interest or his play taken as a guiding principle in education : it is found formulated in Plato.

(iv) Guidance to guardians—Those who are to undergo the early education and become guardians of the state are to unite in themselves 'philosophy and spirit and swiftness and strength'[1] Throughout their education they are to be watched carefully and tested and tempted in various ways;[2] and those who, after being proved, come forth victorious and pure are to be apponted rulers and guardians of the state, the others remaining auxiliaries or soldiers.

(v) Principles of Qualification for their Education—The qualities required for the higher education[3] or for the philosophic character Plato frequently enumerates. Preference is to be given to 'the surest and the bravest, and, if possible, to the fairest; and, having noble and generous tempers, they should also have the natural gifts which will facilitate their education.[4] Anothe account runs: 'A good memory and quick to learn, noble, gracious, the friend of truth, justice, courage, temperance';[5] again, 'Courage, magnificence, aprehension, memory.[6]

Aim of Higher Education

The aim of the higher education is not a mere extension of knowledge; it is, in Plato's phrase, 'the conversion of a soul from study of the sensible world to contemplation of real existence[32] 'Then, if I am right,,' he explains, 'certain professors of education must be wrong when they say that they can put a knowledge into the soul which was not there before, like sight into blind eyes. Whereas, our argument shows that the power and capacity of

1. Ibid, 376.
2. Ibid, 413.
3. Ibid, 521-41.
4. Republic, & 535.
5. Ibid 487.
6. Ibid, 490

learning exist in the soul already; and that just as the eye was unable to turn from darkness to light without the whole body, so too the instrument of knowledge can only by the movement of the whole soul be turned from the world of becoming into that of being, and learn by degrees to endure the sight of being, and of the brightest and best of being, or in other words, of the good.[1,2]

1. Mathamatical Studies—Such is the aim of the higher education, the education of the philosopher or ruler. Plato, having determined the aim, next proceeds to consider the scope of higher education. It includes number or arithmetic, plane and solid geometry, astronomy, theory of music or harmonics, all preparatory to the highest of the sciences, namely, dialectic. 'Through Mathematics to Metaphysics' might be said to sum up Plato's scheme of higher education.

Principles deciding on the selection of the higher studies. (i) Higher education must lead to reflection rather than deal with the things of sense;[3] (ii) They must likewise be of universal application.[4] The first subject that satisfies these requirements is number, hence Plato concludes.[5] This is a kind of knowledge which legislation may fitly prescribe; and we must endeavour to persuade those who are to be the principal men of our state to go and learn arithmetic, not as amateurs, but they must carry on the study until they see the nature of numbers with the mind only; nor again, like merchants or retail-traders, with a view to buying or selling, but for the sake of their military use, and of the soul herself; and because this will be the easiest way for her to pass from becoming to turth and being'. The main function of number is thus to afford a training in abstraction.

1. Ibid 490.
2. Ibid 518.
3. Ibid 523.
4. Ibid 522.
5. Ibid 525

Search of Universal Notions

The value which Plato assigns to number, as a subject in the training preparatory to philosophy, strikes the explained, however, by the fact that philosophers had then only begun the search for universal or conceptual notions, and the science of number presented itself as satisfying their requirements in a remarkable degree. The Pythagoreans had indeed maintained that number was the rational principle or essence of things, and it is generally agreed that Plato was for some time under Pythagorean influences; in fact, by some it is maintained that by 'Ideas' he understood at one stage in the development of that doctrine nothing other than numbers themselves. At the time of writing the *Republic,* however, he had outgrown the naive identification of numbers with things themselves, for we find him asserting: 'Yet anybody who has the least acquaintance with geometry will not deny that such a conception of the science is in flat contradiction to the ordinary language of geometricians. They have in view practice only, and are always speaking, in a narrow and ridiculous manner, of squaring and extending and applying and the like—they confuse the necessities of geometry with those of daily life; whereas knowledge is the real object of the whole science.[1] If the Greeks, as is implied in Plato's statement, were at times in danger of ignoring the purely conceptual natue of number, we of the present day are in danger of disregarding the practical needs which brought the science into existence and the concrete bases in which numbers were first exemplified.

Principle of Transfer of Training

In insisting on the value of number as a means of training in abstraction Plato gives expression to a statement which implies the doctrine of formal discipline or transfer of training, that is, that a training in one function results in a general improvement of the mind, which in turn favourably influences other functions. Thus he asks: 'Have you further observed, that those who have a natural talent for calculation are generally quick at every other kind of

1. Ibid. 527.

knowledge; and even the dull, if they have had an arithmetical training, although they may derive no other advantage from it, always become much quicker than they would otherwise have been?'[1] When in the same section he adds: 'and inded, you will not easily find a more difficult subject, and not many as difficult', he approximates to the doctrine that the more trouble a subject causes the better training it affords, he fallacy of which is evident in its enunciation by a modern paradoxical philosopher, namely, it matters not what you teach a pupil provided he does not want to learn it. This argement is repeated in almost identical terms in the Laws, 747: 'Arithmetic stirs up him who is by nature sleepy and dull, and makes him quick to learn, retentive, shrewed and aided by art divine he makes progress quite beyond hs natural powers'

In dealing with geometry Plato also remarks that in all departments of knowledge, as experience proves, any apprehension than one who has not.'[2]

Mathematics and Dialectics

These views must nevertheless be qualified by the statement[3] occurring in the discussion of the relation between mathematics and dialectic. 'For you surely would not regard the skilled mathematician as a dialectician? Assuredly not, he said; I have hardly ever known a mathematician who was capable or reasoning.'[4] This qualification, it has been contended,[5] acquits Plato of the responsibility of initiating the doctrine of formal training, but if it does so, it is only at the cost of consisteny. In his defence, however, it may be said, that in Plato's day little was known of, although much was hoped from, the science of number; and no objection could have been urged against him had he said that a knowledge of number 'broadened' rather than 'quickened'

1. **Republic, 526.**
2. **Republic, 752.**
3. **Ibid. 531.**
4. **E.C. Moore, What is Education? (Boston and London: Ginn & Co., (1915), Ch.iii.**
5. **Republic, 526.**

the mind. Number, like language, affords us an invaluable means of mastering and controlling experience, and does not require to be defended on the ground of some hypothetical influence on the mind in general. It must be put to Plato's credit that in interpreting a faculty as a function (*Republic*, 477) he avoided the 'faculty' doctrine which long retarded the development of psychology.

As number is the first subject selected for inclusion in the curriculum of the higher education, so geometry is the second. Its bearing on strategy is acknowledged, but what Plato is concerned about is whether it tends in any degree to make easier the vision of the idea of good.[1] The idea of good, or 'the Form of the Good', is the ultimate principle in Plato's philosophy, at once the source of all Being and of all knowledge. This, he believes, geometry does accomplish; 'geometry will draw the soul towrads truth, and create the spirit of philosophy',[2] consequently those who are to be the rules of the ideal state must be directed to apply themselves to the study of geometry.

The study of solid geometry, or the investigation of space of three dimensions, should, Plato admints, logically follow plane geometry and in turn precede astronomy, or the study of solid bodies in motion, but the unsatisfactory contition of the subject at the time causes him to dismiss it briefly.

REILLUMINATION OF EYE OF THE SOUL

Astronomy is the next of the instrumental subejcts of the higher training, and in enumerating its practical advantages to the agriculturist and navigator Plato remarks: 'I am amused at your fear of the world, which makes you guard against the appearance of insisting upon useless studies; and I quite admit the difficulty of believing that in every man there is an eys of the soul which, when by other pursuits lost and dimmed, is by these purified and re-illumined; and is more precious far than ten thousand bodily eyes, for by it alone is truth seen.'[3] 'Then in astronomy, as in

1. **Ibid. 527.**
2. **Ibid. 528.**
3. **Republic, 527.**

geometry, we should employ problems, and let the heavens alone if we would approach the subject in the right way and so make the natural gift of reason to be any real use.[1] In accordance with this principle the calculation of Neptune into existence by Adams and Leverrier would have been commended by Plato; the verification of its existence by actual observation would have merited his contempt.

Search for Beautiful and Good—The last of the studies preparatory to dialectic is music, not, however, music as an art as dealt with in the early education, but the theory of music, harmonics, the mathematical relations existing between notes, chords, etc., or what we should now probably term the physical bases of music—'a thing', Plato affirms, 'which I would call useful; that is, if sought after with a view to the beautiful and good; but if pursued in any other spirit, useless'.[2]

If a common basis for the mathematical studies just enumerated could be discovered, Plato believes that is would advance the end in view, namely, preparation for the science of dialectic.

Revelation of Absolute Truth—Dialectic is, for Plato, the highest study of all. It is as far removed from the mathematical sciences as they are from the practical arts. The sciences assume certain hypotheses, or make certain assumptions, geometry, for example, assumes the existence of space and does not inquire whether it is a perceptual datum, a conceptual construction or, as Kant maintained, an a *priori* Anschauung. Philosophy, or dialectic as Plato calls it, tries to proceed without presuppositions or, at least seeks critically to examine their validity and to determine the extent of their appliation.

' I must remind you', says Plato, 'that the power of dialectic can alone reveal this (absolute truth), and only to one who is a disciple of the previous sciences.' 'And assuredly', he continues, 'no one will argue that there is any other method of comprehending by any regular process all true existence or of ascertaining what each thing is in its own nature; for the arts in

1. Ibid. 530.

general are concerned with the desires and opinions of men, or are coltivated with a view to production and construction, or for the proservation of such productions and constructions; and as to the mathematical seiences which, as we were saying, have some apprehension of true being—geometry and the like—they only dream abut being, but never can they behold the waking reality so long as they leave the hypotheses which they use unexamined, and are unable to give an account of them. For when a man knows not his own first principle, and when the conslusion and intermediate steps are also constructed out of he knows not what, how can he imagine that such a fabric of convention can ever become science?'[1] In the *Cratylus* Plato defined the dialectician as 'he who knows how to ask questions and how to answer them.' in the *Phaedrus* he indentifies dialectic with the process of division and generalisation, and he adds, *Republic,* 537, 'For according as a man can survey a subject as a whole or not, he is or is not a dialectician.'

'Then dialectic, and dialectic alone, goes directly to the first principle and is the only science which does away with hypotheses in order to make her ground secure; the eye of the soul, which is literally buried in an outlandish slough, is by her gentle aid lifted upwards; and she uses as handmaids and helpers in the work of conversion, the sciences which we have been discussing.'

Dialectic then is the coping-stone of the sciences;[2] no other science can be placed higher; it completes the series. All who would be magistrates in the ideal state must consequently address themselves to such studies as will enable them to use the weapons of the dialectician most scientifically.

No Intellectual Study for Cadets—Having determined the subjects which the philosopher or ruler must study, Plato proceeds to consider the distribution of these studies.[3] For three years after the completion of the early education, that is, from seventeen to twenty years of age, the youths are to serve as cadets, being

1. Ibid. 533.
2. *Republic,* 534.
3. Ibid, 537-41.

brought into the field of battle, and, 'like young hounds, have a taste of blood given them'.

During these years of bodily exercises there is to be no intellectual study, 'for sleep and exercise are unpropitious to learning.'

No Science Study in Youth—At the age of twenty the choice characters are to be selected to undergo the mathematical training preparatory to dialectic. This training is to continue for ten years, and at the age of thirty a further selection is to be made, and those who are chosen are to begin the study of dialectic.[1]

Plato deliberately withholds the study of dialectic to this late age, giving as his reason that 'youngsters, when they first get the taste in their mouths, argue for amusement, and are always contradicting and refuting others in imitation of those who refute them; like puppy-dogs, they rejoice in pulling and tearing at all who come near them.'[2] According Aristotle, "The young man is not a fit student of polities." This study is to be prosecuted for five years, every other pursuit being resigned for it. For the next fifteen years, that is, from thirty-five to fifty years of age, the philosopher or rulers are to return to practical life take the command in war and hold such offices of state as befit 'young men'. After the age of fifty the lives of the rulers are to be spent in contemplation of 'the Good', so that when they are called upon to regulate the affairs of the state, their knowledge of this will serve as a pattern according to which they are to order the state and the lives of individuals, and the remainder of their own lives also; 'making philosophy their chief pursuit, but when their turn comes, toiling also at politics and ruling for the public good, not as though they were performing some heroic action, but simply as a matter of duty; and when they have brought up in each generation others like themselves, they will depart to the Islands of the Blest and dwell there.'[3]

1. **Ibid. The tests for philosophers include intelligence tests. The tests for the guardians are mainly temperament tests.**
2. **Ethics, 539.**
3. ***Republic*, 540.**

Such is Plato's scheme of education as set forth in the *Republic*, and he warns us in conclusion that it is an education for women as well as for men; they are to have the same training and education, a training in music and gymnastic, and in the art of war, which they must practise like men, 'for you must not suppose', he adds, "that what I have been saying appliest to men only and not to women as far as their natures can go."[1]

Women's Education—Plato dismisses as irrelevant the ridicule which would be excited by his proposal that women should share with men the exercises of the gymnasia, maintaining that the question should be decided on principle. The principle, he argues, which applies in this case is that each member of the state should undertake the work for which he is best fitted by nature, and while admitting that physically the woman is weaker than the man, he nevertheless maintains that in respect to political or governing ability the woman is the equal of the man. Had he affirmed that in respect to intellectual ability the woman is *on the average* the equal of the man, he would have anticipated the conclusions of modern research.

Co-Educational Proposal—His coeducational proposal arouses distrust, not so much on its own account but because the second 'wave' the community of wives and children, results from it.[2] The great waves or paradoxes in the construction of Plato's ideal state are—1. the community of goods and of pursuits; 2. the community of wives and children; 3. summarised in the statement—'Until kings are philosophers or philosopher are kings; cities will never case from ill.' To secure and preserve the unity of the state, Plato was forced to destory the family as the social unit; the family with its bonds of kinship and ties of natural affection was the only institution which he feared might challenge the supremacy, or lead to the disruption, of the state, and the pains he displays to eliminate every trace of family influence are witness of its power. Plato can only secure the unity of the state at the cost of sacrificing all differences; he makes a wilderness and calls it peace. This is the

1. **Ibid. 540.**
2. ***Republic*, 457.**

great defect of his ideal state, and on this ground his communistic scheme has been effectively criticised by Aristotle.[1]

A similar criticism has been appled by Rousseau, who says : 'I am quite aware that Plato, in the *Republic*, assigns the same gymnastics to women and men. Having got rid of the family, there is no place for women in his system of government, so he is forced to turn them into men. That great genius has worked out his plans in detail and has provided for every contingency; he has even provided against a difficulty which in all likelihood no one would ever have raised; but he has not succeeded in meeting the real difficulty. I am not speaking of the alleged community of wives which has often been laid to his charge;....I refer to that subversion of all the tenderest of our natural feelings, which he sacrificed to an artificial sentiment which can only exist by their aid.'

Role of Educator

In Plato's plan of education, the educator is considered to have greatest importance. He is like the torch bearer who leads a man, lying in a dark cave, out of the darkness into the bright light of the outside world. His task is to bring the educand out of the darkness of the cave into the light of the day. He is thus the guide.

In his methods of teaching Plato believes imitation to be of the greatest importance, for he realizes that the child learns a great deal through imitation. He will acquire the behaviour of the people among whom he is make to live. Hence, keeping in mind the status of the child, he should be made to live among people from whom he can learn good habits and avoid bad ones.

Education According to Classes

Plato's plan of education does not envisage uniform education for one and all. He accepted the concept of social stratification, and suggested that since different individuals had to perform different tasks in society, they should also be educated differently, in order to train each one in his own respective sphere. He believed that different individuals are made of different metals.

---

56. ***Politics*, ii, 3.**

Those made of gold should take up administration and government, while those made of silver were best suited for trade and defence. Others made of iron and baser metals should become labourers and agriculturists. The state must make different arrangements for the education of these different kinds of people, although Plato implicitly agrees that education of governing classes is of the greatest importance. The education of the other classes in society does not concern him very much.

Faced with the problem of determining the class of each individual, Plato suggested various kinds of tests to be conducted at different age levels. In the first place, primary education will be given to all between the ages of seven and twenty, following which a test shall be administered to everyone. Those who failed the test are to be sent to labour in the various occupations and productive trades. The successful candidates will be sent to the armed forces where training will be imparted to them for the next ten years. This will again be followed by a test, the failures will be compelled to remain in the armed forces while the successful ones will be sent to join the governing. Then this governing class will be subjected to further education in science. Later on, one from among the government class will be subject to further education in science. Later on, one from among the governing class will be elected as the philosopher administrator whose task will be to look after the government and education of the state. This individual will occupy the highest position in the land, his word will be the law of the land. Apart from this supreme individual, all other members of the governing class will continue to receive education throughout their lives, most of this education consisting of teachings in philosophy. It is thus evident that Plato granted the highest place to philosophy in his educational scheme.

Evaluation

Rousseau was correct when he commented that Plato's *The Republic* is the finest textbook on education. But it must be admitted that Plato's scheme of education suffers from certain defects and shortcomings, which have been enumerated below—

1. Little Education for the Productive Classes—In any society the labouring or productive class is invarably the largest in size. In Plato's scheme of education, this class is granted only primary education, which implies that higher education of all kinds is intended only for the soldiers and the governing classes, assuming that the labouring class has no need for such an education. Plato's dictum was that the productive class actually required no more than primary education.

2. Absence of Variety—Plato's educational plan pays no attention to the individual differences between one individual and another. He sugested the same kind of education to be given to an entire class of people, according to a uniform curriculum. This will inevitably lead to the creation of only one kind of citizens, thus inevitably leading to deadening monotony and lack of variety, which kills all future progress.

3. Stress on Philosophy—Some people get the impression that Plato's insistence on philosophy is exaggerated, and that it could only lead to an increase in the number of contemplative individuals at the expense of more practical members. But it must be remembered that Plato has stressed the importance of both bodily and mental development and in this respect, he has achieved a remarkable harmony of both.

4. Neglect of Literary Education—Plato's curriculum also neglects training in literature by stressing the importance of training in mathematics.

In spite of the above defects, Plato's concept of education has influenced educational philosophy in almost all ages. In particular, his influence can be seen in the idealist philosophy of education. And many of the finest teachers still consider Plato as their only true guide.

LIMITATIONS OF PLATO'S PRINCIPLES OF EDUCATION

Plato established the humanistic tradition in Western education. His influence on later education throught can be traced in Quintilian in the medieval curriculum, the studies constituting the *trivium* (grammar, rhetoric, logic or dialectic) **and the** quadrivium (music, arithmetic, geometry, astronomy), if different in order, being practically identical with those prescribed by Plato for the philosopher, in More's *Utopia*, Elyot's *Governour* and other renaissance writers, in the educational scheme of *The Book of Discipline* ascribed to John Knox, Rousseau's *Article on Political Economy* and in Ficthe's *Addresses to the German Nation.* Whether this influence has been for good or evil has been vigorously debated. That different interpretations can be derived from the writing of a thinker so original and fertile as Plato is only to be expected.

1. Static View of State—Thus, his static view of the state, with divisions into clearly demarcated classes, each of which is required to keep as much as possible to itself, has been condemned as undemocratic.

2. Neglect of Technical Education—Another evil side of Platonic culture, according to Whitehead, was its total neglect of technical education as an ingredient in the complete development of ideal human beings.

Contribution of Plato

On the other hand, Whitehead recognises that the Platonic ideal has rendered imperishable service to European civilisation by encouraging art, by fostering that spirit of disinterested curiosity which is the origin of science and by maintaining the dignity of mind in the face of material force. Dewey likewise acclaims Plato's procedure of untrammelled inquiry, remarking: "Nothing could be more helpful to present philosophising than a 'Back to Plato' movement, but it would have to be back to the dramatic, restless, co-operatively inquiring Plato of the *Dialogues*, trying one mode of attack after another to see what it might yield; back to the Plato whose highest flight of metaphysics always terminated with a social and practical turn, and not to the artificial Plato constructed by unimaginative commentators who treat him as the original university professor."

2

Aristotle

"In its scope, Aristotle's philosophy is perhaps the most comprehencive synthesis of knowledge ever achieved by the mind of man. No other thinker, ancient, medieval, or modern-with the possible exception of the German philosopher Hegel-has incorporated into his system so great a bulk of knowledge."

–Frank Thilly.[1]

Among the pioneers of human knowledge Aristotle was undoubtedly, the greatest. His philosophy included almost all the sciences and humanities such as logic, mathematics, physics, biology and psychology, metaphysics and ethics, politics and aesthetics. His range was encyclopaedic, original as well as creative. He was not merely an eclectic. Far from it he was the original genius behind the original growth of not only so many social sciences but also the physical sciences. His influence in philosophy surpassed even that of his master Plato. It could be seen not only on the philosophy propounded by the thinkers of the middle ages but also upon the philosophical systems of the modern western philosophy such as that of Spinoza, Immanual Kant and Hegel. His position in the history of philosophy is unique. From the criteria of breadth, originality and influence Aristotle was undoubtedly, "Master of those who know."

BIOGRAPHICAL SKETCH

Born in 384 B.C., in Stagria, a city of Greece, Aristotle had a silver spoon in his mouth right from his childhood[1]. His father,

Nicomachus, was the court physician of Philip of Macedon.[2] Aristotle entered the famous Academy of the great philosopher Plato at the early age of 17 years. He stayed there for almost 20 years as a student and a teacher. In 347 B.C. after the death of his master Plato, Aristotle left the academy and started travelling. He went to Assos in Mysia and from there to Mitylene. He was called by the king Philip to look after the education of his son Alexander the great, in 342 B.C. For seven years he was the tutor of Alexander after which he returned to Athens to establish the School known as *Lyceum*. It was also known as Peripatetic school because of the habit of Aristotle of walking while lecturing. His method of teaching was not only through lectures but also through dialogues. After the death of Alexander the great he was accused of sacrilege. He left Athens for Euboea where he died in 322 B.C.

Aristotle was a master of dialectic. He was a great observer, a voracious reader and a specialist both in natural sciences as well as in philosophy. Among his writings one finds not only on metaphysics and logic but also on human sciences like psychology and ethics and politics as well as upon natural sciences.

WORKS OF ARISTOTLE

It has been said that Aristotle wrote as many as 400 books.[3] Each book, however, means a chapter of a book as we generally understand by the term 'book' today.

Aristotle's works have been classified into those of logic, metaphysics, ethics, politics, rhetoric, psychology and natural sciences. In these fields his important works are as follows :

1. Logic—Aristotle's views concerning logic are available in his work *Organon*.This work includes categories, rules of interpretations, analytic and fallacies etc. This great work is divided into different books on these different topics.

---

1. Frank Thily, *History of Philosophy*, p. 118.

2. Gomperz *Greek Thinkers*, pp. 18-19.

3. Zeller, *Outlines of the History of Greek Philosophy*, p. 1.58

2. Metaphysics—*On Metaphysics* includes as many as 14 books of Aristotle.

3. Ethics—Aristotle's famous work *Nicomachean ethics* consists of 10 books on different topics concerning ethics. Another important work on ethics is *Eudemian ethics.*

4. Politics—Aristotle's famous book *Politics* consists of 8 books. Besides this important work he also wrote another book entitled *On the Constitution of Athens.*

5. Psychology—Aristotle's famous work *On the soul* consists of 8 books on different topics concerning human psychology. Besides, he also wrote small independent treatises on memory, dream etc.

6. Natural Sciences—Aristotle has a wide influence on almost all the natural sciences due to his pioneer work in different fields. Of these the most important are : *Physics* (eight books of which Book VII is an interpolation); *Astronomy* (four books); *Origin and Decay* (two books); *Meteorology* (four books); *Cosmology* (spurious), Botany (supurious); History of Animals (ten books, book X spurious); *On the parts of Animals* (four books); *On the Progression of Animals* (not genuine, according to some); *On the origin of Animal* (five books); *On the Locomotion of Animals* (spurious).

From the point of view of the period of writing, Aristotle's works are classified into the following three periods :

1. Writings of Platonic Age—These were written during Aristotle's stay in Plato's academy. Of these the most important is–*On the soul.*

2. Writings in the Court of Macedon—While the first class of writings has a clear influence of Plato, the writings during this period were more free and original. Of these the most important are–Aristotle's work on *Metaphysics and Politics.*

3. Writings in Lyceum—These writings were composed in Aristotle's school known as Lyceum. Of these the most important are–*On Creation and Destruction and On Heavens,* etc.

PLATO AND ARISTOTLE

Similarities

It is a common saying in the field of philosopy that a philosopher must be either a Platonist or an Aristotelian. This shows that Plato and Aristotle represented mutually contradictory views. This, however, is far from the fact. No one can deny that Aristotle was sufficiently influenced by hismaster Plato inspite of the fact that he presented so many views contradicting the views of his master. He was undoubtedly the greatest Platonist. His realist philosophy was in a way a purer and better form of Plato's theory of ideas.[1] According to Professor Zeller one can find the following similarities between the philosophical views of Plato and his disciple Aristotle[2] –

1. Objective and Scope of Philosophy—Both Plato and Aristotle believe that the subject of philosophy is Being as such, the essence which is present every where, the universal essence. Both believed that philosophy aimed at finding out the bases and the causes of physical things. This, however, is not the causation as found in sciences. It is the search after the supreme or the ultimate good which is the basis of all things but which in itself is uncaused, self-evident, free and self-sufficient.

2. Value of Objective Knowledge—Both Plato and Aristotle agreed that the philosopher must have sufficient knowledge of things in order to know the ultimate essence or being.

3. Distinction between Knowledge and Opinion—Both Plato and Aristotle distinguished between knowledge and opinion. Knowledge according to them was eternal and necessary, while knowledge and opinion were temporary and charging. Like Plato, Aristotle believed that knowledge is realisation and not only a matter of thinking.

4. Distinction between Knowledge and Experience. Plato believed that knowledge is the knowledge of universals and

---

1. Zeller, *Aristotle*, p. 162.

2. Ibid p. 165.

therefore cannot be subject to perception. Similarly, according to Aristotle, knowledge is different from sense experience. While sense experience gives us the knowledge of 'that', knowledge not only is the information concerning that but also concerning 'what'.

5. Knowledge begins in Wonder. Both Plato and Aristotic believed that all knowledge starts in wonder.

6. Philosophy is the Mother of All Sciences. Both according to Plato and Aristotle, philosophy is the highest knowledge, the mother of all sciences, the supreme and the best knowledge possible for man. This knowledge again, is necessary in order to gain any happiness in human life.

7. Philosophical Method. Both Plato and Aristotle have accepted the Socratic dialectical method and also improved upon it.

Differences

Inspite of the above mentioned similarities, as has been already pointed out in the famous philosophical proverb about their distinction, Plato and Aristotle propounded certain fundamentally different views.[1] According to Prof. Gomperz, the differences between Plato and Aristotle were natural since while the former was the enquirer into ideas, the later was an enquirer into Nature.[2] Therefore, while Plato was more interested in Abstract universal, Aristotle was searching after Concrete individual. Again, Aristotle constantly evaluated and criticised Plato's theory of ideas. According to Prof. Zellar, Aristotle followed the fundamental principles of the theory of ideas advocated by Socrates and Plato, improved upon it, elaborated it, re-defined it and presented it in a form which, inspite of having its similarities, was very much different from the original. According to Zeller, Plato and Aristotle differed in the following fundamental points[3]–

1. Stace, *A Critical History of Greek; Philosophy*, p. 256.
2. Gomperz, *Greek Thinkers*, pp. 77-78.
3. Zeller, *Aristoctle*, pp. 168-180.

1. Difference Concerning Philosophy. Plato defined philosophy in a very wide sense including almost all metaphysical, moral, practical and theoretical aspects of knowledge, though he considered it different from every other activity of human being. On the other hand, Aristotle distinguished philosophy as theoretical knowledge, as distinct from the applied knowledge. The aim of applied knowledge, accoding to Aristotle, is not the search after fundamentals but concerning things. Therefore, it includes sciences rather than philosophy.

2. The Place of Sciences in Philosophy. Plato did not elaborate his concept of creation. His primary aim was concerning theory of ideas. Aristotle agreed with Plato that scientific knowledge is primarily concerned with the universal essences. But then he proceeded to explain the phenomena as well. Thus he found a place for sciences within the realm of philosophy. According to Plato philosophical discusin was intellectual discourse, while according to Aristotle it also included discourse concerning the actual problems and things of everyday life.

3. Dialectical Method—Though Aristotle adopted the dialectical method of Plato, he enquired further in its field and gave it a completely original form. As an observer of Nature, he discovered the method of observation and included it in its philosophical method. To the analytic of Socrates, he gave a more technical form so that it may be utilised in inventions and discoveries. It has been rightly pointed out by Zeller that while Aristotle's dialectic can be used in the explanation of physical facts, the same cannot be said about the dialectic of Plato. Aristotle was not only a speculative thinker but also an accurate observer.

4. Objectivity of Knowledge. Aristotle accepted the Platonic principle that a science is concerned with the concept and the discovery of the essences but then, while according to Plato the seesneces were subjective, according to Aristotle they were objective and cannot be separated from the objects. Thus Aristotle, as contrasted to Plato, does not believe in a world of ideas as distinct and separate from the world of things. According to him the idea and the thing cannot be separated from each other, and knowledge is not only subjective but also objective.

5. Factual Interest. Thus it can be said that as compared with the philosophical interest of Plato, Aristotle had more factual interest. He always aimed at exact and accurate scientific knowledge. He was always prepared to gather facts though they may be found in any science. Therefore, Francis Bacon has wrongly concluded that Aristotle has neglected facts conerning nature.

6. Definite Knowledge. Besides being a philosopher. Plato was also a poet. Therefore one finds myths, imaginations and poetry along with mysticism in his philosophical writings. Aristotle, on the other hand, favoured exact knowledge.

7. Distinction Concerning Language—Thus Plato and Aristotle differed in their styles of writing and language. Plato had extra-ordinary mastery over language and words. But Aristotle did not pay much attention to the beauty of style or language. As contrasted to Plato, Aristotle's writings do not have that artistic eminence and linguistic excellence. He kept his works absolutely free from all literary and artistic learings. He attended more to the meaning and communication through the words. Therefore, though his style is often crude and even sometimes ugly, it helps in the understanding of concepts. He selected definite words to convey definite meanings and where such words were not available, he coined words himself. Therefore, Aristotle is known as one of the greatest linguists of the world. In fact he was the pioneer of the philosophical language and technical dictionary. Words coined by him are still very much used not only in philosophy but in so many sciences in order to convey abstract and subtle ideas. This does not mean that Aristotle's writings are absolutely devoid of poetic beauty. On the other hand, some of his writings are even more beautiful than that of Plato. In fact, Aristotle wanted to keep art and science as distinct and used different languages in their communication. A mixture of them, according to him, was injurious to both. If art is made subservient to reason, beauty will be destroyed. On the other hand, if philosophy is communicated through poetic language, it will not meet its purpose. In order to search beauty we must follow the path of art while in order to discover truth we must treat the path of reason.

EPISTEMOLOGICAL BACKGROUND OF EDUCATION

The Nature

The most important contribution made by Aristotle in the field of knowledge is in the sphere of logic. In the words of Frank Thilly "There is no parallel case in the whole history of man's intellectual pursuits in which a single thinker has brought to completion a new science". Though some effort was made concerning the science of logic even before Socrates, Aristotinle in fact was the first to lay a scientific foundation for it. Since his time to the present day traditional logic means Aristotelian logic. According to Aristotle logic is an important instrument for the acquisition of knowledge. It is the study of the first philosophy, the science of the essence of things, which requires a sound knowledge of the principle of logic. Thus logic is a preliminary science. It is a science of the method employed in persuit of knowledge. It is the science of sciences. It is a preparation for the study of all sciences. It is a tool or instrument of scientific research. It is the science of correct thinking.

The Subject Matter

Scientific truth is necessary. In the words of Aristotle it is, "Something which cannot be other than what it is." It must be proved that the opposite is impossible. Thinking consists in reasoning or scientific demonstration. Inferences are composed of judgements. Judgements expressed in language are propositions. Judgements are made up of concepts and expressed in terms. Concepts, however, have not been dealt exhaustively in Aristotle's logic. His primary concern was the logic of judgements or propositions. He has discussed the nature and kinds of judgements, their inter-relations and proofs. He was the first to discover syllogism or a series of syllogisms. Syllogism is a discourse in which from certain premises something new is concluded. Therefore, it consists of two premises major and the minor and a conclusion. According to Aristotle syllogism is the form in which educations are made. The goal of knowledge is demonstration through valid syllogism. Thus scientific knowledge rests upon syllogism. In the process of induction, according to Aristotle, we know the primary premises. The basic principles of logic are inherent in reason itself. Thought and being coinside. Rational knowledge is implicit in the mind and is made explicit by experience. Universals are the last things in-our thinking and the first in Nature. Induction is a preparation for deduction. According to Aristotle experience and reason have different functions in knowledge. Scientific knowledge is a body of necessary truths which are based upon and guaranteed by intuition. Logic concerns itself with the thought forms. Thought is directed towards some objects or the other. Thus from logic we proceed to metaphysics.

The Categories

Aristotle's theory of categories is a part of his metaphysics. Categories are fundamental concepts of thought and also basic features of reality. Thought is not possible without categories. They are however, not subjective, but given in Nature. Substance is the first category. By it Aristotle means, "That which is neither predicable of a subject nor present in a subject". By the category he means the most fundamental and universal predicate, categories, according to him, are ten of which sometimes only eight are mentioned. We can say of a thing what it is (man : substance) how it is constituted (white; quality), how large it is (two yards long; quantity), how related (greater, double : relation), where it is (in the Lyceum : space), when it was yesterday: time) what posture it assumes (lies, sits : position), the condition it is in (armed state), what it does (burns : activity), and what it suffers (is burned : passivity) Science deals with the category of substance, which therefore is the most important.

Aristotle's theory of category has been criticised by Stoice, by Neo Platonists and philosophers like Plotinus. The German philosopher Immanual Kant has pointed out that Aristotle has described the ten categories as he pleased without any system. According to the German philosopher Hegel Aristotle threw categories at a place at random. J.S. Mill has also criticised the concept of categories by pointing out that it is an effort to divide animal beings into human, quadrupeds, horses, donkies and mules. Now, these criticisms of Aristotelian categories are not absolutely pointless. While conceiving categories Aristotle's aim was not the arrival at highest concepts nor was it simplification. He has himself admitted that the category of quality cannot be distinguished from the category of relation. He was, however, satisfied that the category of quality is required in certain forms of descriptions. He has also admitted that the same term can be classified into two categories. The classification of categories, according to Aristotle, was based upon linguistic expediency. Therefore he did not use them to achieve philosophical aims. Hence J.S. Mill's objection that in Aristotle's logic the distinction between categories is merely linguistic is both right and wrong.

PSYCHOLOGICAL BACKGROUND

Body and Soul

Aristotle is known as the founder of systematic and comparative zoology. His biology is opposed to quantitative and mechanical conception of nature. According to him it is qualitative, dynamic and teleological. The body is an *organon* or instrument of the soul. It is meant for the use of the soul. Soul moves body and determines the principle of life. Thus, Aristotle's biology has been termed as vitalism. Body and soul form an indivisible unity. In this unity the soul is the controlling guiding principle. The whole is prior to the parts and the parts realised the purpose of the whole. Thus the body is the instrument for the realization of the purposes of the soul. Where there is life, there is soul. Thus, corresponding to different forms of life, there are different grades or degrees of soúl. As soul and body constitute one unit, neither can there be a body without soul nor a soul without body. Again, since every being has a different body and therefore a different soul, a human soul cannot enter the body of a horse. In this series of souls there is a gradual ascending order from lowest to the highest. This series starts from the plant soul and rises to the human soul. In man the plant soul governs the functions of nutrition, growth and reproduction while the human soul governs higher powers.

Mind-Body Dualism

In the field of psychology Aristotle has discovered ideas concerning sensations, perception, imagination, feelings, memory, emotions, thinking and almost all other psychological processes. The soul of man, according to him, resembles the plant soul so far as it controls the lower vital functions. The animal soul in man works through the faculties of perception. Sense perception is a change produced in the soul by the perceived thing. The soul is informed about the qualities of things through the sense organs. Heart is the organ of common sense. It is the meeting place of all the sensations which are then combined to form total picture of an object. Heart again, gives an idea concerning number, size, shape, motion and rest etc. The feelings of pleasure and pain are connected with perception. When functions are furthered we feel pleasure and when impeded we feel pain, Feelings again, arouse desire and aversion. Desire is the result of perception of desirable object. It is accompanied by deliberation or rational will. Reason, again, is the characteristic of human soul. It is the faculty of conceptaul thought. It is initially potential and is actualised in thinking. Aristotle has distinguished between active and passive reason. Active reason is creative, pure actuality like the pure soul of Plato. While passive reason is the matter, active reason is the form of thought and concepts are the result of the combination of both. Thus, Aristotle's dualism of form and matter continues in his psychology. The same dualism is found in body mind relationship. Perception, imagination and memory are connected with the body. Creative reason, however, is connected with the soul. It is immaterial, imperishable and therefore, immortal. It is the spark of divine in human soul. It does not arise with man nor perish with him. It is not individual reason but the universal in man.

SOCIETY AS EDUCATOR

In an early dialogue of Plato's the *Protagoras,* Socrates asks Protagoras why it is not as easy to find teachers of virtue as it is to find teachers of swordsmanship, riding or any other art. Protagoras' answer is that there are no special teachers of virtue, becaue virtue is taught by the whole community. Plato and Aristotle both accept the view of moral education implied in this answer. In a passage of the *Republic* (492 b) Plato repudiates the notion that the sophists have a corrupting moral influence upon young men. The public themselves, he says, are the real sophists and the most complete and thorough educators. No private education can hold out against the irresistible force of public opinion and the ordinary moral standards of society. But that makes it all the more essential that public opinion and social environment should not be left to grow up at haphazard as they ordinarily do, but should be made by the wise legislator the expression of the good and be informed in all their details by his knowledge. The legislator is the only possible teacher of virtue.

VALUE OF EDUCATION IN THE STATE

Aristotle assigns the paramount political importance to education. It is the great instrument by which the legislator can ensure that the future citizens of his state will share those common beliefs which make the state possible. The Greeks with their small states had a far clearer apprehension than we can have of the dependence of a constitution upon the people who have to work it.

If the state is the organisation of men seeking a common good, power and political position must be given to those who can forward this end. This is the principle expressed in Aristotle's account of political justice, the principle of "tools to those who can use them." As the aim of the state is differently conceived, the qualifications for government will vary. In the ideal state power will be given to the man with most knowledge of the good; in other states to the men who are most truly capable of achieving that end which the citizens have set themselves to pursue. The justest distribution of political power is that in which there is least waste of political ability.

According to Aristotle the virtue of a good citizen and good governor is the same as of a good man; and that every one before he commands should have first obeyed, it is the business of the legislator to consider how his citizens may be good men, what education is necessary to that purpose, and what is the final object of a good life.

Now life is divided into labour and rest, war and peace; and of what we do the objects are partly necessary and useful, partly noble; and we should give the same preference to these that we do to the different parts of the soul and its actions, as war to procure peace; labour, rest; and the useful, the noble. The politician, therefore, who composes a body of laws ought to extend his views to everything; the different parts of the soul and their actions; more particularly to those things which are of a superior nature and ends; and in the same manner, to the lives of men and their different actions. They ought to be fitted both for labour and war, but rather for rest and peace; and also to do what is necessary and useful, but rather what is fair and noble. It is to those objects that the education of the children ought to tend, and of all the youths who want instruction.

EDUCATION OF THE CHILD

When a child is born the strength of its body will depend greatly upon the quality of its food. People who desire that their children should acquire a warlike habit, feed them chiefly with milk, as being best accommodated to their bodies, but without wine, to prevent any distempers; those motions which are natural to their age are very serviceable; and those should be prevented which makes their limbs crooked. On account of their extreme ductility, some people use particular machines that their bodies may not be distorted. It is useful to ensure them to the cold when they are very little; for this is very serviceable for their health; and to enure them to the business of war; whatever it is possible to accustom children to, it is best to accustom them to it at first, but to do it by degrees; besides, boys have naturally a habit of loving the cold, on account of the heat.

No Education Upto Five Years

According to Aristotle, these, then, and such-like things

ought to be the first object of our attention; the next age to this continues till the child is five years old; during which time it is best to teach him nothing at all, not even necessary labour, lest it should hinder his growth; but he should be accustomed to use so much motion as not to acquire a lazy habit of of body; which he will get by various means and by play also; his play also ought to be neither illiberal nor too labourious nor lazy.

Imitation Theory of Play

Their governors and preceptors of children should take care what sort of tales and stories it may be proper for them to hear; for all these ought to pave the way for their future instruction for which reason the generality of their play should be imitations of what they are afterwards to do seriously. They too do wrong who forbid by laws the disputes between boys and their quarrels, for they contribute to increase their growth; as they are sort of exercise to the body. The struggles of the heart and the compression of the spirits give strength to those who labour, which happens to boys in their disputes. The preceptors also ought to have an eye upon their manner of life, and those with whom they converse; and to take care that they are never in the company of slaves.

Home Education

At this time and till they are seven years old it is necessary that they should be educated at home. It is also very proper to banish, both from their hearing and sight, everything which is illiberal and the like. The legislator should banish every indecent expression out of the state : for from a permission to speak whatever is shameful, very quickly arises the doing it, particularly with young people. Let them never speak nor hear any such thing. If it appears that any freeman has done or said anything that is forbidden before he is of age to be thought fit to partake of the common meals, let him be punished by disgrace and stripes : But if a person above that age does so, let him be treated as you would a slave on account of his being infamous. As we forbid child speaking everything which is forbidden, it is necessary that he neither sees obscene stories nor pictures. The magistrates should take care that there are no statues or pictures of anything of this nature, except only of those gods to which the law allows persons of a certain age to pay their devotions, for themselves, their wives, and children. It should also be illegal for young persons to be present either at iambics or comedies before they are arrived at that age when they are allowed to partake of the pleasure of the table. "Indeed a good education will preserve" them from all the evils which attend on these things."

According to Aristotle, what we meet with first pleases best : for which reason children should be kept strangers to everything which is bad, more particularly whatsoever is loose and offensive to good manners. When five years are accomplished, the two next may be very properly employed in being spectators of those exercise they will afterwards have to learn.

TWO PERIODS OF EDUCATION

According to Aristotle, there are two periods into which education ought to be divided, according to the age of the child; the one is from his being seven years of age to the time of puberty; the other from puberty till he is twenty-one. Those who divide ages by the number seven are in general wrong : it is much better to follow the division of nature; for every art and every instruction is intended to complete what nature has left defective.

Thus, Aristotle, like the sages of India of his time considered good sanstomes as the most important in the early education of the children. Today, when children are being indiscriminately exposed to all type of experiences, particularly through the media, it is a point with consideration by those who are concerned with the education of the children. It is unfortunate that today, almost all over the world the contemporary pedagogues are neglecting this common wisdom of East and West.

EDUCATION OF MAGISTRATES

Aristotle say, "No one can doubt that the magistrate ought greatly to interest himself in the care of youth; for where it is neglected it is hurtful to the city, for every state ought to be governed according to its particular nature; for the form and manners of each government are peculiar to itself; and these as they originally established it, so they usually still preserve it." Universally, the best manners produce the best government. Besides, as in every business and art there are some things which men are to learn first and be made accustomed to, which are necessary to perform their several works. So it is evident that the same thing is necessary in the practice of virtue.

UNIFORM SYSTEM OF EDUCATION

According to Aristotle, as there is one end in view in every city, it is evident that education ought to be one and the same in each; and that this should be a common care, and not the individual's, as it now is when every one takes care of his own children separately, and their instructions are particular also, each person teaching them as they please; but what ought to be engaged in ought to be common to all." Besides, no one ought to think that any citizen belongs to him in particular, but to the state in general; for each one is a part of the state, and it is the natural duty of each part to regard the good of the whole. Aristotle praised Lacedaemonians for they give the greatest attention to education, and make it public. "It is evident, concludes Aristotle, then, that there should be laws concerning education, and that it should be public."

CURRICULUM OF CHILD EDUCATION

According to Aristotle, "What education is, and how children ought to be instruted, is what should be well-known; for there are doubts concerning the business of it, as all people do not agree in those things they would have a child taught, both with respect to their improvement in virtue and a happy life : nor is it clear whether the object of it should be to improve the reason or rectify the morals."

From the present mode of education continues Aristotle "we cannot determine with certainty to which men incline, whether to instruct a child in what will be useful to him in life; or what tends to virtue, and what is excellent : for all these things have their separate defenders." As to virtue, there is not particular in which they all agree : for as all do not equally all virtues, it reasonably follows that they will not cultivate the same. It is evident that what is necessary ought to be taught to all : but that which is necessary for one is not necessary for all; for there ought to be a distinction between the empkloyment of a freeman and a slave. The first of these should be taught everything useful which will not make those who know it mean. According to Aristotle, "Every work is to be estreemed mean, and every art and every discipline which renders the body, the mind, or the understanding of freemen unfit for the habit and practice of virtue : for which reason all those arts which tend to deform the body are called mean, and all those employments which are exercised for gain; for they take off from the freedom of the mind and render it sordid." There are also some literal arts which are not improper for freemen to apply to in a certain degree; but to endeavour to acquire a perfect skill in them is exposed to the faults.

Aristotle points out that there are four things which it is usual to teach children; reading, gymnastic exercise, and music, to which (in the fourth place) some add painting. Reading and painting are both of them of singular use in life, and gymnastic exercise, as are productive of courage. As to music, some persons may doubt, as most persons now useit for the sake of pleasure; but those who oiginally made it part of education did it because, nature requires that we should not only be properly employed, but to be able to enjoy leisure honourably. According to Aristotle "But, though both labour and rest are necessary, yet the latter is preferable to the first; and by all means man ought to learn what he should do when at rest : for he ought not to employ that time at play; for then play would be the necessary business of his lives. Play is more necessary for those who labour than those who are at the rest : for he who labours requires relaxation; which play will supply : for as labour is attended with pain and continued exertion, it is necessary that play should be introduced, under proper regulations, as a medicine : for such an employment of the mind is a relaxation to it, and cases with pleasure. Now rest itself seems to partake of pleasure, of happiness, and an agreeable life : but this cannot be theirs who labour, but theirs who are at rest; for he who labours, labours for the sake of some end which he has not. According to Aristotle, "Happiness is an end which all persons think is attended with pleasure and not with pain : but all persons do not agree in making this pleasure consist in the same thing; for each one has his particular standard, correspondent to his own habits; but the best man proposes the best pleasure, and that which arises from the noblest actions." To live a life of rest there are some things which a man must learn and be instructed in. The object of this learning and this instruction centres in their acquisition. The learning and instruction which is given for labour has for its object other things. The ancients made music a part of education; not as a thing necessary, for it is not of that nature, not as a thing useful, as reading, in the common course of life, or for managing of a family, or for learning anything as useful in public life. Painting also seems useful to enable a man to judge more accurately of the productions of the finer arts : nor is it like the gymnastic exercise, which contribute to health and strength; for neither of these things do we see produced by music. The employment of our rest, they had in view who introduced it. It is proper employment for freemen.

It is evident, then, that there is a certain education in which a child may be instructed, not as useful nor as necessary, but as noble and liberal, We have the testimony of the anicents in our favour, by what they have delivered down upon education—for music makes this plain. Moreover, it is necessary to instruct children in what is useful, not only on account of its being useful in itself, as, for instance, to learn to read, but also as the means of acquiring other different sorts of instruction. Thus, they should be instructed in painting, not only to prevent their being mistake in purchasing pictures, or in buying or selling of vases, but rather as it makes them judges of the beauties of the human form. According to Aristotle, "To be always hunting after the profitable ill agrees with great and freedom souls." Whether a boy should be first taught morals or reasoning, and whether his body or his understanding should be first cultivated, it is plain that boys should be first put under the care of the different masters of the gymnastic arts, both to form their bodies and teach them their exercises.

3

Ignatious Loyola

"The Jesuit educational system is likewise a phase of the renaissance movement, and the general practice of the Jesuit schools corresponded with the practice of all Western and Central Europe of whatever religion." ***-R. Schwickerath***

THE JESUIT SOCIETY

Ignatius Loyola, knight of noble birth, recognised that all available gifts of intellect and birth would be required for the crusade which the Company of Jesus was enrolled to wage. Consequently it gave him peculiar satisfaction when the tests imposed on candidates for admission to the Society were passed by youths of noble birth. The Society devoted itself mainly to higher education. Its aim was to arrest the disintegrating forces in the religious life of Europe. To effect this it was necessary to attack the evils at their source, namely, in the universities, hence the Society's concern for higher education.

According to the *Constitution* of the Society instructing others in reading and writing would be a work of charity if the Society had a sufficient number of persons available, but on account of dearth of teachers it is not ordinarily accustomed to undertake this.

PUBLIC EDUCATION

The Jesuits extoled Public education. As T. Hughen puts it, "For this moral strengthening of character, no less than for the invigorating of mental energies, the system of Ignatius Loyola prescribes an education which is public – public, as being that of many students together, public as opposed to private tutorism, public, in fine, as requiring a sufficiency of the open, fearless exercise both of practical morality and of religion."[1]

After his surrender to the Christian life, it was early borne in on Loyola, that without proper education his labours would be of no avail. When over thirty years of age, he resolved to acquire from the beginning the Latin rudiments and patiently to learn his lessons among the ordinary pupils. Bringing to his studies an adult mind of a surprisingly practical type and an unerring judgement, he could reflect upon the methods employed, and from his own initial failures deduce a procedure from which other might profit. Francis Thomposon writes, one knows not whether more to admire his astonishing determination or his astonishing mental power, when it is reflected that he carried through his philosophical studies at the age of forty-four, having begun his whole education from the very elements others acquire in boyhood."

On the 3rd May 1539, a series of resolutions was adopted by the few companions to whom Ignatius Loyola had communicated his ideas of founding a society, agreeing : (1) to take an explicit vow of obedience to the Pope ; (2) to teach the Commandments to children or anyone else; (3) to take a fixed time – an hour more or less – to teach the Commandments and Catechism in an orderly way ; (4) to give forty days in the year for this work.

THE CONSTITUTION

Ignatius set forth the fundamental principles of the Society in the Constitution. It consists of ten parts, the fourth and largest of which presents in outline the plan of studies which was later more

---

1. T. Hughes, Loyola, p.99.

fully elaborated in the *Ratio Studiorum.* In part I of the *Constitutions,* Ignatius prescribes the conditions of admission to the Society. In Part II he recounts the causes justifying the dismissal of probationers or of members of the Order. According to Ignatius, the Society should demand of its entrants the qualities which Plato in the *Republic* required of his philosophers. "It is needful', Ignatius states, 'that those who are admitted to aid the Society in spiritual concerns be furnished with these following gifts of God. As regards their intellect : of sound doctrine, or apt to learn it; of discretion in the management of business, or, at least, of capacity and judgment to attain to it. As to memory : of aptitude to perceive, and also to retain their perceptions. As to intentions : that they be studious of all virtue and spiritual perfection ; calm, steadfast, strenuous in what they undertake for God's service; burning with zeal for the salvation of souls, and therefore attached to our Institute; which directly tends to aid and dispose the souls of men to the attainment of that ultimate end, from the hand of God, our Creator and Lord. In externals : facility of language, so needful in our intercourse with our neighbour, is most desirable, a comely presence, for the edification of those with whom we have to deal. Good health, and strength to undergo the labours of our Institute. Age to correspond with what has been said; which in those admitted to probation should exceed the fourteenth year and in those admitted to profession the twenty-fifth. As the external gifts of nobility, wealth, reputation and the like are not sufficient, if others are wanting; so, if there be a sufficiency of others, these are not essential ; so far, however, as they tend to edification, they make those more fit for admission, who, even without them, would be eligible on account of the qualities before mentioned; in which, the more he excels who desires to be admitted, so much the more fit will be be for this Society, to the glory of God our Lord, and the less he excels, so much the less serviceable will he be. But the sacred unction of the divine Wisdom will instruct those who undertake this duty to His service and more abundant praise, what standard should be maintained in all these things."

PHYSICAL EDUCATION

In Part III of the *Constitutions,* a chapter is included 'Of the Superintendence of the Body'. Speaking from his own experience, Loyola frequently warned his companions against the subversive influence of an enfeebled bodily condition. The charge frequently made against the Jesuit system of education, that it does not regard the physical care of the pupil, is accordingly not warranted by the *Constitutions* of the Society.

EDUCATIONAL ORGANISATION AND MANAGEMENT

The fourth Part of the *Constitutions* is devoted to the regulations governing the instruction in literature and other studies of those who remain in the Society after their two years' period of probation. The first ten chapters of this Part are concerned with the organisation and management of the colleges, the remaining seven with unversities.

Aim and scope of the work of colleges

As the object of the doctrine to be acquired in this Society is by the divine favour to benefit their own and their neighbours' souls, this will be the measure in general and in particular cases, by which it shall be determined to what studies our scholars should apply, and how far they should proceed in them. And since, generally speaking, the acquisition of diverse languages, logic, natural and moral philosophy, metaphysics, and theology, both scholastic as what is termed "positive", and the Sacred Scriptures assist that object, they who are sent to our colleges shall give their attention to the study of these faculties; and they shall bestow greater diligence upon those subjects which the supreme Moderator of the studies shall consider most expedient in the Lord to the aforesaid end, the circumstances of times, places, and persons being considered."[1]

1.Constitutions, Pt. IV, ch. V, S I.

Order of Studies

The order of studies to be followed is first the Latin language, then the liberal arts, thereafter scholastic, then positive theoglogy. The sacred scriptures may be taken either at the same time as the foregoing or afterwards.[1]

The Scholars

The scholars to be assiduous in attending lectures, and diligent in preparing for them; and when they have heard them, in repeating them ; in places which they have not understood, making inquiry ; in others, where needful, taking notes, to provide for any future defect of memory.[2] Latin was commonly to be spoken by all, but especially by the students in humanity. Since the habit of debating is useful, especially to the students in arts and scholastic theology, instructions are given as to when and how these debates or disputations are to be arranged and conducted. There should be in each college be given to those who ought to have it. Besides these, however, every one should have such other books as are necessary.[3]

Those scholars who intend to devote their lives to the work of the Society are further instructed in the performance of the ordinances of the Church; "and to discharge this duty, let them labour to acquire thoroughly the vernacular tongue of the country."

The Universities : Curriculum

"The universities which the Society shall establish or maintain shall consist of the three faculties : languages, arts and theology'[4] "the study of Medicine and of the Law shall not be engaged in within the Universities of our Society; or at least, the Society shall not take that duty upon itself, as being remote from our Institute."[5] The curriculum in arts shall extend over three and

1. Constitutions, Pt. Iv, ch. vi.

2. Ibid.

3. Ibid Ch. viii.

4. Ibid Ch. xviii.

5. Ibid Ch. xii.

a half years, and that in theology over four years. In the arts curriculum reference is made to the natural sciences which 'dispose the mind to Theology, and contribute to its perfect study and practice, and of themselves assist in the same object'. It is further enjoined that the natural sciences, 'be taught by learned professors, and with proper diligence, sincerely seeking the honour and glory of God in all things".

Modification Positive

Provision was made by Ignatius Loyola in the *Constitutions* for modification of his outline plan of studies according to circumstances. This concession should not be abused. The uniformity of the system should not destroyed. It was considered expedient that an authoritative yet more detailed plan of studies than that outlined in the *Constitutions* should be issued for the guidance of the schools and colleges of the Society.

The *Ratio Studiorum,* was accordingly prepared as the main source of the educational doctrines of the Society. Jouvancy's *Ratio Discendi et Docendi* is regarded as the official complement to, and commentary on, the *Ratio Studiorum.*

Ratio Studiorum

Unlike the *Constitutions* the *Ratio Studiorum* deals exclusively with education. It sets forth the following rules and regulations :

1. Regulations which are to direct the Superior of a Province in dealing with education in his Province.

2. The regulations which the Rector of a college is to apply in governing a college.

3. The guidance of the prefect of Studies.

4. General regulations for the professors of the higher faculties–theology and philosophy.

5. Special rules for the professors of each subject in the faculties : sacred writings, Herbrew, scholastic theology,

ecclesiastical history, canonical law and moral or practical theology, moral philosophy, physics and mathematics.

6. Regulations for the Prefects of the Lower studies.

7. Regulations for the conduct of written examinations and for the awarding of prizes.

8. The general regulations for the professors of the lower classes.

9. Detailed regulations for the professors of rhetoric, humanity and higher, intermediate and lower grammar.

10. Rules for the pupils for the management of Academies, etc., are added.

The *Ratio Studiorum* comprehends all subjects from the principles governing the educational administration of a Province to the fixing of school holidays, the textbooks to be used in teaching Latin grammar and the method of correcting exercises.

The general organisation of the educational work of the society

It may be gathered from the regulations issued for the direction of the Provincial that the theological course of four years is the highest. It is preceded by a course of philosophy extending over three years. The Provincial shall not send pupils to philosophy before they have studied rhetoric for two years. All students in the philosophical course must attend lectures in mathematics. Students, who show special proficiency in any subject, should have the opportunity of extending their study of that subject. The classes for the Lower Studies are not to exceed five : one for rhetoric, another for humanity and three for grammar. These classes are not to be confused with one another. Parallel classes for the various grades are to be instituted if the number of pupils warrants.

Regulations for the Rector of a college

The need of trained teachers even for the lowest classes is recognised. The teachers of the lower classes should not take up the work of teaching without training. The Rector of the college should select some one specially skilled in teaching. Towards the end of their future teachers should come to him three times a week for an hour to be trained for their calling in methods of exposition, dictation, writing, correcting and all the duties of a good teacher.

Prefect of Studies

In colleges the Rector appoints a Prefect of Studies as his assistant, his position somewhat analgous to that of the Dean of a Faculty. He is responsible to the Rector for the proper organisation of studies and the regulating of classes so that those who attend may make as much advancement as possible in uprightness of life, the arts and doctrine. The Prefect of Lower Studies aids the Rector in ruling and governing schools in such a way that those who attend may progress no less in uprightness of life than in the liberal arts. In day schools the Prefect of Studies is ordinarily responsible for both studies and discipline. In boarding schools he exercises both functions within class hours. Prefect of Studies may have as assistant a Prefect of Discipline whose duties in a boarding school would be somewhat analogous to those of a Bursar in an English Public School or in a University College.

General Regulation for Professors

The educational aim of the Society is recalled in the general regulations for all the professors of higher faculties. It is to lead the pupil to the service and love of God and to the practice of virtue. Each professor is required to offer up a suitable prayer before beginning his lecture. Directions are given as to how far authorities are to be followed and used by the professors in lecturing, and how they are to lecture that the students may be able to take proper notes. After each lecture the professor is to remain a quarter of an hour for the student interrogations about the substance of the lecture. At the end of each session a month is to be devoted to the repetition of the course. The last general rule for all the professors is that the professor is not to show himself more familiar with one student than with another ; he is to disregard no one, and to further the studies of the poor equally with the rich ; he is to promote the advancement of each individual student.

Detailed directions follow for the professors of each of the subjects in the faculties of theology and philosophy. In the 1832 revision of the *Ratio*, special provision was made for the teaching of physics, which had previously been treated under the general title philosophy. The regulations for the teaching of mathematics were modernised.

The rules for the Prefect of the Lower Studies

He is to help the masters and direct them. He is to be especially cautious that the esteem and authority due to them be not impaired in the least. Once a fortnight he is to hear each one teach. He is to see that the teacher covers the class-book in the first half-year, and repeats it from the beginning in the second term. Promotion is generally given after the long vacation. Where it would appear that a pupil would make better progress in a higher class, he is not to be detained in the lower, but to be promoted at any time of the year after examination. When there is a doubt whether a pupil should ordinarily be promoted, his class records are to be examined, and his age, diligence and the time spent in the class are to be taken into consideration. While intimating promotions the names of pupils gaining special distinction are to be announced first ; the others are to be arranged in alphabetic order. To further the literary training of the pupils, the Prefect is to institute Academies or school societies. In these on specified days the pupils are to hold lectures, debates, etc., amongst themselves. A Censor is to be appointed, one who is held in esteem by his fellow-pupils and who shall have the power to impose small penalties. For the sake of those who are wanting in diligence and in good manners and on whom advice and exhortation have no effect, a Corrector, who is not to be a member of the Society, is to be appointed. When reformation is despaired of, and the pupil is likely to become a danger to his fellows, he is to be expelled.

Rules for Professor of Lower Studies

Among the general regulations for the professors of the Lower Studies are those dealing with the Praelectio, or method of exposition of a subject or lesson, and those concerning emulation. Four stages were in exposition of a lesson or passage; (1) The whole passage, when not too long, is to be read through. (2) the argument is to be explained, also, when necessary, the connection with what went before. (3) Each sentence is to be read, the obscure points elucidated ; the sentences are to be connected together, and the thought made evident. (4) The whole is to be repeated from the beginning.

Through out the *Constitutions* and the *Ratio* anything likely to excite contention or produce invidious distinctions is deprecated. Graduates are not to occupy special seats in the university classes, and the class lists are to be in alphabetic order. That emulation is not a dominant or integral part of the Jesuit system may be judged from the fact that only four regulations are here devoted to it. It was merely one among other devices to enliven instruction and develop in the pupils a ready command of the knowledge which they had acquired. The directions governing its use state that the *Concertatio*, or contest, is usually so conducted that either the teacher puts the question, and the *aemulus* or adversary corrects the answer, or the adversaries question one another. The contest is to be held in the highest regard. It is to take place as frequently as time permits, so that a noble emulation, may be fostered which is a great incitement to study. The contest may be engaged in by one or more on either side, especially by the better pupils of the class against one another. A contest of one against many may even be allowed. An average pupil may sometimes challenge a distinguished pupil. If he overcomes, he succeeds to the superior office. Public contests may be allowed on occasion, but only for the better pupils. One class may contend with the class next to it on a common subject of study, both teachers presiding.

Though the *Ratio* is not the work of Ignatius; it nevertheless represents more fully, and doubtless more justly, his views on, and practices in, education than his *Constitutions,* in which the subject could be treated only as part of the general work of the Society.

Contribution of Jesuits

To the Jesuits must be given the credit of providing education with a uniform and universal method. "So far as the evidence of history extends," said loyola "an organised caste of priests, combining the necessary leisure with the equally necessary continuity of tradition, was at all times indispensable to the beginnings of scientific research."[1] The need of a uniform and universal method in teaching was thus declared in the Proem to the 1586 *Ratio* : 'Unless a ready and true method be adopted much labour is spent in gathering but little fruit .... We cannot imagine that we do justice to our functions, or come up to the expectations formed of us, if we do not feed the multitude of youths, in the same way as nurses do, with food dressed up in the best way, for fear they grow up in our schools, without growing up much in learning."[2]

Role of Teacher

The Jesuits system does not, however, exalt the method at the expense of the teacher. In the selection of teachers something of the same discrimination as Ignatius exercised in his choice of the first members of the Society is still demanded. The selected candidates are subjected to a training. Yet the educational authorities in many modern countries have failed to realise the importance of thorough professional training for all engaged in higher education, including university teaching.

Value of Training

The value of training was recognised in the draft *Ratio* of 1586 in the statemnet : "It would be most profitable for the

---

1. T. Gomperz, Greek Thinkers, English transalation (London, John, Murray, IgoI), vol. i, p.43.

2. Pachtler, vol. v, p. 27.

schools, if those who are about to be preceptors were privately taken in hand by some one of great experience, and for two months or more were practised by him in the method of reading, teaching, correcting, writing, and managing a class." If teachers have not learned these things beforehand, they are forced to learn them afterwards at the expense of their scholars; and then they will acquire proficiency only when they have already lost in reputaton; and perchance they will never unlearn a bad habit. Sometimes such a habit is neither very serious nor incorrigible, if taken at the beginning; but if the habit is not corrected at the outset, it comes to pass that a man, who otherwise would have been most useful, becomes well-nigh useless. There is no describing how much amiss preceptors take it, if they arecorrected, when they have already adopted a fixed method of teaching; and what continual disagreement ensues on that score with the Prefect of Studies. To obviate this evil, in the case of our professors, let the Prefect in the chief college, whence our professors of humanities and grammar are usually taken, remind the Rector and Provincial, about three months before the next scholastic year begins, that, if the Province needs new professors far versed in the art of managing classess, whether he be at the time actually a professor or a student of theology or philosophy, and to him the future masters are to go daily for an hour to be preared by him for their new ministry, giving dirlections in turn, writing, dicaing, correcting and discharging the other duties of a good teacher."

Place of Classics

The predominant place assigned to classics in the Jesuit curriculum has historical justification. The Society has not bound itself slavishly to a seventeenth-century curriculum. The widening of the conception of culture to connote not only the classical languages but also a precise use of the mother tongue, an appreciation of modern literatue, the principles of mathematics and the methods of natural science, has been recognised by the Jesuits. The new subjects, when admitted to the curriculum, have been taught with the same thoroughness as the old.

Successive Teaching

In order of time the mathematical subjects follow the classical subjects. The subjects are taught sucessively, not simultaneously. On pedagogical grounds the Jesuits defend the successive teaching of different branches of instruction in preference to the simultaneous treatment of a number of subjects. However, they modify this procedure when any government system requires this. Their arrangement is partly recognised in the demand of present day educators who advocate successive periods of 'intensive study' of the various school subjects.

1. Dramatic Method—In retaining the drama as an educational instrument the Jesuits anticipated the modern movement represented by the dramatic method of teaching history.

2. Direct Method—In insisting on the speaking of Latin they like wise anticipated the direct method of teaching the classics.

3. Repetition—In repeating the work of the class twice in the year, and thus enabling the abler pupils to spend only half a session in a grade and thus be promoted more rapidly, they introduced a procedure now adopted by some modern school systems.

4. Discipline—The Jesuits' contribution to school discipline was notable. To the early Jesuits we owe the substitution of supervision for compulsion. The principle implied is that prevention is better than cure. They did not, however, dispense with punishment altogether. The *Ratio* of 1599 recommended the introduction of a Corrector, who was to administer chastisement when such was necessary. The office of Corrector was later dispensed with, but the principle of dissociating punishment from teaching has been retained. Gentleness is especially enjoined towards the pupils. Ignatius prescrbing as the maxim of the Society that it must always govern by love.[1] That obedience is one of the vows taken by the members of the Society must lighten the work of teaching.

---

1. Ibid vol. v, p. 154; Schwickerath, pp. 432-3.

5. Moral and Religious Education—In the Confession and the Communion the Society possesses powerful instruments for the moral and religious education of the pupil. Through the communion the Society secures practice in worship, an exercise which distinguishes the religious from the moral attitude to life, and a training in which is essential to a complete and generous eduation.

6. Changing System—The Jesuit system has survived since its approval by the Pope in 1540. It has adapted itself with a certain measure of success to changing conditions.

7. Universal System—As its exponents are not merely educators, but missionaries of a religious faith, it has been applied in almost every country in the world. The Jesuit educational system has taught the world the value of a uniform and universal method in education, and the economy of a cultured and highlytrained teaching profession.

Writing of Loyola – Fancis Thompson says : "When he spoke, it was not what he said, it was the suppressed heat of personal feeling, personal conviction which enkindled men. This has ever been the secret of great teachers, were they only school–masters; it is the communication of themselves that avails."[1]

❑❑❑

---

1. Francis Thompson, Saint Ignatius Loyola, p. I81.

4

John Amos Comenius

"Comenius proposed to teach all things to all men', but also set about planning a universal system of education in a practical fashion devising methods of teaching which would hasten the attainment of his ideal; even preparing school books to illustrate how his principles should be applied in practice."

—R.R. Rusk

According to Comenius, God is the deal of education. Education includes knowledge concerning the world and its relationship with man. Thus, Comenius was influenced by the religious aims of education. However, he also opened the gates of secular ideal of education. Education, according to him, starts in the lap of the mother. The mother makes a significant contribution to the first six years of the child development. The development of his tendencies in the next six years very much depends upon the school. In the next six years more intelligent students may be allowed to study in the Latin schools. Those who successfully pass through it may study at the university for another six years. The method of education, according to Comenius, should adhere to the rules of child's nature. His interests should be developed and intellectual development should be realised through the use of his senses. Perception should be given emphasis in learning.

SOURCES OF KNOWLEDGE

According to Comenius there are three sources of knowledge–inner knowledge, observation and idea. The means of attainment of knowledge are : sense, intelligence and talent. The three aims of education are :

1. To give knowledge to man for success in life.
2. To give wisdom for moral and character development.
3. To create devotion to God in man.

PRINCIPLES OF EDUCATION

From the point of view of teaching methds, Comenius has laid down the following principles meant for the reform of the educational system of his time :

1. Whatever is to be taught to the child should be told in direct and clear words.
2. The thing to be taught should have practical utility.
3. Education should not be complex.
4. The purpose of whatever is to be taught should be clearly stated.
5. General rules should be explained before-hand.
6. It is necessary to teach everything or all aspects of a subject in a proper order, proper place and proper relationship.
7. All subjects should be taught in a proper order.
8. The subject should not be left unless the child understands it properly.

Rules for the Development of the Child

The above principles were summarised in the following rules for the development of the child :

1. Proceed from concrete to abstract.
2. If possible, present mutual co-relation.
3. Adopt result method.
4. Prompt the interest of the child.
5. It is necessary to proceed towards 'to prove' instead of 'to assure'; 'to see' instead of 'to discuss' and 'to know' instead of 'to believe'.

SCHOOL MANAGEMENT

Comenius has classified schools according to different stages of the development of the child. Thus, school may be organised for infants, children, adolescents and the adults. Infancy schools may admit infants from birth to six years of age. Childhood schools may admit children from six years to twelve years to be taught through mother-tongue. Adolescence schools provide education to adolescents from 12 to 18 years of age through Latin. These are also called Latin schools. Beyond 18 years of age the educand may be admitted to schools for adulthood. The functions of all these categories of schools are :

1. To teach language.
2. To develop faculties through the study of science and art.
3. To develop morality.
4. To create true devotion in God.

NEW SYSTEM OF EDUCATION

The following characteristics show that Comenius established a new system of education in seventeenth century :

1. Practical—Children should be taught practical things having utility in their life and at the same time they should understand them as well.

2. Self-experience—The child should understand the reality by his self-experience, should explore things himself and should not depend on others.

3. Mother-Tongue—The medium of education should be mother-tongue. Only then education will be enjoyable, easy and useful.

4. No Pressure—No pressure should be exerted on the child. If the child does not take interest in studies, it means there is some defect in the teaching method of the teacher.

5. No Punishment—The child should not be given corporal punishment, if he is unable to read.

6. Equal Opportunities. Boys and girls should be given equal opportunities for education.

7. Physical Development. It is necessary to make proper arrangement for the physical development of children. Provisions of games only is not sufficient.

8. Greek and Latin. It is necessary to teach Greek and Latin through the mother-tongue. But these languages should be taught only to those who have interest in them.

9. Scientific Methods. Education is a science. All subjects should be taught by scientific methods. By finding natural law and order it is necessary to base education on them. Object knowledge should be given first and then word-knowledge. In order to develop the mind of children properly, it is better to discuss about the things before telling them the rule.

10. Psychological Education. First easy and then difficult things should be taught. Proceed from concrete to abstract with objects so that they can understand them well. The children should take interest in analysis and should not study books only.

Plato and Aristotle had confined their attention to the training of the governing classes of the community. Until thet time of Comenius, idealists like More hazarded the suggestion that 'all in their childhood be instruct in learing .... in their own native tongue'. It was not on the grounds of an abstract political principle like the equality of man that he based his belief. He advocated that education should be accessible to all not on the religious grounds rather by reason of the infinite possibilities in human nature and of the uncertainty about the position to which providence might call this or that man. Such a faith in the universal education of the people could at that time be based on the idea of universalising education, proved more difficult of realisation than could have been foressen by Comenius. As M. Spinka says about Comenius, "He became an educational reformer more by accident than by primary design; and it would be doing him less than justice if we were to fail to recognise his primary and dominant life-motive."[1]

---

1. **Utopia, 88 182, 18z.**

THE LABYRINTH

As M. Spinka said about Comenius, he exerted to succour his persecuted and exiled people by his endeavours to assuage the bitter dissensions between the factions of the Reformed Church. His most influential gift to the religious life of his nation was *The Labyrinth of the World and the Paradise of the Heart,* the supplementary title of which reads – 'a book that clearly shows that this world and all matters concerning it are nothing but confusion and giddiness, pain and toil, deceit and falsehood, misery and anxiety, and lastly, disgust of all things and despair; but he who remains in his own dwelling within his heart, opening it to the Lord God alone, will obtain true and full peace of mind and joy."[1]

SUBJECT MATTER OF LABYRINTH

The Labyrinth was in many respects analogous to Bunyan's *Pilgrim's Progress.* It became a classic in Czech literature. It was one of the great books of mystical devotion. The sections in *The Labyrinth* having educational significance are those in which Comenius described the current pedagogical practice and what he regards ought to be the practice. "I speak not of their pouches", he said "but of their skins which had to suffer, for fists, canes, sticks, birch rods struck them on their cheeks, heads, backs and posteriors till blood streamed forth, and they were almost entirely covered with stripes, scars, spots and weals."[2] In the ideal state, the paradise of the heart, however, Comenius described how he found "no few learned men, who, contrary to the customs of the world, surpassed the others in humility as greatly as they did in learning, and they were sheer gentleness and kindness. It befell that I spoke to one of them, from whom it was thought no earthly learning was concealed, yet he bore himself as a most simple man,

---

1. **John Amos Komensky, *The Labyrinth of the World and the Paradise of the Heart* (1623). Edited and translated by Count Lutzow (Łondon : Swan Sonnenschein & Co., 1901).**
2. **Count Lutzow's translation, pp. 116-17.**

sighing deeply over his stupidity and ignorance. The knowledge of languages they held in slight value, if the knowledge of wisdom was not added to it. For languages, they said, give not wisdom, but have that purpose only that by means of them we can converse with many and diverse inhabitants of the terrestrial globe, be they alive or dead. Therefore, not he, they said, who can speak many languages, but he who can speak of useful things, is learned. Now they call useful things all God's works, and they said that arts are of some use for the purpose of understanding Him; but they also say that the true fountain of knowledge is Holy Writ, and the Holy Ghost our teacher, and that the purpose of all true knowledge is Christ, He who was crucifieed."[1]

PANSOPHISM

Comenius's efforts for eduational reform were inspired by religious motives, However, the great interest of his life, apart from religion, lay in a scheme of universal knowledge or pansophism. This influenced, and some times diverted him from his educational activities. Pansophism is not mere encyclopaedism, as Kenneth Richmond said in The Permanent Values in Education[2] Kenneth Richmond pointed out : "Encyclopaedic teaching is neither practicable nor desirable; pansophic teaching is both. The one aims at making the learner an inexhaustible mine of information upon every subject, the other would make him capable of wisdom in his regard for any subject and able to see any subject in relation to others and to general principles.[2] Pansophism is not 'the correlation of sciences in a unity' as Laurie proposes in his *Comenius.*[3] Correlation is, after all, a somewhat artificial and external process. Pansophism is best understood when expressed in modern terms as a recognition of the organic conception of knowledge – the 'flower in the crannied wall'. According to Comenius himself, Pansophism is an accurate

1. ***The Labyrinth*, pp. 335-6.**
2. **K. Richmone Oolite London : Constable & Co. Ltd., 1917, p. 36.**
3. **S.S. Laurie, *John Amos Comenius* (Cambridge University Press, 1899), p.20.**

anatomy of the universe, dissecting the veins and limbs of all things in such a way that there shall be nothing that is not seen, and that each part shall appear in its place and without confusion". The purpose of Pansophism as Comenius explains in *The Way of Light*,[1] is not so much to make men learned as to make them wise, to give them understanding of their own ends and of the end of all things.

Pansophic conception reflects the influence of Bacon. It recalls the *New Atlantis* rather than the scientific method of the *Advancement of Learning* or the *Novum Organum*. In the *New Atlantis* the central feature is Salomon's House, 'which house or college is the very eye of the kingdom'. Its foundation is the embodiment of the scientific spirit which Bacon hoped might bring happiness to humanity. Salomon's House is a great laboratory equipped with all of scientific instruments. Associated with it is an organised army of scientific investigators. All the processes of nature are there artifically reproduced. The results are made to serve mankind. Comenius failed to appreciate the value of experiment in science on which Bacon insisted. He believed that the progress of humanity could be materially advanced by the collection of all available knowledge of God, nature and art, and by its reduction, to a system called Pansophia or Universal Wisdom.

The Great Didactic,[2] belongs to the earlier period of Comenius' life. This period was religious rather than pansophic. According to Adamson, The Great Didactic setting forth the whole Art of Teaching all Things to all Men", nevertheless reveals "the desire for omniscience" which is very rarely absent in the seventeenth century writers.[3] The sub-title formulates Comenius's

---

1. **John AmosComenius, *The Way of Light* (1968). Translated into English with Introduction by E.T. Campagnac (The University Press of Liverpool, 1938), pp. 148-51.**
2. **M.W. Keatinge, *The Great Didactic of John Amos Comenius* (London : A. & C. Black, 1910). Cf. V. Jelinek, *The Analytical Didcatic of Comenius* (University of Chicago Press, 1954).**
3. **J. W. Adamson, *Pioneers of Modern Education* (Cambridge University Press, 1905), p. 149.**

democratic attitude. It runs: "a certain Inducement to found such schools in all the Parishes, Towns and Villages of every Christian Kingdom that the entire youth of both sexes, none being excepted, shall quickly, pleasantly and thoroughly become learned in the Sciences, pure in Morals, trained to Piety, and in this manner instructed in all things necessary for the present and for the future life."

EDUCATIONAL OF REVOLUTION

It is evident from the complaint about the condition of the schools of their day common to all the pedagogical writers of the period that a reorganisation of educational institutions and a revolution in educational methods were urgent.

CONDITIONS OF CONTEMPORARY SCHOOLS

About these schools Comenius wrote, "they are the terror of boys and the slaughter houses of minds–places where a hatred of literature and books is contracted, where ten or more years are spent in learning what might be acquired in one, where what ought to be poured in gently is violently forced in, beaten in, where what ought to be put clearly and perspicaciously is presented in a confused and intricate way, as if it were a collection of puzzles–places where minds are fed on words."[1]

EDUCATION FOR BOTH BOYS AND GIRLS

In *The Great Didactic* Comenius dismissed existing schools more succinctly as 'terrors for boys and shambles for their intellects'. In accordance with the ideal of the universal school expressed in the sub-title of *The Great Didactic* Comenius wanted to establish a system of education that all the young, 'not the children of the rich or of the powerful only but all alike, boys and girls, both noble and ignoble, rich and poor, in all cities and towns, villages and hamlets, should be sent to school. Let none therefore be excluded unless God has denied him sense and intelligence."[2]

---

1. **Quoted S. S. Laurie, *John Amos Commenius*, p. 55.**
2. ***The Great Didactic, ch. ix.***

About the education of girls Comenius said; "They are endowed with equal sharpness of mind and capacity for knowledge, and they are able to attain the highest positions since they have often been called by God Himself to rule over nations. Why, therefore, should we admit them to the alphabet, and afterwards drive them away from books?"

IMPORTANCE OF SCHOOL EDUCATION

According to Comenius school education is preferable to home education. Schools are necessary since it is seldom that parents have adequate ability or the necessary leisure to instruct their children. To quote his words "Although there might be parents with leisure to educate their own children, it is nevertheless better that the young should be taught together and in large classes, since better results and more pleasure are to be obtained when one pupil serves as an example and a stimulus for another. For to do what we see others do, to go where others go, to follow those who are ahead of us, and to keep in front of those who are behind us is the course of action to which we are almost naturally inclined. Young children especially are always more easily led and ruled by example than by precept. If you give them a precept, it makes little impression; if you point out that others are doing something, they imitate without being told to do so.[1] Comenius has advocated a common school for all. He said, "We wish all men to be trained in all the virtues, especially in modesty, sociability and politeness, and it is therefore undesirable to create class distinctions at such an early age, or to give some children the opportunity of considering their own lot with satisfaction and that of others with scorn."[2]

SCHOOL ORGANISATION

Comenius wanted to organise schools on the following plan : a Mother or nursery school for children up to the age of six, a vernacular or primary school in every village for pupils of six to

1. *Ibid. ch. viii,* 817.
2. *Ibid.* ch. xxix, 82.

twelve, a Latin or secondary school in every city for pupils of twelve to eighteen, and a university in every kingdom or province for youths from eighteen to twenty-four, preparing for the professions. Promotion was be given for ability.

According to Comanius, "When boys are only six years old, it is too early to determine their vocation in life, or whether they are more suited for learning or for manual labour. At this age neither the mind nor the inclinations are sufficiently developed. The Latin school admission too should not be reserved for the sons of rich men, nobles and magistrates, as if these were the only boys who would ever be able to fill similar positions. The wind blows where it will, and does not always begin to blow at a fixed time"[15] University entrance is to be more stringently restricted :[16] "The studies will progress with ease and success if only select intellects, the flowers of mankind, attempt them. The rest had better turn their attention to more suitable occupations, such as agriculture, mechanics or trade".[2]

DEFECTS OF EXISTING SCHOOLS

Comenius was distressed by the lack of internal organisation of the existing schools. Comenius pointed out, or Among the defects were that each school, even each teacher, used a different method, that one procedure was followed in one language and another in a second, and even in the same subject the method was so varied that the pupil scarcely understood the way in which, he was expected to learn. There was a no method by which instruction could be given to all the pupils in a class at the same time : The individual alone was taught.[3]

To remedy these defects, Comenius proposed that there should only be one teacher in each school or at any rate in each class; only one author should be used for each subject studied; the same exercises should be given to the whole class; all subjects and languages should be taught by the same method; everything

1. *The Great Didactic,* ch. xxix 82.
2. *Ibid.* ch. xxi, 84.
3. *Ibid.* ch. xix, 88, 7, 8.

should be taught thoroughly, briefly and pithily; all things that are naturally connected ought to be taught in combination; every subject should be taught in definitely graded steps, that the work of one day may thus expand that of the previous day, and lead up to that of the morrow; and finally, everything that is useless should be invariable discarded.[1]

Besides making instruction more methodical Comenius also made it more agreeable to the pupil. He suggested that the school should be situated in a quiet spot, far from noise and distraction.[2] He said, "The school itself should be a pleasant place, and attractive to the eye both within and without. Within the room should be bright and clean, and its walls should be ornamented by pictures. These should be either portraits of celebrated men, geographical maps, historical plans, or other ornaments."[3] Without, there should be an open place to walk and to play in (for this is absolutely necessary for children), and there should also be a garden attached, into which scholars may have be allowed to go from time to time and where they may their eyes on trees, flowers and plants. If this be done, boys will in all probability go to school with as much pleasure as to fairs, where they always hope to see and hear something new."[4]

EDUCATION OF SENSES

Comenius reiterated the principle that the child should be first instructed in things before being taught to express them in language, that everything should be first learned through the medium of the senses.[5] According to Comenius, "Men must, as far as possible, be taught to become wise by studying the heavens, the earth, oaks, and beeches, but not by studying books; that is to say, they must learn to know and investigate the things themselves,

1. *Ibid.* ch. xix, S 14.
2. Ch. xvi, 8 56 (ii).
3. Ch. xvii, S 17.
4. *ibid, S 42.*
5. Ch. xvii, 12 (viii). Cf. 838 (iii).

and not the observations that other people have made about the things. We shall thus tread in the footsteps of the wise men of old, if each of us obtain his knowledge from the originals, from things themselves, and from no other sources".[1] And Echoing Bacon, Comenius added, that "no information should be imparted on the grounds of bookish authority, but should be authorised by actual demonstration for the senses and to the intellect."

The common school for all pupils from six to twelve years of age necessitates that the teaching of other languages should be carried on through the mother tongue.[2] Direct instruction in the mother tongue itself should also be given. To quote Comenius, To attempt to teach a foreign language before the mother tongue has been learned is 'as irrational as to teach a boy to ride before he can walk. Cicero declared that he could not teach elocution to those who were unable to speak, and, in the same way, my method confesses its inability to teach Latin to those who are ignorant of their mother tongue, since the one paves the way for the other. Finally, what I have in view is an education in the objects that surround us, and a, brief survey of this education can be otained from books written in the mother tongue which embody a list of the things that exist in the external world. This preliminary survey will render the acquisition of Latin far easier, for it will only be necessary to adapt a new nomenclature to objects.[3]

CURRICULUM

Comenius's curriculum included 'all those subjects which are able to make a man wise, virtuous and pious'. He required that every pupil should have a universal insight into things and the qualification which he adds is apparent rather than real. As he said. "But do not, therefore, imagine that we demand for all men a knowledge (that is to say, an exact or deep knowledge) of all the arts and sciences. It is the principles, the causes, and the uses of

---

1. **Ch. xviii, 828. Cf. ch. xx.**
2. **Cf. ch. xvii, 88 27, 28.**
3. **Ch. xxix, 88 3-4.**

all the most important things in existence that we wish all men to learn ; all, that is to say, who are sent into the world to be actors as well as spectators. For we must take strong and vigorous measures that no man in his journey through life may encounter anything unknown to him that he cannot pass sound judgement upon it and turn it to its proper use without error."[1]

PRINCIPLES OF ORDER

Comenius assumed, that all the errors of the past could be avoided and all his aims achieved, by the adoption of the principles of order. Order was education's, as well as heaven's, first law : Accordingly Comeniu's contended that the art of teaching demands nothing more than the skilful arrangement of time, of the subjects taught and of the method. Comenius failed to recognise the importance of the teacher in education as Bacon believed that by his method truth could straightway be attained. He assumed that which could be easily conveyed to all. Thus he added : "As soon as we succeed in finding the proper method it will be no harder to teach schoolboys in any number desired than with the help of the printing press to cover a thousand sheets daily with the neatest writing.[2]

1. Follow Nature. Comenius believed that the right order, or proper method, can be secured if, after the manner of the writers of his time, we 'follow nature'. Thus he declared : "That order which is the dominating principle in the art of teaching all things to all men, should be, and can be, borrowed from no other source but the operations of nature. As soon as this principle is thoroughly secured, the processes of art will proceed as easily and as spontaneously as those of nature."[3] For Comenius, "following nature" consists in adducing analogies from natural processes in support of preconceived and independently acquired principles. The analogies are in many instances quite fanciful and lend no authority to the maxims of method which are supposed to be based

1. *Ibid.* ch. x, 81.
2. *Ibid. ch.* xxx, & 15. Cf. ch. xix, 88 16-29
3. Ch. xvi, 88 7-10

on them. Thus : '*Nature observes a suitable time*'.

For example : a bird that wishes to multiply its species, does not set about it in winter, when everything is stiff with cold, nor in summer, when everything is parched and withered by the heat; nor yet in autumn, when the vital force of all creatures declines with the sun's decliniong rays, and a new winter with hostile mien is approaching; but in spring, when the sun brings back life and strength to all....

2. Imitation. In the same way the gardener takes care to do nothing out of season....

3. Deviation. In direct opposition to this principle, a twofold error is committed in schools.

(i) The right time for mental exercise is not chosen.

(ii) The exercises are not properly divided, so that all advance may be made through the several stages needful, without any omission.

4. Rectification. We conclude, therefore, that

(i) The education of men should be commenced in the springtime of life, that is to say, in boyhood.

(ii) The morning hours are the most suitable for study (for here again the morning is the equivalent of spring........)

(iii) All the subjects that are to be learned should be arranged so as to suit the age of the students, that nothing which is beyond their comprehension be given them to learn.

TEACHING METHODS

Among following statements of Comenius may be found some of the traditional maxims of teaching method :

1. Easy to Difficult. 'Proceed from what is easy to what is more difficult'.

2. General to Particular. Instead of the maxim 'Proceed from the particular to the general' we find 'Proceed from the general to the particular'.

3. The principle of correlation or integration of studies.

This is implied in the statements : 'Great stress [should] be laid on the points of resemblance between cognate subjects'; and 'all things that are naturally connected ought to be taught in combination'.[1]

4. The inductive method of teaching. This is expressed thus[2] : 'It is necessary that examples come before rules'.

5. Doctrine of interest. It is anticipated in such remarks as : 'The desire to know and to learn should be excited in the boy in every possible manner;[3] 'Every study should be commenced in such a manner as to awaken a real liking for it on the part of the scholars"[4]

6. Principle of Development. Although Comenius's own psychology was of the most primitive type, he anticipated the psychological principle of Pestalozzi when he affirmed that nothing should be taught to the young, unless it is not only permitted but actually demanded by their age and mental strength.

NOT NATURALISM

The misapplications of natural analogies by Comenius has misled some writers[5] into regarding him as a naturalist in philosophy. There is no doubt that Comenius was influenced by the new scientific movement initiated by Bacon, This however, does not justify the ascription of naturalist to him. In his *History of Western Education* Boyd is nearer the truth when he affirms that the religious bent of Comenius' mind inclined him to lay the main stress on the idealistic view of mental development[6] Spinka clinches the issue by designating Comenius 'the incurable idealist'.[7]

CRITICAL EVALUATION

1. Ibid, ch. xix 814.
2. The Great Didactic, ch. xvi, & 19.
3. *Ibid* ch. xvii, & 13.
4. Ch. xviii, & 16. Cf ch. xix, & 20 (ii).
5. J. Adams, *Thwe Evolution of Educational Theory* (London : Macmillan & Co.,1912) p. 267.
6. W. Boyd, *History of Western Education* (London) : A. & C. Blacm 1921). p. 263.
7. Spinha, John Amos Comenius, p. 146.

The value of Comenius's principles must be estimated independently of the analogies from nature given in support of them. The procedure he adopts while apparently securing uniformity in presentation actually results in a most unsystematic arrangement of the principles of school organisation and of educational method. His claim to present an a *priori* system is far from justified. His criticism of his predecessors' collections of a *posteriori* precepts are not inapplicable to his own work.

COMPARISON WITH JESUITS

Some of the principles and methods recommended by Comenius are common to him and to the Jesuits, the success of whose practices he cited in support of the procedures he advocated[1]. He advised that care should be exercised in the selection of texts put into pupils' hands : He maintained that the books which the scholars use should be such as can rightly be termed sources of wisdom, virtue and piety : He deplores the fact that more caution has not been exercised in the matter. The *Ratio Studiorum* instructs the Provincial to secure that school books which might do harm to virtue or good morals should be withheld from pupils till the offensive passages are expurgated. The professors of the Lower Studies are advised to refrain from introducing words prejudicial to good morals, not only to abstain from expounding these but also to deter pupils from reading them out of school as far as possible. Comenius also recommended[2] the use of epitomes, and they criticised use of the Jesuits. The following extracts from *The Great Didactic* read almost like a translation of the Jesuit regulations : If the scholars are to be interested, care must be taken to make the method palatable, so that everything, no matter how serious, may be placed before them in a familiar and attractive manner; in the form of a dialogue, for instance, by pitting the boys against one another to answer and explain riddling questions, comparisons and fables..." "The civil authorities and the managers of schools can kindle the zeal of the

1. ***Ibid* pp. 129-30.**
2. *Cf. A. P. Farrell,* **The jesuit Code of Liberal Education,** ***pp. 248-51.***

scholars by being present at public performances (such as declarations, disputations, examinations and promotions), and by praising the industrious ones and giving them small presents (without respect of person).' Even emulation is commended by Comenius as 'by far the best stimulus[1] with school pupils.

SCHOOL DISCIPLINE

Comenius held enlightened views on school discipline. His recommendations follow the principles enunciated by Quintilian on this subject. Thus he affirmed. "That no blows be given for lack of readiness to learn for, if the pupils do not learn readily, this is the fault of no one but the teacher, who either does not know how to make his pupil receptive of knowledge or does not take the trouble to do so."[2] In his chapter 'Of School Discipline' Comenius said, "A musician does not strike his lyre a blow with his fist or with a stick, nor does he throw it against the wall, because it produces a discordant sound; but, setting to work on scientific principles, he tunes it and gets it into order. Just such a skilful and sympathetic treatment is necessary to instil a love of learning into the minds of our pupils, and any other procedure will only convert their idleness into antipathy and their lack of industry into downright stupidity."

TEXT BOOKS

Comenius felt the need of suitable textbooks. Like the other educators of his time and in spite of the prominence he assigned to the teaching of the vernacular, Comenius was condemned to devote attention to the teaching of languages, especially of Latin. Here, he met with his greatest practical success. The manuals he prepared to facilitate the learning of Latin won ready acceptance, His *fanua Linguarum Reserata* was the most celebrated school book ever published. His *Orbis Pictus* was one of the earliest to introduce visual aids.

Though there is much repetition and contradiction among

1. **The Great Didaetic**
2. ***Ibid* ch. xvii, & 41, (i)**

the principles of Comenius; but his writings evince a sincere sympathy with childhood. They start with an earnest aspiration to make education available to all, to lighten the drudgery of learning for the child, and to introduce into schools a humane treatment of the pupil. It has even been claimed by Kandel that the establishment of the United Nations Educational, Scientific and Cultural Organisation marks the culmination of a movement for the creation of an international agency for education which began with the following statement by Comenius. 'Universal harmony and peace must be secured for the whole human race. By peace and harmony, however, I mean not that external peace between rulers and peoples among themselves, but an internal peace of mind inspired by a system of ideas and feelings. To guarantee the stability of the world there must be 'some universal rededication of minds' begining in the schools of each nation."[1]

EVALUATION

Though it is undeniable that reforms suggested by Comenius made all-round improvement in the existing system of education, criticisms have been advanced by educationists upon the philosophy of education given by Comenius. The most important evaluation has been advanced as follows :

1. He considered the child as inheritor of human-race but could not present an educational system accordingly. He forgot ancient culture in his zeal for scientific study. He thought it necessary to teach the works of contemporary authors only.
2. Comparison is useful only when it is explained. In his principles he takes inspiration from nature and compares man to trees and birds. But he forgets human nature. He begins to give importance to nature, without man. Reality lies in proof.
3. On the basis of Divine-voice, he imagined that man should

1. I.L. Kandel in 'National education in an Internatinal World', *N.E.A. Journal* (April 1946), p. 175.

learn everything, but did not estimate 'knowledge' and 'human power' properly. This made his educational system defective. Later on, in his old age Comenius admitted that his books did not fulfil the need of the time.

4. It is not proper to give the essence of 'worldly knowledge' to the children.
5. It is not proper to explain general rules first.
6. Comenius was of the view that the essence of language should be taught to the child, but this is not suitable because there are many words in the language which we do not know nor is there any need of knowing.

In spite of the above mentioned criticism, it should be remembered that Comenius has been compared to Copernicus and Newton in science so far as his contribution to education is concerned.

❑❑❑

5

John Locke

'Locke's influence far exceeds his fame. Most of his followers do not know their master. His point of view coincides so completely with that of the ordinary intelligent man in the street that his following in all English-speaking countries is infinite".

—Adams

John Locke was born in a religious family living in an English village in 1632. He was sent to Oxford for his higher education, where he studied philosophy and Greek literature with complete absorption. In 1660 he was presented with an opportunity for demonstrating his scholarship. He was appointed professor of philosophy and Greek literature at Oxford itself, but immediately after a complete change in his life and outlook compelled him to give up this profession. Political philosophy of the day claimed him and he became engrossd in it, so much so that he joined the warring faction, left England and exiled himself in Holland for some time. At this time he was beset with other difficulties as the death of his father forced him to assume all the responsibilities of his family. He returned home from Oxford in order to study medicine but could find no real satisfaction in it. An accidental meeting with Lord Shaftesbury placed him on the post of a secretary which he gratefully accepted. While engaged in this work he revived his intellectual life, and wrote his classic work *'Essay Concerning Human Understanding'* in 1690. Concerning the composition of this great classic of deductive reasoning and elegant prose it is said that Locke one evening went to an inn for his evening tea. In the course of conversation a question that came up for consideration was how man gained knowledge of universal truths. Locke made this the subject of his research, and the book consequent upon it has gained tremendous importance in philosophical circles. Locke's own philosophy and his entire knowledge of science have gone into its making. He passed the rest of his days in study and the pursuit of knowledge and breathed his last in 1704.

PUBLISHED WORKS

Collected Works, 1853; philosophical works, edited by St. John in Bohn's Library. *An Essay Concerning Human Understanding;* ed. by A. C. Fraser, 2 vols, 1894; *Treatise on Civil Government and a Letter Concerning Toleration,* Charles L. Sherman. ed, 1937; M.W. Calkins, ed., *John Locke-Selections;* 1917; S.P. Lamprecht, ed., *John Locke-Selctions,* 1928. Among important work on Lock's philosophy are : 1. H. R. Fox Bourne, *Life of Locke,* 2 vols., 1876; 2. T. Fowler, *Locke,* 1880; 3. A.C. Fraser, *Locke*, 1890; 4. S Alexander, *Locke,* 198; 5. M.M. Curits, *Outline of Locke's Ethical Philosophy,* 1890; 6. J Gibson, *Locke's Theory of Knowledge and Its Historical Relations* 1917; R I Aaron, *John Locke, 1937;* 8. W. Kendall, John Locke *and the Doctrine of Majority Rule,* 1941 : 9. C. R. Morris, *Locke, Berkeley, Hume,* 1946.

The publication of Locke's *An Essay Concerning Human Understanding* in 1690 has been said to mark the opening of an epoch in the history of education. It initiated a new era in philosophic thought. The importance of Locke's professedly educational writings have likewise been variously assessed. Adamson in his Introduction to the *Educational Writings of John Locke* maintains that they have proved much less influential than his philosophy. His influence on education on the Continent has been considerable.

When resident in Holland and engaged on the great *Essay,* in the latter half of 1684, Loke wrote to his friend Edward Clarke of Chipleigh House in Somerset, giving advice on the upbringing of his friend's children, especially the eldest boy–Edward. These

'Directions' served as the first draft of Locke's *Some Thoughts concerning Education.* The work, as Locke acknowledges in the concluding paragraphs of the *Thoughts*, does not pretend to be a complete account of the subject of education. But the author hopes that it may give some light to those who venture to consult their own reason in the education of their children rather than wholly rely upon old custom.'

Locke did not offer a comprehensive education for all the children of all the people. After being appointed Commissioner of Trade in 1696 Locke drew up a comprehensive plan for making workhouses useful institutions; it included a project for the maintenance and upbringing of pauper children.[1] This provided for working schools to be set up in every parish where such children from three to fourteen years of age would get meals in return for their labour in spinning or knitting. The schools were to be self-supporting. The proposal was not, however, adopted.[2]

EDUCATION ACCORDING TO CLASSES

Locke believed that different classes in the community should have different types of education. He said "I think a prince, a nobleman, and an ordinary gentleman's son, should have different ways of breeding".

EDUCATION OF YOUNG GENTLEMAN

Although he makes incidental reference to the education of other classes, Locke's main concern is with 'the breeding of a young gentleman'. Classification has conception of the ideal gentleman of Locke. We cannot but be pleased with a humane, friendly, civil temper wherever we meet with it. "A mind free and master of itself and all its actions, not low and narrow, not haughty and insolent, not blemished with any great defect is what every one is taken with."[3]

1. **See R.H. Quick, *Some Thoghts concerning Education by John Locke* (Cambridge University Press, 1895), Appendix A.**
2. **217.**
3. **Ibid. 66.**

CHOICE OF GOVERNOR

About the problem whether the young gentleman should be educated at home under a tutor or sent to a public school. 'I cannot but prefer breeding of a young gentleman at home in his father's sight under a good governor as much the best and safest way to this great and main end of education when it can be had and is ordered as it should be. Much, of course, depends on the choice of a tutor, and about this Locke said, "the great work of a governor is to fashion the carriage and form the mind to settle in his pupils good habits and principles of virtue and wisdom, to give him little by little a view of mankind and to work him into a love and imitation of what is excellent and praiseworthy, and in the prosecution of it to give him vigour, activity and industry".[4]

IMPORTANCE OF EDUCATION

Locke believed that mind is a *tabula rase*. All minds are identical in structure and the differences found amongst men are the result of education. In the opening sections of the *Thoughts* he says : "that of all the men we meet with, nine parts of ten are what they are, good or evil, useful or not, by their education. "Tis that which makes the great difference in mankind'. And he repeated : That the difference to be found in the manners and abilities of men is owing more to their education than to anything else.[5] Later in the *Thoughts* he qualified his statement averring 'God has stamped certain characters upon men's minds which, like their shapes, may be a little mended, but can hardly be totally altered and transformed into the contrary"[6] In *Of the Conduct of Understanding* – a work published posthumously Locke was equally emphatic that there are innate individual differences and that the contribution of education is almost negligible. He said, Amongst men of equal education there is great inequality of parts."[7]

1. **Ibid 88-94.**
2. **Ibid $ 32.**
3. **Ibid, $ 66.**
4. ***Locke's Conduct of the Understanding*, by Thomas Fowler (Oxfor University Press, 1901), $ 2.**

ROLE OF FORMAL TRAINING

Formal training is inconsistent w4ith Locke's general empiricist philosophy. It implies the existence of mental faculties. Locke is usually cited as a critic of the faculty hypothesis in psychology, more especially in regard to memory. He said, "Memory is so necessary to all parts and conditions of life, and so little is to be done without it, that we are not to fear it should grow dull and useless for want of exercise, if exercise would make it grow stronger. But I fear this faculty of the mind is not capable of much help and amendment in general by any exercise or endeavour of ours, at least not by that used upon this pretence in Grammar Schools..."

TRANSFER OF TRAINING

Locke rejected transfer of training in the *Conduct of the Understanding* he said : "We see men freuqently dexterous and sharp enough in making a bargain who, if you reason with them about matters of religion, appear perfectly stupid.[8] And later he explained : "The mistake is that he that is found reasonable in one thing is concluded to be so in all, and to think or say otherwise is thought so unjust an affront, and so senseless a censure, that nobody ventures to do it."[9]

HABIT FORMATION

According to Locke the practice-effect is specific, not general in habit formation. He said the legs of a dancing master and the fingers of a musician fall as it were naturally, without thought or pains, into regular and admirable motions. Bid them change their parts, and they will in vain endeavour to produce like motions in the members not used to them and it will require length of time and long practice to attain the same degree of a like ability.[10]

---

1. **Sp. City.**
2. **Ibid. p. 20.**
3. **Ibid.**

UTILITARIAN CRITERION

To the question "To whom should Grammar be taught?" Locke answered : 'Men learn languages for the ordinary intercourse of society and communication of thoughts in common life, without any farther design in the use of them. And for this purpose the original way of learning a language by conversation not only serves well enough, but is to be preferred as the most expedite, proper and natural. Therefore, to this use of language one may answer that grammar is not necessary. Others there are, the greatest part of whose business in this world is to be done with their tongues and with their pens; and to these it is convenient, if not necessary, that they should speak properly and correctly, whereby they may let their thoughts into other men's minds the more easily, and with the greater impression. Upon this accont it is, that any sort of speaking, so as will make him to be understood, is not thought enough for a gentleman. He ought to study grammar amongst the other helps of speaking well........ And to this purpose grammar is necessary; but it is the grammar only of their own proper tongues, and to those only who would take pains in cultivating their language, and in perfecting their styles.' 'There is a third sort of men, who apply themselves to two or three foreign, dead, and (which amongst us are called the) learned languages, make them their study, and pique themselves upon their skill in them. No doubt, those who propose to themselves the learning of any language with this view, and would be critically exact in it, ought carefully to study the grammar of it.' Grammar is throughout regarded purely as an instrumental subject and ancillary to language; its formal training value is ignored. Logic and rhetoric, are dismissed by Locke on the utilitarian because of the little advantage young people receive from them."[1]

Locke also suggested that there is no transfer between ability in Latin and in English ; in Latin "the manner of expressing of one's self is so very different from ours that to be perfect in that

1. **Thought 188.**

would very little improve the purity and facility of his English style."[1]

VALUE OF MATHEMATICS

Locke followed the fashion of his times in regarding mathematical reasoning as the ideal method of attaining truth. In doing so he makes admissions which might justify the charge of formal training. He said, "Would you have a man reason well, you must use him to it betimes, exercise his mind in observing the connection of ideas and following them in train. Nothing does this better than Mathematics, which therefore I think should be taught to all those who have the time and opportunity, not so much to make them mathematicians as to make them reasonable creatures."[2]

In the *Thoughts* Locke maintained that practice in one phase of memory does not result in improvement in other aspects, that the learning of one language may adversely affect the learning of another, and that training in grammar does not improve the mind in general. In the *Conduct of the Understanding* a similar conclusion is deduced in respect of reasoning and of habit formation. Thus, the weight of evidence is against the charge that Locke supports formal training.

PRAGMATISM

Locke's positon might be regarded as pragmatic, where he said, we shall not have reason to complain of the narrowness of our mind, if we will but employ them about what may be of use to us.[3]

This pragmatic attitude of Locke is reflected in his emphasis on practical studies. In the Introduction to the *Essay* he said, "Our business here is not to know all things, but those which concern out conduct". In the *Thoughts* he said it is not the tutor's business

---

1. **Ibid, 172.**
2. **Locke, *Conduct of the Understanding,* p. 20.**
3. **John Locke, *Essay Concerning Human Understanding,* Introduction.**

'to teach them all that is knowlable'. In his essay 'Of Study' he elaborated "The extent of knowledge of things knowable is so vast .... that the whole time of our life is not enough to acquaint us with all those things, I will not say which we are capable of knowing, but which it would not be only convenient but very advantageous to know".

FREQUENCY OF LIFE

In accordance with this view Frequency of use Locke formulated, a principle extensively exploited by modern curriculum makers known as `frequency of use' He said, "And since it cannot be hoped that he [the pupil] should have time and strength to learn all things, most pains should be taken about that which is most necessary, and that principally looked after which will be of most frequent use to him in the world."

SOUND MIND IN SOUND BODY

A sound mind in a sound body is a short but full description of a happy state in this world. He that hath these two, has little more to wish for; and he that wants either of them, will be but little better for anything else. Such were the opening sentences of the *Thoughts*. Locke dispose first of health education, advocating a hardening regime which is the natural lot of the children of the poor. "Plenty of open air, exercise and sleep, plain diet, no wine or strong drink, and very little or no physic, not too warm and strict clothing, especially the head and feet kept cold, and the feet often used to cold water and exposed to wet."[15]

IDEAL PERSONALITY

According to Locke, four things, are necessary in fashioning ideal type of personality virtue, wisdom, breeding and learning.[2]

1. Wisdom. Wisdom is beyond the reach of children since it implies natural good temper, application of mind and experience.[3]

---

1. **Thoughts.**
2. **Ibid 134.**
3. **Ibid, 140.**

2. Virtue. Of virtue Locke said : "This virtue, then, direct virtue, which is the hard and valuable part to be aimed at in education....All other considerations and accomplishments should give way and be postponed to this. This is the solid and substantial good [on] which tutors should not only read lectures, and talk of, but the labour and art of education should furnish the mind with, and fasten there, and never cease till the young man had a true relish of it, and placed his strength, his glory, and his pleasure in it."[1] The foundations of virtue are to be laid in religion : "There ought to be imprinted on his mind a true notion of God as of an independent supreme being, author and maker of all things, from Whom we receive all our good, Who loves us, and gives us all things".

3. Breeding. Breeding is largely a matter of right company. Its aim is to secure 'a carriage suitable to his rank'. The rule to be observed here is : "Not to think meanly of ourselves, and not to think meanly of others."[2]

4. Learning. Learning Locke puts last, "Regarding it as the least part of education. .... This may seem strange in the mouth of a bookish man; and this making usually the chief, if not only hustle and stir about children, this being almost that alone which is thought on when people talk of education, makes it the greater paradox."[3]

The explanation that Locke gave in *Thoughts Concerning Reading and Study for a Gentleman* was that 'a gentleman's proper calling is the service of his country, and so is most properly concerned in moral and political knowledge; and thus the studies which more immediately belong to his calling are those which treat of virtue and vices, of civil society and the arts of government, and will take in also law and history."

1. Ibid.
2. Ibid, 94.
3. Ibid, 147.

But if the young gentleman is not to remain 'more ignorant than the clerk of our parish', he must learn to read and write. Various contrivances for learning his letters are described by Locke; after mastering these he is to proceed to reading. After reading comes writing. In dealing with the acquisition of this skill Locke enunciate the principle that if one would do anything well he should not attempt to do two parts of an action at the same time if they can be separated. Learning to hold the pen must accordingly be taught independently of learning to form the letters. Representational drawing is added not for any aesthetic but merely for its practical value.

PLACE OF LANGUAGE

In spite of his general pragmatic standpoint Locke did not evade the issue of the place of languages in the education of his pupil. After English, French is proposed. The reason for its priority over Latin is that it is a living language and can be acquired by the direct method. Latin, too, absolutely necessary to a gentleman. But it should be taught by the direct method and not after the traditional grammatical manner. No man can pass for a scholar who is ignorant of the Greek tongue.

IMPORTANCE OF MOTHER TONGUE

Locke is a convinced believer in 'English for the English'. Care is to be taken when the boy is learning French and Latin, that his English is not neglected .... 'since' tis English that an English gentleman will have constant use of, that is the language he should chiefly cultivate .... I am not here speaking against Greek and Latin; I think they ought to be studied, and the Latin at least understood well by every gentleman. But whatever foreign languages a young man meddles with (and the more he knows the better), that which he should critically study and labour to get a facility, clearness and elegancy to express himself in, should be his own; and to this purpose he should daily be exercised in it.

CURRICULUM

To complete his curriculum Locke adds arithmetic, astronomy, geometry, geography, chronology, history, ethics, law, natural philosophy. Other accomplishments include dancing and music, and wrestling is preferred to fencing. Locke also recommended a trade. He said, "And yet I cannot forbear to say I would have him learn a trade, a manual trade, nay two or three, but one more particularly .... I should propose one, or rather both these, namely gardening or husbandry in general, and working in wood as a carpenter, joiner or turner, these being fit and healthy recreations for a man of study or business."[21] A young gentleman should learn to keep accounts, "though a science not likely to help a gentleman to get an estate, yet possibly there is not any thing of more use and efficacy to make him preserve the estate he has."[22]

IMPORTANCE OF METHOD

Locke recognise the importance of method in education. He said, "This I am sure, nothing so much clears a learner's way, helps him so much on in it, and makes him go so easy and so far in any inquiry, as a good method. His governor should take pains to make him sensible of this, accustom him to order, and teach him method in all the applications of his thoughts; shew him wherein it lies, and the advantages of it; acquaint him with the several sorts of it either from general to particulars, or from particulars to what is more general, exercise him in both of them, and make him see in what cases each different method is most proper, and to what ends it best serves." Starting his own general principle Locke said, "He that hath found a way how to keep up a child's spirit easy, active and free, and yet at the same time to restrain him from many things he has a mind to, and to draw him to things that are uneasy to him; he, I say, that knows how to reconcile these seeming contradictions, has, in my opinion, got the true secret of education.

---

1. **Ibid. 201, 204.**
2. **Ibid 210.**

PLAY WAY IN EDUCATION

Locke anticipated the play-way in education. He said "Were matters ordered right, learning anything they should be taught might be made as much a recreation to their play as their play is to their learning." A condition of realising this fortunate state of affairs is that the task should be begun at the psychological moment, when the pupil is in the right mood for it. "The favourable seasons of aptitude and inclinations be heedfully laid hold of." It should not be prolonged till exhaustion or aversion sets in : 'Care should be taken that what is of advantage to them they should always do with delight; and before they are wearied with one they should be timely diverted to some other useful employment."[1]

ROLE OF TEACHERS

In the course of the task "masters and teachers should raise no difficulties to their scholars but on the contrary should smooth their way and readily help them forwards where they find them stoop."[2] As constant attention is one of the hardest tasks that can be required of children, "he that requires their application should endeavour to make what he proposes as grateful and agreeable as possible, at least he ought to take care not to join any displeasing or frightful idea with it". "The great skill of a teacher is to get and keep the attention of his scholar; whilst he has that, he is sure to advance as fast as the learner's abilities will carry him, and without that, all his hustle and bother will be to little or no purpose. To attain this he should make the child comprehend (as much as may be) the usefulness of what he teaches him, and let him see by what he has learnt that he can do something which he could not do before, something which gives him some power and real advantage above others who are ignorant of it. To this he should add sweetness in all his instructions, and by a certain tenderness in his whole carriage make the child sensible that he loves him

1. I08.
2. Ibid. 167.

and designs nothing but his good, the only way to beget love in the child which will make him hearken to his lessons and relish what he teaches him."[1]

The aim should be to create in the pupil "a liking and inclination to what you propose to them to be learned and that will engage their industry and application".[2] This, Locke adds, should be no hard matter if children are handled as they should be. They are to be treated as rational creatures.[3]

PRINCIPLES OF GUIDANCE

Locke was one of the first to express the guidance point of view : "He that is about children should well study their natures and aptitudes and see by often trials what turn they easily take and what becomes them; observe what their native stock is, how it may be improved, and what it is fit for; he should consider what they want, whether they be capable of having it wrought into them by industry and incorporated there by practice, and whether it be worth while to endeavour it. For in many cases all that we can do, or should aim at, is to make the best of what nature has given, to prevent the vices and faults to which such a constitution is most inclined, and give it all the advantages it is capable of. Everyone's natural genius should be carried as far as it could, but to attempt the putting another upon him, will be but labour in vain, and what is so plastered on will at best sit untowardly and have always hanging to it the ungracefulness of constraint and affectation."[4]

DISCIPLINE

A firm believer in teaching without tears Locke held advanced views on child discipline. He said, "I am very apt to think that great severity of punishment does but very little good, nay, great harm in education; and I believe it will be found that

1. Ibid, 167.
2. Ibid, 72.
3. Ibid, 54.
4. Ibid, 66.

alteris paribus those children who have been most chastised seldom make the best men."[1] Strongly opposing the use of the rod Locke said, "The usual lazy and short way by chastisement and the rod which is the only instrument of government that tutors generally know, or ever think of, is the most unfit of any to be used in education."[30] This sort of correction, naturally breeds an aversion to that which 'tis the tutor's business to create a liking to. If it needs be that offences come, then Locke offered advice suggesting the employment of a Corrector after the manner of the Jesuits, but repeating : "Beating is the worst and therefore the last means to be used in the correction of children and that only in cases of extremity after all gentle ways have been tried and proved unsuccessful."[2]

FEMALE EDUCATION

In a covering letter attached to a fair copy of the early draft of the *Thoughts* sent in 1684 to his friend, Edward Clarke, Locke contemplated dealing with the education of girls, the last sentence running : "Be therefore both you and your lady as severe as may be in examining these rules, doubt as much as you can of every one of them, and when upon a scrupulous review we have settled this part and supplied what possibly you may find wanting. I shall be ready to talk my mind as fully to Madame concerning her daughters, if she continues to be of the mind that may be worth her patience to hear it." And in the *Thoughts* he explained "I have said *he* here because the principal aim of my discourse is how a young gentleman should be brought up from his infancy, which in all things will not so perfectly suit the education of daughters though where the difference of sex requires different treatment, 'twil be no hard matter to distinguish".[3]

❑❑❑

---

1. Ibid, 43.
2. Ibid 47.
3. Ibid, 83-7.

6

Pestalozzi

Education is the inner development of the child. Therefore it should not be imposed from outside. The principles of education should be discovered through obsevation and experiment in the field of education. The success of the teacher depends upon teaching according to the interests of the child. Childhood is the most important period in a person's education. Education is the birth right of every individual. It aims at the all-round development of his capacities and abilities. The teacher should not only know various subjects but should also be conversant with best teaching methods."

—Pestalozzi

Among the great educators, Pestalozzi appears a man afflicted with new ideas which he found himself unable to formulate or to put effectively into practice. In his *Swansong* (1826) he admited. "My lofty ideals were pre-eminently the product of a kind, well-meaning soul, inadequately endowed with the intellectual and practical capacity which might have helped considerably to further my heartfelt desire. It was the product of an extremely vivid imagination which in the stress of my daily life proved unable to produce any important results."[1] Pestalozzi arrived at his principles mostly by intuition. In one work he described his educational ideal in the form of a romance. In another, he is, metamorphosed into a pedantic drillmaster in arithmetic pleased with himself for having filled a thick book with

1. ***Pestalozzis Educational Writings*, edited by J. A. Green (London : Edward Arnold, 1912), p. 228.**

the multiplication table. However, his reputation attracted philosophers like Fichte and Herbart who not only critically examined his system but also published their versions of it. In fact, no great European educator has ever had such a succession of distinguished visitors to his schools.

EDUCATIONAL AIM IN LIFE

Pestalozzi's aim in life was to ameliorate the lot of the poor. As Herbart commented : "The welfare of the people is Pestalozzi's aim....He did not seek the wealth of merit in your mansions but in their hovels." His humanitarianism was reinforced by his reading of Rousseau's works in early youth. This aim compelled him to concentrate on the fundamentals of education, for, as Herbart remarks, "the most pressing needs are the more universal"[1]. Pestalozzi was thus forced to formulate a practical scheme of education suitable for all, and, to lay the foundation of elementary school system. In the *Letters to Greaves* he states. "It [the end held out as the highest object of all man's efforts] must embrace all mankind, it must be applicable to all, without distinction of zones, or nations in which they may be born. It must acknowledge the rights of man in the fullest sense of the word...They embrace the rightful claims of all classes to a general diffusion of useful knowledge, a careful development of the intellect, and judicious attention to all the faculties of man—physical, intellectual and moral"[2].

Echoing Rousseau's dictum' "Life is the trade I would teach him"· That the ultimate end of education is not a perfection in the accomplishments of the school but fitness for life, he elaborated in *How Gertrude Teaches Her Children*: "We have spelling schools, writing schools, catechism schools, and we want—men's schools."

First Experiment

Pestalozzi settled at Neuhof in 1774 and introduced a number

1. **Herbart, *Minor Pedagogical works,* pp.36.**
2. **Pestalozzi, *Letters on Early Education,* Eng. Tray. London, Sherwood, Gilbert and Paper, 0827, p. 88**

of beggar children into his house to rescue them from their degraded condition, hoping to restore their self-respect and manhood – to educate the poor for poverty–but the scheme failed and the institution was closed in 1779. In his *Ansichten and Erfahrungen* he explained that he not only tried to find work for the poor children, but also wished to warm their hearts and to develop their minds, and through self-instruction to elevate them to a sense of the inner dignity and worth of their nature. He also acknowledged his failure, admitting that he took upon his own shoulders a burden which he could not bear and which he should have left to others, and therby exhausted himself, plunged himself into domestic confusion and brought indescribable suffering on himself.

After the failure at Neuhof a literary interlude ensued. Pestalozzi's *Evening Hours of a Hermit* and *Leonard and* Gertude: *A Book for the People* both appeared in 1780. The former, was to serve as a preface to all that Pestalozzi should write in the future. In it he warned parents not to hurry their children into working at things remote from their immediate interests, and after the manner of Rousseau, not to anticipate the ordinary course of their development. The danger lies in children's lessons dealing with words before they have actually encountered the real things. Hermann Krusi, one of Pestalozzi's coadjustors, in *My Educational Recollections,* writes how before his meeting with Pestalozzi at Burgdorf he held the system in high estimation which could elicit answers from the children by dexterous questions. He continues : 'Having read in educational writings that Socrates had possessed this faculty in a high degree, the term "to socratize" presented to me an almost magic charm. When I communicated my views on this subject to Pestalozzi he could not refrain from a knowing smile. "This art," he then said quite earnestly, "when applied at the proper time and place, has its own value, but it is utterly worthless for teachers and children in the public schools. Socrates was surrounded by young men who had a background in the knowledge of words and things. If you take pains to give your children first this background, then the necessary questions about things within their own observation will be naturally suggested. Without this background every attempt to elicit proper answers from the children by artfully put questions is merely thrashing of straw, and leades to sore deception or discouragement which may even deprive you of faith in yourself. "

Leonard and Gertrude described how, mainly by means of education, the regeneration of a small community was effected by the noble efforts of a pious woman, the wife of a village mason in humble circumstances. In the village of Bonnal, the home of Leonard becomes the model educational institution, and Gertrude, the mother of the children, the ideal educator. This home-education represents Pestalozzi's idea. It was only the circumstances in which he laboured that compelled him in practice to adopt class-teaching methods. These he regarded as a necessary but temporary expedient till mothers in sufficient numbers should be adequately educated to superintend the instruction of their own children.

As yet there was no formal analysis but the 'contact with realities' for which Pestalozzi pleaded in his *Evening Hours of a Hermit* as is exemplified in the procedure of Gertrude. "Yet she never adopted tone of instructor toward her children; she did not say to them : "Child, this is your head, your nose, your hand, your finger" ; or "Where is your eye, your ear?" but instead she would say : "Come here, child, I will wash your little hands", "I will comb your hair", or "I will cut your finger nails". Her verbal instruction seemed to vanish in the spirit of her real activity, in which it always had its source. The result of her sytem was that each child was skilful, intelligent, and active to the full extent that his age and development allowed.

EARLY EDUCATION IN REALITIES OF LIFE

"The instruction she gave them in the rudiments of arithmetic was intimately connected with the realities of life. She taught them to count the number of steps from one end of the room to the other, and two of the rows of five panes each, in one of the windows, gave her an opportunity to unfold the decimal relations of numbers. She also made them count their threads while spinning, and the number of turns on the reel, when they wound the yarn into skeins. Above all, in every occupation of life she taught them an accurate and intelligent observation of common objects and the forces of nature."

ANOTHER EXPERIMENT

Between December 1798 and June 1799 another opportunity, presented itself to Pestalozzi to put his ideas into practice, this time at Stanz. About eighty children, left destitute after the village had been reduced to ashes by the French troops, were put in Pestalozzi's charge. But the population being Catholic were naturally hostile to the representative of a government which had brought ruin upon them. The retreating French forces commandeered the convent where Pestalozzi was established, and ended the experiment. Nevertheless some measure of success attended his efforts. It illustrated the truth of his view that education should be based on love. The great human sympathy for children with which Pestalozzi was endowed in a singular degree had prevailed. But affection, even when it is reciprocal, is not enough. The pupil must be trained to independence. As Herbart insists : "something more than a love for a subject is required of the youth ; a well balanced, many-sided interest is demanded."[1]

VENTURE OF BURGDORF

Pestalozzi's next venture was at Burgdorf (1799-1804). It was here that he developed and formulated his teaching technique. The Burgdorf of period produced Pestalozzi's most important treatise on educational method *How Gertrude Teaches Her Children* or *Letters to Gessner* (1801). Reviewing this work, Herbart states : "It is his intention to place in the hands of wholly ignorant teachers and parents such writings as they need only to cause the children to read off and learn by heart, without adding anything of their own. What he believed could be carried into effect most immediately he prererred; he must have his levers sturdy enough not to break even in clusmy hands. The book in which, under the form of letters to a friend, he describes the outlines of such a plan, belongs really in the hands of such men

1. Herbart, *Minor Pedegogical Words*, pp. 74-6.

as have influence on the organisation of the lowest schools and upon parents of the lowest social ranks. Such men would be able to spread his actual school books, which are to be published in the future. What is faulty in the whole publication therefore is, perhaps, its title, which brings it immediately into the hands of women, of mothers."[1]

Pestalozzi's intention, as he himself conceived it was to discover the nature of teaching itself, to found popular instruction on psychological principles, to produce a general method of instruction following a psychologically ordered sequence.

Although the title and the form of Pestalozzi's chief work mentioned above were unfortunate, it was nevertheless the main source of his contributions to the psychology, sociology and philosophy of education. Of the Pestalozzian method Herbart says: "Its peculiar merit consists in having laid hold more boldly and more zealously than any former method of the duty of building up the child's mind, of constructing in it a definite experience in the light of clear sense-perception, not acting as if the child had already an experience but taking care that he gets one..... The Pestalozzian method, therefore, is by no means qualified to crowd out any other method but to prepare the way for it. It takes care of the earliest age that is capable of receiving instruction."[2]

CONCEPT OF ANSCHAUUNG

Herbart here refers to Pestalozzsi's conception of Anschauung, a term for which there is no precise English equivalent. By Anschauung is to be understood the immediate experience of objects or situations. Terms used by English and American writers to convey the same idea include : immediate awareness, direct acquaintance, direct appreciation, concrete experience, personal contact first hand impressions, face-to-face knowledge, the direct impact of things and persons.

Anschauung is the basis of all knowledge and experience. It is not, however, restricted to mere awareness of objects. It

1. **Ibid. pp. 37-8**
2. **Ibid. p. 61**

comprises also spontaneous appreciation of moral actions and direct realisation of situations. It emphasises the immediacy of the experience, but does not imply simplicity in the process. Negatively it excludes the intervention of any object or process between the subject and his experience. Its primary purpose, for Pestalozzi, was to further the converse of man with his world.

For Kant the forms of Anschauung were space and time. In his *Letters to Greaves* Pestalozzi accepts Kant's classification. "The relations and proportions of number and form constitute the natural measure of all those impressions which the mind receives from without. They are the measures, and comprehend the qualities of the material world; form being the measure of space and number the measure of time." Earlier, and generally, he distinguished three aspects of Anschauung, namely, form, number and name. How he arrived at this division he recorded as follows: Living, but vague, ideas of the elements of instruction whirled about in my mind for a long time...At last, like a *Deus ex machina*, came the thought–the means of making clear all knowledge gained by sense-impression comes from number, form and language. It suddenly seemed to throw a new light on what I was trying to do.Now, after my long struggle, or rather my wandering reverie, I aimed wholly and simply at finding out how a cultivated man behaves, and must behave, when he wishes to distinguish any object which appears mistery and confused to his eyes, and gradually to make it clear to himself.

1. How many, and what kinds of objects are before him.
2. Their appearance, form or outline.
3. Their names; how he may represent each of them by a sound or word.

Three fold Observation

In this case he will observe three things :

1. How many, and what kinds of objects are before him.
2. Their appearance, form or outline.
3. Their names ; how he may represent each of them by a sound or word.

Threefold Powers

The result of this action in such a man manifestly presupposes the following ready-formed powers :

1. The power of recognising unlike objects, according to the outline, and of representing to oneself what is contained within it.
2. That of stating the number of these objects, and representing them to himself as one or many.
3. That of representing objects, their number and form, by speech, and making them unforgettable.

Threefold Principle

I also thought number, form and language are, together, the elementary means of instruction, because the whole sum of the external properties of any object is comprised in its outline and its number, and is brought home to my consciousness through language. It must then be an immutable law of the technique of instruction to start from and work within this threefold principle

1. To teach children to look upon every object that is brought before them as a unit, that is, as separated from those with which it is connected.
2. To teach them the form of every object, that is, its size and proportions.
3. As soon as possible to make them acquainted with all the words and names descriptive of objects known to them.

CULTIVATION OF PRIMARY FACULTIES

And as the instruction of children should proceed from these three elementary points, it is evident that the first efforts of the technique of instruction should be directed to the primary faculties of counting, measuring, and speaking, which lie at the basis of all accurate knowledge of objects of sense. We should cultivate them with strictest psychological technique of instruction, endeavour to strengthen and make them strong, and to bring them, as a means of development and culture, to the highest pitch of simplicity, consistency and harmony.'

Apprehension of form was developed by Pestalozzi mainly through drawing, on the ground that children are ready at an earlier age for knowledge of proportion and for the guidance of the slate-pencil than for guiding the pen and making tiny letters.

Pestalozzi, built all power of doing, even the power of clear representation of all real objects, upon the early development of the ability to draw lines, angles, rectangles and curves. Thus he states that by exercises in lines, angles and curves, a readiness in gaining sense impressions of all kinds is produced in the children, as well as skill of hand, of which the effect will be to make everything that comes within the sphere of their observation gradually clear and plain." Against the tendency for the means to obscure the aim, and for drawing to become an end in itself, Pestalozzi protested, saying "Nature gives the child no lines, she only gives him things, and lines must be given him only in order that he may perceive things rightly. The things must not be taken from him in order that he may see only lines."[1] And concerning the danger of rejecting Nature for the sake of lines, on another occasion he angrily exclaimed : "God forbid that I should overwhelm the human mind and harden it against natural sense-impressions, for the sake of these lines and of the technique of instruction, as idolatrous priests have overwhelmed it with superstitious teaching, and hardened it against natural sense-impressions."[2]

TEACHING WRITING

By basing writing on drawing, separating the acquisition of the forms from the commmand of the instrument, and using the skill acquired in writing for the expression of significant ideas Pestalozzi anticipated in many points the Montessori method of teaching writing. The defect of his method, as in language teaching, is that he carried his analysis to its ultimate limits. What is psychologically simple to the child is not necessarily what remains when analysis cannot be carried further . In writing, the unit is the word or the letter, not the so called element of the letter.

1. Ibid. p. 69.
2. Ibid.

TEACHING OF ARITHMATIC

Scope for the application of Pestalozzi's principle of concreteness was readily found in arithmetic. Reviewing Krusi's development as a teacher, Pestalozzi writes : "For instance, when he asked in arithmetic, How many times is seven contained in sixty-three, the child had no real background for his answer, and must with great trouble dig it out of his memory. Now, by the plan of putting nine times seven objects before his eyes, and letting him count them as nine servents standing together, he has not to think any more about this question; he knows from what he has already learnt, although he is asked for the first time, that seven is contained nine times in sixty-three. So it is in other departments of the method."[1] The general principle of Anschauung as applied to arithmetic Pestalozzi formulated in these terms : "That by exercising children beginning to count with real objects, or at least with dots representing them, we lay the foundation of the whole of the science of arithmetic, and secure their future progress from error and confusion."[2]

LANGUAGE TEACHING

With the language aspect of Anschauung Pestalozzi concerned himself more particularly, although he did not quite regard the name as coordinate in rank with form and number. Fichte complains[3] that acquaintance with the word-sign adds nothing to the knowledge of an object but simply brings it within the sphere of what can be communicated to others. Herbart nevertheless comes again to the defence of Pestalozzi arguing that to young children a word, a name, is not as to use merely the sign of a thing. The word itself is the thing. They linger upon the sound. Not until the latter has become commonplace to them do they learn to forget it in attention to the thing itself. Pestalozzi reasoned that the child must learn to talk before he can be taught to read, and recognised the child's need for a full and facile vocabulary. Thus he affirmed: "The advantage of a fluent and early nomenclature is invaluable to

---

1. **Pestalozzi, *How Gertru Teaches her Children.* p.54**
2. **Ibid. p. 51**
3. ***Fichte, Addresses to the German Nation,* Eng. Tran. p.166**

children. The firm impression of names makes the things unforgettable, as soon as they are brought to their knowledge; and the stringing together of names in an order based upon reality and truth develops and maintains in them a consciousness of the real relation of things to each other. Certain it is that when a child has made the greater part of a scientific nomenclature his own, he enjoys through it at least the advantage that a child enjoys who in his own a great house of business, daily becomes acquainted from his cradle upwards with the names of countless objects."[1] Pestalozzi does not propose that the child should acquire a stock of names merely for their own sake but as a means to the mastery of things, a function which the name has had from the earliest times. He complained" That in the lower schools for more than a century there had been given to empty words a weight in the human mind that not only hindered attention to the impressions of nature, but even destroyed man's inner susceptibility to these expressions."[2] His own method, he explained was "like Nature with the savage, I always put the picture before the eye, and then sought for a word, for the picture."[3]

Pestalozzi reduced language to words or names, and the latter he resolved into sounds. For each stage he constructed formal exercises, beginning with syllables which he regarded as the irreducible elements. The first exercises took the form, for example, a–ab–bab, etc., much after the manner of the present day phonic methods of teaching to read. Lists of names of the most important objects in all divisions of the kingdom of nature, history, geography, human callings and relations he required to be memorised, and lastly sentences had to be formed in various ways. Pestalozzi's analysis was carried to extremes and evoked censure. The redeeming feature of his method was nevertheless that it based reading on sounds and not on spelling, and thereby prepared the way for modern methods.

In *The Mother's Book*, Pestalozzi was misled into beginning with the child's body, arguing that the first object of the child's

1. ***How Gretrude Teachers Her Children*, p. 33**
2. **Ibid. p. 113**
3. **Ibid. p. 55**

knowledge must be the child himself. Immediate experience is generally confused and must be made definite; it must likewise be generalised.

In his *Letters to Greaves* Pestalozzi explains : "But if a mother is to teach by THINGS, she must recollect also that to the formation of an idea more is requisite than bringing the object before the senses. Its qualities must be explained ; its origin must be accounted for ; its parts must be described, and their relation to the whole ascertained ; its use, its effects or consequences must be stated. All this must be done, at least, in a manner sufficiently clear and comprehensive to enable the child to distinguish the object from other objects, and to account for the distinction which is made."[1]

NO GAPS IN INSTRUCTION

In the progressive development no step must be missed. There must be no gaps in instruction. This is Pestalozzi's principle of unbroken sequence, second in significance only to his doctrine of Anschauung. It was the feature of his teaching that appealed to and was championed by Herbart : "Not a useless word is heard in his school the train of apperception is never interrupted. The teacher pronounces for the children constantly. Every faulty letter is expunged from the slate immediately.The child never dwells on its mistakes. The right track is never departed from ; hence every moment marks progress."

Although *How Gertrude Teaches Her Children* is mainly concerned with the nature and development of knowledge, Pestalozzi would not have it thought that this is the aim of education, for he says : "To have knowledge without practical power, to have insight, and yet to be incapable of applying it in everyday life, what more dreadful fate could an unfriendly spirit devise for us"[2]

THE EDUCATIONAL PROCESS

Of the threefold division of the educational process–the physical, the intellectual, the moral-religious—the first comprises not merely physical culture but also artistic skill and technical dexterity since all involve the physical organs. Fichte approved

1. Ibid. p. 123
2. Ibid. p. 173

of the inclusion by Pestalozzi of the development of the pupil's bodily powers, quoting a passage from *How Gertrude Teaches Her Children.* But he complained that Pestalozzi has failed to supply a graduated scheme of physical exercises.

VIEW ABOUT ART

While mental development in general consists in the inner organisation of impressions received from without, art reverses the process in so far as it modifies the external world by means of inner impulses and tendencies. The basis of all art is partly internal, partly external; partly mental, partly physical. Artistic skill comprises the effort to embody the products of the human mind, to give expression to the impulses of the human heart, to exercise the dexterities required in domestic and social life. Such is Pestalozzi's view of art as expounded in the *Swansong.* The development of dexterity follows the same laws as the development of knowledge.

MORAL EDUCATION

Following Rousseau, Pestalozzi believed that the child is born good. But we must nevertheless take his education out of the hands of blind nature, as the world he enters is a world meant for the innocent enjoyment of the senses and for the feelings of his inner nature.[1] The moral faculty is present in infancy. "God has given the child a spiritual nature, that is to say, He has implanted in him the voice of conscience; and He has done more, He has given him the faculty of attending to this voice."[2] The moral virtues originate in the relations existing between the child and his mother. In them too lies the whole essence of the natural germ of that state of mind which is peculiar to human dependence on the Author of our being.

EQUALITY OF DIVISIONS

In his earlier writings Pestalozzi stressed the equality rather than the correlation of his three main divisions of education–the physical, the intellecutal and the ethicoreligious, or – the physical, the intellectual and ethicordigious, or – the physical, the technical,

1. **Ibid. p. 187**
2. **J. A. Green, *Pertalozzi educational writings,* p. 281**

the aesthetic, the intellectual, the moral and the religious aspects of quality. In his later writings he insists that the three aspects should be coordinated by one spiritual princple. Thus in the *Swansong* he definitely characterised the relationship between them as one of harmony. "The education of all three sides of our nature proceeds on common lines in equal measure, as is necessary if the unity of our nature and the equilibrium of our powers are to be recognised from the outset."[2] And in the *Letters to Greaves* : "The powers of man must be so cultivated that no one shall predominate at the expense of another, but each be excited to the true standard of activity ; and this standard is the spiritual nature of man."[1]

Earlier *in How Gertrude Teaches Her Children* the idea of harmonious development was mentioned. "The aim of all instruction is, and can be, nothing but the development of human nature, by the harmonious cultivation of its powers and talents, and the promotion of manliness of life." Emphasis on harmonious development or on well balanced training, should not blind us to the fact that education should respect individuality. In the *Swansong* Pestalozzi advises : "Unusual capacity should be given every possible chance, and, above all, it should be rightly guided." In 1805, Pestalozzi went from Burgdorf to Yverdon, where he remained till 1827. He had by now acquired international fame. Princes visited his institution.

CRITICAL EVOALUATION

Froebel said : 'What I saw was to me at once elevating and depressing, arousing and also bewildering .... "The powerful, indefinable, stirring and uplifting effect produced by Pestalozzi when he spoke, set one's soul on fire for a higher, nobler life, 'Writes Froebel, "although he had not made clear or sure the exact way towards it, nor indicated the means whereby to attain it. Thus did the power and many sidedness of the educational effort make up for the deficiency in unity and comprehensiveness; and the love, the warmth, the stint of the whole...and benevolence of it replaced the want of clearness, depth, thoroughness, extent, preserverance, and steadiness"...

1. Ibid. p. 18

Pestalozzi's efforts in education were tentative. Although lacking the scientific precision demanded to-day, they were experimental. His results had not that consistency which obtains in a purely *a priori* scheme of education, nor did they command that respect which attaches to the conclusion of a philosophical theory. As the products of hard-won experience they nevertheless possess a reliability which many other more pretentious systems do not. To conclude in the word of Robert R. Rusk." With Pestalozzi it may truly be said that necessity was the mother of invention. It was this necessity that constrained him to make Anschauung the common starting-point of all instruction, to insist that teaching should follow an orderly sequence, to formulate a general method based on psychological principles, to recognise the practical and emotional aspects of personality, to lay the basis of our elementary school system and to reinforce the democratic tradition in education."[1]

IMPORTANT EDUCATIONAL IDEAS OF PESTALOZZI

1. Aim of Education. Education is "the natural, progressive and harmonious development of all the powers and capacities of human being."

2. Methods of Instruction. Pestalozzi remarked, "I wish to psychologise education." He advocated that a child should be studied thoroughly and therafter appropriate methods of instruction should be used.

3. Sense Perception or 'Anschuung'. He was a believer in the value of sense perception.

4. Use of Object Lesson. He said, "Man's knowledge must be founded on sense impression." Again he writes, "Teach him nothing by words that you can teach him by things themselves.

5. Nature as an Educator. Pestalozzi remarked, "nature teaches better than men."

6. Discipline. Pestalozzi forced nothing upon students from without. He guided them to control themselves. He gave them his love and affection.

❑❑❑

1. **Rusk, R. R., *The doctrine of Great Educators,* 1954, London Macmillan, p. 208.**

7

Jean Jacques Rousseau

"I want that some wise man should tell us the art of counselling the child. This art will be valuable for us. The teachers have not learnt even its elementary rule"

—Jean Jacques Rousseau

"What must we think then, of that barbarous education which sacrifices the present to an uncertain future, which loads a child with chains of every sort and begins by making him miserable in order to prepare for him long in advance, some pretended happiness, which it is probable, he will never enjoy."

"Nature wants that the child should remain a child before he becomes an adult. By changing this sequence we shall get raw fruits which shall soon perish. The child has his own ways of seeing, thinking and experiencing. We should not impose our own methods on him. It will be a folly."

Jean Jacques Rousseau was born in 1712, in Geneva of parents of French protestants ancestry, in a middle class family. His father was a watch maker but became a dance master and went to Constantinople leaving his mother who urged him to come again. After this reunion Rousseau was born, ill and weak and her mother died. Issac, the father of Rousseau brought him up without giving him proper education, but forced him to read about erotic romantic impressions of life."

At the age of ten his father entrusted Rousseau to his uncle's care and left Geneva. Upto the age of 13, Rousseau had to work as an apprentice under a cruel engraver. When 16, Rousseau left home and led a life of vagabound for 20 years wandering at different places. In 1742, he tried many trades but met with no success. He was very much disappointed but with the help of his friend, he got a post in the French Embassy at Vienna. But he was soon dismissed. He again came to Paris and opened a hotel. Here Cauasser, a servant in hotel became his real and lasting friend.

In the year of 1742, The Acadancy of Dizon announced a prize for the best essay on the subject "Has the progress of science and arts contributed to corrupt or purify morals?" Rousseau presented his thesis that the progress of sciences and arts tended to degrade the human morality. He wrote an essay which depicted an early state of society in which all men lived under conditions of simplicity and innocence and traced the present evils of society to the thirst of knowledge and to the education of artificialities of civilization. He won the prize which made a great sensation. It was the first ramble of revolution. In 1753, Rousseau wrote another essay on "What is the origin of inequality among men and is it authorized by natural laws?"

Later on in 1755-1761 Rousseau wrote many of his important books. In 1762, he left Paris and led a life of vagabond for 16 years. This was a period of gloom, failing health, broken spirit, haunting terrors, paralysing illusions and of accumulating despair according to Hearnshaw.

ROUSSEAU'S WRITINGS

1. *Two essays written for Acadamy.*
2. *Contract Social or The Principles of Political Right*—published in 1762 is most famous.
3. *Émile* dealing with education.
4. Few Hèloìse
5. *The progress of Arts and Sciences*
6. *Confessions*
7. *The Dialogues*
8. *The Reveries*—Published between 1762-1770

Rousseau's books rebelled against the rational thinking of his age. He brought out the problems and conflicts inherent in civilised societies.

According to R.R. Rusk, Rousseau is the most maligned and most misunderstood figure in the history of education, and for this he has himself largely to blame.

He had no children of his own, no schooling and little or no experience of teaching. Towards the end of 1735 he was reprimanded by his father for his shiftless existence. He reported by expressing his inclination to become a tutor : 'Finally, I might in a few years and with a little more experience become tutor to some young men of quality......I confess frankly that is the estate for which I feel some inclination'.[1]

Such an opportunity did present itself later, and although his experience of tutoring two of the sons of M. de Malby, Provost of Lyons, revealed to Rousseau his unfitness for the task,[2] it engaged his interest in education, and led him to prepare his first treatise on the subject, name by the *Project for the Education of M. de Sainte-Marie,* Sainte-Marie being the elder of the two boys. 'The end that one should set before oneself in the education of a young man', states Rousseau in the *Project,* 'is to form his heart, his judgment and his mind—in the order in which I have named them', thus echoing the precept in Locke's *Thoughts* : 'Tis virtue, then, direct virtue, which is the hard and valuable part to be aimed at in education, and not a forward pertness or any little art of shifting. All other considerations and accomplishments should give way and be postponed to this. This is the solid and substantial good [on] which tutors should not only read lectures, and talk of, but the labour and art of education should furnish the mind with, and fasten

1. **A.L. Sells, *The Early Life and Adventures of J.J. Rousseau* (Cambridge : Heffer and Sons, 1929), p. 103.**
2. **Of. Emile, Everyman translation, pp. 86, 18. After a similar experience but extending over nine years kant likewise confessed there was hardlyever a tutor with a better theory or a worse practice. T.K. Abbott, Kant's Critical of Practical Reason, p. xvi.**

there, and never cease till the young man had a true relish of it, and placed his strength, his glory and his pleasure in it.' Concerning the position and function of a tutor, we have in the *Project* anticipations of the *Émile,* but the great attention which he devotes in this treatise to the early social training of Sainte-Marie proves that Rousseau had not yet adopted his anti-social attitude which is characteristic of his later political and educational writings.

During Stay in Paris

During his stay in Paris the announcement in the *Mercure de France* of the subject of the prize essay set by the Academy of Dijon in 1750—'Has the Restoration of the Arts and Science contributed to the Purification of Morals?'—gave Rousseau his opportunity. The success attending his effort marked the beginning of his literary fame and of his anti-social bias. This anti-social attitude was temperamental, a defence mechanism against his gaucherie. His attempt to put the simple life into practice estranged the literary coterie with whom he was consorting. This, added to his general introvertive tendencies. It created the misundderstandings which embittered his life and caused it to be one of increasing misery.

At the Hermitage

Having come within the ambit of Madame d'Épinay's circle in 1747, he was provided by her with the Hermitage on the estate of d'Épinay at Montmorency which he occupied from April 1756 til December 1757. The Hermitage afforded a happy interlude in his troubled life. Madame d'Epinay had conceived the idea of writing for the edification of her little son, then nine years old, a series of lettes, and had submitted some of these to Rousseau for observations. He approved of the idea but objected that the purpose, being too apparent, would defeat itself. According to Mrs. Frederika Macdonald's researches, Rousseau's replies have been deliberately mutilated to discredit him; he is reported in the falsified version to have said that fathers and mothers are not made educators by nature nor are children made to be educated and to have maintained the 'bizarre thesis' that no education is advisable.

As contrasted with the published text of Madame d'Épinay's *Memoirs* the true version according to the original manuscript is as follows :

'I have read, madame, with great attention your letters to your son; they are good, excellent; but entirely unsuited to him. Allow me to tell you this with all the sincerity I owe you. In spite of the tenderness and earnestness with which you adorn your counsel, the general tone of these letters is too serious. They show your purpose is to improve him—and if the purpose is to succeed, the child must not suspect it. I think the idea of writing to him a very happy one, that may help to form his heart and mind; but two conditions are necessary for this; he should understand you; and he should be able to reply to you. These letters should be written for him alone—and these you have sent me would do for almost anyone but him! Believe me, keep them until he is older. Tell him stories and fables, that he can find out the moral of, and, above all, that he can apply to himself. **Avoid generalities** : *one only arrives at poor results, or at none at all, by putting maxims in the place of facts.* It is from what he has actually seen whether of right or of wrong, that you must start; when his ideas begin to form themselves, and when you have taught him to reflect, and to compare them, by degrees, you will change the tone of your letters, suiting it to his progress, and to the faculties of his mind. But if you tell your son now that your object is to form his heart and mind, and that you wish, whilst amusing him, to teach him the truth and his duties, he will be on his guard against everything you say : he will see a lesson in every word you utter, everything, even his top, will become an object of suspicion of him. Try to instruct him whilst amusing him but keep the secret to your self....Here, Madame, you have it. I hope it may not vex you; for it is not possible for me to give you another. If I am not deceived in you, you will forgive my brutality; and you will begin your task over again with more courage, and more success than ever.'

The ***Discourse on the Arts and Sciences*** expresses Rousseau's **anti-social doctrine** or rather his protest against the false conventional standards which controlled current society.

In the *Discourse* Rousseau writes 'in praise of ignorance'. He assembles instances to prove that the decline and fall of ancient peoples coincided with the growth of knowledge among them. He argues that the days of their poverty, simplicity and ignorance were also the days of their strength, their happiness and their innocence.

DISCOURSE ON THE ORIGIN OF INEQUALITY

The extravagances against which Rousseau inveighed in his *Discourse on the Arts and Sciences* he seeks to account for in his *Discourse on the Origin of Inequality.* They are the results of man's sense of possession and desire for private property; would be but few inequalities in social life. To sustain his contention Rousseau defined the original nature of man. It is this part of the *Discourse on Inequality* that has educational interest.

Rousseau emphasises the common nature of mankind. He said, "If all human knowledge were divided into two part, one common to all, the other peculiar to the learned, the latter would seem small compared with the former".

Ignoring the comparative treatment Rousseau attacks directly the question of the nature of man; he frankly warns us that he is likewise not following the historical method—'Let us begin then by laying facts aside, as they do not affect the question'. The plan he adopts is the hypothetical or conjectural.

Animal behaviour can be explained by the laws of mechanism, but man, according to Rousseau, is a free agent, and has some share in his own operations. Rousseau would even go the length of attributing ideas and intelligence to animals, allowing man in this respect to differ only in degree from them, but he adds that it is not so much the understanding that constitutes the specific difference between the man and the brute as the human quality of free agency. According to Rousseau it is particularly in the consciousness of this liberty that the spirituality of man's soul is displayed. In his analysis of human endowment Rousseau thus gives priority to the higher spiritual values, the existence of which modern psychologists are apt to ignore. To freedom he links progress, or self-improvement.

A DISCOURSE ON POLITICAL ECONOMY

In *A Discourse on Political Economy,* the subject is the principles of political obligation, Rousseau formulates the differences between public and domestic administration and lays down the principles of public education. His plan of public education is communistic, recalling the schemes set forth by Plato in the *Republic* and the *Laws,* and anticipating the communistic arrangement advanced by Fichte in *Address to the German Nation.* But for the most eloquent refutation of Rousseau's communistic view we do not require to go outside Rousseau's own writings, for in the *Émile* he asks: 'Will the bonds of convention hold firm without some foundation in nature? Can devotion to nature exist apart from the love of those near and dear to us? Can patriotism thrive except in the soil of that miniature fatherland, the home? Is it not the good son, the good husband, the good father, who makes the good citizen?'

Influence of Greece

If we ignore the communistic aspect of the *Discourse on Political Economy,* Rousseasu's view of national education accords with Greek theory and Spartan practice. He agrees with Aristotle who declares that service to the state as a whole has single end, it is plain that the education of all must be one and the same, and that the supervision of this education must be public and not private.....public training is wanted in all things that are of public interest. Rousseau echoes Aristotle, asserting : "Public education under regulations presented by the government, and under magistrates established by the Sovereign, is one of the fundamental rules of popular or legitimate government'.

In his *Letters à M. de Malesherbes* Rousseau designates the *First Discourse* that on Inequality and the treatise on Education [*Émile*] his three principal works, and indicates that they are inseparable and together constitute a complete whole. For his educational views it could equally well be said that three at least of his works should be consulted, namely, the *Nouvelle Hèloïse,* the *Emile* and the *Considerations on the Government of Poland.*

CONSIDERATION ON THE GOVERNMENT OF POLAND

In his *Considerations on the Government of Poland* Roussseau applied his principles of national education, and although it is a departure from the historical order to consider it before the *Nouvelle Hèloïse* and the *Émile, it* is a natural and logical order. The precedence thus accorded to it may help to counteract the popular belief that Rousseau was an individualist in education as a cursory reading of the *Émile* might suggest.

In the *Émile* Rousseau distinguishes three phases of education—the natural or negative; the social or moral; the civic or political. Only in dealing with Émile's experience of foreign travel does Rousseau refer in the *Émile* to the third aspect. In the *Considerations on the Government of Poland* he makes this civic aspect the chief aim; in it he preaches the most aggressive nationalism which, however necessary for the preservation of the national spirit of Poland at that time and for the later emancipation of that country, is now outmoded. The spirit of the *Considerations on the Government of Poland* is the spirit of Fichte's *Addresses to the German Nation* which misled Germany into two world wars.

In this treatise Rousseau recognises the importance and recommends the inclusion of physical exercises, emphasising their moral value and the social training to be derived from participation in common games. He cites with approval an arrangement at Berne by which pupils acquire a training for the public duties which will later fall to their lot. Of intellectual studies there is practically no mention, the whole scheme being planned to develop a national character. Education should be virtually free and teaching should not be a profession but rather a civic duty undertaken at the outset of a career of public service. The administration of education was to be under the control of a council of magistrates, as advocated by Plato in the *Laws* and as earlier practised at Sparta. Throughout the *Considerations on the Government of Poland* Rousseau, as he repeatedly does in the *Émile,* reverts to the tradition of the ancients when he is required to give practical form to his proposals, for, as he maintains in the *Émile,* 'the ancients are nearer to nature and their genius is more distinct'.

COMPARISON BETWEEN PUBLIC AND PRIVATE EDUCATION

Sometime between the publication of the *Émile* and his flight from England, that is, between 1762 and 1767, Rousseau had prepared a *Comparison between Public and Private Education.* Rousseau recognised that such a comparison was requisite in any complete system of education and had intended to incorporate it in a revised edition of the *Émile.*

Nouvelle Hèloìse

In the *Considerations on the Government of Poland* Rousseau dealt with education from the national standpoint. In the *Nauvelle Hèloìse* he presents an account of private or domestic education, or what we should call home education. Locke in the *Thoughts* had suggested, as stated above, that the principles determining physical upbringing 'might all be dispatched in this one short rule, namely, that gentlemen should use their children as the honest farmers and substantial yeomen do theirs'. This maxim Rousseau adopted and elaborated in the *Nouvelle Hèloìse,* admitting as much when he says : 'Accustomed like the children of peasants to expose themselves to the heat and cold they grow as hardy; are equally capable of bearing the inclemencies of the weather; and become more robust as living more at their ease. This is the way to provide against the age of maturity, and the accidents of humanity.' The idyllic picture which in the *Nouvelle Hèloìse* Rousseau delineated of the early education of her own two boys and her cousins' daughter at the hands of Madame de Wolmar served as the model for Pestaozzi's *Leonard and Gertrude,* Pestalozzi merely making of necessity a virtue and transposing Roussau's conception into the terms of an under-provileged class.

The Émile

In the ***Émile*** Rousseau distinguishes various stages in the pupil's development : (1) infancy characterised by habit and the training of the emotions; (2) childhood characterised by 'necessity' and the training of the senses; (3) boyhood characterised by 'utility' and the training of the intellect; (4) adolescence, the stage of 'morality', and of moral, aesthetic and social education. In the *Nouvelle Hèloìse* he treats at greater length and in more detail of the childhood stage—'till his understanding ripens', when the child will be placed under a tutor, as was Émile; but up to the age of understanding, which he puts much earlier than in the *Émile,* namely, at six instead of at twelve years of age, Rousseau would in the *Nouvelle Hèloìse* have the children educated at home by the mother, introducing even a girl cousin and approving of coeducation till the boys are the age to come under the care of a tutor when the girl would become the special care of her instructress and be thereafter educated on quite other lines.

FUNDAMENTAL PRINCIPLES OF EDUCATION

The fundamental principles of education set forth in the *Nouvelle Hèloìse* are identical with those of the *Émile,* the *Nouvelle Hèloìse* for this reason being the natural and best introduction to the *Émile.* Rousseau regards that the original nature of the child is good. He assumes an intital equality among pupils, inequalities being the result of intercourse with a perverted society. Education, he contends, is necessary—'the best disposition must be cultivated'. Like Plato, Rouseau believes that it cannot begin too early—'the first and most important part of education, precisely that which all the world neglects, is that of preparing child to receive education'. The aim of education is the liberty and happiness of the child, but Rousseau recognises that liberty and constraint are compatible, and does not attempt to minimise the influence of the 'heavy yoke of necessity' which nature lays upon the pupil at this stage. The education is given imagination through things. It is so whether at twelve years of age or even at fifteen the pupil is totally ignorant of book knowledge. Throughout the whole work there is eloquent plea for the predominance of environmental over hereditarian influences.

When he was writing *The Social Contract* Rousseau was not conscious that he was initiating a political revolution. Nevertheless when penning the *Émile.*[1] he was under the impression of effecting a revolution in education. 'My thoughts are not those of others', he declares in the Author's Preface, and later in regard to method he counsels: 'Reverse the usual practice and you will almost always do right'. In spite of these protests Rousseau owed much to the past and to earlier writers in his view of a rational principle governing the universe he derived

NATURALIST PHILOSOPHY

Rousseau's naturalist philosophy shows three forms : Social naturalism, Psychological naturalism and Physical naturalism. In his social naturalism he devises education as a method to develop society. According to him one cannot become a man and citizen at the same time. Every new culture is born out of the old. The past mistakes or evils must be removed though old ideals may be honoured. As a bitter critic of society Rouseau condemned old traditions opposing new reforms. He said, "Whatever is generally banned today you should do just the opposite, then you will find the right path". Rousseau's social naturalism may be found in his book *Social Contract*. His aim is man making and not the making of social man and citizen. In man making the man should follow his own inner feelings and natural tendencies. The child should be left to behave naturally. He learns in the contact of plants, animals, birds and natural objects. Society and man spoil the child. From moral and physical point of view the city is opposed to human good. The people should organise government to fulfill their needs. Wealth should not be concentrated in few hands. Thus, Rousseau pleaded for liberty and equality. According to him education means, "natural development of organs and power of the child".

NEGATIVE EDUCATION

According to Rousseau, the first education ought to be purely negative. It consists not at all in teaching virtue or truth but in shielding the heart from vices and mind from errors. Thus, Rousseau was against imparting any education to the child. According to him, "In childhood the aim of education is not to utilise time but to loose it". Elsewhere he said, "A twelve-year old child should know nothing. The teacher should pay attention to the child only and not to knowledge."

In Rousseau's time the children were given moral and religious education through various types of books in order to prepare them for adult life. Explaining his new system of education, Rousseau said, "Give me a twelve-year old child who does not know anything. By 15 years of age, I will teach him so much as other children read in 15 years of early life. The only difference will be that your student remembers only knowledge and my student will be able to use it in practical life." Thus, Rousseau precisely reversed the old order. As he said, "Take the reverse of the accepted practice and you will almost always do right". This was what he called, negative education.

CRITICISM OF CURRENT EDUCATIONAL SYSTEM

Criticising the educational system of his time Rousseau said, "What must we think then, of that barbarous education which sacrifices the present to an uncertain future, which loads a child with chains of every sort and begins by making him miserable in order to prepare for him long in advance, some pretended happiness, which it is probable, he will never enjoy". This was positive education emphasising the mind and trying to make the child an adult. Negative education, on the other hand, strengthens the sense organs and the power of reasoning. As Rousseau said, "Nature wants that the child should remain a child before he becomes an adult. By changing this sequence we shall get raw fruits which shall soon perish. The child has his own ways of seeing, thinking and experiencing. We should not impose our own methods on him. It will be a folly". We do not understand the child and assume our ideas as his ideas. Elsewhere he said, "I want that some wise man should tell us the art of counselling the child. This art will be valuable for us. The teachers have not learnt even its elementary rule".

Thus, negative education is self-education. It is the education of sense organs and body. This may be more possible in the playground rather than in the classroom. As Rousseau said, "We give too much importance to words. We produce by chattering education chatterers only. If you are all the time teaching morals to the child, you will make him a fool. If your mind is always giving instruction to the child, then his mind will become useless. Whatever the child learns in playground is four times more useful than what he learns in the classroom."

FOUR STAGES OF DEVELOPMENT

According to Rousseau man's development may be classified into the following four stages—

1. *Infancy*, from birth to 5 years of age.
2. *Childhood*, from 5 years to 12 years of age.
3. *Adolescence*, from 12 years to 15 years of age.
4. *Youth*, from 15 years to 20 years of age.

Rousseau has suggested suitable education in all these stages in his book *Émile*.

AIMS OF EDUCATION

In the opinion of Rousseau, education aimed at the natural development of the child's inner faculties and powers. Educations should help the child to remain alive. Life implies not merely the taking of breath but working. To live is to work, to develop and to properly utilise the various parts of the body, the sense organs and the various other powers of the body. In his book *Émile*, Rousseau seeks to train Émile in the profession of living so that he may become a human being before becoming a soldier, a churchman or a magistrate. Education, thus, in Rousseau's opinion, must aim at making the child a real human being.

But the aims of education change at different stages of the child's development, because at each stage something different needs strees. The following are the various aims of education according to each level of the child's development—

1. Infancy—This stage begins at birth and continues upto five years of age. The chief objective during these five years is bodily development, the development and strengthening of every part of the body. This is essential if the child is to grow up healthy and strong. It forms the basis of subsequent healthy development of the mind. Rousseau expressed the opinion, "All wickedness comes from weaknes. The child should be made strong so that he will do nothing which is bad." When the child is allowed to freely engage in playing and exercising his body, he remains active and has no time to indulge in undersirable activities. Nothing need be done to develop his instincts in other than to give him complete liberty. If such freedom is given, he naturally develops his own instincts.

2. Childhood—This stage lasts from the fifth year to the twelth and it is the period of developing the child's sense organs. This development is achieved through experience and observation. Hence, the child should be made to observe and experience those things in his environment which will assist the development of his sense organs.

3. Adolescence—For Émile, adolescence was believed to last from the twelfth to the fifteenth year. The chid has, by this time, achieved the development of his body and his sense organs, and is, therefore, prepared, for systematic education. At this stage, education aims at developing the adolescent personality through hard work, guidance and study. During adolescence the individual should be given knowledge of various kinds so that he is enabled to fulfil his needs.

4. Youth—The individual passes through his youth between his fifteenth and twentieth year and undergoes development of emotions and sentiments. Rousseau pointed out, "We have formed his body, his sense and intelligence, it remains to give him a heart." Development of the sentiments will lead to development of moral and social qualities, but is is essential to pay attention to the development of religious emotions also. Summing up, the aim of education is to achieve the bodily, sensory, mental, social and moral development of the individual.

CURRICULUM OF EDUCATION

It is possible to arrive at Rousseau's concept of a curriculum from an analysis of the various stages of development described in his Emile. Even in framing the curriculum, Rousseau paid attention to these four stages in development, and it will be better to consider the curriculum in the same fashion.

1. infancy—Rousseau was very critical of the contemporary curriculum laid down for the education of infants, because he stressed the fact that infants should be treated as infants and not as instincts and tendencies are dissimilar to those of the adult. For this reason, it is imperative to first understand child psychology and then to frame a curriculu. Instead of giving him controlled information of various subjects at this stage, it is far more important to pay attention of the development of his body and his sense. Before thinking of making the child a successful engineer or doctor, it is desirbale to make him a healthy and self-sufficient young animal. In this age, the child can be taught a great deal through normal conversation carried on in the child's mother-tongue. This will develop his linguistic ability. It is better not to try and instil any kind of habits in the child at this stage. Rousseau stated, "The only habit the child should be allowed to contract is that of having no habits."

2. Childhood—Even in childhood, Rousseau objected to the use of any textbooks for education, because he wanted to keep Emile away from books of any kind upto the twelfth year. He thought in necessary go give the child a chance to learn everything through direct experience and observation. Education of this kind is based on the concept of negative education which suggested that the child's mind should not be stuffed with information of different kinds. Instead he should be given liberty to learn through experience, because experience develops the sense organs which in trung lead to mental development, reason and development of the power of argument and reasoning. When the child is free to play, move, act at his own will during his childhood, he goes through a variety of experiences and learns all kinds of activities. During childhood, the child should not be given any verbal lessons on history, geography or even language. It is not desirable even to do any moral preaching. Rousseau opined that the child will learn his morality by the natural consequences of his own actions. Hence, upto the childhood stage no curriculum of any kind is required.

3. Adolescence—Having arrived at the appropriate level of bodily and sensory development, the child can now be exposed to teaching according to a formal curriculum consisting of education in natural science, language, mathematics, woodwork, music, painting, social life and some kind of professional training. Even here, Rousseau opined, more stress should be laid on the use of the sense orans than books. The very object of training in all these various subjects is the training and development of the sense organs. The study of science will enhance the child's curiosity and his inclination towards research, invention and self-education. Painting helps to train the muscles and eyes. handicrafts help in developing the ability to work, apart from the mental development which is part of the process. Passing through various phases of social life, the individual learns that men depend upon each other, and thereby the child learns to assume and fulfil social responsibility. Rousseau gave it as his opinion that books do not give knowledge, but only train one to talk. Hence, it is better if the curriculum for adolescence is based on active work than on books. During this period the adolescent must get adequate opportunity and time for hard work, education and study.

4. Youth—In the curriculum for youth, special stress has been laid on moral and religious education. But even moral education is to be derived through actual experience rather than through formal lectures. The youth learns a moral lesson when the sight of a physically handicapped person arouses in him the emotions of pity, sympathy and love. Religious education also follows the same pattern, but it can be assisted by the teaching of history, mythological stories and religious stories. The youth derives many lessons from these stories. Apart from moral and religious education, Rousseau gave appropriate importance to education in bodily health, music and sex.

SELF EDUCATION

Pointing out the importance of experience in education Rousseau said, "To be alive does not mean to breathe, but it means to work and to develop our organs, senses and other powers. That man is not happy who has a long life but happy is one who has gained experiences of life." As the method generally pursued in education in his time was mainly oral and theoretical, Rousseau criticised the present teaching methods. He said, "I wand that some wise man should tell us the art of counselling the child. This art will be valuable for us. The teachers have not learnt even its elementary rule." Rousseau wanted to adopt playway method in education in place of verbal teaching. He maintained, "Education should be practical rather than oral. The child will not have to read through books, he will have to stop reading words." Then, what should be the proper method of teaching the child? For Rousseau education to the child should be provided by play. "Thus, real education is self-education. The infant himself learns to develop by utilisation of his sense organs and reacting to the environment."

PRINCIPLES OF EDUCATION

Rousseau is a naturalist in his methodology of education just as much as he is a naturalist in the curriculum of education. He has stressed the importance of the two following principles governing the process of education.

1. Learning through self-experience—Rousseau wanted to educate Émile through experience and not through book. He was opposed to bookish education, because he contended that books try to teach one to talk abou those things which one does not in fact, know. That is why he wanted to keep Emile away from books for twelve years, so much so that he did not want Émile even to know what a book is. Rousseau has praised only one book, *Robinson Crusoe*, because it presents the natural needs of human beings in such a simple manner that the child can easily comprehend them. From this book the child can also learn the manner in which these needs are to be satisfied.

2. Learning Through Doing—Rousseau opposed the rote method of learning on the ground that knowledge acquired through actual doing or actual experience is far more permanent that knowledge acquired through wrods. He wanted the child's power of reasoning and not his power of memorising things to be developed. That is why, Rousseau was so severely critical of the existing methods of education. He wanted the child to become educated through his own observation. Experience and analysis Instead of stuffing the child's mind with his own knowledge, the educator's task is to arouse the child's curiosity so that the child is inspired to find out things for himself, thus developing his own mind. Science is best taught through curiosity and desire to experiment and research. Rousseau's insistence on these elements was later manifested in the evolution of the Heuristic method. If the child is to give moral education to himself he must be active. Long lectures bore the child, and instead of contributing to his education, only hinder it because they blunt the child's appetite for new things. Hence, instead of delivering long lectures to the child, it is better to give him the opportunity to act for himself. In education, the object is more important than the word. It is undersirable to fashion a method of education and to mould the child accordingly.

DISCIPLINE

Rousseau, being a naturalist, wanted complete freedom as the first step towards inducing discipline in the child. He wanted a total absence of any restraints on the child, because he felt that they hindered the development of discipline. It is better to leave the child free environment so that he can develop his natural powers. Rousseau's plan also did not include any arrangement for punishment, because he felt that punishment should be the natural outcome of their own mistakes. This is the naturalist conception of punishment. In this theory it is assumed that the child has no knowledge of good and bad, but he suffers pain when he makes a mistake and pleasure when he does something right. Hence, he gets the reward of his actions. This is the natural pattern of punishment and it is this which will instil discipline in the child. This is natural discipline, which implied obedience of natural laws, because neglect or violation of these laws invariably leads to pain and suffering. Hence, it is not necessary to lecture to the child. He is naturally possessed of a fine character, and this character is defiled by long lectures. He will learn better discipline, if he is left to himself.

SCHOOL ORGANISATION

The title given above may be a little misleading because Rousseau object to the system of school education. He contended that the child is born innocent and pure, that he is only defiled and distorted by the defective environment of the school. In fact, the only suitable environment of every kind is defective and impure. It is better to separate the child from his parents, to take him away from school, and leave him by himself in a natural environment. The educator's only task is to look after the child, because in natural surroundings the child will himself look after the development of his natural abilities. Even if schools are created, they can be utilised by stressing the natural surroundings instead of insisting on creating a social atmosphere. In the predominantly natural surroundings the child will be able to develop naturally.

From the Stoics, as he did also his anti-social views. His political ideas are developments of Locke's, and his early educational views also owe to Locke.

Rousseeau counsels us to live according to nature, and in education to follow the order of nature.

For Rousseau 'nature' has several connotations. When rousseau says that 'education comes to us from nature from men or from things' he is regarding nature as equivalent to 'endowment' — the inherited dispositions and capacities of the individual. Before our innate tendencies are warped by our prejudices, they are what Rousseau terms 'nature'. Nature in this sense, is beyond our control: 'Now some hold that we become good by nature, some we become so by habit, and others that it is by teaching. As to nature. That it is by teaching. As to nature, that is clearly not in our power; it is something vouchsafed to the truly fortunate by some divine cause.

THREE MEANINGS OF NATUR

1. Education according to nature is frequently interpreted to meannothing more than the spontaneous development of the innate dispositions of the child, nothing more than what modern psychologists term 'maturation'. In the sense of endowment, Education according to nature, leads to the non-interventionist policy in education, a hands-off procedure for which, however, there is no warrant in the *Émile.* Rousseau may regard Education as an evil, but it is a necessary evil. In fact, he specifically warns us against such misconception : 'Things would be worse without this education. . . . Under existing conditions a man left to himself from birth would be more monster than the rest.' Later he says : 'When I want to train a natural man, I do not want to make him a savage and to send him back to the woods, but that living in the whirl of social life it is enough that he should not let himself be carried away by the passions and prejudices of men; let him see with his eyes and feel with his heart, let him own no sway but that of reason'. He repeats: 'Émile is no savage to be banished to the desert, he is a savage who has to live in the town'.

2. The second meaning attached to the term 'nature' in the *Émile* is a negative one, a consequence of Rousseau's adoption of the anti-social attitude. Society, for Rousseau, is not a natural, but an artificial, product, the outcome of a contract. And for Rousseau what is natural is good, and what is conventional or artificial is evil. Nature and society thus become opposed to each other; nature is accordingly defined negatively to society. A natural or a negative education does not mean no education; it signifies

simply a non-social education. Rousseau's natural or negative eduation this becomes what we should call a preventive education; it is not a preparation for life but rather a preparation against the social conditions in which, Rousseau fully realises, Émile must later play his part. Gradually and sadly does he seek to disillusion Émile as to the wicked world into which he is born.

Full soon the soul shall have its earthly freight
And custom lie upon thee with a weight
Heavy as frost and deep almost as life.

Rousseau does not aim at producing an unsocial creature; he hopes to establish in Émile an ethical constancy before his inevitable entrance into society. The ultimate aim is nevertheless to reconcile the natural and the social training : 'If their teaching conflicts, the scholar is ill-educated and will never be at peace with himself; if their teaching agrees, he goes straight to his goal, he lives at peace with himself, he is well-educated'.

3. The third meaning attached by Rousseau to the term 'nature' is a positive one, inherited from the Stoics who in turn derived it from Plato. Nature or the universe is governed by a divine providence. To live 'according to nature' is to live in accordance with the rational principle of the universe, to live according to reason; 'he who obeys his conscience is following nature'. A divine will sets the universe in motion and gives life to nature; a divine intelligence exist 'not merely in the revolving heavens, not in the sun which gives us light, not in myself alone but in the sheep that grazes, the bird that flies, the stone that falls, and the leaf blown by the wind'.

Not only is the ultimate principle of the universe spiritual, as idealism contends, but human nature is likewise spiritual and is not to be accounted for on mechanical or biological lines. 'For physics may explain', as Rousseau maintains in *The Origin of Inquality,* 'in some measure the mechanism of the senses and the formation of ideas; but in the power of this power of willing or rather of choosing, and in the feelings of this power, nothing is to be found but acts which are purely spiritual and wholly inexplicable by the laws of mechanism.' And whereas instinct may govern man in a state of nature, that is, before morality has emerged and men are bound by social ties, thereafter the voice of duty takes the place of physical impulses, and reason must be consulted before he listens to his inclinations. Or, as Rousseau says in the *Émile,* 'Distrust instinct as soon as you cease to rely altogether upon it. Instinct was good while he acted under its guidance only; now that he is in the midst of human institutions, instinct is not to be trusted; it must not be destroyed, it must be controlled which is perhaps a more difficult matter.'

NATURALISM

Rousseau is almost universally regarded as a naturalist in philosophy, the result of a superficial rendering of 'living according to nature' whereas from the interpretation given above and from the articles of faith formulated in the Creed of the Savoyard Priest he is manifestly an idealist. He serves as the bridge between the Stoics and Kant. The *Émile* is likewise not a word on individual education, as might at first sight be inferred, but actually propounds a universal system. At the outset of the *Émile* he states that education comes from nature, from men or from things, that is, the problem of education is the relationship of man to his physical and social environment. Emphasis may be laid either on the individual or on the social aspect of education. 'Two conflicting types of educational systems spring from these conflicting aims. One is public and common to many, the other private and domestic.' If rousseau refers the reader of the *Émile,* to Plato's *Republic* for an account of public education, it is because he himself had evidently studied the *Republic* not without profit. In the *Émile,* however, he professes to restrict himself to 'the education of the home', but the scheme he there presents is a scheme suited not to one individual only but to all; it is a universal scheme, and for this reason has become the fount of democratic education.

Rouseau's primary conception of man is, in a sense, individualistic, that is, it is individualistic in the sense of the Stoics in which the claims of the individual are based on the fact that he is in himself a *universal*.'

Many of the features nevertheless contribute to obscure this fact. The introduction of the individual pupil suggests the contrary interpretation, but it was merely the exigencies of exposition that compelled him to particularise and personify his principles in Émile ; as Rousseau himself warns us : 'Lest my book should be unduly bulky I have been content to state those principles the truth of which is self-evident. But as to the rules which call for proof I have applied them to Émile or to others, and I have shown in very great detail how my theories may be put into practice. Such at least is my plan.' And elaborating this literary technique he adds : 'At first I have said little about Émile, for my earliest maxims of education, though very different from those generally accepted, are so plain that it is hard for a man of sense to refuse to accept them, but as I advance, my scholar . . . appears upon the scene more frequently, and towards the end I never lose sight of him for a moment'. Rousseau maintains too that we must look at the general rather than the particular, and consider our scholar as man in the abstract; he further explains : 'I have discarded as artificial what belongs to another; and I have regarded as proper to mankind what was common to all, in any station, and in any nation whatsoever. He also believes in fitting a man's education to his real self, not to what is no part of him. That Rousseau is propounding a universal and not an individualist system is confirmed by his choice of a pupil : 'If I had my choice', he says, 'I would take a child of ordinary mind. . . . It is ordinary people who have to be educated, and their education alone can serve as a pattern for the education of their fellows'; he repeats : 'I assumed that my pupil had neither surpassing genius nor a defective understanding. I chose him of an ordinary mind to show what education can do for man.' Another assumption postulated in regard to the pupil for whom Rousseau proposes to presctibe and education, is that he should be 'a strong, well-made, healthy child'. Rousseau would not undertake the care of a feeble sickly pupil, for a healthy body is not only a condition of healthy mind, but also the basis of moral character. The ideal of the superman of Plato, Quintillian and others gives space with Rousseau to the ideal of the common or natural man ; the great souls, he believes, can find their way alone.

Further difficulties are created by Rousseau's selection of Émile from among the rich and by his introduction of a tutor for Émile. Rouseau's apology for choosing his scholar form among the rich is — 'we shall have made another man ; the poor may come to manhood without our help'. And if Émile comes of a good family so much the better — 'he will be another victim snatched from prejudice'. He proposes to give the sons of the rich a natural education that whatever might befall them in later life they would be independent of fate or fortune. A more penetrating interpretation is that the education which Rousseau proposed would be accepted as suitable for the poor, whereas by demonstration that it was quit appropriate for the children of the rich Rousseau established that it was an education for all. It is necessary to emphasis this fact, that Rousseau is expounding a universal system of education, for frequently the *Émile* is regarded as an account of an individualistic scheme of education, and difficulty is thereby encountered in explaining how the democratic systems of Pestalozzi and others originated in the *Émile*.

Although the intervention of the tutor recalls Locke's procedure in the *Thoughts Concerning Education,* Rousseau disclaims any similarity in standpoint : 'I have not the honour of educating a young gentleman'. The introduction of the tutor is indeed something more than a mere literary expedient; it is, in fact, a stroke of genius on the part of Rousseau. Their must be only one voice if the scheme proposed is to be a coherent whole. It may be mistaken but it will at least be consistent, whereas when the child is subject to two parents his education may be both mistaken and inconsistent; in fact, as is now recognised, it is the dissensions and estrangements of parents that constitute one of the most serious obstacles in the upbringing of their children, and Rousseau obviates this by placing Émile under the sole charge of a tutor.

ANTI-SOCIAL BIAS

The anti-social bias of Rousseau first enunciated in the *Discourse on the Arts and Sciences* is reflected in the Émile and divides the work into two contrasting sections — the natural or negative education up to adolescence, and the moral or social thereafter. Aristotle had declared in the *Politics* that man is by nature a social or political animal and that the state is creation of nature. In the perfect state, too, the good man would also be the good citizen. For Rousseau, however, nature and society are eternally at strife — 'Forced to combat either nature or society, you must make your choice between the man and the citizen, you cannot train both'. Rousseau should nevertheless have added 'at the same time', for the *Émile* is an attempt first to train the man, then to train the citizen. 'Man's proper study', he explains, 'is that of his relation to his environment. So long as he only knows that environment through his physical nature, he should study himself in relation to things; this is the business of childhood; when he begins to be aware of his moral nature, he should study himself in relation to his fellow men; this is the business of his whole life.' Again : 'We are working in agreement with nature, and while she is shaping the physical man, we are striving to shape his moral being; Thus the aim of education for Rousseau, as for Herbart later, was virtue or morality, the natural or physical education being but the preparatory stage.

The definite break, even direct opposition, between the natural or negative stage of education and the social or positive stage is the extreme instance of Rousseau's doctrine of the serial emergence of the faculties. That it cannot be completely effected Rousseau is forced to confess : 'I think it impossible to train a child up to the age of twelve in the midst of society without giving him some idea of the relations between one man and another, and of the morality of human actions. It is enough to delay the development of these ideas as long as possible, and when they can no longer be avoided to limit them to present needs, so that he may neither think himself master of everything nor do harm to others without knowing or caring.' The impossibility of isolating Émile entirely from the moral and social order should have led Rousseau to revise his view of human development as demarcated into well-pronounced stages, but his retention of it is not without its compensations.

It necessitated the adoption of what has come to be known as the psychological standpoint in education. This is one of Rousseau's fundamental principles. 'My method', he says 'does not depend on my examples; it depends on the amount of a man's powers at different ages and the choice of occupations adapted to these powers.' 'There is a time for every kind of teaching and we ought to recognise it, and each has its own dangers to be avoided.' 'Every stage, every station in life, has a perfection of its own.' 'Childhood has its own ways of seeing, thinking and feeling.'

The principle is also expressed negatively. 'We know nothing of childhood; and with our mistaken notions the further we advance the further we go astray. The wisest writers devote themselves to what a man ought to know, without asking what a child is capable of learning. They are always looking for the man in the child, without considering what he is before he becomes a man.' 'Nothing is useful and good for him which is unbefitting his age.'[1] 'Beware of anticipating teaching which demands more maturity of mind.'[2] 'Man's lessons are mostly premature.'[3] Émile 'should remain in complete ignorance of those ideas which are beyond his grasp. My whole book is one continued argument in support of this fundamental principle of education.'[4]

A consequence of the psychological standpoint was the acceptance of the 'participation' as opposed to the 'preparation' view of education. Rousseau argued that the possibilities of each stage of life should be fully exploited before proceeding to the next stage, a principle assumed later by Froebel and Montessori, although generally associated with the name of Dewey. Thus

1. p. 212.
2. p. 165.
3. p. 76.
4. p. 141.

Rousseau says : 'What is to be thought of that cruel education which sacrifices the present to an uncertain future, that burdens a child with all sorts of restrictions and begins by making him miserable in order to prepare him for some far-off happiness which he may never enjoy'. Again : 'What a poor sort of foresight to make a child wretched in the present with the more or less doubtful hope of making him happy at some future day'.

The perfect adaptation to his capabilities of the tasks undertaken by the pupil creates interest, and Rousseau by providing for this anticipates Herbart's doctrine of interest and its present-day equivalents — the Play Way and the Project Method. Thus Rousseau claims to be justified in saying of Émile : 'Work or play are all one to him; his games are his work ; he knows no difference'.

EDUCATION AS GUIDANCE

Education becomes for Rousseau a matter of guidance. In detailing the qualifications of the tutor he introduces the very term[1] : 'I prefer to call the man who has this knowledge master rather than teacher, since it is a question of guidance rater than instruction.' For the same reason Montessori latter substitutes 'directress', 'The art of teaching', Rousseau further explains,[2] 'consists in making the pupil wish to learn.' Or negatively expressed:[3] 'We learn nothing from a lesson we detest'. He summarises his guidance programme for Émile in the statement:[4] 'Surround him with all the lessons you would have him learn without awaking his suspicions'.

INNATE GUIDANCE OF CHILD

'Mankind has its place in the sequence of things; childhood has its place in the sequence of human life; the man must be treated as a man and the child as a child. Give each his place.' It was because Rousseau was the first to give the child his rightful place that the *Émile* was characterised by Lord Morley as the charter

1. p. 126.
2. p. 19.
3. p. 210.
4. p. 209.

of youthful deliverance, and that led Frederika Macdonald to write : 'Throughout Europe Rousseau's voice went proclaiming with even more restless eloquence than it had proclaimed the *Rights of Man,* the *Rights of Childhood.* Harsh systems, founded on the old medieval doctrine of innate depravity, were overthrown. Before Pestalozzi, before Frobel, the author of *Émile* laid the foundation of our new theory of education, and taught the civilised world remorse and shame for the needless suffering and the quenched joy that throughout long ages had darkened the dawn of childhood.' Rousseau's own panegyric on childhood reads thus[1]: 'Love childhood indulge its sports, its pleasures, its delightful instincts. Who has not sometimes regretted that age when laughter was ever on the lips, and when the heart was ever at peace ? Why rob these innocents of the joys which pass so quickly, of that precious gift which they cannot abuse? Why fill with bitterness the fleeting days of early childhood, days which will no more return for them than for you ? Fathers, can young tell when death will call your children to him ? Do not lay up sorrow for yourselves by robbing them of the short span which nature has allotted to them. As soon as they are aware of the joy of life, let them rejoice in it, so that whenever God calls them they may not die without having tasted the joy of life.'

What 'the delights of liberty' signify Rousseau explains in the statement : 'That man is truly free who desires, what he is able to perform, and does what he desires. This is my fundamental maxim. Apply it to childhood, and all the rules of education spring from it.' Rousseau's aim is 'a well-regulated liberty', the same as Montessori later adopts. Rousseau is well aware of the distinction between liberty and licence, for he retorts to those who object to this aim : 'If such blundering thinkers fail to distinguish between liberty and licence, between a merry child and a spoilt darling, let them learn to discriminate'. He would train his pupil to be 'as self-reliant as possible', whereas he contends that the ordinary educator 'teaches him everything except self-knowledge and self-control, the arts of life and happiness'.

---

1. Émile, p. 43.

What simplifies the problem for Rousseau is his assumption of the innate goodness of the child. 'Man is by nature good', he says. 'God makes all things good', and 'what is, is good'. 'Our first impulses are always good.' Locke had claimed that the mind instead of being by nature evil and desperately wicked was a clean slate. Rousseau goes further and maintains 'that the first impulses of nature are always right; there is no original sin in the human heart, the how and the why of the entrance of every vice can be traced'. Dealing with the education of Sophy in Book V, he repeats that all our natural inclinations are right.

If we accept Rousseau's position and assume that our endowment is good and all our natural inclinations right, the task of education should be simple; we have merely to fix the inborn propensities by habit, for, as Rousseau declares, 'If the voice of instinct is not strengthened by habit, it soon dies', Habit is all that is needed, as we have nature on our side. He says, speaking of Sophy's education, "Education, then, being but habit, care must be taken to see that only right habits are established, and Rousseau issues his warning in the form of a contradiction : 'The only habit', he says, 'the child should be allowed to contract is that of having no habits'. Later he says of Émile : 'No doubt he must submit to rules; but the chief rule is this — be able to break the rule if necessary'.

Heedless of Rousseau's warning — 'I must admit that my words are often contradictory, but I do not think there is any contradiction in my ideas', Commentators have seized on Rousseau's apparently incompatible statements to score easy triumphs, but Rousseau's antinomy is resolved when we recognise that he distinguishes two types of habit, the natural and the social, and that while he advocates establishing natural habits — 'leave his body its natural habit'— he protests against making his pupil 'a mere slave of public opinion'. Thus he explains : Always distinguish between natural and acquired tendencies', and again : 'The only useful habit for children is to be accustomed to submit without difficulty to necessity, and the only useful habit for man is to submit without difficulty to the rule of reason. Every other habit is a vice.'

To attain liberty education must act both negatively and positively. The negative training consists in restricting the child's desires, the positive in supplying the pupil with the strength he lacks so far as it is required for freedom, not for power. Rousseau effects the former by keeping the child dependent on things. 'Keep the child dependent on things only' is his prescription. 'By this course of education you will have followed the order of nature.' 'There are two kinds of dependence ; dependence on things which is the work of nature and dependence on men which is the work of society. Dependence on things, being non-moral, does no injury to liberty, and be gets no vices, dependence on men, being out of order, gives rise to every kind of vice.'

Keeping the child dependent on things has two aspects—**intellectual and moral.** The intellectual aspect is the basis of Pestalozzi's Anschauung — the direct awareness of objects or the immediate experience of situations. Negatively it implies the postponement of book knowledge. 'Give your scholar no verbal lessons; he should be taught by experience alone.' 'Reading is the curse of childhood. . . . When I thus get rid of children's lessons I ger rid of the chief cause of their sorrow.' 'I hate books; they only teach us to talk about things we know nothing about.'[1] 'I am pretty sure Émile will learn to read and write before he is ten, just because I care very little whether he can do so before he is fifteen.'[2] Languages he dismisses as among the useless lumber of education,[3] geography is only learning the map;[4] as a real knowledge of events cannot exist, apart from the knowledge of their causes and effects, history is beyond their grasp. And more generally he says:[5] 'I do not like verbal explanations. Young people pay little heed to them, nor do they remember them. Things! Things! I cannot repeat it too often. We lay too much

1. Emile, p. 147

2. Ibid. p. 81.

3. p. 73

4. p. 74

5. p. 143

stress upon words; we teachers babble, and out scholars follow our example.' And he sums up:[1] 'Never substitute the symbol for the thing signified unless it is impossible to show the thing itself.'

Moral Aspect of Negative Education

The moral aspect of Rousseau's negative education consists not in teaching virtue or truth, but in preserving the heart from vice and from the spirit of error,[2] and takes the form of 'the discipline by natural consequences'. The value of such impersonal punishments is to give to Émile's character a certain stability, for natural laws are consistent and inevitable; the weakness of the doctrine is that it ignores the social consequences of action. 'Children should never receive punishment as such', recommends Rousseau,[3] 'it should always come as the natural consequence of their fault.' 'He must never act from obedience, but from necessity.'

Not only are there to be no direct moral lessons but there are to be no indirect moral lessons. Thus in contrast to Plato, who advocated beginning with the false first, Rousseau protests against young children learning fables. 'Men may be taught by fables; children require the naked tuth.'[4] The reason he adds is that the child is attracted by what is false and misses the truth, and the means adopted to make the teaching pleasant, prevent him profiting by it. Rousseau does not, however, propose to proscribe fables altogether; he would merely postpone their introduction; till such time as they could be properly understood and applied, that is, till the adolescent stage; 'the time of faults is the time for fables. When we blame the guilty under the cover of a story we instruct without offending him, and he then understands that the story is not untrue by means of the truth he finds is its application.'[5]

---

1. **Emile, p. 133.**
2. **Ibid. p. 57.**
3. **p. 65.**
4. **Ibid. p. 210.**
5. **p. 57.**

The importance of the negative aspect of education may be inferred from the statement that 'the most dangerous period in human life lies between birth and the age of twelve,'[1] and from the attention Rousseau devotes to it.

Positive Education

The positive education of the childhood period comprises physical[1] and sensorys training. The physical education is modelled on that of Sparta. 'This was the education of the Spartans; they were not taught to stick to their books, they were taught to steal their dinners. Were they any the worse for it in after life? Ever ready for victory, they crushed their fores in every kind of warfare, and the prating Athenians were as much afraid of their words as of their blows.' But for a temporary reinstatement by some of the early humanists this reversion to Greek practice initiated in Europe a new development in physical culture which had suffered from the medieval doctrine of the mortification of the flesh.

Physical Training

The importance of physical condition for the moral and mental training of the child is frequently insisted on by Rousseau. It is, as with Plato, 'the body for the sake of the soul'. Rousseau remarks:[2] 'A feeble body makes a feeble mind.' 'All Wickedness comes from weakness.' 'The weaker the body, the more imperious its demands; the stronger it is, the better it obeys.' 'Would you cultivate your pupil's intelligence, cultivate the strength it is meant to control? Give his body constant exercise, make it strong and healthy, in order to make him good and wise; let him work, let him do things, let him run and shout, let him be always on the go; make a man of him in strength, and he will soon be a man of reason.' 'As he grows in health and strength he grows in wisdom and disecurement. This is the way to attain to what is generally incompatible, strength of body and strength of mind, the reason of the philosopher and the vigour of the athlete.'

---

1. p. 82.
2. Emile, pp. 21, 33, 21, 82, 84.

TRAINING OF SENSES

The other aspect of the positive education during the age of childhood is the training of the senses. Man's first reason is, in Rousseau's opinion, a reason of sense experience. Our first teachers are our feet, hands and eyes. 'To substitute books for them does not teach us to reason, it teaches us to use the reason of others rather than our own; it teaches us to believe much and know little.'[1] Training the senses does not, however, for Rousseau consist in practising formal exercises; it implies judgment by their means in concrete situations encountered in life, and is accordingly not open to the objections which have been urged on psychological grounds against some doctrines of sensory training. Thus he promises such tasks as determining whether a ladder is big enough to reach the cherries on a tree, whether a plank is long enough to bridge a stream, the length of line required for fishing or how much rope to construct a swing. In running races the distances are made unequal, and Émile has to estimate their length so that he may choose the shortest.

No Predetermined Curriculum

The main concern of earlier educators was to assist pupils to acquire the contents of a prescribed course of study. The outstanding feature of the *Émile* is the complete abandonment of a predetermined curriculum. Émile was to be educated entirely through activities and by firsthand experience. Kant claimed that he was effecting a Copernican revolution in metaphysics by assuming not that knowledge should conform to objects, but that objects should conform to our method of knowing. Rousseau's attempt to shift the centre of gravity from the curriculum to the child may be regarded as a parallel revolution in education. This new standpoint has been adopted by later writers, for example, by Nunn : 'The school must be thought of primarily not as a place where certain knowledge is learnt, but as a place where the young are disciplined in certain forms of activity, namely, those that are of greatest and most permanent significance in the wider world'.

1. **Emile p. 90.**

The Consultative Committee's Report on *The Primary School* repeats : the curriculum is to be thought of in terms of activity and experience rather than of knowledge to be acquired and facts to be stored.

CHILDHOOD UP TO 12 YEARS OF AGE

Another surprising feature of the *Émile* is the prolongation of childhood up to twelve years of age. The long preparatory period recalls Greek education, and could hardly be justified in a more complex age. Rousseau keeps protesting that he is not educating Émile but merely preparing him for education. The art of teaching, at this stage, 'is to lose time and save it' 'Give nature time to work', he advises, 'before you take over her business, lest you interfere with her dealings. You assert that you know the value of time and are afraid to waste it. You fail to perceive that it is a greater waste of time to use it ill than to do nothing, and that a child ill-taught is further from virtue than a child who has learned nothing at all. . . . Do not be afraid, therefore, of this so-called idleness. What would you think of a man who refused to sleep lest he should waste part of his life ? You would say, "He is mad; he is not enjoying his life, he is robbing himself of part of it; to avoid sleep he is hastening to his death". Remember that these two cases are alike, and that childhood is the sleep of reason.' The result that Rousseau expects from this course he formulates thus : 'His ideas are few but precise, he knows nothing by rote but much by experience. If he reads our books worse than other children, he reads far better in the book of nature; he has less memory and more judgment; he can only speak one language, but he understands what he is saying, and if his troughts are not in his tongue but in his brain; deeds are better.' 'He has reached the perfection of childhood; he has lived the life of a child; his progress has not been bought at the price of his happiness ; he has gained both.'

STAGE OF BOYHOOD

During the years of transition between childhood and adolescence, the boyhood stage between twelve and fifteen, the lost ground must be recovered and education accordingly speeded up. 'Time was long during early childhood; we only tried to pass our time for fear of using it ill; now it is the other way; we have not time enough for all that would be of use.' Rousseau is accordingly compelled to restrict Émile's training ton what is useful. 'What is the use of that ? This is the sacred formula.' 'This is the time for work, instruction and inquiry. And note that this is no arbitrary choice of mine, it is the way of nature herself.' The experiences must likewise be preselected; they are not quite haphazard: 'take care that all the experiments are connected together by a chain of reasoning, so that they may follower an orderly sequence in the mind'.

METHOD OF EDUCATION

The occupations rejected at the previous stage must now be reviewed in the light of the principle of utility and to those that stand the test Émile is to be introduced. They comprise practical science, geography and manual work. Rousseau accordingly plies Émile with concrete problem and engineers him into situations which challenge explanation. These satisfy the definition of the project— a practical problem in its natural setting. The aim is not 'to teach him the various sciences, but to give him a taste for them and methods of learning them when this taste is more mature'. Against the formalism of abstract science Rousseau protests : 'The scientific atmosphere destroys science', 'among the many short cuts to science we badly need someone to teach us the art of learning with difficulty'. The apparatus Émile uses in his investigations is to be self-invented : 'We should make all our apparatus ourselves. . . . I would rather our apparatus was somewhat clumsy and imperfect, but our ideas clear as to what the apparatus ought to be, and the results to be obtained by means of it.'

COMPARISON WITH HEURISTICS METHOD

The method which Rousseau recommends is commonly identified with the heuristic method. Rousseau's heurism nevertheless is not strictly a heuristic method; it is a method of discovery , but it does not necessitate following the order of the original discoverers. It is more akin to Dewey's experimental procedure. It is formulated thus : 'Let him know nothing because you have told him, but because he has learnt it for himself'. 'You have not got to teach him truths so much as to show him how to set about discovering them for himself.'

LEARNING GEOGRAPHY

Geography is to be learnt by observation of natural phenomena. 'His geography will begin with the town he lives in and his father's country house, then the places between them, the rivers near them, and then the sun's aspect and how to find one's way by its aid. Let him make his own map, at first containing only two places; others may be added from time to time, as he is able to estimate their distance and position. You asee at once what a good start we have given him by making his eye his compass.'

NEEDS OF A TRADE

Rousseau would prescribe a trade for his pupil. Locke had proposed gardening or husbandry in general, and working in wood as carpenter, joiner or turner, these being fit and healthy recreations for a man of study or business. Rousseau requires Émile to learn a trade that with any change of fortune he might be independent economically, for its social value in recognising the dignity of labour and in helping him to overcome the prejudices which otherwise he would acquire, and to aid generally in training the mind. 'In society'. Rousseau maintains, 'a man either lives at the cost of others or he owes them in labour the cost of his keep; there is no exception to this rule. . . . Man in society is bound to work; rich or poor, weak or strong, every idler is a thief.' 'Remember' Rousseau counsels, 'I demand to talent, only a trade, a genuine trade, a mere mechanical art, in which the hands work harder than the head, a trade which does not lead to fortune but makes you independent of her.' The trade which most completely satisfies Rousseau's demands is that of the carpenter: 'It is clean and useful; it may be carried on at home; it gives enough exercise; it calls for skill and industry, and while fashioning articles for everyday use, their is scope for elegance and. taste'. Not content with this

Rousseau contends that technical training has a transfer value : 'If instead of making a child stick to his books I employ him in a workshop, his hands work for the development of his mind. While he fancies himself a workman, he is becoming a philosopher.' 'He must work like a peasant and think like a philosopher, if he is not to be as idle as a savage. The great secret of education is to use exercise of mind and body as relaxation one to another.'

LEARNING BY DOING

The general principle governing Émile's education during these transition years is that of learning by doing. 'Teach by doing whenever you can, and only fall back upon words when doing is out of the question.' 'Let all the lessons of young people take the form of doing rather than talking; let them learn nothing from books which they can learn from experience.'

There is nevertheless a significant exception, the one book which to Rousseau's thinking 'supplies the best treatise on an education according to nature'. It is *Robinson Crusoe.* 'This is the first book Émile will read; for a long time it will from his whole library and it will always retain an honoured place. It will be the text to which all talks about natural science are but the commentary.'

Émile's knowledge is still restricted to nature and things : 'The very name of history is unknown to him, along with metaphysics and morals. He knows the essential relations between men and things, but nothing of the moral relations between man and man. The résumé of his training up to fifteen runs thus: 'Having entered into possession of himself our child is now ready to cease to be a child. He is more than ever conscious of the necessity which makes him dependent on things. After exercising his body and his senses you have exercised his mind and his judgment. Finally we have joined together the use of his limbs and his faculties. We have made him a worker and a thinker; we have now to make him loving and tender-hearted, to perfect reason through feeling.'

STAGE OF ADOLESCENCE

To adolescence, the crown and coping-stone of education', Rousseau was doubtless the first great educator to devote special attention; he complains : 'Works on education are crammed with wordy and unnecessary accounts of the imaginary duties of children; but there is not a word about the most important and most difficult part of their education, the crisis which forms the bridge between the child and the man's The period when education is usually finished is, he insists, just the time to begin; it is our second birth for 'we are born so to speak twice over; born into existence, and born so to speak twice over; born into existence, and born a man'.

Adolescent education is designed to prepare Émile for the moral and social order in which he must play his part. Instead of studying himself in relation to things he must now study himself in relation to his fellow-men: 'As there is a fitting age for the study of the sciences, so there is a fitting age for the study of the ways of the world'. 'We have reached the moral order at last; we have just taken the second step towards manhood.' 'What then is required for the proper study of men ? A great wish to know men, great impartiality of judgment, a heart sufficiently sensitive to understand every human passion, and calm enough to be free from passion. If there is any time in our life when this study is likely to be appreciated it is this that I have chosen for Émile; before this time men would have been strangers to him; before this time men would have been strangers to him; later on, he would have been like them.'

Émile's earlier social contacts were restricted to casual encounters with village boys; there was occasional cooperation with other youths, but no opportunity for companionship with boys of his own social class. There were visits to hospitals which would create disgust in Émile at mankind. The early education was largely a preparation against the hazards of life. It demanded estrangement from society. Émile was in the social order, but not of it. Rousseau had condemned Plato's communistic scheme contending that the home was the best training ground for governing the state; he should have recognised that companionship with other boys of his own age would have been Émile's best preparation for associating with them in later manhood. Any social training Émile received was like learning to swim without going into the water, with the same result, as Dewey tells, to the youth so taught.

SOCIAL TRAINING

Even the social training to which Rousseau would introduce Émile at the adolescent stage is to be acquired second-hand, through the experiences of other, in contrast with the early education which was to be first-hand. The hazards involved in participation are too great; people cannot be left to learn the laws by breaking them. In the moral sphere there may be no second chance; one mistake may only lead to another, not to its elimination; social training must be given in advance of the situation, for example, in matters of sex. Instruction before experience is the order here. 'We must take the opposite way from that hitherto followed and instruct the youth rather through the experience of other than through our own.' The attitude Rousseau would have Émile adopt, reads; 'I would have you so choose the company of a youth that he should think well of those among whom he lives, and I would have you so teach him to know the world that he should think ill of all that takes place in it. Let him know that man is by nature good, let him feel it, let him judge his neighbour by himself; but let him see how men are depraved and perverted by society; let him find the sources of all their vices on their preconceived opinions; let him be disposed to respect the individual, but to despise the multitude; let him see that all men wear almost the same mask, but let him also know that some faces are fairer than the mask that conceals them.'

MORAL TRAINING

The moral training was not only to be at second-hand, but it was also to be indirect, through history, fables, etc. The studies which Rousseau had previously dismissed as premature and inappropriate are now reinstated; for the realistic subjects of the transition years the humanistic subjects are now substituted. There is, in fact, a complete inversion of the earlier education just as Plato's higher education necessitated the conversion of the soul from the sensible to the intelligible aspects of the world.

TEACHING OF HISTORY

This is accordingly the time to introduce the pupil to history: 'With its help he will read the hearts of men without any lessons in philosophy; with its help he will view them as a mere spectator, dispassionate and without prejudice; he will view them as their judge, not as their accomplice or their accuser'.

Of the difficulties in turning history to moral account Rousseau is fully conscious. The first is that history records the evil rather than the good: 'It is revolutions and catastrophes that make history interesting; so long as a nation grows and prospers quietly in the tranquillity of a peaceful government, history says nothing. . . . History only makes them famous when they are on the downward path. . . . We only hear what is bad; the good is scarcely mentioned. Only the wicked become famous, the good are forgotten or soughed to scorn, and thus history, like philosophy, is for ever slandering man-kind.'

A further difficulty which Rousseau recognises is that 'history shows us actions rather than men, because she only seizes men at certain chosen times in full dress; she only portrays the statesman when he is prepared to be seen; she does not follow him to his home, to his study, among his family and his friends; she only shows him in state; it is his clothes rather than himself that she describes'.

Against the use of the figures of history as moral examples for the instruction of youth Morley has protested in the following terms : 'The subject of history is not the heart of man but the movements of society. Moreover the oracles of history are entirely dumb to one who seeks from them maxims for the shaping of daily conduct, or living instruction as to the motives, aims, caprices, capacities of self-restraint, self-sacrifice of those with whom the occasions of life bring us into contact.' Even this objection was foreseen by Rousseau: 'History in general is lacking because it only takes note of striking and clearly marked facts which may be fixed by names, places and dates; but the slow evolution of these facts, which cannot be noted in this way, still remains unknown. We often find in some battle, lost or won, the ostensible cause of a revolution which was inevitable before this battle took place. War only makes manifest events already determined by moral causes, which few historians can perceive.'

The dilemma with which we are confronted in attempting to exploit history as a means of moral instruction is that the more scientifically history is treated the more is it regarded as history of great movements and general tendencies, a matter of principles rather than of personalities, and consequentiality the less adapted does it become to provide moral examples; whereas, even assuming that the historical heroes are worthy moral examples, to secure biographical material for moral lessons we are compelled to distort the presentation of history. The choice is therefore between the incompatible alternatives, history or moral instruction.

These difficulties limit the field of choice, and Rousseau is reduced to commending the ancient writers of historical biographies, especially Plutarch, the modern biographies being too conventional.[1] The spectacles of history portrayed in such biographies are to serve the pupil sometimes as warnings, sometimes as forms of 'catharsis', as the vicarious expression of his own passions; thus 'the play of every human passion offers lessons to any one who will study history to make himself wise and good at the expense of those who went before'[2]. The examples of history are thus not to be regarded as models for imitation, 'for he who begins to regard himself as a stranger will soon forget himself altogether'.

In spite of all the care exercised on the training of the pupil it must needs be that offences come. Their correction, Rousseau suggests, should be secured indirectly. 'The time of faults is the time for fables';[4] for 'when we blame the guilty under the cover of a story we instruct without offending him.' The moral of the fable should accordingly not be formulated. 'Nothing is so foolish and unwise as the moral at the end of most fables; as if the moral was not, or ought not to be, so clear in the fable itself that the reader cannot fail to perceive it.'

TEACHING OF RELIGION

Till now Émile has scarcely heard the name of God;[5] 'at fifteen he will not even know that he has a soul, at eighteen even he may not be ready to learn about it.' Some instruction is now inevitable, Rousseau recognises, and this he formulates in The Creed of a Savoyord Priest. Rousseau does not explain why a creed is advisable.

The Creed of a Savoyard Priest makes no pretext to be the theoretical formulation of the tenets of revealed religion, and the title is unfortunate. After relating the obstacles in the way of accepting any theological dogma Rousseau turns back to the book of nature. Rousseau's aim was to refute the materialistic philosophy of his age,

Rousseau refers to the materialist as one 'who prefers to say that stones have feelings rather than that men have souls'. He likewise rejects the naturalist's contention that there is no difference between intelligent behaviour on the perceptual level and the abstract reasoning of which only men are capable: 'It is not in my power to believe that passive and dead matter can have brought forth living and feeling beings, that blind chance has brought forth intelligent beings, that which does not think has brought forth thanking beings' to re-establish the validity of the concepts, God' freedom and immortality, and to reaffirm the principles of right conduct. The materialists regarded matter as inert and lifeless; they postulated motion without accounting for its origin. Rousseau rejecting the idea of self-initiated or self-perpetuating motion contended that voluntary action was the only type of motion of which we had direct experience, hence the first article of his creed: 'There is a will which sets the universe in motion and gives life to nature'. As the universe is an orderly system, he is led to infer the second article of his creed—the proof of God's existence from the well-known argument from design: 'If matter in motion points me to a will, matter in motion according to fixed law points me to an intelligence'. And he adds : 'This being who wills and can perform his will, this being active through his own powers, this being who moves the universe and orders all things, is what I call God'.

FREEDOM

As man's will is determined by his judgment, and his judgment by his intelligence, the determining cause of action is in himself and he is accordingly free. Freedom, for Rousseau, is thus self-determinism. The third article of his creed is : Man is therefore free to act and as such he is animated by an immaterial substance. Rousseau adds that it is not the word freedom that is meaningless, but the word necessity.

JUSTICE AND GOODNESS

Justice and goodness are inseparable, Rousseau claims, for that love of order which creates order we call goodness, and that love of order which preserves order we call justice. To redress the apparent disparity between justice and goodness in this life an infinite time is required; such is Rousseau's argument for the immortality of the soul. 'Had I no other proof of the nature of the righteous in this world would be enough to convince me.'

In support of his objections to innate ideas Locke cites instances to illustrate the diversity of human behaviour; Rousseau condemns this procedure assailing these writers who venturing to reject the clear and universal agreement of all peoples, and setting aside this striking unanimity in the judgment of mankind seek out some obscure exception known to them alone. He challenges Montaigne to tell him if their is any country upon earth where it is a crime to keep one's plighted word, to be merciful, helpful and generous, where the good man is scorned and the traitor held to honour. Contrariwise Rousseau emphasises the universality of the principles of good conduct and assumes an innate principle of goodness: 'Do you think there is anyone upon earth so depraved that he has never yielded to the temptation of well-doing ?'[1]

MORAL EDUCATION

The ultimate sanction of the moral laws [2] is to be found in religion, but after eloquently recounting the obstacles in the way of accepting any definite religious belief Rousseau turns again to the book of nature[3] : 'In this good and great volume I learn to serve and adore its Author. Their is no excuse for not reading this book, for it speaks to all in a language they can understand.' Such is the method to be adopted in reasoning with Émile on religion. 'So long as we yield nothing to human authority nor to the prejudices of our native land, the light of reason alone, in a state of nature, can lead us no further than to natural religion; and this is as far as I should go with Émile. If he must have any other religion, I have no right to be his guide; he must choose for himself.[4]'

The Creed of a Savoyard Priest is frequently regarded as an unwarranted interpolation in the *Émile,* but a review of Rousseau's religious doctrines as expressed in this section of his work is necessary to make intelligible, or to justify, the postponement of religious instruction till the adolescent stage. If it is necessary for Émile to have an intelligent appreciation of the proofs of God's existence, of freedom and of immortality, then it is not to be wondered at that at fifteen he need not have heard the name of God nor even known that he had a soul. Rousseau has evidently ignored the fact that he is legislating for the ordinary man who takes his creed on trust and does not usually trouble to justify it on rational grounds.

STUDY OF AESTHETICS

In addition to instruction in ethics and religion, Rousseau would prescribe for the adolescent the study of aesthetics, the philosophy of the principles of taste. Rousseau's account of these principles is somewhat vague; but this is not surprising when we remember the state of the development of the science of the beautiful at the time he wrote. The simplicity of taste which goes straight to the heart is, in Rousseau's opinion, only to be found in the classics[1], and these Rousseau would employ for purposes of instruction in aesthetics as he previously had recommended them for instruction in morals.

During the cirtical period of adolescence, Émile's physical training is not neglected. He is required to engage in an occupation which keeps him busy, diligent and hard at work, an occupation which he may become passionately fond of, one to which he will devote himself entirely. For this purpose Rousseau recommends the chase,[2] although he does not even profess to justify the cruel passion of killing; it is enough that it serves to delay a more dangerous passion.

SEX EDUCATION

Rousseau believes it necessary to prescribe for Émile direct moral exhortation on chastity, although he admits that he has had to abandon the task of giving examples of the form which the lessons should take. The general plan of sexual instruction he outlines in the following passage[3] : 'If instead of the empty precepts which are prematurely dinned into the ears of children, only to be scoffed at when the time comes when they might prove useful, if instead of this we bide our time, if we prepare the way for a hearing, if we then show him the laws of nature in all their truth, if we then show him the sanction of these laws in the physical and moral evils which overtake those who neglect them, if while we speak to him of this great mystery of generation, we join to the idea of the pleasure which the author of nature has given to this act the idea of the duties of faithfulness and modesty which surround it, and redouble its charm while fulfilling its purpose; if we paint to him marriage, not only as the sweetest from of society, but also as the most sacred and inviolable of contracts, if we tell him plainly all the reasons which lead men to respect this sacred bond, and to pour hatred and curses upon him who dares to dishonour it; if we give him a true and terrible picture of the horrors of debauch, of its stupid brutality, of the downward road by which a first act of misconduct leads from bad to worse, and at last drags the sinner to his ruin; if, I say, we give him proofs that on a desire for chastity depend health, strength, courage, virtue, love itself, and all that is truly good for man— I maintain that this chastity will be do dear and so desirable in his eyes, that his mind will be ready to receive our teaching as to the way to preserve it; for so long as we are chaste we respect chastity; it is only when we have lost this virtue that we scorn it.'

The sexual instinct must be sublimated by redirecting it to the affection for an ideal of true womanhood which Rousseau would picture for Émile with all the eloquence and emotion he could compass, and this ideal he would personify and assign to it a name, the name Sophy. Before, however, introducing Émile to Sophy, Rousseau considers it necessary to describe the education in accordance with which the wife of Émile should be trained.

Émile's education is not even yet complete. Between his betrothal to Sophy and his marriage he is required to travel, the object being that he should get to know mankind in general.

EDUCATION OF WOMEN

The education of woman had by most early educators been treated much after the manner of Locke who in his *Thoughts* wrote; 'I have said *he* here because the principal aim of my discourse is how a young gentleman should be brought up from his infancy which in all things will not so perfectly suit the education of daughters though where the difference of sex requires different treatment, 'twill be no hard matter to distinguish'. Rousseau, however, at least paid woman the compliment of realising that her education demands independent treatment, and for this a alone must be forgiven much

DIFFERENT VOCATIONS

Rousseau was congenitally even more unfitted than most other men to understand woman, and his views are accordingly even more contradictory. In his earliest writings his belief was that the hand that rocks the cradle rules the world; thus in the *Discourse on the Arts and Sciences* he maintains that men will always be what women choose to make them, and in the *Discourse on the Origin of Inequality,* addressing 'the amiable and virtuous daughters of Geneva' he repeats : 'It will always be the lot of your sex to govern ours. . . . Continue, therefore, always to be what you are, the chaste guardians of our morals, and the sweet security for our peace.' Disillusioned, nevertheless, by his somewhat unfortunate experience of the sex, he came to modify his views and in the *Nouvelle Hèloìse* and the *Émile* to emphasis the training of the heart rather than of the head; the aim of woman's life as expressed in these works might be summed up in the popular precept, slightly modified : Be good, sweet maid and let who will, be clever. And for the place of woman in the scheme of things Rousseau might have quoted Milton to the effect that God made woman for marriage but marriage for man. Thus in the *Nouvelle Hèloìse* Rousseau explains : 'I have still the same difficulty in supposing that there can be buit one common model of perfection for two beings so essentially different. Attack and defence, the assurance of the men and modesty of the women, are by no means effects of the same cause, as the philosophers have imagined, but are natural institutions which may be easily accounted for and from which may be deduced every other moral distinction. Besides, the designs of nature being different in each, their inclinations, their perceptions ought necessarily to be directed according to their different views; to till the ground and to nourish children require very opposite tastes and to nourish children require very opposite tastes and constitutions. A higher stature, stronger voice and features, seem indeed to be no indispensable marks of distinction; but this external difference evidently indicates the intention of the Creator in the modification of the mind. The soul of a perfect man ought to be no more alike than their faces.' And again; 'Husband and wife were designed to live together but not to live in the same manner. They ought to act in concert, but not to do the same things. The kind of life which would delight the one would be insupportable to the other; the inclinations which nature has assigned them; they differ in their amusements as much as in their duties. In a word, each contributes to the common good by different ways, and the proper distribution of their several cares and employment is the strongest tie that cements their union.' In the *Émile* he repeats: The man should be strong and active; the woman should be weak and passive'. 'A man seeks to serve, a woman seeks to please; the one needs knowledge, the other taste'; What will people think is the grave of a man's virtue and the throne of a woman's', and even goes the length of affirming that woman is made for man's delight. He wavers once, and admits the frailty of the male when he concedes: What is most wanted in a woman is gentleness; formed to obey a creature so imperfect as man, she should early learn to submit injustice and to suffer the wrongs inflicted on her by her husband without complaint; she must be gentle for her own sake, not his.

Different Education

As men and women have different vocations their education must be different : 'When once it is proved that men and women are and ought to be unlike in constitution and in emperament, it follows that their education must be different'. Women's education is to be planned in relation to, and to be made subservient to, that of man. its aim is : 'To be pleasing in his sight, to win his respect and love, to train him in childhood, to tend him in manhood, to counsel and console, to make his tend him in manhood, to counsel and console, to make his tend him in manhood, to counsel and console, to make his life pleasant and happy, these are the duties of women for all time, and that is what she should be taught while she all time, and that is what she should be taught while she is young'. The woman's education is also conditioned by the fact that she never attaiin the age of reason; hers is a case principles and if men had as good heads for detail, they would be mutually independent.' 'The search for abstract and speculative truths, for principles and aximoms in science, for all taht tends to wide generalisation, is beyond a woman's grasp; their studies should be thoroughly practical. It is their business to apply the principles discovered which lead men to discover those principles. 'Speaking generally if it is desirable to restrict a man's studies to what is useful, this is even more necessary for women, whose life, though less labrious, should be even more industrious and more uniformaly employed in a variety fo duties, so that one talent should not be encouraged at the expense of others.'

Different Physical Trainning

That supply's physical training should be different from that of Émile is understandable, the one aiming at grace, the other at strength, but it is inexcusable to infer that since little boys should not learn to read, still less.

❑❑❑

8

John Friedrich Herbart

"Freedom is of the utmost direct importance of character provided it issues in well weighed and successful action."

– J. F. Herbart

Herbart was a great German educator, philosopher and teacher. He was the first great educator to base education upon the science of psychology. He carried on experiments to find out the foundations of true psychological insight.

MAIN FEATURES OF EDUCATIONAL PHILOSOPHY OF HERBART

1. Three Important Ideas about Teaching-Learning— Herbart put forth the following ideas :

(a) Lesson must be connected with the salient ideas in the child's mind.

(b) The teacher must help the child to retain the new ideas.

(c) For relating new ideas the teacher must pay attention to the interests of the child.

2. Apperception—Herbart initiated this idea. Apperception means the assimilation of new ideas by means of ideas already acquired. Accordingly the teacher should know the child's mind.

3. Interest—According to Herbart, interest is a motive power for attaining some worthwhile end. Understanding of the interests ofthe child is a keynote in Herbart's psychology.

4. Lesson Plan—Herbart is the originator of the formal steps of teaching—

(a) Preparation or Introduction or Motivation.

(b) Presentation which includes (i) Comparison or Association, and (ii) Generalisation.

(c) Application.

The ideal of education, according to Herbart, is the development of moral character in the educand. Moral education is helped by the education in history, literature, science and mathematics. The child's interest is the most important basis of his education. As long as he does not take interest, education cannot realise any significant aim in him. Various subjects of teaching are correlated. Preparation is the first step in teaching. After it teaching proceeds by presentation, comparison, generalisation and application. Thus in aims and ideals, methods of teaching, curriculum and school organisation Herbart presented an idealistic system of education.

According to "Herbart PEADAGOGY as a science is based on practical philosophy and on psychology. The former points out the aim of culture, the latter the way, the means and the obstacles." In *Observations of a Pedagogical Essay* Herbart furhter explains, "I have for twenty years employed metaphysics, mathematics, and side by side with them self-observation, experience and experiments, merely to find the foundations of true psychological insight. And the motive for these not entirely effortless investigations has been, and is, in the main my conviction that a large part of the enormous gaps in our pedagogical knowledge results from lack of psychology."

NEGATIVE OR CRITICAL PSYCHOLOGY

Herbart disposed of both mental faculties and formal training. Uncompromising polemic against innate faculties, activities and predispositions as the mos striking negative feature of his psychology. "The soul', says Herbart, 'has no innate tendencies nor faculties.' Again 'it is an error, indeed, to look upon the human soul as an aggregate of all sorts of faculties.' The faculties are, indeed, 'nothing real, but merely logical designations for the preliminary classification of psychical phenomena.'

TRAINING OF THE FACULTIES

In the *Brief Encyclopaedia of Practical Philosophy* Herbart remarks : "Those, however, who have no proper psychological insight seldom grasp anything about the rules of education. They cling to the old idea that there are certain powers or faculties in the soul which have to be exercised, and it does not matter what they are exercised on. The exercises might well belong to the same category as gymnastic exercises, because men have only one kind of muscle, and by gymnastics the muscles of the body become strong and pliable. In actual fact every apperceptive system comprises elements of imagination, memory and reason, though naturally not all in equal proportions. In one and the same person there can quite easily be, and usually there is, an apperceptive system composed predominantly of intellectual elements, while another is rich in imagination, while in a third memory plays the greatest part. Intense feeling may colour one apperceptive system, whereas apathy characterises another. What educators call formal training is accordingly a complete chimera, since it presupposes the exercise of powers existing only in the imagination of those who hold such views on psychology." According to Herbart the assumption that mental powers can work in isolation is still the commonest fallacy in psychology.

UNITY OF MENTAL LIFE

He has been credited by Merz of preserving the unity of mental life for the psychologists who have been influenced by him "Thus it is a characteristic of all psycho-physical writers who have come under the influence of Herbart, that however much they may be occupied with detailed description of physiological processes, with the analysis of sensations, or the direction of the data of experience, they never lose sight of the underlying mental unity which is the central phenomenon of psychology and of psycho-physics, just as it must be the central problem of biology to arrive at some definition of life ...... It seems to me that, in Germany at least, it is through Herbart, more than through any other thinker, that we have been preserved from a threatening disintegration of psychological research."

NATURE OF SOUL

'The simple nature of the soul, accurance to 'is totally unknown. It is as little an object of speculative as of empirical psychology." In so far as the soul is endowed with the power of presentation, it may be regarded as mind. In Herbart's psychological investigation, the abstract metaphysical unity of the soul becomes transformed into a concrete unity pervading and connecting the manifold variety of individual experience. Passions or feelings arise from ideas. Satisfation or uneasiness is associated with thought. "Feelings are but passing modifications of the existing presentation'. 'Feelings and desires are conditions, and for the most part changeable conditions of presentation.

In the mental life when a presentation meets with a presentation opposed to it, an unpleasant feeling results. But pleasure results if its realisation is facilitated.

The intellectualism of Herbart's psychology is intensified by his use of the term 'Empfindungen' to signify both sensation and feeling. In the Introduction to the *Alilgemeine Padogogik* he says that out of thoughts arise feelings (*Empfindungen*), and, from these, principles and modes of action.

According to erbart the circle of thought is no mere intellectual structure. It is interwoven throughout with feelings and volitional impulses. The task of educative instruction is to anchor this circle of thought in the youth's soul.'

DEPENDENCE OF EMOTION ON IDEAS

Herbart's view of the dependence of emotion on ideas has important educational consequences. There can be no education of the feelings *per se*. Herbart was not content to rely on the emotionalism of Rousseau or the sentimentalism of Pestalozzi for moral training. He demanded a surer foundation. He found it in 'the circle of thought'. He said, "the disposition of the heart has its source in the mind."

The Herbartian system of ideas is pure mechanism, for 'presentations must be regarded as forces whose effectiveness depends upon their strength, their opositions, and their combinations, all of which are different in degree.' Herbart's doctrine of psychical mechanism has become the common possession of scientific psychologists. He diverted attention from mental contents to mental activities or forces, to the interaction among presentations. Instead of viewing the mental life as a succession of states of consciousness or as a stream of consciousness he conceived it as a mental system.

ROLE OF SUBJECTIVE FACTORS

Herbart's main contribution to psychology is the emphasis he lays on the part subjective factors play in the mental process. Thus, to account for perception we have to assume reinstated or revived experiences constituting the prepercept. In perception this coalescing is known as assimilation or complication.

Apperception

Apperception is an analogous process on a higher level. It is the interpretation of a percept by a system of ideas. In the words of Herbart : "Apperception or assimilation takes place through the reproduction of previously acquired presentations and their union with the new element." It implies the dependence of the new on the old, or the interpretation of the new by the old. It is not confined to sense-perception but embraces 'inner perception' as well. One presentation-mass may exert a determining influence on another. Thus what we notice depends not so much on the strength of the external stimulus or on the susceptibility of the subject as on the context, the mental system dominant at the time. This accounts for the fact that different people or the same person at different times have different perceptions under the same external conditions. As Herbart remarks : "Even in the same surroundings every man has his own world."

Thus apperception emphasises the significant part that old knowledge plays in the acquisition of the new knowledge which should always be a development of previous knowledge.

AIM OF EDUCATION

Although psychology provides the means, philosophy dictates the end of education. While Herbart confesses that education has no time to make holiday till philosophical questions are once for all cleared up, he admits : 'To teach completely how life is determined by its two rules, Speculation and Taste, we must seek for a system of philosophy, the keystone of instruction', and he also claims that the true perfection of education is philosophy.

In the opening sentences of Dissertation on the Aesthetic the World as the main function of Education Herbart affirms: "The one and the whole work of education may be summed up in the concept – morality." But he goes on to explain that "I therefore believe that the mode of consideration which places morality at the head is the most important, but not the only and comprehensive standpoint of education." He regards an aesthetic interpretation of the world as the ideal of education.

EXALTATION OF PERSONALITY

Neither ethics nor aesthetics can, however, determine fully the end of education. Education must include the ideals of truth and righteousness as well as of goodness and beauty. Intellectual inquiry and religious reverence are as natural to man and as necessary to him for the full realisation of his personality as are ethical endeavour and aesthetic enjoyment. The aim of education as of life itself cannot be formulated in any more succinct phrase than that of Eucken, namely, to exalt personality.

According to Herbart we need not go beyond experience to see that there is a great diversity in intellectual talents. The educability of the child is limited by his individuality. In the *Minor Pedagogical Works'* he says it is a chief requisite of a good pedagogical plan that it be flexible enough to fit the various capacities.

Herbart, however, seeks to avoid that individuality should develop into eccentricity. Where this occurs, a state of society results in which each brags of his own individuality, and no one understands his fellows." Herbart does not make the development of individuality the aim of education. Individuality is one of the data of education, not the end. It has to be fashioned into personality. This is achieved through the development of a variety of interests and their integration.

THE ASPECTS OF HUMAN ACTIVITY

Human activity, for Herbart, has two main aspects : many-sided interest and moral character. Many-sided interest is further qualified by 'evenly balanced'. This is equivalent to the popular statement – the harmonious expansion of all the powers of the individual. Many-sidedness is opposed not only to one-sidedness but also to discursiveness. It must be distinguished from its exaggeration – dabbling in many things.

TWO ASPECTS OF INTEREST

Interest has two aspects – a subjective or psychological, and an objective. The objective aspect comprises the various activities in which the individual participates or the different aspects of the environment to which he react. It consists of the two main divisions (i) knowledge, and (ii) sympathy, although Herbart explains that the environment of objects for knowledge embraces nature and humanity and that only certain expressions of humanity belong to what he terms sympathy.

DIVISION OF KNOWLEDGE

Herbert divides into knowledge (1) actual phenomena, (2) scientific laws, (3) aesthetic relations (or the empirical, the speculative and the aesthetic), representing different attitudes to our natural environment or different aspects of experience. He divides sympathy into (i) human, (2) social and (3) religious, representing different attitudes in social intercourse or different aspects of our spiritual environment. These constitute the six facets of a many-sides interest. When properly exploited they provide a liberal training or an all-round education.

THE SOURCES OF PRESENTATION

Presentation masses emanate from two main sources – experience and social intercourse. Through experience we acquire knowledge, and through intercourse we develop sympathy. While we cannot dispense with experience and intercourse they must be supplemented by instruction, for, a Herbart claims, experience seems to expect that instruction will follow her to analyse the material which she has amassed and to collect and arrange her scattered and formless fragments. To sums up : "Interest arises from interesting objects and occupations. Many-sided interest originates in the wealth of these. To create and develop this interest is the task of instruction which carries on and completes the preparation begun by intercourse and experience." Instruction alone, adds Herbart, can lay claim to cultivate a well-balanced, all-embracing many sidedness. It is for this reason that Herbart keeps reiterating that he has no conception of education without instruction; conversely, he does not acknowledge any instruction which does not educate.

"The chief means of positive education lies in instruction taken in its widest sense". Not all instruction is, however educative. The types of instruction which are not educative are those which afford only temporary pleasure or light entertainment, and such studies as remain isolated and do not lead to continued effort.

THE FORMS OF INSTRUCTION

Instruction may take two main forms — synthetic and analytic. The child's experience may be augmented through the teacher's description of events or activities. This is narrative instruction. It has but one law — to describe in such a way that the pupil believes he sees what is described. Or the teacher may avail himself of the pupil's experience eliciting the facts which he requires for his exposition. These facts require to be organised according to the purpose the teacher has in view. Both these forms of exposition— narrative and educative — are classed by Herbart as synthetic. The pupil's experience may not only be inadequate; it may even be erroneous. In this case the teacher must dissect it to utilise the elements in a new systematic whole. This Herbart terms analytic instruction, and he adds : "The pupil ought properly to provide the material for analytic instruction, especially in later years". The various forms of presentation or exposition are not mutually exclusive, but may be combined in the same lesson as occasion requires.

In his Serence of Education Herbart illustrates how the analytic and synthetic types of instruction may be employed in the respective fields of interests — empirical, scientific, aesthetic, human, social and religious. But his treatment, is too general to provide a curriculum which must arrange the opportunities provided in accordance with the needs of the pupils and the individual powers of the teacher. Earlier, Herbart had suggested the principle of recapitulation as a guide to the organisation of a teaching material. This doctrine plays a prominent part in Herbartian literature : "If pupils would continue the work of their forefathers they must have travelled the same way; above all, they must have learned to recongise these forefathers as their own from their early years".

DOCTRINE OF INTEREST

The interests which constitute the main divisions of education are interests of one person Herbert, warns us : 'Do not forget interest among interesting things". It is with the doctrine of interest in this sense, that Herbart's name has come to be associated in Britian and in America.

According to Herbart, "The word interest stands in general for that kind of mental activity which it is the business of instruction to create. Mere information does not suffice; for this we think of as a supply or store of facts which a person might possess or lack, and still remain the same being. But he who lays hold of his information, and reaches out for more, takes an interest in it."

Interest is thus a concomitant of mental activity. 'Interest', says Herbart means self-activity. But not all self-activity, only the right degree of the right kind is desirable, else lively children might very well be left to themselves. There would be no need of educating or controlling them. It is the purpose of instruction to give the right *direction* to their thoughts and impulses, to incline these toward the morally good and true." Interest opposed to indifference. It displays a preference over mere perception for certain objects by arousing in the mind analogous presentations and involuntarily suppressing others. It differs from certain other mental processes by depending on its object and referring to the present.

It should not be confused with amusement. "The teafcher", says, Herbart 'should not be misled into turning instruction into play, nor designedly into work; he sees before him a serious business and tries to forward it with gentle but steady hand." That which is too simple must be avoided. "Instruction must be comprehensible and yet difficult rather than esay, otherwise it causes *ennui*".

'Interest depends partly on native capacity which the school cannot create; but it depends also on the subject-matter of instruction," and also on its arrangement. We must know both what to teach and how to teach it.

When presentations arise spontaneously in the pupil's mind, the pupils are said to be attentive and the instruction has an interest for them. When attention has to be enforced, it is doubtful whether an interest in the subject can ever be evoked. As Herbart explains : "Presentations that must by effort be raised into consciousness because they do not rise spontaneously, may become spontaneous by gradual strengthening. But this development we cannot count on unless instruction, advancing step by step, bring it about."

Knowledge is likewise likely to be inanimate if it remains detached or dissociated from a general system of ideas. Herbart warns us — 'If the facts of knowledge are allowed to fall asunder ..... instruction endangers the whole of education." Thus, Herbart emphasises the correlation of studies.

CONCENTRATION AND COORDINATION

No matter what subject-matter is selected or what method of exposition is adopted, the same sequence must be followed in instruction if interest is to ensue. Herbart insisted that teaching procedure shoulsd be adapted to the stages discernible in the development of knowledge. He first ditinguished two phases — an intensive and an extensive. *Vertiefung*—absorption in or concentration on a subject, and *Besinnung*—coordination and systematisation of the results of *Vertiefung*. In one of his Aphorisms Herbert explains that *Vertiefung* or concentration occurs when a thought so dominates the mind that is suppresses the ordinary contents of consciousness, and *Besinnung*—coordination when these ordinary contents re-establish themselves; coordination is essneital not only to collect and combine the effects of concentration but also to prevent a lop-sided development.

As these two concepts are too general for practical purposes Herbart finds it necessary to subdivide concentration into clearness and association, and coordination into system and method. Clearness, association, system and method thus become Herbart's formal steps in teaching.

"In order always to maintain the mind's coherence,' Herbart argues, "instruction must follow the rule of giving equal weight in every smallest possible group of its objects to concentration and reflection; that is to say, it must care equally and in regular succession for clearness of every particular, for association of the manifold, for coherent ordering of what is associated, and for a certain practice in progression through this order. Upon this depends the distinctness which must rule in all that is taught."

CLEARNESS AND ASSOCIATION

Under clearness Herbart includes the analysis and synthesis of the given. Through association the new knowledge presented to the pupil is connected with the old. Implies the apperceptive process. It is analogous to the preparation stage of the Herbartian five formal steps. Its purpose is to secure a proper orientation of the subject to be taught. 'For Association', Herbart tells us, 'the best mode of procedure is informal conversation, because it gives the pupil an opportunity to test and to change the accidental union of his thoughts, to multiply the links of connection, and to assimilate, after his own fashion, what he has learned. It enables him, besides, to do at least a part of all this in any way that happens to be the easiest and most conveninet." Association prepares the way for system, which is 'the perfect order of a copious co-ordination'. 'By exhibiting and emphasising the leading principles', Herbart adds, "System impresses upon the minds of pupils the value of organised knowledge." In the generally accepted Herbartian tradition system is termed generalisation. A system is not to be merely learned it is to be used, applied and often needs to be supplemented by additions inserted at appropriate places.

Herbart's formal steps apply to method-wholes, instructional units or centres of interest not to individual lessons. They are stages in the exposition of a topic which has a unity and completeness in itself. It was the mechanical application of the formal steps in each and every lesson that brought the Herbartian method into discredit.

INTEREST AND DESIRE

In introducing the concept of many-sidedness of interest Herbart believed that one aspect of human activity was being neglected; namely, action, and, what immediately impels thereto—desire. The two spheres of human activity are accordingly interest and desire, knowing and willing. They are nevertheless not unconnected, being linked through instruction.

CIRCLE OF THOUGHT

Just as instruction creates a many-sided interest, so it has also the task of developing 'the circle of thought'. The section dealing with the influence of the circle of thought on character is the central point of the Science of Education. It is the vantage point from which the whole should be viewed.

According to Herbart the chief seat of the cultivation of character lies in the circle of thought, and that in it lies the main part of education. Character training is uable to accomplish its work unless in conjunction with instruction. "It will be seen when the task of setting forth the whole of virtue is renewed in its completeness that the main things are accomplished by instruction." In the Introduction to the Science of Education Herbart affirms : "Those only wield the full power of education who know how to cultivate in the youthful soul a large circle of thought closely connected in all its parts, possessing the power of overcoming that which is unfavourable in the environment, and of dissolving and absorbing into itself all that is favourable". In his reply to Jackmann's review Herbert repeats : "Instruction will above all form the circle of thought and education the character. The latter is nothing without the former—herein is contained the whole sum of my pedagogy," In his *Brief Encyclo paedia* Herbgart takes credit for introducing the term 'an educative instruction'. The principle of the determination of the inner aspect of character by means of instruction is Herbart's chief contribution to educational thought, "Moral education", he sums up, "is not separable from education as a whole."

VALUE OF WILL

While instruction is thus the central theme of Herbart's doctrine he never allows us to forget that man's worth does not lies in his knowing but in his willing. He is however, against all constraint upon moral will. "It may be doubted", he explains, "whether the treatment of discipline in the sense of constraint belongs to pedagogy or should not more appropriately be appended to those parts of practical philosophy which treat of government in general. Moral improvement is not brought about by the constraint of government. Education can only begin after control has done its work. Later on in he nevertheless concedes that control may have both an indirect and a direct bearing on character; it partly helps to make that instruction possible which will influence the subesequent formation of character, and it serves to create through action or inaction a beginning of character.

CONTROL OR CONSTRAINT

Control or constraint need not be repressive, Herbart review the various means of keeping order—supervision, the threat of punishment and compulsion : He concludes : When the environment is so arranged that childish activity can of itself find the road to the useful and expend itself thereon, then control is jmost successful.

Control or constraint is necessary evil, doubtless better than anarchy, but its defect is that it weakens while education seeks to strengthen. It is negative and inhibitive, whereas education should be positive and purposive. Herbart's distinction between good behaviour secured by administrative regulations and gentlemanly conduct exercised by voluntary self-restraint has much significane in education.

FOUR STAGES IN CHARACTER TRAINING

Corresponding to the four formal steps in intellectual instruction are the four stages in character training : these are Merken (to imprint), Erwarten (to anticipate), Fordern (to desire), Handeln (to act). Although Herbart affirms that character is the embodiment of the will, he does not include the will as a separate function among the subjective aspects of character training. The will, for him, is not something apart from desire; 'action generates the will out of desire. The teacher's task is to assist the pupil to acquire the right desires, for whan opportunity presents itself and the pupil desires, for when opportunity presents itself and the pupil realises that he can attain his end, action follows. "Will is desire combined with the consciousness of the attainment of what is desired."

TO CONCLUDE WITH ROBERT R. RUSH

To conclude with Robert R. Rush, "Educators previous to the time of Herbart had made the training of character the end of education while others had recognised the importance of instruction, but it was left to Herbart to connect instruction with character training through interest and to provide techniques based on psychological considerations for the attainment of both. He made the proper selection of the content of instruction and the right method of presenting the selected content moral duties incumbent on the teacher, and contributing factors to the achievement of the aim which he set up for himself."

9

Friedrich August Froebel

"Come, let us live for the Children" ***—Froebel***

Fredrich August Froebel was born on April 21, 1782, in the village of Oberweis— back in South Germany. He lost his mother when he was only of nine months. His father remarried. His father was not very affectionate to him. The unfair treatment of his step-mother made his childhood all the more miserable. Deprived of parental affection, the poor chap was left at the mercy of God. Froebel grew moody and subjective. He turned towards the natural phenomena–hills, trees, flowers and clouds etc., for companionship. His father, who was a clergyman, influenced him indirectly.

EDUCATION

Froebel did not receive much education at schol where he was considered a dunce. At the age of 15 he was appointed an apprentice to a forester. He spent two years there. Thus the neglected child came into intimate contact with nature. He spent a good deal of his time all alone in the forest. Here he received his real education and his love for nature grew. The religious influence of his father and the contact with nature cultivated in him a spirit of idealism. The new idea developed in him a love for the study of natural sciences. So he joined the University of Jena where he was profoundly influenced by the idealistic philosophy of Fitche and Schelling. Unfortunately he could study for about two years only. The varsity doors were closed for him on account of his poor financial position. Again, for four years he remained on 'career-wandering'. He wandered from place to place, engaging in professions of different nature and failing miserable in them, one after the other.

At Frankfert, Froebel began to study architecture. There he developed some intimacy with Dr. Gruner who was the Director of a model school. The Director discovered that Froebel could become an excellent teacher and he persuaded him to join his school. This marked a turning point in his life. Froebel was greatly satisfied. He found his 'long missed life element' and was 'inexpressibly happy'. He declared, "for the first time I found something I had always longed for, but always missed, as if my life had at last discovered its native element. I felt as happy as a fish in the water or a bird in the air."

CONTACT WITH PESTALOZZI

After spending three years at Frankfurt, Froebel paid a visit to Pestalozzi's institute at Yverdun. There he learnt the principles and methdos of Pstalozzi.

Objections against traditional Education.

1. The school lacked organisation.
2. There was no unity in the whole work.
3. The subject of studies lacked integration.
4. In the early education of children, co-operation of mothers was not forthcoming.

However, it must be admitted that his contact with Pestalozzi prepared him for his own educational reforms.

FROEBELS SCHOOL

Froebel established a small school in 1816 at Grie Sheim. Later on this was transferred to Keihan. Froebel incorporated his main principle of elementary education in the school. Instead of 'impression', 'expression'through play and art work was his chief consideration at this place.

PUBLICATION OF 'THE EDUCATION OF MAN'

In 1826, Froebel published his famous book *The Education of Man*. In this he says, "The true method of education consists in considering the mind of the child as a living whole in which all the parts work together to produce harmonious unity." After this he started many scholls in Germany. The Government suspected the revolutionary ideas of Froebel. An enquiry was conducted. The Inspector gave a favourable report. "I found here a closely united family of some sixty members held together in mutual confidence and every member seeking the good of the whole —The aim of institution is by no means knowledge and science merel, but free self-active development of the mind from within."

IN SWITZERLAND

Due to some financial difficulties, Froebel shiftwed his work to Switzerland in 1830. Swiss Government appreciated his work and sent their teachers for training. He then moved to Burgdrof. There he became a superintendent of an orphanage. He continued his work of training teachers. He realized that due to non-availability of education in the pre-school age the school suffered and did not get good raw material—the educand.

RETURN TO GERMANY

In 1836 Froebel returned to Germany and founded his first kindergarten in 1849 in the village of Blankendurg. He spent his whole time in the founding and devising his apparatus for kindergartens.

His views were not accepted by the German Government. He was forbidden from establishing any school. This was a great stock for the good teacher and he could not survive long. Froebel died in 1892, in poverty, misery and agony. His grave is marked by a slab with a cube, a cylinder and a sphere on it.

The great aim and purpose of his life is summed up in his famous saying : "Come let us live for children".

PUBLICATIONS OF FROEBEL

1. Education of Man.
2. Pedagogies of Kindergarten.
3. Education by Development.
4. Mother Play and Nursery Songs.

Froebel also devised some famous nursery rhymes such as 'Jack and jill' 'Humpty Dumpty' and 'Cyndrella."

PRINCIPLES OF FROEBEL'S PHILOSOPHY

Froebel has been considered to be the most idealistic philosopher of education. He believed that right since birth man possesses dormant capacities and abilities. The sole function of education is to arouse these dormant capacities and abilities and leave them to complete development. Therefore, education should be based upon the natural principles of inner development. As God is the source of creation, therefore there may be one common element among all living beings. Hence, the child should realise integrated development of his powers. According to Froebel self activity is the chief method of child's education. Therefore, his creativity must be encouraged. The school is a mini-society and social environment is very much important for the development of the child. These ideas of Froebel have been found to be particularly important in the field of primary education.

1. The Law of Unity—According to Froebel there is one eternal law–the law of unity–that governs all things, men and nature. He said, "In everything there works and stirs 'one' life because of all, one God has given life. God is the one ground of all things. God is the all comprehending, the all sustaining. God is the essential nature, the meaning of the world. All things, animate or inanimate, originate from God. Man and nature are one. They are simply the different forms of the unity which is God. There is unity in diversity and diversity in unity. Each of these is an individuality and also a unity. All things have come from the Divine Unity (God) and have their origin in the Divine Unity. All things live and have their beings in and through the Divine Unity". The unity is three-fold.

(i) Unity of Substance. There is only one substance from which all things come.

(ii) Unity of Origin. There is one source, that is God, from which all things come.

(iii) Unity of Purpose. All things strive towards perfection, *i.e.*, God.

2. The Principle of Development—This principle is based upon the first. We are marching towards the same unity. The movement is continuous and upward. Everything is, therefore, changing growing and marching towards the same unity. Froebel maintained that mind evolves from within. All the child is ever to be and to become, can be attained only through development from within. By 'Development', he meant an increase in bulk or quantity, increase in complexity or structure, an improvement in power, skill and variety in the performance of natural functions.

3. The Principle of Self-activity—It is only through self-activity that the real growth and development is possible. Forced activity is artificial and unnatural. An acute observer can know what the child is or what he is to become. All this lies in the child and can be attained through development from within.

4. Development Through Social Institutions—According to Froebel, the school is a miniature school. He remarked, "No community can progress while the individual remains behind." He believed that the individual is not apart from the life of the society.

PHILOSOPHY OF EDUCATION

1. Creativeness of Childhood—Froebel derives a new conception of childhood. Childhood is not merely preparation for adulthood; it is valuable in itself. It possesses its own creativeness. It participates in the divine whole with the same rights of its own as adulthood, and therefore it can claim the same respect on the part of the educator. The adult has no right to feel himself superior and to interfere with the natural conditions of childhood; rather, he must combine guidance with the capacity of waiting and understanding. Here Froebel is line with Rousseau and Herbart.

2. Inner Relatedness of all Education—The second postulate which Froebel derives from his idea of unity is that of the inner relatedness of all education. This means that the educator ought to lead the child through such situations as will help him to relate his experiences organically one with another. Only thus can the child realize his own personal unity and the unity inherent in the diversity of live.

3. Totality of Educational Endeavour—In order to realize athe divine character of the universe and his part in it, man needs his senses and emotions as well as reasons. They are all windows of the soul. Hence Froebel emphasizes the totality of educational endeavour.

4. Concept of Play—The finest expression of Froebel's idea of harmony in diversity is found in his concept of play. For Froebel, play is not merely a means of distraction; it is the most important phase in the spontaneous development of the child, because it allows him to exercise harmoniously all his physical, emotional and intellectual qualities. Play combines attention with relaxation, purpose with independence, and rule with freedom. For the child it is as ethical as devotion to his work is for the adult.

5. Education of the Pre-School Child—One might rightly ask why Froebel, with his comprehensive training in so many fields of knowledge and his philosophical interests, finally concentrated his efforts particularly on the education of the pre-school child. There are two reasons for it. One is psychological. Froebel had great insight into the importance of the early experiences of childhood for the future development of the personality. The other reason is of sociological nature. Froebel lived in the preiod of the Napoleonic wars, with all their destructive influences, upon which followed the early period of capitalism and a series of social revolutions. He saw that in all these crises nobody was so imperilled as the children.Therefore he fought for the establishement of Kindergarten.

AIM OF EDUCATION

1. Aim of Education—Froebel maintained that the aim of education is not to make the mind of the child a jumble of words. The aim of education is to enable the child to realize the unity in diversity. The functions of education, according to Froebel, may be summed up as "Education should lead and guide man to clearness, concerning himself and in himself to peace with nature, and to unity, with God. It should lift him to knowledge of himself, to mankind, to a knowledge of God and of nature, and to the pure and holy life."

2. Education Through Play—The chief means of education is the child's own activity. Play is an essential factor in the growth of the child. The free and unfettered natural development of the child takes place through play.

3. Education According to the Nature of the Child—Education should be in conformity with child's nature and needs.

4. Education Through Freedom—The child should be educated in free atmosphere. Freedom means obedience to self-imposed law.

5. Education Through Assistance—The teacher is like a gardener who carefully nurses and protects children in order to secure their full and free development along most desirable lines. The educator assists the educand who is developing according to the law of his nature.

6. Education Through Group Life—Froebel stressed the social aspect of education also. He believed that all social institutions like the home, the school, the church and the State, etc., are the agencies of development of the individual.

7. Education Through Gifts—He devised songs, gestures and construction as the chief means of stimulating the imagination of the child.

8. Functions of Education—The functions of education, according to Froebel, may be summed up these words "Education should lead and guide man to clearness, concerning himself and in himself to peace with nature, and to unity with God. It should lift him to knowledge of himself, to mankind, to a knowledge of God and of nature, and to the pure and holy life."

Like Kant's categorical imperative Froebel says "in its inner essence the living thought, the eternal spiritual ideal, ought to be and is categorical and mandatory in its manifestations. The ideal becomes mandatory only where it supposes that the person addressed enters into the reason of the requirement with serene, childlike faith, or with clear, manly insight. It is true, in word or example, the ideals is mandatory in all these cases, but always only with reference to the spirit and inner life, never with reference to outer form."

MEANING OF FREEDOM

As for Hegel "freedom is the truth of necessity, so for Froebel in good education, in genuine instruction, in true training, necessity should call forth freedom; law, self-dertermination; external compulsion, inner free-will; external hate, inner love. Where hatred brings forth hatred; law, dishonesty and crime; compulsion, slavery; necessity, servitude; where oppression destroys and debases; where severity and harshness give rise to stubbornness and deceit—all education is abortive. In order to avoid the latter and to secure the former, all prescription should be adapted to the pupil's nature and needs, and secure his co-operation. This is the case when all education in instruction and training, in spite of its necessarily categorical character, bears in all details and ramifications are irrefutable and irresistible impress that the one who makes the demand is himself strictly unavoidable subject to an eternally ruling law, to an unavoidable eternal necessity, and that, therefore, all despotism in banished."

STAGES OF DEVELOPMENT

The stages recognised by Froebel, namely, infancy,

childhood, boyhood, youth, corresponded to Rousseau's division in the *Emile*.

1. *Infancy*—For Rousseau the activity characteristic of infancy is habit; for Froebel it is sensory development. Froebel's account of sensory development is highly artificial, the result of an attempt to impose on it the dialectical form.

2. *Childhood*—Childhood, the second stage, is distinguished from infancy by the appearance of language; it is then that the child begins to represent the internal outwardly. Actual education now begins, attention andf watchful care, being less directed to the body than to the mind. Speech training should now be begun. Each object should be given its appropriate name, and each word should be uttered clearly and distinctly. On pedagogical grounds Froebel supports Pestalozzi, maintaining that to the child names are still on with the thing, and that the name creates the thing for the child. In The *Pedagogies of the Kindergarten* he adds that the name defines the object by connecting it with something familiar.

PLAY WAY OF CHILD EDUCATION

It is in treating of childhood in *The Education of Man* that Froebel formulates his plea for the significane of play in education. *Play is the characteristic activity of childhood.* "It is," says Froebel, "the highest phase of child-development of human development at this period; for it is self-active representation or the inner representation of the inner from inner necessity and impulse. Play is the purest, most spiritual activity of man at this stage, and, at the same time, typical of human life as a whole of the inner hidden natural life in man and all things. It gives, therefore, joy, freedom, contentment, inner and outer rest, peace with the world. It hold the source of all that is good."

GUIDANCE IN PLAY

To have educative value the play of the child *must not be a purposeless activity.* His play impulses must be directed and controlled by the use of definite material necessitating an orderly sequence in the feelings engendered and in the activities exercised.

'Without rational conscious guidance', Froebel said, "childish activity degenerates into aimless play instead of preparing for those tasks of life for which it is detained...... In the *Kindergarten* the children are guided to bring out their plays in such a manner as really to reach the aim desired by nature, that is, to serve for their development .... Human education needs a guide which I think I have found in a general law of development that rules both in nature and in the intellectual world. Without lawabiding guidance, there is no free development.

WORK IN ADOLESCENCE OR BOYHOOD

Law of Oposites

At the transition from childhood to boyhood, Froebel proposes an inversion. Whereas the period of childhood is characterised as predominantly that of life for the sake of living, for making the internal external, the period of boyhood is predominantly the period for learning, for making the external internal. Here we have an illustration of Froebel's law of opposites. Education is not to be endowment determined. It is to be environmentally determined. It is not to be child-centred; it is to be curriculum-centred. Actually, it is both endowment and environmentally determined from the outset. In *The Pedagogies of the Kindergarten* Froebel virtually admits this through his recognition of a third or synthesising stage. "Another fundamental idea is that all knowledge and comprehension of life are connected with making the internal external, the external internal, and with perceiving the harmony and accord of both."

Work in Boyhood

While play is the characteristic activity of childhood, work is that of boyhood. Interest in the process gives place to interest in the product. In the words of Froebel, "What formerly the child did for the sake of the activity, the boy now does for the sake of the result or product of his activity." If activity brought joy to the child, work now gives delight to the boy". For while during the previous period of childhood the aim of play consisted simply in activity as such, the aim lies now in a definite, conscious purpose. This contract is forced and invalid. Work is regarded as directed and purposive, whereas, in disregard of Froebel's previous statements on play, play is now simply an 'activity as such'. The more extended range of the pupil's environment has provided him with new patterns of activity in the shape of vocational occupations to be imitated. For the boy there are another forms of play, not work in the sense of his parents' work. The pupil's activities at the boyhood stage are self-selected, their products have no economic significance, and their features are characteristic of play. In childhood the pupil imitates domestic activities, in boyhood neighbourhood occupations. His development is determined by the widening range of environment rather than by a sudden transition from inner experience to outer. For Froebel there is, a unity transcending the opposition between play and work, for both he regards as means to the individual's self-realisation. "Man works", he affirss, "only that his spiritual divine essence may assume outward form, and that thus he may be enabled to recognise his own spiritual, divine nature and the innermost being of God."

PROJECT ACTIVITIES

The activities in which the boy engages have all the characteristics of projects—practical problem involving co-operative effort and affording intellectual and moral training. "If in his former activity (in childhood) he emulated phases of domestic life, in his present activity (in boyhood) he shares the work of the house-lifting, pulling, carrying, digging, splitting". According to Schlipp Froebel, particularly in his *Education of Man*, has given the world no mean-anticipation of Dewey's own school.

INSTRUCTION

The other main feature of boyhood education is instruction. It also serves to mark the transition from making the internal external to making the external internal. 'Instruction is conducted not so much in accordance with the nature of man as in accordance with the fixed, definite, clear *laws* in the nature of things, and more particularly the laws to which man and things are equally subject. It is conducted in accordance with fixed and definite conditions lying outside the human being.

SCHOOL CURRICULUM

In describing his pupil's life and education from the development standpoint Froebel proposes various educational occupations and expounds his attitude to these. The subjects are not to be regarded as ends in themselves; they are merely instrumental to the full realisation of the pupil's personality.

MANUAL INSTRUCTION

Froebel was an early advocate of the inclusion of *manual instruction* in the school curriculum. It is a necessary condition of the realisation of the pupil's personality. Through it he comes to himself. "Every child, boy, and youth, whatever his condition or position in life, should devote daily at least one or two hours to some serious activity in the production of some definite external piece of work .... Children—mankind, indeed—are at present too much and too variously concerned with aimless and purposeless pursuits, and too little with work, Children and parents consider the activity of actual work so much to their disadvantage, and so unimportant for their future conditions of life, that educational institutions should make it one of their most constant endeavours to dispel this delusion. The domestic and scholastic education of our time leads children to indolence and laziness; a vast amount of human power thereby remains undeveloped and is lost."

OTHER SUBJECTS

Froebel also recommends the introduction of such subjects as drawing, nature study and school gardening. He insists on an all-round development as the aim of education. As the main divisions of an educational curriculum he enumerates :

(i) religion and religious instruction
(ii) natural science and mathematics
(iii) language,
(iv) art and objects of art.

Human education requires the knowledge and appreciation of religion, nature and language with reference to the aim of instruction in art Froebel states "Its intention will not be to make each pupil an artist in some one or all of the arts, but to secure to each human being full and all-sided development".

KINDERGARTEN

Meaning

In the form of Kindergarten, Froebel made an important contribution to the theory and practice of education. He realising the paramount importance of childhood he opened the first Kingergarten, an institution of children of age 4 to 6, at Blankenburg in 1837. Kindergarten is a German word which implies a children's garden. Froebel conceived the school as a garden, the teacher as the gardener and the students as tender plants. The teacher like the gardener is to look after the little human plants and water them to grow to beauty and perfection. Froebel discovered much similarity between a child and a plant. He believed that the process of growth and development of the plant and the child is the same. The plant grows from within according to the seed that is within. In the same way the child grows from within. He unfolds his tendencies and impulses from within.

Objectives

Froebel outlined the following objectives of Kindergarten :

1. To the children enjoyment in agreement with their nature.
2. To strengthen the bodies of children.
3. To exercise their senses.
4. To awaken their minds.
5. To acquaint them with nature and their fellows.
6. To lead them to unity.

MAIN CHARACTERISTICS

1. Self-Activity—Froebel stressed that the child should be given full freedom to carry out his activities. The growth of the child is directed by inner force in the child. Education, said Froebel, "should provide for free self-activity and self0-determination on the part of the man—being created for freedom in the image of God."

The following points should be noted regardng activity :

1. It should not be vague.
2. It should be a sublimated or ontrolled activity.
3. Social atmosphere is essential in order to secure meaningful results.
4. Self-activity may take the form either of work or of play.

An Inspector reported about this self-activity—"Self-activity of the mind is the first law of this institution. The instruction steadily goes on from the simple to the complex, from the concrete to the abstracts, so well adapted to the child and his needs. He goes as easily to his learning as to his play."

2. Play—According to Froebel, "Play is the purest, most spiritual activity of man at this stage .... It gives, therefore, joy, freedom, contentment, inner and rest, peace with the world." Froebel recognised that play needs to be organised and controlled on definite materials so that it may not degenerate into aimless play instead of preparing for those tasks of life for which it is destined". There should be rational, conscious guidance. Conseequently, Froebel has given seven gifts to children to play with.

3. Songs, Gestures and Construction—Froebel saw an organic relationship between songs, gestures and construction. He regarded these as three co-ordinate forms of expression in the child. What is to be learnt by the pupil is first expressed in a song, then it is dramatised or expressed in gesture or movement and lastly illustrated through some constructive work such as paper or clay. Thus, a balanced development of the mind, the speech organs and the hands is aimed at. The three activities provide exercise to the senses, limbs and muscles of the child.

In Froebel's book *"Mother and Nursery Songs"*. There are fifty play songs. The idea of the introduction of songs is to enable the child to use his senses, limbs and muscles and also to familiarise him with the surroundings. The child begins to use language through these songs. Each song is accompanied by a game, such as 'Hid and Seek'. The selection of the song is determined by the teacher in accordance with the development of the child. There are three parts in a song :

1. A motto for the guidance of mother or teacher.
2. A verse accompanied by music.
3. A picture illustrating the song.

The song for drill is:
Let us have a drill to-day,
March along grande array,
And whoever steps the best
Shall be captain over the rest,
And lead us on our way.

4. Gifts and Occupations—To provde activities, Froebel devised suitable materials known as gifts. The gifts suggest soje form of activity and occupations. These have been carefully graded. They possess all the novelties of play things. The order of the gift is devised in such a way as it leads the child from the activities and thought of one stage to another.

SEVEN GIFTS

1. ***First Gift***—The first gift consists of six coloured balls contained in a box. The balls are of different colours. The child is to roll them about in play. The occupation consists in rolling them. The balls are intended to give the students an idea of colour, materials, motion and direction. The rhymes accompanying of the rolling of the ball are :

Oh, see the pretty ball

So round so soft and small
The ball is round and rolls each way,
The ball is nice for baby's play.

2. *Second Gift*—It consists of a sphere, a cube and cylinder made of hard wood. They are contained in a box. The child plays with them and notices the difference between the stability of the cube and the mobility of the sphere. He learns that the cylinder is both movable and stable and it harmonies the quaility of both.

3. *Third Gift*—It is a big wooden cube subdivided into light wooden cubes. The child can have an elementary idea of addition and substraction through these.

4. *Fourth Gift*—It consists of large cubes divided into eight oblong prisms in each of which the length is twice the breadth and the breadth is twice the thickness. The assists the child to construct different kinds of buildings and pattens when combined with the third gift.

5. *Fifth Gift*—It is very much similar to the third gift. It consists of a large cube divided into twenty seven small cubes, three of which are again divided diagonally into halves and three into quarters. The child can construct many beautiful patterns and forms by combining the third, fourth and fifth gift. This gift is also useful in learning form and number.

6. *Sixth Gift*—It is very much like the gift four. It is a large cube divided into eighteen whole and nine small oblong blocks. Many designs in forms and construction can be made by the child. It is also useful in teaching numbers.

7. *Seventh Gift*—It is a set of square and triangular tables made of fine wood in two colours. It provides material for many exercises in geometrical forms and mosaic work.

5. The place of Teacher. The teacher is not to remain passive. He has to suggest the idea of occupation when gifts are offered to children. He is also required to demonstrate certain activities to them. He also sing a song with a view to helping the child to form appropriate idea.

6. Discipline–A teacher has important responsibilities to perform. He has to inculcate sympathetically values like love, sympathy, humility, co-operation and obedience to elders. He has to avoid external restraint and bodily punishment. The child should be made to realize that discipline depends upon his love for order, goodwill and mutual understanding. Froebel stressed that women should be trained for training children at this stage.

7. Curriculum. The divisions of the curriculum are :

(i) Manual work.

(ii) Religion and religious instruction.

(iii) Natural science and mathematics.

(iv) Language

(v) Arts and objects of work

Philosophy of Kindergarten

Three fold Division of Philosophy.

There are three distinct philosophies of kindergarten—

1. First of all, there is the philosophy of the activity centred curriculum. Here pupils are actively involved in selecting goals, learning opportunities and appraisal procedure. A variety of materials to learn from are readily apparent in a stimulating learning environment.
2. A second philosophy stressed the importance of pupils learning subject matter. Definite subject matter is prescribed for pupils to attain. The scope and sequence of the kindergarten curriculum is prescribed for the young learner. Subject matter to be learned is strongly emphasized in the pre-determind scope and sequence.
3. A third philosophy emphasizes measurement driven instruction. Precise objectives are developed first in the kindergarten curriculum. The teacher then selects and aligns learning activities which guide kindergarten pupils to attain the objectives. Evaluation is emphasized only in terms of the measurably stated objective(s). Ideally, the stimuli in the learning activity should not exceed what is

contained in the measurably states objective. Emphasis is placed upon measuring observable outcomes of instruction.

A synthetic view point.

To synthesize diverse philosophies and beliefs in the Kindergarten curriculum, it is recommended that the pupils are provided—

1. Ample opportunities to choose interesting sequential learning opportunities.
2. Stimulating experiences which develop intrinsic motivation for learning.
3. Opportunities to learn to read and write when readiness is in evidence.

OPEN CURRICULUM IN THE KINDERGARTEN

The most popular philosophy of the kindergarten is to emphasise a very informal curriculum in to-day's schools. The teacher then becomes a guide or stimulator. His/her job is to motivate, encourage, challenge and secure pupil interest in learning. The informal classroom structure may emphasize the use of learning situations in the classroom. Each situation is quite open ended in terms of what pupils may achieve. The following are examples of the kinds of situations contained in the classroom.

1. A Library Book Centre—Here, pupils may listen to a story being read by the teacher in a stimulating manner. Illustrations are shown to learners in the book as the contents are read orally by the teacher or an aid. Selected objects on the table relate to content in the library books. Thus, a few model animals at this stage relate directly to the content being read from the library books. The models are also discussed with pupils.

2. A Drawing Centre—Diverse art media are at this centre. The media include pencils, crayons, magic marker, coloured pencils and watercolours. Creatively the learner chooses what to portray as an art product on paper. Spontaneity and uniqueness of expression are desired in terms of processes emphasized in art work. Pupils may wish to tell the content in the finished art product. Sharing of ideas with other learners is to be encouraged.

3. A Model Centre—Models of animals, buildings and people should be housed here. Learners may take the models to build diverse scenes. The models may also be discussed in terms of characteristics and traits. Pupils may secure additional ideas about each model by consulting picture books with large illustrations. Ideas secured should be shared with other leaners. Oral communication needs to be encouraged at each situation.

4. Role Playing Centre—Toy dishes, plates, utensils, a kitchen sink and refrigerator among other items may well provide stimulating materials for pupils. Spontaneity of learners needs to be encouraged as they prepare and serve food to each other in a stimulated setting. Quality of positive interactions is important in role playing activities.

Addiational situations for the kindergarten pupil include :

(a) A reference materials place containing illustrated content for pupils.

(b) A costume place. Here, Kindergartners may dress up in different costumes such as in adult dresses, suits, slacks, shoes and hats.

In the words of Froebel the object of a Kindergarten is "to give the children employment in agreement with their whole nature, to strengthen their bodies, to exercise their senses, to engage their awakening mind and through their senses to make them acquainated with nature and their fellow creatures. It is specially to guide aright the heart and the affections, and to lead them to the original ground of *all life*, to unity with themselves."

MERITS OF FROEBEL'S KINDERGARTEN

1. Kindergarten laid emphasis on pre-school or nursery education.
2. Kindergarten stressed the importance of play in early education.

3. Kindergarten broadened the concept and scope of the school as an essential social institution. Forebal regarded school as a miniature society where children get training in important things of life. They learn the virtues of co-operation, sympathy, fellow-feeling responsibility etc.
4. Kindergarten stressed the necessity of the study of child's natu his instincts and impulses.
5. The gift and occupations of the kindergarten give a new method of teaching.
6. The inclusion of productive work in the school make children productive workers.
7. There is sufficient scope for activity in a kindergarten.
8. Various gifts provide sensory training.
9. The inclusion of nature study in the curriculum helps to develop love for nature and world in the mind of the students.

Limitations

1. Kindergarten expects too much from the child. It is not possible for the child to be able to understand abstract ideas of organic unity while paying with gifts.
2. In the kindergarten, too much stress has been laid on the development from within. The importance of the environment has not been fully recognised.
3. Songs as given by Froebel are out of date. These cannot be used in every school.
4. The gifts of Kindergarten are formal in nature. The order of presentation of gifts is arbitrary. They do not serve much purpose of sense training.
5. The kindergarten does not provide for the study of the individual child.
6. There is little of correlation in the teaching of various subjects in kindergarten.

7. It is not possible to accept his kindergarten excessive emphasis on play in education as it is likely to detract the child from serious learning.

FROEBEL'S INFLEUCNE ON MODERN EDUCATION

Froebel invited people to live for their children and love them. The schools for young children are not jails and the children are not passive learners. All the tendencies in the modern educational thought and practice find their roots in Froebel's conceptions. He helped to make the society conscious of education for young children. Following chief field in which he influenced the modern education.

1. Emphasis on Nursery or Pre-Primary Education—The present educator recognises the importance of the education in the early years. Today there are a large number of schools catering to the needs of such children. Froebel often said, "until the education of nursery years was reformed nothing solid and worthy could be achieved."

2. New Concept of School—Kindergarten school was a little world where responsibility was shared, by all, individual rights respected by all, brotherly sympathy developed and voluntary co-operation practised by all. Kindergarten school was a society in miniature.

3. Respect for the Child's Individuality—Froebel had profound love and sympathy for children. He lived for children, worked for childaren and died for children.

4. Stress on the Study of the Child—Froebel stressed the need for the study of the nature of the child, his instincts and impulses. Modern education is very careful to see that adequate scope is provided for the free play of the impulses and instincts of children.

5. Education Through Play—Froebel believed that play is the highest phase of self-development. He introduced play way in the activities of the school. Today the principle of play way has been accepted by every educator. We teach children through songs, movements, gestures, dramatisation, hand-work etc.

6. Sense Training—Froebel introduced gifts for the training of the senses of children. With the help of these gifts he wanted to give the idea of shape, form, colour, size and number. Audio-visual aids form an integral part of the present system of eduation.

7. Activity in Education—Froebel was the first educator to make self-activity the basis of education. 'Learning by doing is the slogan of the day. The present school has become a place of activity and joy for children. We provide activities to students so that they may satisfy their instincts of construction, manipulation curiosity and acquisition.

8. Nature Study in Education—For Froebel nature study was a means of bringing the child nearer God. He adovacted a syllabus of nature study to enable the child to understand the world in which he lived and to develop habits of careful observation. This idea has taken such a strong hold today that we do not regard any school worthy of name if it does not provide for nature study.

9. Women Teachers at the Nursery Stage—It is due to the influence or Froebel that there is a trend to entrust the education at the pre-primary or pre-basic stage to women teachers who are considered to be more suited for this task of instruction at this stage.

10

Maria Montessori

'By education must be understood the active help given to the normal expansion of the life of the child's.'

—Maria Montessori

Montessori's House of Childhood was situated in the slums of Rome, a European capital. She "*established the centre of gravity of her system in the environment". In her the Secret of Childhood* she affirms: 'Our own method of education is characterised by the central importance that we attribute to the question of environment'; it is well-known how our pedagogy considers the environment so important as to make it the central point of the whole system."

The Roman Association for Good Building was formed to remove the social evils of the poorest quarters of Rome. Its plan was to acquire tenements, remodel them, put them into a productive condition and administer them in the interests of the occupier. The care of the reconstructed tenements was given to the tenants and they did not abuse their trust. Difficulties however, arose in regard to young children under school age. Left to themselves during the day, unable to appreciate the motives which led their parents to respect the property. there children spent their time defacing the buildings. In order to cure ths evil it the Director General of the Roman Association for Good Building planned to gather together in a large room, all the little ones between the ages of three and seven, belonging to the families living in the tenement. They play and the work of these children were to be carried on under the guidance of a teacher who should have her own apartment in the tenement house. Thus came to be instituted the House of Childhood-the school within the tenement on 6th January 1907. In accordance with the general self-supporting principle of the reconstruction scheme the expenses of the new institution were met by the sum that the Association would otherwise have been forced to expend upon redecoration and repairs.

THE MONTESSORI METHOD

The Director General of the Roman Association of Good Building entrusted to Montessori the organisation of the infant schools in the model tenements in Rome towards the end of 1906; She adopted method according to her training and previous experience. Having graduated in Medicine, she was for a time in charge of the training of mentally defective children. She taught a number of such children to read and write so efficiently that they were able to be presented for examination with normal children of the same age. This phenomenal result she attributed to an improved method. She therefore conjectured that if this method is applied in the training of normal children, it would yield even more surprising results.

To be successful, these methods should obviously be applied in the training of infants. At this period of life the child has not acquired the coordination of muscular movements necessary to enable him to perform dexterously the ordinary acts of life. His sensory organs are not fully developed, his emotional life is still unstable and his volitional powers irresolute. About the significance of the pedagogical experiment for which the institution of the House of Childhood afforded the facilities, Montessori wrote : "It represents the results of a series of trials made in the education of young children, with methods already used with deficients."

PRINCIPLES OF MONTESSORI METHOD

The first principle is to train the pupil to be independent of others in respect of the ordinary practices of life. It necessitates approach children, an appeal to the senses rather than to the intellect. With physically defective children it implies training one sense to function icariously for another. The ultimate reference is to the sense of touch, which is regarded as fundamental and primordial. The Montessori system accordingly becomes an 'education by touch'. Montessori maintains that the sense of touch is fundaments. It undergoes great development during the early years of life. If neglected at this age, it loses its susceptibility to training.

The Psychological Method

Montossori "psychological method in education implies that the educative process is adapted to the stage of mental development of the child, and to his interest. It is not wholly subordinated to the necessities of a curriculum or to the teacher's sscheme of work. By education', says Montessori, 'must be understood the active help given to the normal expansion of the life of the child." The 'psychological moment' in the educative process comes when consciousness of a need arises in the child mind. In the Monsessori method, 'It is necessary then to offer those exercises which correspond to the need of development felt by an organism, and if the child's age has carried him past a certain need, it is never possible to obtain, in its fulness, a development which missed its proper moment. If a child fails to perform a task or to appreciate the truth of a principle, the teacher must not make him conscious of his error by repeating the lesson. She must assume the task has been presented prematurely. Before again presenting the stimulus, she must await the manifestation of the symptoms which indicate that the need exists. The duration of a process is determined not by the exigencies of an authorised time-table, but by the interval which the child finds requisite to exhaust his interest. Thus in a Montessori school one may find a pupil working unremittingly at a self-imposed task for several days on end.

No Prizes

In the Montessori system there are no prizes. The pupils's sense of mastery is his highest reward: "His own self-development is his true and almost his only pleasure". Such correction as is admitted in the Montessori system comes from the material, not from the teacher. "From the "Children's Houses the old-time teacher who wore herself out maintaining discipline of immobility and wasting her breath in loud and continual discourse, has disappeared, and the didactic material which contains within itself the control of errors is substituted, making auto-education possible to each child. It is an intellectual discipline by consequences."

Perfect Freedom

The psychological method implies the perfect freedom of the child, which consists in absolute obedience to the laws of the development of his own nature. According to Montessori, "The method of observation (that is, the psychological method) is established upon one fundamental base–the liberty of the pupils in their spontaneous manifestations. This liberty necessitates independence of action on the part of the child. "Whoever visits a well kept school is struck by the discipline of the children. There are forty little beings from three to seven years old, each one intent on his own work; one is going through one of the exercises for the senses, one is doing an arithmetical exercise, one is handling the letters, one is drawing, one is fastening and unfastening the pieces of cloth on one of the wooden frames, still another is dusting. Some are seated at the table, some on rugs on the floor."

Adapted Environment

As instruction should be adapted to the stage of development of the pupil, Montessori advocates that the environment should likewise be so adapted. She gave the child an environment in which everything be so adapted. She gave the child an is constituted in proportion to himself and let him live therein. Thus, will develop within the child that "active life" which has caused so many to marvel because they see in it not only a simple exercise performed with pleasure but also the revelation of a spiritual life. Such an environment "should contain the means of auto-education. He who speaks of liberty in the schools, ought at the same time to exhibit object–approximating to a scientific apparatus which will make such liberty possible."

PRACTICES OF MONTESSORI METHOD

The practices of the Montessori method fall into three classes: (A) the exercise of practical life; (B) the exercises in sensory training; and (C) the didactic exercises.

(A) The Exercise in Practical Life—Freedom, according to Montessori, does not consist in having others at one's command to perform the ordinary services, but in being able to do these for oneself, in being independent of others. Thus in the House of Childhood the pupils learn how to wash their hands, using little wash-stands with small pitchers and basins, how to clean their nails, brush their teeth and so on. Exercise are also arranged to train the child in the movements necessary in dressing and undressing. The apparatus for these exercises consists of wooden farms, mounted with two pieces of cloth or leather, which are fastened by means of buttons and buttonholes, hooks and eyes, eyelets and lacing or automatic fasteners. After some practice in fastening and unloosening the pieces of cloth with the various types of fasteners, the child finds that he has acquired a dexterity which enables him to dress and undress himself : Not content with the satisfaction derived from such independence, his consciousness of the possession of a new power excites in him a desire to assist in dressing the whole family. All the furniture in the House of Childhood, tables, chairs, etc. are of such a size and construction that the pupils can handle them easily. They learn to move them deftly and without noise, and are thus afforded a training in motor adjustment.

Montessori devised certain formal gymnastic exercises to develop coordinated movements in the child. She disapproved of the child practising the ordinary gymnastic exercises arranged for the adult. She maintained "We are wrong' if we consider little children from their physical point of view as little men. They have, instead, characteristics and proportions that are entirely special to their age." A new set of exercise has been evolved in caccordance with the general montessori principles, by observing the spontaneous movements of the child. One piece of apparatus, is the little round stair. It is a wooden spiral stairway enclosed on one side by a balustrade on which the children can rest their hands. The other side being left open, enables the children to habituate themselves to ascending and descending stairs without holding on, it teaches them to move up and down with poised and self-controlled movement. The steps are very low and shallow. The children can thereby learn movement which they cannot execute properly in climbing ordinary stairway in their homes, where the proportions are suited to adults. The new exercises give the pupils of the House of Childhood a gracefulness of carriage which distinguishes them from other children.

(B) Exercises in Sense Training—For the method and the apparatus of her scheme of sensory training, Montessori is largely indebted to the tests and apparatus employed by the experimental psychologist. However, Montessori is not interested in measuring the powers but in furthering their development. Practice-effects frequently disclose themselves. In the application of tests by psychologists, especially when the investigation extends over a long period, these are disturbing factors to the psychologist which he must estimate and eliminate. However, it is just these practice-effects that sensory education strives to secure.

'To make the process one of self-education', Montessori explains in *The Advanced Montessori Method*, "it is not enough that the stimulus should call forth activity, it must also direct it. The child should not only persist for a long time in an exercise; he must persist without making mistakes. All the physical or intrinsic qualities of the objects should be determined, not only by the immediate reaction of attention they provoke in the child, but also by their possession of this fundamental characteristic, the control of error, that is to say, the power of evoking the effective collaboration of the highest activities (comparison, judgment).

In sensory training the senses are isolated whenever that is possible. This procedure is suggested by the education of physically deficient children. The pupils of the Montessori schools are blindfoded, a feature of the training which seems to add zest to their efforts. The auditory exercises are given in an environment not only of silence, but even of darkness.

Material used in Sensory Training

(1) For Perception of Size—A series of wooden cylinders varying in height only, in diameter only or in both dimensions at once, are employed, likewise blocks varying regularly in size, and rods of regularly graded lengths.

(2) For Perception of Form—In it are used geometrical insets in metal, in wood or the shapes of the insets drawn on paper.

(3) For Discrimination in Weight—It was tablets of wood similar in size but differing in weight.

(4) For Touch—All highly polished surface and a sand-paper surface is used.

(5) For Sense of Temperature—Here are used small metal bowls with caps.

(6) For Auditory Acuity—Cylindrical sound boxes are used containing different sbstances.

(7) For the Colour Sense—A graded series of coloured woods is used.

(8) Tactual Activity—Similar methods are adopted in developing in the child's tactual acuity, and in training him to discriminate differences in temperature and in weight. In these exercises the child is blindfolded or is enjoined to keep his eyes closed during the tests; he is encouraged to do so by being told that he will thus be able to feel the differences better.

Exercises Directed to the Development of Senses

(1) The first exercise is to sort out of a heap of bricks and cubes such as are employed by Froebel. Young children come to recognise the forms of these merely be grasping them; they do not require to trace the contour. This exercise may be varied by the use of different materials, as for examples, by the use of coins, and so expert do the children become that they can distinguish between small form which differ but little from one another, such as corn, wheat and rice.

(2) The real training in the perception of form begins, when the child passes to the exercises of placing wooden shapes in spaces made to receive them, or in superimposing such shapes on outlines of similar form.

(3) Geometric insets of various designs, the initial ones strongly contrasted, the later ones merely dissimilar forms of the same figure, as for example, the triangle, are mixed up and have to be sorted out by the children and fitted into the frames made to receive them. The frames furnish the control necessary to test the accuracy of the work. Montessori method is determined purely from the pedagogical standpoint. The objects most commonly used are table tops, doors, window frames, etc.

In learning to fit the geometric insets into the spaces provided for them the child employs not only the visual sense but also the tactual and muscular senses. He is taught to run the index finger of the right of the frame into which the insect fits. It is frequently observed that children who cannot recognise a shape by looking at it do so by touching it. According to Montessori, "The association of the muscular-tactile sense with that of vision aids in a most remarkable way the perception of the forms and fixes them in memory."

(4) From the exercises with the solid insets in which the control is absolute, the child passes to exercises in the purely visual

perception of form. The wooden insets have to be superimposed on figures cut out of blue paper and mounted on cards. In a further series of exercises the figures are represented by an outline of blue paper, which for the child represents the path which he has so often followed with his finger. Finally, he is required to superimpose the wooden pieces on figures whose outlines are represented merely by a line. He thus passes from the concrete to what is relatively abstract, from solid objects to plane figures represented merely by lines and perceived only visually.

Through such exercises the forms of the various figures, circles, ellipses, triangles, rectangles etc. come to be known. When the need for them becomes urgent the names of the figures are given. As no analysis of the forms is undertaken, no mention made of sides and angles, the teaching of geometry is not being attempted at this stage.

THE DIDACTIC EXERCISES

The methods adopted in training the perception of from prepare the way for the teaching of writing and of the other didactic processes.

Popular interest was aroused in the Montessori method by the success attending the application of the didactic processes of writing, reading and numbers. At the inception of the system it was not intended that such exercise should be included. Therefore, the results were incidental.

(1) Teaching of Writing—In the Montessori system the teaching of writing precedes the teaching of reading. Montssori maintained that in normal children the muscular sense is most easily developed in infancy, and this makes the acquisition of writing exceedingly easy for children. In writing of dictation the child translates sounds into material signs and perfors certain movements, the latter process being easy usually affording pleasure to the child.

In accordance with her general principle, Montessori adopts psychological standpoint in respect to writing. "Let us observe an individual who is writing and let us seek to analyse the acts he performs", she proposes; and again : "It goes without saying that we should examine the individual who writes, not the writing, the subject, not the object."

According to the Montessori view, writing is not a mere copying of head-lines, but the writing of words which express ideas. In writing are involved two diverse types of movement, the movement by which the forms of letters are resproduced and that by which the instrument of writing is manipulate. In addition, the phonetic analysis of spoken words into their elementary sounds is also necessary. Preparatory exercise for each of these factors must be devised and practised independently before writing is actually commenced.

As the children has alredy learned to know the forms of the geometric insets by running their fingers round the contours, so, to teach the forms of the letters, Montessori got the pupils to trace with the finger the shapes of the letters cut out in sand-paper and pasted one cards, the roughness of the sand-paper providing a the finger the shapes of the letters cut out in sand-paper and pasted control for the accuracy of the movements. As soon as they have acquired facility in this tracing of the forms of the letters, the children take great pleasure in repeatign the movement with closed eyes. Thus the forms of the letter are not learned and impressed on the minds of the pupils by visual analysis and retained by visual imagery, but by tactual and motor experiences and grapho-motor imagery.

The phonetic sounds of the letters are taught at the same time as the tracing of the forms, the steps in the lesson following the three-stage procedure illustrated. The audio-motor imagery helps to reinforce the grapho-motor and to faciliate the retention of the forms of the letters. The children are also practised in analysing the spoken word into its sounds and in reconstructing the word with sand-paper letters.

The control of the pen is also attacked indirectly. Recourse is had for this training to the geometric insets, of which mention has already been made. Taking one of the metal frames into which the inset fits, the child daws on a sheet of paper with a coloured crayon around the contour of the empty frame. Within the figure which results he places the metal inset, and with a crayon of a different colour traces figures in different colours. With another crayon of his own selection the pupil fills in the figures which he has outlined. In making the upward and downward strokes he is taught not to pass outside the contour. Variety is lent to the task by the choice of different coloured crayons and by the use of different insets, the employment of the latter also training him to make upward and downward strokes of various lengths. Gradually the lines tend less and less to go outside the enclosing boundary until at last they are perfectly contained within it. Both the centre and the frame are filled in with close and uniform strokes. The child is now master of the writing instrument: The muscular mechanism necessary to its manipulation is established.

Now the three prerequisites to writing are at the pupil's command, that is he has acquired control of the writing instrument, he can reproduce the forms of the letters moving his fingers in the air, and the composition of words out of the isolated sounds of letters can be effected psychically. At this point the imitative tendency in the child arouses in him the impulse to write. Now a pupil who has given no previous indication of having developed ability in this direction begins straightway to write.

(2) Teaching of Reading—The way to the teaching of reading is prepared in the Montessori system by the procedure adopted in the teaching of writing. In the exercises preparatory to writing is included word-building with sand-paper script characters representing the sound of the spoken word. Reading demands the inverse process, that is, the reproduction of the sound from the symbols and the fusion of these sound into words.

The proper accentuation of the syllables is also necessary for the correct enunciation of the word. This comes only with recognition of the meaning. Montessori refused to give the name 'reading' to anything less than this. Just as writing is something more than mere copying pothooks and head-lines, so reading is not a mere 'braking at print' but the recognition of the meanings represented by the visual characters. She says, "What I understand by reading, is the interpretation of an idea from the written sings." Until the child reads a transmission of ideas from the written words the does not read."

The didactic material for the lessons in reading consists of slips of paper or of cards upon which are written words and phrases in clear large script.

The lessons begin with the reading of names of objects which are known or which are present. The child is given a card on which a name is written in script. He translates the writing slowly into sounds. If the interpretation is exact the directress restricts herself to saying 'Faster'. The child reads more quickly the second time, but still often without understanding. The teacher repeats, 'Faster, faster'. The child reads 'faster' each time, repeating the same accumulation of sounds : Finally the word emerges in consciousness. When the child has pronounced the word, be places the card under the object whose name it bears, and the exercise is finished. It is a lesson which proceeds very rapidly since it is only presented to a child who is already prepared through writing.

Sentences describing actions or expressing commands are likewise written on slips of paper, The children select these and carry out the requests contained in them. The child does not read the sentences aloud. The aim of reading is to teach the child to discover ideas in symbols, hence the reading should be silent and not vocal. According to the Montessori analysis, 'reading aloud' implies the exercise of two mechanical forms of language–articulate graphic–and is a complex task. The child, therefore, who begins to read by interpreting thought should read mentally." 'Truly', claims Montessori, "we have buried the tedious and stupid ABC primer side by side with the useless copy-books."

The period intervening between the commencement of the writing process and the appearance of the ability of read is about a fortnight. Facility in reading is, however, arrived at much more slowly than in writing. Normal children trained according to the Montessori method begin to write at four years of age and at five know how to read.

(3) Teaching of Number—In the teaching of number in the Montessori system is used the 'long stair', a set of ten rods, the first being one meter in length, the last one decimetere, the intermediate rods diminishing in length by decimeters. The rods are divided into decimetre parts, the spaces on the rods being painted alternately red and blue. When arranged in order they form what is called the 'long stair'. They are utilised in the sensory exercises for training the children in discrimination of length. In these exercises the rods are mixed up, and the teacher grades them in order of length, calling the child's attention to the fact that the stair thus constructed is uniform in colour at one end. The child is then permitted to build it for himself.

After the child has had practice in arranging the rodes in order of length he is required to count the red and the blue division, beginning with the shortest rod, thus : one ; one, two; three; always going back to one in the counting of each rod and starting from the same end. He is then required to name the various rods from the shortest to the longest, according to the total number of divisions each contains, at the same time touching the rods on the side on which 'the stair' ascends. The rods may they he called 'piece number one', 'piece number tow', and so on, and finally they may be spoken of in the lessons as one, two, three.

The graphic signs for the numbers are cut in sandpaper, and by the three-period lesson arrangement previously illustrated, the pupil is taught to associate the names of the numbers with their graphic forms. The graphic signs are then related to the quantity represented.

(4) Teaching of Arithmetics—Addition may then be taught by suggesting to the child to put the shorter rods together in such a way as to form tens; I is aded to 9, 2 to 8 and so on. Subtraction, multiplication and division can also be introduced by means of the same didactic material, and later on the child is allowed to express graphically his operations with the rods.

The means and methods of dealing with the larger denominations of number and the higher arithmetical processes are dealt with in *The Advanced Montessori Method.* It also deals with the teaching of drawing, music, grammar and prosody.

Recapitulation Principle

Montessori accepts the recapitulation principle in education : The child follows the nature way of development of the human race. In short, such education makes the evolution of the individual harmonise with that of humanity." In *The Advanced Montessori Method*, however, Montessori rejects the recapitulation principle discussing it as 'a materialistic idea now discredited."

ROLE OF TEACHER

The Montessori method requires the employment of teachers possessed of a training in child psychology and in its application to young children. According to Montessori, "The broader the teacher's scientific culture and practice in experimental psychology, the sooner will come for her the marvel of unfolding life, and her interest in it". "The more fully the teacher is acquainted with the methods of experimental psychology, the better will she understand how to give a lesson." The training of the teacher should enable her to know when to intervene in the child's activities, and when to refrain from intervening. According to Montessori "In the manner of this intervention lies the personal art of the educator." Montessori has substituted the term 'directress for the title 'teacher' she says "instead of facility of speech she has to acquire the power of silence; instead of teaching she has to observe; instead of the proud dignity of one who claims to be infallible she assumes the vesture of humility."

Sir John Adam attributed to Montessori the credit of sounding the death-knell of class teaching as the most significant feature of the system is the individualisation of instruction.

11

John Dewey

"Education is a constant recognising and reconstructing of experience."

—John Dewey

John Dewey greatest of the pragmatists and generally recognised as the most outstanding philosopher his country has yet produced, made significant contributions to virtually every field of philosophy as well as to such other areas of inquiry as education and psychology. Active for 70 years as a scholar, he was a prolific writer publishing approximately fifty books and more than eight hundred articles. Many of these have been translated into varius foreign languages. New volumes are still coming out with more Dewey material, mainly correspondence; and books and articles on him are appearing at a rapidly increasing rate.

Some Dewey material is at present available only in Chinese. In February and March of 1919 he lactured at the Imperial University of Tokyo, and these lectures were published as *Reconstruction in Philosophy.* While in Japan he was invited to lecture in Chine also, and he spent from May 1, 1919 to July, 1921 there, finding the developments there of extremely great interest. He lectured extensively in Peking, Nanking, and Shanghai, speaking in English from brief lecture notes; and his lectures were translated and recordes in full on the spot in Chinese by his former students. Dr. Hu Shih, for example, translated his Peking lectures. According to Dr. Hu Shih's account in "John Dewey in China,"[1] Dewey provided the translators and recorders with his typed lecture

1. **Charles A. Moore, ed., *Philosophy and Culture—East and West* (Honolulu, University of *Hawali* Press, 1962); pp. 762-769.**

notes in advance of each lecture so that they could study them and think out suitable Chines words and phrases before the lecture and its translation. The translation was checked against his notes before publication in newspapers and periodicals or later publication in book form. What was known as "Dewey's Five Major Series of Lectures" in Peking, some 58 lectures on Modern Tendencies in Education, Social and Political Philosophy, Philosophy of Eduction, Ethics, and Types ofThinking according to Hu Shih,went through ten large reprintings in book form before Dewey left China, and continued to be reprinted for at least three decades before government authorities on the mainland put a stop to them. There were also series on such other topics as Democratic Developments in America, Experimental Logic, History of Philosophy, and (as an introduction to Russell's lectures there in 1920). Three Philosophers of the Modern Period, James, Bergson and Russell.

Fortunately, the Institute for Advanced Projects East-West Center, University of Hawaii, with Professor Robers W. Clopton as special consultant has undertaken to translate these materials, and in the fall of 1964 Dr. Tsuin-Chen Ou as the first of a team of translators began the work of translation. When his material is available in may well shed significant new light on various areas of Dewey's thought.

The southern Illinois University Co-operative Research Project on Dewey publications has discovered a number of previously unlisted publications by Dewey, and it has assembled the most complete collection in existence of works by and about him. Under the direction of its Editorial Board—Professors George E. Axtelle, Je Ann Boydstonm Joe R. Burnett (University of Illinois), S. Morris, Eames, and Lewis E. Hahn—the project, with the cooperation of a number of other leading Dewey scholars, is planning a definitive edition in forty or more volumes of all his published writings (books and articles).[1] The materials are to be arranged chronologically with careful textual editing but with a

---

1. The Editorial Board has the assistance of a larger Advisory Committee under the chairmanship of professor charles Moore, Chairman of the Philosophy Department Southern Illinois University

minimum of interpretive comment. The editorial and textual work connected with this pioneering venture for a major American philosopher will extend over many years, but it was hoped that the first volumes will be ready from the Southern Illinois University Press in 1967. Accompanying *The Works* was to be a one-volume *Readers' Guide* with interpretive essays by eminent Dewey scholars on the main subject areas of his though and writing. It was expected that this volume will be completed by 1967 so that it may be used throughout the publication period of *The Works*.

Further evidence of the contemporary relevance of Dewey, especially in education broadly conceived, may be had in connection with the activities of the John Dewey Society for the Study of the Education and Culture. Organized at Atlantic City in February, 1935, it exists to promote the study of the educational aims and educated methods of a democratic society. Regular meetings are scheduled in connection with the annul meetings of the National Society of College Teachers of Education. Much of the work of the Society is carried on through its Commissions on Meetings and Communications, Monographs in Educational Theory, and Annual John Dewey Lectures. It helped launch the journal, *Educational Theory,* and it has had a distinguished series of year-books going back to 1937 when William H. Kilpatrick edited the first one on *The Teacher and Society.* Among the other editors for this series are Harold D. Alberty, Christian O. Arndt. George E. Axtelle, Harold Benjamin, Theodore Brameld, Bovd H. Bode, John S. Brubaeher, Samuel Everett, Hollis L. Caswell, H. Gordon, Hullfish, Virgil Clift, Archibald Anderson, Ernest O. Melbv, Harold Rugg, Willam Van Til , Harold G. Shane, Lindly J. Stiles and William W. Wattenberg. The Annual Dewey Lectures have included Ordway Tead, Oscar Handlin, Seymour Harris. Gardner Murphy, Loren Eiseley, R. Freeman Butts, and Huston Smith. Arthur G. Wirth is current Chairman of the Society Commission on Publications.

For one who has written so voluminously and who has made major contributions in so many different areas, no brief summary can be fully adequate. Selecting a few emphases, moreover, is especially dangerous in connection with the through of one who commonly transcended conventional categories and boundaries and who habitually saw special topics in terms of larger contexts. And yet if one is to discuss this complex thinker as well as a group of others in a single chapter, a high degree of selectivity is required. It can only hoped that many readers will be led to turn to extensive reading in his works to supplement these remarks.

PHILSOPHICAL BACKGROUND

1. Analysis of Reflective Inquiry—Perhaps the most important single emphasis of John Dewey is his insistence upon applying reflective or critical inquiry to problems or indeterminate situations. What is involved in problem solving or thinking through a problem? What is critical inquiry ? How does one apply intelligence to human affairs? Dewey's answer to these questions is set forth in its simplest terms in *How we Think*; and a more sophisticated version is given in *Logic : The Theory of Inquiry.* In a sense the phases or steps in a complete act of reflective thinking afford an outline for each of his major works; and he had a life-long concern with what is involved in reflective thinking.

(a) The first step in a complet act of reflective thinking is the appearance of the problem. This may be marked by a more or less vague sense of something having gone wrong, a breakdown in habitual responses or modes of action. One of our beliefs is questioned, or acting upon it leads to a conflict or perplexity. (b) The second step or phase is clarification of the problem. Through analysis and observation we gather sufficient data to formulate the difficulty or define the problem. If for example, a belief is disputed, questioning or analysis may indicate what precisely is in dispute. (c) With problem clearly stated we pass to the stage of appearance of suggested solutions or hypotheses as to how to solve the problem. Various ideas occur to us as to how it may be solved. (d) The fourth stage is that of deductive elaboration. We reason out the implications of the various hypotheses. If we take the first hypothesis, we may expect such and such consequences; or need to make additional observations or gather more information to see what may be expected. It we take the second one, we may expect such and such other consequences; and so on. On the basis of a survey of the implications of the various proposed solutions we decide which to test in action. (e) The fifth step is that of verification. Through observation or experiment we check out the hypothesis or hypotheses which looked most promising to us. If one of the hypotheses works out, the indeterminate situation is replaced by a determinate one in which stable lines of action are possible; instead of the problematic situation or perplexity we have a resolved or clarified one.

These steps or stages do not necessarily come one right after another in the sequence in which these have been listed here. For example, the first three stages may be telescoped in such a fashion that we do not get a clear indication of the stages, but in general, the more difficult the problem, the more likely the stages are to be clearly outlined before it is solved. Or, again, after we have reached the stage of deductive elaboration, we may discover that we need to go back and further clarify the problem or think of additional ways of trying to solve it.

Thought this pattern is somewhat oversimplified, in fundamentals it is basically accurate. This is what is involved in problem solving activity whether it is a personal problem, an important social conflict, or a weighty scientific problem. When we solve a problem in this way, moreover, we have not merly a solution to our difficulty but also some descriptive or explanatory statements about how it was solved.

2. View of Experience—Experience is one of the central concepts in Dewey's thought, occurring and recurring throughout his writing. Though he finally concluded that he might have done better to use another term, many of his most important works are concerned with clarifying it—for example, his Carus Lectures, *Experience and Nature, or his Art as Experience or Experience and Education.* For him experience constitutes the entire range of men's relations to, or transactions with the universe. We experience nature and things interacting in certain ways make up experience.

For a brief presentation Dewey's views can perhaps best be

summarized in terms of a contrast with what he calls the orthodox view of experience, that is accepted by both the traditional empiricists and their opponents.[1] Whereas the orthodox view treats experience primarsly as a knowledge affair, Dewey speaks of it as intercourse between a living being and its physical and social environment. The traditionalists regard as subjective inner affair, separate and distinct from objective reality; but Dewey has always thought of experience as being of a piece with the objective world, which enters into the actions and sufferings of man and which, in turn, may be modified through human response. Instead of a gulf between disparate inner and outer realms of being, one may move freely from experience to that which surrounds, supports, and maintains it. The proponents of the orthodox view have been preoccupied with what is 'given' in a bare present, whereas Dewey was more concerned with what might be done to change what is given or taken, in furtherance of human purposes. The older empiricists thought in terms of what has been or is given, looking toward the past if they passed beyond the present. For Dewey the salient trait of experience is its connection with a future. If change is what we are interested in, we look primarily towards the future, and not recollection but anticipation is central for the experimental form of experience.

One of the main differences between Dewey's and the orthodox view of experience, however, turns about the latter's particularism, its concern with sense data to the neglect of connections and continuities, and its supposition that relations and continuities are either foreign to experience or are dubious by-products of it. Dewey, like James, emphasized the relations. The contextual, situational, transactional, or field character of experience stands out in his account. The traditional view opposed experience and thought in the sense of inference, but for Dewey experience is full of inference, as might be expected for one who sees the directional and relational character of experience. Where one seeks to control what is to come through employing present

1. See "The Need for a Recovery of Philosophy" In John Dewey and others, *Creative Intelligence, Essays in the Pragmatic Attitude* (New York Henry Holt and Co., 1917), pp. 3—69.

environmental supports to effect changes which would not otherwise occur, inference is of vital importance. From the standpoint of the future life-activity of the organism environmental incidents are favourable or hostile; and if one is to eliminate the latter and insure the former, an imaginative forecast of the future is essential for guidance in this process.

The structure of experience, however, comes out most clearly on Dewey's view in aesthetic experience. There we have experience in full, vivified clarified, and intensified.

3. View of Knowledge—Dewey rejects the traditional epistemology which sets up a knower outside the world and then asks about the possibility, extent, and validity of knowledge in general. He laughingly suggests that we might equally well have a problem of digestion in general—its possibility, extent, and genuineness—by assuming that the stomach and the food-materials were inhabitants of different world. The significant problem is not how such a knower is somehow to mirror the antecedently real out but rather one how one set of experienced events is to be used is signs of what we shall experience under another set of conditions. The important distinction, moreover, is not between the knower as subject and the world known as object. Instead it is between different ways of being in the movement of things, between an unreflective physical way and a purposive, intelligent one.

On Dewey's view knowledge needs to be placed in the context of the problematic or indeterminate situation and reflective inquiry. Knowledge is more than immediate awareness or the presence of a set of sense data. Having qualities before us does not constitute knowing. Knowledge is always inferential, and the problem is how the processes of inference are to be guided to trustworthy or warranted conclusions. It involves operations of controlled observation, testing, and experimentaiton. It is a product of inquiry—the stems in a complete act of reflective thinking. Dewey liked Bacon's idea that knowledge is power and it may be tested by the promotion of social progress.

4. Conception of Philosophy—In "The Need for a Recovery

of Philosophy" Dewey declares that philosophy must cease to be "a device for dealing with the problems of philosophy" and become 'a method, cultivated by philosophers, for dealing with the problems of men." But the problems of man as he sees them cover a range broad enough to include in one way or another most of the traditional problems as well as many others. The method involves treating philosophy as vision, imagination and reflection; and though the clarifying process may show that certain epistemological problems a pseudo-problem, the fact that they are raised may point to genuine cultural crises. If action at all levels needs to be informed with vision, imagination and reflection to bring clearly to mind future possibilities with reference to attaining the better and averting the worse, there is more than enough for philosophy to do.

Developing an adequate conception of the place of intelligence in human affairs is one important task for philosophy. How can intelligence which is a creation of a culture also be a creator or forming influence on that culture? How can it define the larger patterns of continuity between stubborn past and an insistent future? How can philosophy adjust the body of traditional beliefs to scientific tendencies and political aspirations which are novel and incompatible? These are tasks which involve the application of reflective inquiry on the broadest scale possible, and in applying it we need to remember Dewey reminds us in the little essay of *Philosophy and Civilization*, than in philosophy we are occupied with meaning rather than truth. This, of course, is not to deny either the crucial importance of truths as a sub-class of meanings or the relevance of existence to meanings. It is rather to suggest that imaginative sweep, values and significance are our primary concern.

In *Reconstruction in Philosophy.* Dewey stresses the social function of philosophy, holding there that the task of philosophy is to clarify men's minds as to the social and moral issues of their day, to enlighten the moral forces which move mankind, and to contribute to the aspirations of men to attain a more ordered and intelligent happiness.

For Dewey, in general, philosophy is both a product of human culture and a process of criticising or—clarifying it, distinguishing meanings within it and helping give it direction and form. In *Experience and Nature* he speaks of philosophy as criticism or criticism of criticism; as the "critical operation and function become aware of itself and its implications." It becomes a kind of theory of criticism—a consideration of alternating ways of critically evaluating values and beliefs. Meaning and values are focal in Dewey's conception of philosophy and this aspect is not lost when he treats pohilosophy as general theory of criticism. For him we criticise for the sake of instituting and perpetuating more enduring and extensive values; and each of the various philosophical disciplines, metaphysics no less than the others, makes its distinctive contribution to this end.

5. Biologism—What is sometimes referred to as Dewey's biologism reflects (a) his emphasis on the genetic point of view, and (b) his conviction that inquiry has a biological matrix. He was interested in how ideas originate and become more complex, in the parallels between human responses and low levels, and in the continuity of different species of organic life from the lowest forms to man. To understand the present situation, he held, we inqure into its specific condition as well as into its probable consequences.

Darwin and James helped Dewey to see the focal importance of the living creature adjusting or adapting to its environment and to view intelligence as a distinctive form of behaviour—one concerned with choosing appropriate means for the attainment of future ends. Whatever else mind may be, it is at least a means of controlling the environment in relation to ends of the life process. Within this framework the senses are not primarily gateways to knowledge but stimuli to action, and sensations are not so many pellets of knowledge but signals to redirect action, or signs of problems to be solved. In *The Influence of Darwin on Philosophy* Dewey suggests that the philosophic lesson of Darwin is that philosophy itself becomes a method of locating and interpreting the most serious of the conflicts that occur in life and a method of projecting ways of dealing with them.

6. Experimentalism—Dewey's experimentalism relates to his analysis of reflective inquiry for which hypotheses, prediction, and experimentation are central. An experiment is a programme of action to determine consequences. It is a way of introducing intelligence into a solution. It is an intelligently guided procedure for discovering what adjustments an organism must make to its environment to ward off ill or secure goods. Experimentation for Dewey is relevant not merely on the individual biological level, but wherever planned reconstruction of a situation may help effect desired transformation for example, in social planning or in education. The more important the issues at stake, the more clearly is experimentation seen to be preferable to such alternative as authoritarianism, simple guesswork or merely waiting for events to run their course.

In some ways the best contrast with Dewey's experimentalism is the quest for certainty. Whereas Descartes sought demonstrable proof or certainty through reason and Berkeley took sensory awareness as the bedrock of certainty, Dewey argued that what we are really after is not certainty of any sort but security in the face of a hostile environment. We are trying to stabilize responses or adjust successfully to a hostile environment.

7. Instrumentalism—Dewey's instrumentalism also stems from his analysis of reflective inquiry. Ideas are not copies, images, or visions of external objects but rather tools or instruments to facilitate an organism's behaviour. They are instruments for operating on things or on stimuli. Things or objects are what we can do with them, and we can distinguish among them by the behaviour reactions they make possible.

Truth, accordingly, is adverbial. It is a way ideas work out in practice. It is a matter of whether hypotheses lead to predicted consequences, an affair of verified predictions warranted assertions.

Dewey's instrumentalism encourages a new respect for instruments, or means. The more we value ends or goals, on his view, the greater is our attention to the means which may bring them about. The separation of goods into natural and moral or into instrumental and intrinsic may have the harmful consequence of making moral and intrinsic goods more remote from daily living besides encouraging us to think that we can have the intrinsic without having to concern ourselves with the instrumental. Viewing any good as merely instrumental, moreover, is fairly sure not to do it justice.

8. Relativism—Dewey's relativism is to be opposed to absolutism and is a way of stressing the importance of context, situation, relationships. To take things out of relations is to deprive them of value and meaning. Absolutes are ruled out on his view, and unqualified generalizations are likely to be misleading. An economic policy or a plan of action is a good relative to a specific situation which makes it desirable. A knife may be good for sharpening pencil and bad for cutting a rope : but to speak of it without qualification as good or bad is quite misleading.

9. Meliorism—In ethics, according to Dewey's account in *Reconstruction in Philosophy,* the emphasis should be placed on improving or bettering our present situation rather than upon good or bad in some absolute sense. The good, if one is to speak of the good rather than the better, is what will enable us to solve the problem or difficulty. Thus what is usually referred to as a moral end or standard becomes on his view a hypothesis as to how to overcome a moral problem. Since every problematic situation is unique, values are also unique; but if one is to specify an end, then growth, education, or problem solving would be that end. Instead of treating acquisition of skill and attainment of culture as ends, we should see them as marks of growth and means to its continuing difficulties or furthering growth.

In the *Quest for Certainty, Dewey*'s Gifford Lectures, we find a somewhat different approach, stressing the construction of the good; and in this construction, it is argued, we have to test our likings, enjoyments and desires. We do this by checking on the conditions and the results of certain forms of enjoyment of liking, and this involves running through the steps in a complete act of reflective thinking. It is not simply a question of whether as a matter of fact we do not enjoy or like something but whether this enjoyment or liking meets the test of reflection. It is not merely enjoyed or desired but also desirable or enjoyable in the sanse of being worthy of being desired or enjoyed? When we say that something is desirable we are claiming that future consequences will be such as to meet the test of reflection.

Further discussion of Dewey's views on valuation and some of the questions growing out of his view may be found in the *Theory of Valuation*[1] and in Ray Lepley, Editor, Value : *A Co-operative Inquiry* in which Dewey, H. D. Aiken, C.E. Ayaes, A.C. Garnett, G.R. Geiger, L.E. Hahn, B.E. Jessup, H.N. Lee, Rao Lepley, E.T. Mitchell, Charles Morris, D.H. Parkar, S.C. Pepper, and P.B. Rice re-examine fundamental issue of value.

10. Humanism—Dewey's humanism stems from his acceptance of the Baconian view that knowledge is tested by promotion of human intelligence based in good part on the experience of modern science for the sake of bettering the human situation. Supernaturalism and the usual dogmas of revealed religion have no place in Dewey's view. As he tells us in *A Common Faith,* the things of greatest value in civilization exist by the grace of the continuous human community in which we are a link, and we have the responsibility of conserving, transmitting, rectifying and expanding our heritage of values of in order that those who come after us may share it more generously and more securely. Our common faith draws its main stand from our attempt to carry our his responsibility.

Dewey's humanism is expressed also in his democratic outlook. As he saw it, democracy as a way of life is controlled by a working faith in the possibilities of human nature. Granted proper conditions, and Dewey devoted a lifetime to working for them, human intelligence can work out aims and methods by which experience can grow in richness. His faith in discussion, persuasion, education and conference techniques as opposed to force or coercion as a way of resolving differences was at one with

1. *In International Encyclopedia of Uni.fied Science* **(Chicago University of Chicago press, 1939), 11 No. 4.**

his democracy or his faith in human nature. With free inquiry, free assembly, and free communication of ideas. The convinced, reflected inquiry is self-corrective.

11. Art as Experience—On Dewey's view' as set forth in *Art as Experience,* there is an aesthetic quality to all experience and not merely to works of art. His account stresses the continuity between everyday experience and art. Wherever experience is vivified, clarified, intensified and unified, we have an aesthetie experience more meaningfully, more coherently, and with greater vividness, clarity, and intensity, then daily life ordinarily mainifests. The humdrum and the routine are the chief enemies of the aesthetic. Ordinarily, we simply recognize objects for this use, but if we can have full perception of them, take in their full quality for its own sake, then we have an experience in a distinctive sense.

If any experience has the potentiality of becoming something appreciated for its own quality, moreover, human intelligence has the responsibility of applying aesthetic principles, not merely in art, but to our houses, our machine products, our cities, our highways and our general environments.

PHILOSOPHY OF EDUCATION

Most of the major theses in Dewey's general philosophy find expression in his philosophy of education. Reflective inquiry is as central for education, on his view, as for any other phase of life or experience. Indeed, for him education is a problem solving process and we learn by doing, by having an opportunity to react in real life situation. In education not indoctrination, but inquiry is focal. Not simply amassing facts priority. Education must be experimental without being simply improvisation.

The reconstructive purpose is as much at work in education as any where else in experience. As he put in *Democracy and Education,* "Education is a constant recognizing and reconstructing of experience". Present experiences must be so guided as to make future experiences more meaningful and worthwhile. Though the values and the knowledge of the past are transmitted, they must be done in such a fashion as to broaden deepen and otherwise improve them. Criticism and not simply passive acceptance is demanded.

Dewey equates education and growth. As teacher we start with the child where he now is, with his present stock of interests and knowledge and seek to help him expand and enrich both his interests and his knowledge and grow as a person in his community and his society. He learns to work responsibly for his own development and for social conditions which will encourage a similar development for all other members of his society. Education must not be simply a means to something else. It should not be merely preparation for the future. As a process of growth it should have its own enjoyable and intrinsically rewarding features at the same time that it helps further continued education, and, on Dewey's view, the test of our social institutions may be found in their effect in furthering continued education on growth.

Dewey himself had considerable reservations over some features of "progressive education, but he continued to emphasize some of the strengths of the newer education as compared with the traditional outlook. His humanism and meliorism are richly exemplified in his account of the theory and practice of education. His philosophy of education stresses the social nature of education, its intimate and multiple relations to democracy, and its cultural significance.

AIMS OF EDUCATION

According to Dewey the aim of education is he development of child's powers and abilities. It is impossible to lay down any definite principle for a particular kind of development, because this development will differ from one child to the next, in conformity with the unique abilities of the individual. The educator should guide the child according to the abilities and powers he observes in it. It is better, in Dewey's opinion, to leave the question of educational objectives unanswered. If a definite aim is ascribed to education, it may do very great harm by compelling the teacher to guide the educand in a particular direction, not in keeping with the innate abilities of the child. In general, the aim of education is to create an atmosphere in which the child gets an opportunity to be active in and contribute to the social awakening of the human race. From the pragmatic standpoint, education aims at creating social efficiency in the child. Man is a social being who must develop within the confines of society, outside which he cannot develop at all. For this reason, education must aim at creating social efficiency and skill.

Pragmatic education aims at instilling democratic values and ideals in the individual, at creating a democratic society in which there is no distinction between one individual and another, each individual is completely independent and willing to cooperate with others. Every individual must be given the freedom to develop his own desires and achieve his ambitions Every individual must be equal to every other member of society. Such a society can be created only when there is no fundamental difference between the individual and collective interest. Hence, education should create cooperation and harmony among individuals, instilling democratic values in school-going children. In fact, the school itself is a miniature form of a democratic society in which the child undergoes various form of development, of which education and development is the most important. Morality can be developed through active participation, because such participation in the activities of the school trains the child in shouldering responsibility. This develops the individual's character and grants him social skill. Equality of opportunity in the school helps to develop boys and girls according to their own individual traits and inclinations.

Pragmatic education is basically practical inasmuch as it aims at preparing the individual for future life in such a manner that he can fulfil his requirements and achieve contentment. Future life in the pragmatic sense implies not merely individual life but also social life. Dewey was critical of the contemporary modes of education because they tend to drive the child away from democratic life by giving advantages to a small section of society. It also lays more stress on book or formal teaching than is really desirable. This mode of teaching compels the education to listen long lectures which blunt his own mental powers. Hence, Dewey laid the foundations of a progressive education in the form of a Progressive School which aimed at establishing democratic values and developing the child's personality.

CURRICULUM

Dewey believed that the educational process has two aspects—psychological and social.

(a) ***Psychological***—The curriculum and the method of education should be determined by the child's instincts and abilities. The child should be educated according to his interest and inclination. Education should be attempted only after discovering the interests of the child, and these should be used as the basis for determining the curricula for the various stages of education.

(b) ***Social***—All education has its beginnings in the individual's participation in the social consciousness of the race. Hence it is necessary to create an atmosphere in the school which will allow the child to take an active part in the social awakening of his group. This improves his conduct and develops his personality and abilities.

Dewey has stressed the following four principles as underlying the formation of educational curricula—

1. Utility—The curriculum imposed on the child must have some utility, meaning thereby that the curriculum should be based on the child's interests and inclinations during various stages of his development. In general, the child evinces four major interests—the desire to talk and exchange ideas, discovery, creation and artistic expression. The curriculum should be conditioned by these four elements, and designed to include the teaching of reading and writing, counting, manual skill, science, music and other arts. It is not desirable to introduce the child to all these subjects at once, but to teach a subject only when it is desired at a particular stage of mental development.

2. Flexibility—It is better for the curriculum to be flexible and predetermined and rigid. It must be capable of accommodating the changes in the child's interests and inclinations.

3. Experiential—The curriculum should be related to the child's contemporary experiences, and these can be multiple and reinforced by presenting different kinds of activities in the guise of problems which inspire the child to attempt a solution. In this way, the variety of his experiences can be increased. As far as possible, the teaching of each subject should be related to the content of the child's experiences.

4. Close to life—As far as possible, the curriculum should include only those subject which can be related to the child's pattern of life at that particular stage. This proximity to life can help in creating a distinctive unity in the knowledge imparted to him and thereby some harmony can be created in the teaching of history, geography, mathematics and language, etc. Dewey was very critical of the contemporary method of dividing knowledge into separate compartments, because he felt that such fragmentation of knowledge was unnatural. As far as possible the various subjects in the curriculum should be harmonized.

EDUCATIONAL METHOD

Dewey, himself a successful educational psychologist, has presented many novels and useful ideas on educational methods in his two books, '*How We Think*' and *Interest and Efforts in Education*.' The most well-known principle enunciated by him is the theory of learning by doing, in which the child learns best when he himself performs action related to particular subjects. The educator is not to stuff the child's mind with information he himself has gathered throughout his life, but to guide the child to those activities by which the child can develop his own natural abilities and qualities. The child should be acquainted with facts while he is engaged in activity relating to those facts. Besides, the child should be confronted with practical difficulties and problems which he should try to solve. Problem solving is a good technique because it adds to the child's experience.

Dewey is of the opinion that there should be integration between the child's life his activities and the subjects he studies. All subjects to be taught to the child should be arranged around his activities in such a manner that he acquires knowledge in the process of doing activities to which he is accustomed. Dewey's principle was later on adopted by Mahatma Gandhi in his plan of basic education.

The next question that arises is that of designing the method of teaching according to the child's interests. Dewey considers interest and effort to be of supreme importance in the process of education. The educator must understand the child's interest before organising the activities which are useful for the child. Given the opportunity to formulate programmes on their own, children will be able to make programmes according to their own interests. It is better if this effort is free of any fear or compulsion, because only then can the children make a programme independently. Once this is done, all school activity takes on the form of self willed activity. Dewey's ideas on educational methods later on led to the evolution of the project method in which the child was made to indulge in those activities which helped in the development of enthusiasm, self-confidence, self-reliance and originality.

In a democratic educational pattern, the child should be made to participate in collective activity which can help in evolving a cooperative and social spirit.

This method of education is apparently very suitable inasmuch as it meets the requirement of educational psychology. But in fact it has one inherent shortcoming that if the education of the child is fashioned exclusively according to the child's natural inclination he will remain ignorant of many subjects. Besides, even his knowledge of other subjects will remain disorganised, objections which are accepted by Dewey himself.

SCHOOL ORGANISATION

Dewey has commented in detail upon the organisation of schools as follows—

Role of the Educator

Pragmatic education grants considerable importance to the educator, who is conceived as a servant of society. His task is to create in the school an environment which will help in the development of the child's social personality and enable the child to become a responsible democratic citizen. Dewey considers the educator to be so important that he goes so far as to call him God's representative on earth.

In determining the educator's own behaviour in the school, Dewey accepts democratic principles and educational psychology as suitable guides for shaping the educator's conduct. In order to realise the values of equality and independence in the school, the educator should not treat himself as superior to the children. He must also consciously abstain from imposing his own ideas, interests, views and tendencies on the children. He must confine his own activity to an observation of the child's own natural inclinations and personality traits, to engaging the child in suitable activities which will help in developing these traits. Hence, it is essential for the educator to pay constant attention to the individual differences of the children. If this is dine, administration of the school becomes easier. The educator must also try and engage the children in activities which compel them to think and reason out things for themselves.

Discipline

If the educator conducts himself on the lines suggested above, discipline in the school becomes easy. Difficulties arise only when discipline takes the form of an external force employed to restrains the child from expressing his natural desires. This is the traditional concept of discipline, which was serverely criticised by Dewey. He argued that discipline depends not only upon the child's own personality but also upon the social environment in which he is placed. True discipline takes the form of social control and this is evolved when the child engages in collective activity in the school. It is therefore desirable to create an atmosphere is the school which encourages the children to live in mutual harmony and cooperation. Discipline and regularity of habit can be induced in children by making them act in consonance with each other in try in to achieve a single objective. This objective may be social, moral, intellectual or purely physical. School programmes go a long way in creating the child's character. It is therefore better to provide the child with a social environment and a mode which inspire him to self-discipline rather than to subject him to long lectures. By methods such as these the child can be turned into a really social being. A peaceful atmosphere is undoubtedly conducive to good and rapid work, but peace is only a means, not an end in itself. The educator's real task is to engage the children in work which suits their natural inclination. If, in the process, the children come into conflict with each other, it is not desirable to scold them and compel them to be peaceful. Self-discipline is a better weapon, and this can be taught through responsibility. When the educand is faced with the responsibility of looking after most of the work of the college or school he automatically evolves self-discipline.

Participation in social activity is an essential part of educational training, in Dewey's opinion. The school itself is are rudimentary form of society. If the child is encouraged to take part in all collective activities in the school, he will not only be able to maintain discipline in the school, he will also be simultaneously trained for many activities he must perform in social life. Thus he will also learn to lead a disciplined life as an adult.

CRITICISM

although Dewey's views on educational principles were enthusiastically received, they were also subjected to critieism on the following grounds—

1. Difficulties of not accepting truth to be permanent— Pragmatist philosophy does not treat truth as permanent and objective. Instead, as Dewey explains, all truth is relative to time and space. No philosophy is always true or correct. It has its utility only in a particular set of circumstances. And utility is the final criterion of truth. In actual practice, of course, Dewey's philosophy is fairly useful, but when his own principles a applied to his own theories, the latter also become relative to time and space and thus have only a limited utility. Hence, he principle of pragmatism itself becomes only relatively true because it does not accept truth as something permanent.

2. Materialistic bias—Pragmatism was born out of reaction to idealism, and consequently it manifests a distinctly materialistic bias, in contradiction of the spiritual bias of idealist philosophy. At the same time, Dewey wants to realize democratic ideals of freedom, equality and fraternity through education. But it is difficult to understand how this can be done unless he accepts and idealistic basis for his system of education. If worldly success is the only criterion of truth, few if any people will concern themselves with moral superiority, since the later has no obvious relationship with material success.

3. Absence of any aim of education—The achievement of democratic ideals through education seems to be implicit in Dewey's educational philosophy, because he rerely ascribes particular aim to education in explicit terms. For him, education is life itself, and it is not possible to determine any objective for it. Most scholars disagree with this opinion because they believe that education can progress only when it has some definite aim and objective. There is always some definite purpose in sending he educand to school. And even though school resembles society in many ways, it has a distinct existence within the larger framework of society. Hence, the aims of education must be difined.

4. Excessive emphasis upon individual differences—Modern educational psychology accepts in principle that the curriculum of education must take into account the individual differences of children and that children must be educated according to their individual and unique interests and inclinations both in respect of curriculum and also of the method of teaching. While in theory this is quite acceptable, any attempts to apply it in practice lead to immediate complications. It is almost, if not completely impossible to provide a separate educational plan for every individual child in a school. It is for this reason that all schools nowadays provide a uniform pattern of education imparted in the same manner. Besides, the teacher may have to educate the educand in a subject in which the latter is not at all interested. Thus, it is not possible to eliminate many complex and difficult subjects from the curriculum only because the student is not interested in them.

5. Limitations of learning through doing—There is no doubt that the child should learn by actually doing things, as Dewey suggested yet the theory has its limitations. Many facts known to an individual are acquired from another person. It is almost impossible for one individual to experience every fact known to him. Thus, the educand should also try to benefit from the experience of his teacher, educator and colleagues. The educator must also supplement the educand's efforts at self-education with guidance and communication of his own experience.

DEWEY'S INFLUENCE ON MODERN EDUCATION

Many of Dewey's ideas have had great impact on modern education. Some important facts in this connection are—

1. Impact on the aims of education—Now a days, one of the important aims of education is the teaching of democratic values. Dewey insisted on developing social qualities in the child. In modern schools these aims of education have been accepted as valid.

2. Impact on educational methods—The greatest impact of Dewey's ideas is seen in the methods of education in more recent times. Dewey suggested that education should be based on the child's own experience, and also that the method of teaching should vary according to the interests and inclinations of each individual child. These ideas influenced modern teaching techniques and led to active teaching in schools. One such school is the Activity School. The project method is also a result of Dewey's ideas. Even in the other schools, attention is paid to the principles of child psychology which guide the educator in creating an atmosphere suitable for developing social consciousness in the educand.

3. Impact on curriculum—The impact of Dewey's ideas on the subject of curriculum led to the introduction of manual skill subjects into modern curricula. Special importance is now being attached to various kinds of games, objects, the use of certain tools and implements, etc. In selecting the subjects to be taught, attention is now paid to the individual interests and abilities of the child.

4. Impact of discipline—As a result of Dewey's theorising on the subject of discipline, now the educand is entrusted with much of the work done in the school. In this manner the educand is trained in self-control and democratic citizenship. Apart from this, once the educand has to face responsibility, he is compelled to think scientifically and reason out things for himself.

5. Universal education—Dewey's thinking and ideal also led to faith in universal and compulsory education. Education aims at the development of personality. Hence every individual must be given the opportunity to develop his personality through education. The current stress on the scientific and social tendency owes much to Dewey's influence. He pointed out that education was a social necessity, in that it was not merely a preparation for life, but life itself. It aimed at the development of both the individual as well as society. This leads to the comprehensive development of the individual.

❑❑❑

12

Swami Vivekananda

"Education in the manifestation of the perfection already in man."
—***Vivekananda***

On 12th January 1863 a child was born in the house of Vishvanath Dutt, resident of Gormohan Mukerjee Street in North Calcutta in Bengal, who was know to the world as Vivekananda. The child was named Narendra Nath. Ramakrishna, the teacher of Vivekananda called him by this name. Bhuvaneshwari Devi, the mother of Narendra Nath was a very intelligent and religious lady. She used to recite Ramayana and Mahabharata and performed her house-hold chores with a calm mind. Thus, like M.K. Gandhi, Vivekananda owed some of his religiosity to the influence of his mother.

The early education of Narendra Nath was given through Bengali and English. His mother used to tell him the stories of Ramayana and Mahabharata. The child showed special interest in Ramayana and particularly in the character of Rama. Wherever the story of Rama was recited the child Narendra Nath used to hear it with rapt attention foregetting all childhood plays. Once he meditated in a room of his house with so much rapt attention that the door of the room had to be broken to awaken him. Thus, Yogic consciousness was evident in Vivekananda from the very beginning. He used to have peculiar experiences while sleeping. In these experiences he used to feel light between the eye-brows which gradually spread throughout his body. This experience proved the spiritual power of Narendra Nath. On the other hand, the child used to commit so much childish pranks that his mother used to say that she asked for a son to Shiva but he sent a demon to him. Narendra Nath was particularly intimate with the domestic servants.

At the age of 6, Narendra Nath started going to school. Here within a year he memorised Muktibodha. He also memorised most of the portions of Ramayana and Mahabharata. After a year he was admitted to the educational institution of Ishwar Chandra Vidyasagar. His teachers here were very much impressed by his intelligence and genius and used to praise him very much. Narendra Nath was not only a good student but also a good player. He possessed sound health. In Entrance class Narendra Nath had sufficient knowledge of English and Bangla literature and Indian history. His understanding was deep and memory sharp. He could follow a writer by only reading some of the lines written by him. He could understand the subject of a book by merely reading some portions of it. He passed Entrance examination in first division. After it he entered Presidency College. Here also he very much impressed his teachers. His principal S.W. Hasti used to say that he never saw a genius like Narendra Nath. Narendra Nath had a multisided genius. At the college stage he had achieved an intimate knowledge of English literature, European history, philosophy, science, art, music and medicine.

During this period, Brahmo Samaj was very popular in Bengal. The leaders of Brahmo Samaj had wide influence over the Bengali youth. Narendra Nath was also influenced by Brahmo Samaj and became a member of it. This influence was particularly due to his intellectual outlook. He never agreed to admit a thing without understanding it. He was vehemently against superstitions. He was a staunch supporter of social reform. He had a keen desire to participate in the progress of his country. All these tendencies took him to Brahmo Samaj. However, gradually he became dissatisfied. Once he asked Devendra Thakur, the greatest leader of Brahmo Samaj, "Sir, Have you seen God". He did not receive any satisfactory answer.

During this time Ramakrishna, the priest of the Kali temple of Dakshneshwar had a name in Calcutta. He was a devotee of a high order and it is said that he realised Kali directly. He used to believe in the value of all the religious. He preached that all religions are essentially similar. The principal of the college of Narendra Nath told him about Ramakrishna. Narendra Nath went to Ramakrishna. Ramakrishna identified the spiritual powers of Narendra Nath at the very first sight. He exclaimed that here is an incarnation of Narayan who is born to remove the sufferings of mankind. On the other hand, Narendra Nath felt that Ramakrishna was a bit abnormal. However, he asked the old question. "Sir, Have you seen God?" The reply which he received was never expected. Ramakrishna told him, "Yes, I see him just as I see you here". Narendra Nath was deeply impressed but not completely satisfied. He continued to meet Ramakrishna more often and gradually came under his influence.

In 1884, the father of Narendra Nath passed away due to heart attack. At his time Narendra Nath was only a graduate and studying law. But now the entire financial responsibility of the family came upon his head. His relative used to tease his family. He did not get any job. He could not repay the debts he owed to many persons. Under these hard circumstances Narendra Nath had crisis of faith. However, the adversities, sufferings and troubles subdued his ego and evoked his faith. Like Gautama, the Buddha, he experienced that everywhere there is suffering in this world. This led him to the resolve to remove sufferings of his countrymen. This also increased his faith in Ramakrishna.

Narendra Nath received his initiation in Vedanta from Ramakrishna. Ramakrishna had extraordinary yogic powers. In 1885 he gave Narendra Nath the experience of attributeless Samadhi by his mere touch and ordered him that his first duty is to fulfil the mission of Ramakrishna. Narendra Nath was the leader of the association of the young followers of Ramakrishna. This association was founded with the purpose of spirituality and welfare of humanity. As the leader of this association, called Ramakrishna Mission, Narendra Nath propagated the views of Ramakrishna everywhere. Beloor near Howrah was made the head office of Ramakrishna Mission and the centre of its activities.

Narendra Nath was now known as Vivekananda. He extensively toured the country and tried to understand and solve its problems.

In 1888 Vivekananda left Calcutta alone. He went to Varanasi, Ayodhya, Lucknow, Agra, Vrindavan and Hathras. At Hathras he was accompanied by his disciple Sadanand. Both of them now toured Himalayas. In Himlayas Vivekananda had a vision of the soul of India. After a year Vivekananda again toured several places within the country including Gazipur and Varanasi. In February 1891 he went to Rajasthan, Bombay and Rameshwaram. From Rameshwaram he went to Kanyakumari. There he sat on a rock in the sea and had his realisation of the great unity of India. At present there is on this rock the world famous Vivekananda Memorial.

In 1883 Vivekananda heard that a Parliament of Religions was being organised in Chicago in U.S.A. He decided to participate in this parliament in order to give his message to the World. He was very much pained by the poverty of India and wanted to draw the attention of the West towards this problem. This was one of the important purposes of his visit of U.S.A. Before going to U.S.A. he went to Khetri, the king of this state was his disciple. It was this princely disciple who suggested the name of Swami Vivekananda which was adopted by Narendra Nath.

On May 31, 1893 Swami Vivekananda left Bombay for U.S.A. In the way he went to Ceylon, Penong, Singapore, Hong Kong, Kentan and Nagasaki. Seeing the influence of Indian culture and Sanskrit language at all these places he realised the spiritual unity of Asia. He reached Chicago in mid-July. Seeing the spectacular progress of knowledge and science at U.S.A., he was highly impressed. After twelve days he reached the information office of the proposed parliament of Religions. He was told that the Parliament will be held in the first week of September and his name cannot be included in the list of delegates unit it is recommended by someone in U.S.A. or elsewhere. Vivekananda sent a telegram to his friends to Madras for recommendation but got no success. However, the genius like Vivekananda hardly needed any introduction. His personality was his best certificate. While travelling in the train at Boston Swami Vivekananad met a rich lady of Messachusetts. She called him at her residence and introduced him to Professor J.H. Wright of the department of Greek studies at the Harward University. Wright was very much impressed by Vivekananda and introduced him to Dr. Bros, the chairman of the selection committee of the delegates by writing, "Here is a person who is a greater scholar than all our scholar professors added together." He insisted that Vivekananda should be admitted as the representative of Hinduism at the Parliament of Religions. He also gave Vivekananda rail ticket to Chicago and a letter of recommendation of lodging and boarding. Unfortunately Vivekananda lost these papers during the journey. However, these were received by a lady G.W. Hale who contracted Vivekananda and took him to the Parliament, where he was respectfully admitted as a delegate and arrangements of his stay were made along with other representative form the East.

The Parliament of Religions was inaugurated on 11th September 1883 at Columbus Hall. Religious leader of the world had gathered there to hear Swami Vivekananda in the evening of the first day. They welcomed by prolonged clapping the first words of Vivekananda, "American brothers and sisters." Leaving all formalities of the Parliament Swami Vivekananda presented his ideas in such a direct and clear language that the Parliament was very much impressed. After it he delivered a dozen lectures in U.S.A. which made him famous in the West. New York Herald proclaimed him as the greatest person at the Parliament of Religions and wrote that after hearing him we feel that how much foolish it is to send relgiious missionaires to the nation of such a great scholar. During his lectures Swami Vivekananda repeatedly drew the attention of the West to the problems of India. On the invitation of Bureau he visited several places in U.S.A. and delivered lectures, which had wide influence over Americal intelligentsia. He was offered the headship of department of Eastern philosophy at Harvard University and Sanskrit language at Columbia University which he declined saying that he was a Sanyasin.

On 7th August, 1895 Swami Vivekananda left U.S.A. for

England. The British newspapers compared him to Raja Ram Mohan Roy, Keshabchandra Sen and even Gautama the Buddha. He was welcomed by the heads of various churches and he delivered several lectures on Jnanayoga in London particularly became famous.

On 6th December, 1895 Swami Vivekananda reached New York from England. Here he delivered lectures on Karmayoga and Bhaktiyoga at the residence of Miss S. E. Waldo who later on became his disciple known as Hari Dasi. Vivekananda delivered lectures idn a very informal but influential style. Gradually, the number of his American disciples increased. In February 1896 he laid the foundation of the famous Vedanta Society of New York. He also delivered lectures on Vedanta philosophy in the philosophy department of Harward University. His lecture here on 25th March, 1896 was so impressive that he was offered the chair of Eastern philosophy. Swami Vivekananda had no financial difficulty as he was receiving overwhelming co-operation from all sides.

In April 1896 Swami Vivekananda left America for England and in the month of May delivered 5 lectures per week on Vedanta. He delivered three lectures, at Royal Institute of Painters, Picaddelli. He also spoke at Princess Hall, Annie Besant Lodge and other well-known Clubs and Educational Institutions. Max Muller invited him to his residence at Oxford and was very much influenced by him. From England Swami Vivekananda went to Switzerland on the persuasion of some of his friends. In August 1896 he was invited by Professor Paul Deussen of Kiel University of Germany. Deussen was very much impressed by Vivekananda and accompanied him on his return journey to London. Vivekananda stayed in London for next few months and then left for India with two of his disciples Mr. and Mrs. Sevier.

When Vivekananda reached India he was given a tumultous welcome. A meeting of the disciples of Ramakrishna was called on 1st May, 1897 at Bagh Bazar in Calcutta at the residence of Mr. Balram Bose. Vivekananda explained the problems of the country before this gathering and pleaded for their remedies. The meeting accepted his proposal and Ramakrishna Mission was established on May 5, 1897 with the express mission of serving humanity through the service of followers of various religions. It aimed at trainee missionaries who could propagate Vedanta everywhere. The programme of the mission was entrusted to two department, Indian and Western. Swami Vivekananda was elected president of the mission and Swami Yoganand and Swami Brahmanand were elected Vice-President and president of Calcutta Branch of the Mission respectively.

As president of Ramakrishna Mission Swami Vivekananda toured the whole of the country. He went to historical place in North India, Punjab, Kashmir and Rajasthan. Everywhere he propagated the preachings of the Mission and clarified the problems of the country asking for remedies. His ideas were a combination of Vedanta and science, East and West, ancient and modern, idealism and realism. He discussed the plan of establishment of branch of mission at Kashmir with the king of Kashmir. On 30th March, 1898 he reached Darjeeling but left for Calcutta in April to serve the people suffering from plague epidemic. The service rendered by follows of Ramakrishna Mission to the suffering people of Calcutta was a rare example. However, some members of Ramakrishna Mission did not agree with the precept of Swami Vivekananda about public service. Some of them even remarked that Vivekananda did not go to America for propagation of preaching of Ramakrishana but for his own propaganda. These and other instances shocked Swami Vivekanands.

In order to provide a centre in the Himalayas for practising Vedanta Philosophy by his disciples from East and West, Vivekananda established Advaita Ashram at Mayavati, 50 miles away from Almora on 19th March, 1899. It was at this centre that the chief organ of Ramakrishna Mission came out under the title *Prabudha Bharata.* Besides Advaita Ashram Swami Vivekananda established several other centres of public service in various parts of the country.

On 20th June 1899 Swami Vivekananda again left for West with his disciples Sister Nivedita and Swami Turiyanand. During the course of his journey he established centres at San Francisco,

Aukland and Alamada. He saw symptoms of destruction of humanity in the technological advance of West, which he discussed latter on his various lectures. He returned to Beloor in India on 24th January, 1901, and went to Mayavati Ashram. He also toured other centres of the country. This herculean labour for the propagation of his preachings gradually adversely affected his physical health. He suffered from diabetes and lung diseases. Gradually his condition worsened. On the insistence of his several disciples, he stayed at Beloor for 7 months and transferred all his responsibilities to his disciples. But his keen desire to serve humanity did not allow him rest. Therefore, he went to Bodh Gaya on the insistence of Japanese Artist Okakura. From there he went to Varanasi and established a centre of Ramakrishna Mission there. All this tour adversely affected his health. He used to say, "I will not live for seeing 40." This happened. On 4th July, 1902 Swami Vivekananda left for his heavenly abode at the early age of 39 years.

CRITICISM OF PREVALENT EDUCATIONAL SYSTEM

In the Neo-Vedanta humanistic tradition of contemporary Indian thought, Vivekananda presented a philosophy of education for man-making. Among the contemporary Indian philosophers of education he is one of those who revolted against the imposition of British system of education in India. He was severely critical of the pattern of education introduced by the British in India. He felt that the current system of education did not confirm to India's culture. He pointed out that such an education only brings about an external change without any profound inner force.

Against the contemporary educational system the chief objection raised by Vivekananda was that it turned men into salves, capable of slavery and nothing else. About the prevailing university education, he remarked that it was not better than an efficient machine for rapidly turning out clerks. It deprived people of their faith and belief. The English educated people believed that *Gita* was false and the *Vedas* were no more significant than rural folklore. Criticising this system of education Vivekananda compared it to the person who wanted to turn his ass into a horse, was advised to thrash the ass in order to achieve this transformation and killed his ass in the process. Vivekananda also criticised the contemporary system of education from the humanistic viewpoint. He was a humanist and pleaded for education for man-making. Such was not the education propounded by the British. Therefore, Vivekananda condemned it. He remarked, "It is not a man-making education, it is merely and entirely a negative education. A negative education or any training that is based on negation, is worse that death. The child is taken to school, and the first thing he learns is that his father is a fool, the second thing that his grandfather is lunatic, the third thing that all his teachers are hypocrities, the fourth, that all the sacred books are lies. By the time he is sixteen he is a mass of negation, lifeless and boneless. And the result is that fifty years of such education has not produced one original man in the three presidencies. Every man of originality that has been produced has been educated elsewhere, and not in this country, or they have gone to the old universities once more to cleanse themselves of superstitions."[1]

AIMS OF EDUCATION

1. Self-development—In contrast to the contemporary system of education Vivekananda advocated education for self-development. He said, "By education I do not mean the present system, but something in the line of positive teaching. Mere book learning won't do. We want that education by which character is formed, strength of mind is increased, the intellect is expanded and by which one can stand on one's own feet. What we want are Western science coupled with Vedanta, *Brahmacharya* as the guiding motto, and also *Shraddha*, and faith in one's own self."[2] These words by Vivekananda represent the characteristic India definition of education. Education according to most of the Western educationists aims at man's adjustment with the environment. According to the Indian philosophical tradition, on the other hand, education is the realisation of the knowledge

---

1. ***Swami Vivekananda on India and Her Problems*, p. 48.**
2. ***Ibid.*, p. 51**

inherent in man. True knowledge does not come from outside, it is discovered with the individual, in the self which is the source of all knowledge. To quote Vivekananda again, "All knowledge that the world has ever received comes from the mind; the infinite library of the universe is in your mind. The external world is only the suggestion, the occasion, which sets you to study your mind. The falling of the apple gave suggestion to Newton, and he studied his own mind. He rearranged all the precious links of thought in his mind and discovered a new link among them which we call the Law of Gravitation."[1] Thus,, according to Vivekananda, the function of education is the uncovering of the knowledge hidden in our mind. Education is the process of self-development. In the words of Vivekananda, "You cannot teach a child any more than you can grow a plant. The plant develops its own nature."[2] A person's education is not judged by the number of books he has read but by the thickness of the cover of ignorance on his mind. The thicker is this cover, the greater is the ignorance. As the light of knowledge dawns this cover of ignorance gradually shatters. The teacher's job is to uncover knowledge by his guidance. His guidance makes the mind active and the educand himself unveils the knowledge lying within him.

2. Fulfilment of Swadharma—Vivekananda supported the idea of *Swadharma* in education. Every one has to grow like himself. No one has to copy others. It is hence that he condemned the imposition of foreign education. He asked, "Getting by heart the thoughts of others in a foreign language and stuffing your brain with them and taking some university degree, you can pride yourself as educated. Is this education?" True improvement is self-inspired. There should be no external pressure of any type on the child. External pressure only creates destructive reaction leading to obstinacy and indiscipline. In an atmosphere of freedom, love and sympathy alone, the child will develop courage and self-reliance. He should not be unnecessarily checked in his activities. The educator should no constantly tell him to do this or that. Such

---

1. Vivekananda, *Complete Works* (1984, Vol. I, p. 28.)

2. *Ibid.*, Vol. II, p. 324.

negative directions tend to blunt his intelligence and mental development. He should be talked to stand on his own, to be himself. This is so since as Vivekananda suggests, "if you do not allow once to become a lion, he will become a fox."[2] Therefore, education should be modified to suit the individual child. Each child should be given opportunities to develop according to his own inner nature.

3. Freedom of Growth—Thus Vivekananda is against any type of external pressure upon the child. He is a staunch champion of freedom in education. Freedom is the first requirement for self-development. The child should be given freedom to grow, according to his own nature. In the words of Vivekananda, "You cannot teach a child any more than you can grow a plant. All you can do is on the negative side—you can only help. You can take away the obstacles, but knowledge comes out of its own nature. Loosen the soil a little, so that it may come out easily. Put a hedge around it, see that it is not killed by anything, and there your work stops. You cannot do anything else. The rest is a manifestation from within its own nature."[3] The teacher should not exert any type of pressure on the child. The child should be helped in solving his problems himself. The teachers should have an attitude of service and worship. Education ultimately aims at realization. It is a means to the establishment of fraternity of mankind.

4. Character Formation—Character is the solid foundation for self-development. The aim of education as self-development, therefore, leads to the aim of education for character. Defining character, Vivekananda said, "The character of any man is but the aggregate of his tendencies, the sum total of the bent of his mind. As pleasure and pain pass before his soul, they leave upon it different pictures and the result of these combined impressions is what is called a man's characther."[4] The aim of education is character

1. *Ibid.,* Vol. III, p. 146.
2. *Ibid.,* p. 20.
3. *Centenary Volume,* p. 474.
4. Vivekananda, *Complete Works,* Vol. I, p. 25.

building. This depends upon the ideals cherished by the individual. The educator should present high ideals before the educands. The best way to develop a character is the personal example of high character set by the teacher. Laying emphasis upon this point Vivekananda said, "Without the personal life of the teacher there would be no education. One would live from his very boyhood with one whose character is like a blazing fire, and should have before him a living example of the highest teaching.... The charge of imparting knowledge should again fall upon the shoulders of *tyagis*."[1] In ancient Indian system of education the teachers used to present high ideals, before the pupils, who in their turn imitated these ideals according to their capacities. Following things are required for character formation—

(i) ***Hard Work***—Character formation, according to Vivekananda, requires hard work. This is not possible by those who have a wish for all types of enjoyments. Struggle is the best teacher in character building. Activity and *purushartha* are the signs of life. Inactivity shows absence of vitality. While living in all types of comforts and escaping from all types of labour, no one can build up high character.

(ii) ***Moral and Spiritual Values***—Besides hard work, character formation requires traits such as purity, thirst for knowledge, perseverance, faith, humility, submission and veneration, etc. These qualities may be developed by the teacher's example and the pupil's efforts. According to Vivekananda, "Without faith, humility, submission and veneration in our hearts towards the teacher, there cannot be any growth in us. In those countries which have neglected to keep up this kind of relation, the teacher has become a mere lecturer, the teacher expecting his five dollars and the person taught expecting his brain to be filled with the teacher's words and each going his own way after this much is done. The true teacher is he who can

1. *Swami Vivekananda on India and Her Problems*, p. 57.

immediately come down to the level of the student and transfer his soul to the student's soul and see through and understand through his mind."[1]

(iii) ***Gurukula System***—Such a relationship between the teacher and the taught is possible only in a Gurukula system of education. Therefore, Vivekananda favoured the ancient Indian Gurukula system of education. In these Gurukulas the pupils served the teacher, who in his turn, helped the pupils everywhere to achieve knowledge. There was hardly any economic relationship between the teacher and the taught, which is the curse of the present system of education.

(vi) ***Formation of Good Habits***—Character is intimately connected with habits. Habits express character. Good habits make for good character. While the contemporary psychologists admit that value of habits in one's life, Vivekananda has pointed out the value of habits on only in this life but in lives to come. A bad habit may be broken by developing the opposite good habit. If a man constantly thinks that he will be courageous and progressive, the may develop confidence for breaking bad habits. It is not the teacher nor the guardian who may reform the habit of a person but only the himself. Man is caught in the net of his own *Karmas* from which he alone can get out, no one else can directly help him. Our own self in us is our best guide in the struggle that is life.

(v) ***Learning Through Mistakes***—The child should be allowed to commit mistakes in the process of character formation. He will learn much by his mistakes. Errors are the stepping stones to our progress in character. This progress requires courage and strong will. Strong will is the sign of great character. Will makes men great. Therefore, there is no occasion to be discouraged or two weep, one

1. *Ibid.*, p. 58

should exercise his will and he will see that things, which he considered to be impossible, become easy and possible. Vivekananda himself was an ideal teacher. His words worked like magic upon men and women. This is possible only in the case of a teacher who has himself risen high. Presenting his own example, Vivekananda asked the people to build up their character and manifest their real nature, which is the Effulgent, the Resplendent and the Ever Pure.

MEANS OF EDUCATION

1. Love—The best means of education, according to Vivekananda is love. Education should be based upon love. Love is best inspiration in character building. The child should be taught through love. This is love for men, for human beings. The only motive in imparting education should be love for the educand, for the man in him. That is why Vivekananda's philosophy of education is known as education for man-making. The teacher's aim should be neither money making nor attainment of fame but only bestowing human love. The spiritual force work through love. This love within the educator is the real source of his influence upon the educand. This may be amply clear by the example of the relationship of Vivekananda with his Guru Ramakrishna. It was the force of spiritual love in Ramakrishna, which helped Vivekananda in God realization. It is this, which makes the educator to take the educand from untruth to truth, darkness to light, death to immortality.

2. Help— The task of educator is to help the educand in manifesting and expressing his abilities and capacities. Educator should help the individual to recognise his cultural heritage and to use it in his struggle of life. The educator can guide the educand because he himself has the experience of treading on this path and knows how to face its difficulties. Vivekananda has not only presented high deals of education but also developed a 'sound system by which these ideals may be achieved.'

3. Guidance—Education is not a bed of roses. Every educand has to face problems peculiarly his own. He solves them by his own efforts and with the guidance of the teacher. The skilled teacher guides the pupil through these difficulties and takes him forward. This requires a sufficient knowledge of human psychology because most of our problems are psychological in nature. The teacher should teach the educand to concentrate his attention, only then can the problems be solved. The greater the attention, the more is the effort effective.

4. Concentration—Concentration, according to ancient Indian though, is the key to true knowledge. Therefore, Vivakananda has placed much emphasis upon focusing of attention. It is only after years of concentration that a man becomes a scholar and a great scientist. The educands should be distinguished according to their abilities, every one of them has to develop concentration. Again, while teaching concentration the educator should keep in mind the varying abilities of concentration is spontaneous and easy, for others it is difficult and requires long training. Hence, the educator must organise his teaching in such a way that he may be helpful to each educand separately. He should attend to every one's difficulties and try to solve them as much as possible. Thus, Vivekananda supported the ancient Indian means of achieving concentration.

5. Brahmacharya—Again, according to ancient Indian thinkers, Brahmacharya or abstinence is the first means of achieving concentration. It gives mental and spiritual powers of the highest kind. It transforms sex drive into a spiritual force. *Brahmacharya* implies purity of thought, deed and action. It helps to improve and sharpen various psychological processes such as learning, remembering, thinking, etc. It helps in achieving power of memory and improve the powers of the mind. Vivekananda therefore strongly emphasized the need for the students to observe *Brahmacharya*. This leads to both mental and physical advantages. Firstly, it takes effective care of all distractions. Secondly, it improves the body and the mind so that they may become effective means of knowledge.

6. Discussion and Contemplation—In addition to

concentration the other means of education are discussion and contemplation. It is only through these that the educand may remove his difficulties. Discussion should be carried out in an informal atmosphere. Contemplation should be practised in a clam and quiet atmosphere with the mind fully alive. In the end the educational process requires faith and reverence of the educand in the teacher and his teachings. Without faith and reverence no true knowledge can be achieved. It is faith and reverence, which are sound foundation for all character development and self-education. The faith and reverence, however, depend not only upon the educand but also upon the high examples by the teacher. In the educational process, therefore, the teacher also occupies a very high place.

MEDIUM OF EDUCATION

1. Mother Tongue—In teaching language Vivekananda laid particular stress upon teaching through the mother tongue. Here he is supported by all other contemporary Indian philosophers of education.

2. Common Language—Besides mother tongue, there should be a common language, which is necessary to keep the country united. This may be taught in addition to the regional languages.

3. Sanskrit—The teaching of Sanskrit forms an important part of the curriculum envisaged by Vivekananda. Sanskrit is the source of all Indian languages and a repository of all inherited knowledge. It is, therefore, absolutely necessary that every Indian should know Sanskrit. Vivekananda appreciated the greatness of Sanskrit in eloquent words when he said that this language granted power, ability and prestige to the nation and that our awareness of our cultural heritage and past greatness depends very much upon our knowledge of this language. He felt that in the absence of this knowledge, it will be impossible to understand Indian culture. If the society has to develop and progress it is necessary that men and women should know this language which is the storehouse of ancient heritage, besides the knowledge of the mother tongue.

TYPES OF EDUCATION

Vivekananda elaborately discussed the teaching methods in physical, moral and religious education. This discussion gives an idea, of types of education as well as methods of teaching.

1. Physical Education—Vivekananda laid particular stress on the value of physical education in curriculum. He said, "You will be nearer to Heaven through football than through the study of *Gita*. You will understand *Gita* better by your biceps, your muscles a little stronger. You will understand the *Upanishads* better and the glory of the *Atman,* when your body stands firm on your feet and you feel yourself as man."[1] Self-realisation or character building is impossible in the absence of physical education. One must know the secret of making the body strong through physical education, for a complete education it is necessary to develop both mind and the body. Vivekananda himself took physical exercise every day. He glorified power and opposed weakness in any form. Power was happiness and weakness a never-ending burden. It is hence that he so such emphasised the importance of physical education particularly for young men and women.

2. Moral and Religious Education—Laying emphasis upon religious education Vivekananda said, "Religion is the innermost core of education. I do not mean my own or any one else's opinion about religion. Religion is as the rice and everything else, like the curries. Taking only curries causes indigestion, and so is the case with taking rice alone."[2] Therefore, religious education is a vital part of a sound curriculum. This religious education is necessary in order to counter effect the evil influence of modern materialism. It is only by synthesis of religion and science that man may reap the advantages of both. As has been already pointed out, religious

---

1. **Vivekananda, *Complete Works,* Vol. III, p. 242.**
2. ***Ibid.,* Vol. IV, p. 358.**

education in itself is never sufficient. It should not be the whole of curriculum but only a part of it. This religion, again, is not any particular dogma or sectarian philosophy, in fact, it is what Tailor called religion of man. It is hence that Vivekananda did not distinguish between secular and religious education. He thought that the former may be given by the latter. He said, "We have to give them secular education. We have to follow the plan laid down by our ancestors, that is, to bring all the ideals slowly down among the masses. Raise them slowly up, raise them to equality. Impart....secular knowledge through religion."[1]

(i) ***High Ideals***—The best way of imparting religious education is to present the high ideals of saints and religious men before the students. They should be taught to worship saints to follow their ideals. Among the great souls, Vivekananda pointed out to Ram Chandra, Krishna, Mahavir and Ramakrishna. In the ideal of Sri Krishna he laid more emphasis on his personality as the author of *Gida*. He said, "Keep aside for the present the Vrindavan aspect of Sri Krishna and spread far and wide the worship of Sri Krishna roaring out the *Gita* with the voice of a lion; and bring into daily use the worship of *Shakti* the Divine Mother, the source of all power. We now mostly need the ideal of the hero with the tremendous spirit of *rajas* thrilling through his veins from head to foot, the hero who will dare and die to know the truth, the hero whose armour is renunciation, whose sword is wisdom; we want the spirit of the brave warrior in the battlefield."[2]

(ii) ***Courage***—Thus, Vivekananda wanted men and women to develop qualities according to their particular sex and their role in society. He asked young men to develop manly qualities. Even in religious practices he considered courage to be a higher quality. Religion is not mere ritualism. It is a progress towards high ideals in the face of extreme difficulties.

1. *Swami Vivekananda on India and Her Problems.* p. 71.
2. Vivekananda, *Complete Works,* Vol. I, p. 303.

(iii) ***Service and Devotion***—Besides courage, Vivekananda prescribed service and devotion in religious education. For this purpose he eulogised the ideal of Hanuman who was living example of service, devotion and courage. He deplores the dramatic imitation of *Ras Lila* because it is against the interest of the country at present. Purity is the real basis of the country at present. Even in music Vivekananda advised young men to adopt manly music so that it may infuse bravery and courage. This, however, does not mean that Vivekananda rejected any particular type of religious practice. He only wanted to adopt religious practices according to the needs of the times. India, according to him, today needs a religion, which should be harmonious with science and teach patriotism, service and sacrifice. Then alone religious education may be useful to the nation. Religion influences total man. It encourages all types of qualities, soft as well as virile. Vivekananda emphasised the inculcation of the latter type of virtues. He exhorted young men by saying, "Never allow weakness to overtake your mind. Remember Mahavir, remember the Divine Mother, and you will see that all weakness, all cowardice will vanish at once."[1]

(iv) ***Self-confidence***—It goes without saying that such a moral and religious education will develop self-confidence among young men and women. Self-confidence, according to Vivekananda, is the real religion. It includes world brotherhood and love of humanity, because a person having self-confidence means having confidence in humanity. Thus, Vivekananda's religion was humanistic. Religion is the source of all powers. It is again, the source of all good. Thus, for vivekananda, ethics and religion are one and the same. God is always on the side of goodness. To fight for goodness is therefore service of God. Weakness is the source of all evils. It is at the root of all violence, hatred

1. ***Ibid.*, p. 232.**

and enmity. If a man sees his own self everywhere he need not fear any one. Fearlessness and power are eternal truths, the real nature of the self.

(v) ***Realisation of Truth***—Thus, Vivekananda pleaded for realisation of trugh through religious practices. Long before Gandhiji identified truth with God, Vivekananda called truth God. The seeker after truth should search for it in every aspect of life. Truth is power, untruth is weakness. Knowledge is truth, ignorance is untruth. Thus, truth increases power, courage and energy. It is light giving. It is, therefore, necessary for the individual as well as collective welfare.

(vi) ***Achievement of Power***—Thus Vivekananda worshipped power. This power, however, was not physical or biological as that of Nietzche. It was spiritual power. Rising high in the tradition of Vedanta, Vivekananda never allowed his feet to leave the solid ground. His teachings influenced the West where materialism was rampant. This was due to the reason that his teachings were based upon universal truths. Modern man is not prepared to leave the world. He wants to enjoy it. Vivekananda, therefore, gave a practical garb to his religion. India in his time was groaning under slavery. Vivekananda, therefore, asked Indian men and women to shed all types of weakness and to march forward courageously. According to him we have to speak less and work more, achieve power first than anything else. To quote Vivekananda, "First of all our young men and must be strong. Religion will come afterwards."[1]

(vii) ***Study of Scriptures***—In the curriculum for religious education, Vivekananda considered *Gita*, *Upanishads* and the *Vedas* as the most important. The study of these scriptures will fill young men and women with courage. These are the eternal sources of the life force of Indian

---

1. ***Ibid.*, Vol. III, p. 242.**

culture. These are the bases of our spiritual education. Vivekananda, however, was not in favour on preaching any particular religious dogmas. Religion for him was self-realisation. Temples, mosques, churches and synagogues do not make religion. Religion is divinization. It is not intellectual development but transformation of total man. It is nothing if it does not teach us service and sacrifice. It is the basis for character formation. It should lead to man-making. In tune with his Guru Ramakrishna, Vivekananda pleaded for unity of world religions. He considered all religions to be equal. A true religion cannot be limited to a particular place or time. The religious books, teachers and institutions are eternal. Their ancient forms are worshipped and their modern forms are respected. Thus, in his moral and religious education Vivekananda pleaded for the education of unity of world religions.

3. Education for Weaker Section of Society—Vivekananda respected human individuality, everywhere and pleaded for freedom for everyone. "Each soul", according to him, "is potentially divine. The goal is to manifest external and internal. Do this, either by work, or worship, or psychic centre or philosophy by one or more or all of these—and before. This is the whole of religion. Doctrines or dogmas, rituals or books, temples or forms are secondary details."[1] It was due to his devotion for the poor and backward people that Vivekananda wanted to make education an instrument for the uplift of the masses. Like Gandhiji after him, Vivekananda, throughout his life, worked for the uplift of backward classes. He pleaded for universal education so that these backward people may fall in line with others. He said, "A nation is advanced in proportion as education and intelligence is spread among the masses. The chief causes of India's ruin have been the monopolising of the whole education among masses."[2] Thus, education should spread

1. *Ibid.*, Vol. I, p. 129.
2. *Ibid.*, Vol. IV, p. 415.

to every household in the country, to factories, playing grounds and agricultural fields. If the children do not come to the school the teacher should reach them. Two or three educated men should team up, collect all the paraphernalia of education and should go to the village to impart education to the children. Thus, Vivekananda favoured education for different sections of society, rich and poor, young and old, male and female.

4. Education of women—In the education for women Vivekananda laid particular stress on chastity and fearlessness. He conceived an ideal institution for women known as Math where literature and religion may be taught. Pointing out to the curricula in this institution he said, "Other matters such as sewing, culinary art, rules of domestic work and upbringing of children will also be taught while *Japa* worship and meditation, etc. shall from an indispensable part of the teaching. The duty of the teaching in school ought to devolve in every respect on educated widows and *Brahmacharinis*. It is good to avoid in this country any association of men with women's school."[1] Thus, he presented a comprehensive curricula for women so that they may develop high character, courage and confidence. He presented the ideal of Sita and lamented that modern Indian women are imitating Western ideals, which had led to all-round degeneration. Like males he advised femalses also to observe *Brahmacharya* which is a solid foundation for any type of education. He was extremely sorry for the lowly condition of Indian women. He considered women to be the incarnation of power and asked men to respect them in every way. He pointed out that unless Indian women secure a respectable place in this country, the nation can never march forward. The regeneration of Indian women, according to him, depends upon proper education. Women's education should be in the hands of women. Clarifying his scheme in this connection he said, "After five or six years' training in this 'Math', the guardians of the girls may marry them. It deemed fit for 'Yoga' and religious life, with the

1. ***Swami Vivekananda on India and Her Problems,* p. 100**

permission of their guardians they will be allowed to stay in this Math, taking the vow of celibacy. These celibate nuns will be in time be the teachers and preachers of the Math. In villages and towns they will open centres and strive for the spread of female education. Through such devout preachers of character there will be the real spread of female education in this country.... Spirituality, sacrifice and self-control will be the motto of the pupils of this Math, and service or 'Seva Dharma' the vow of their life .... If the life of the women of this country be moulded in such fashion, then only will there be the re-appearance of such ideal characters of Sita, Savitri and Gargi."[1]

CONTRIBUTION OF VIVEKANANDA

Our discussion about Vivekananda's concept of the aims and ideals of education, its process and curriculum has made it amply clear that he was a humanist in the true sense of the term. He said, "Look upon every man, woman and every one as God. Blessed you are that this privilege was given to you when other had it not. Do it only as a worship. The only God to worship is the human soul in the human body. Of course, all animals are temples to, but man in the highest, the Taj Mahal of temples. If I cannot worship in that, no other temple will be of any advantage."[2] Vivekananda's humanism, however, was different from naturalistic humanism. It is in this background that his education for man-making should be understood. Man according to him, is the highest of all living being so much so that according to Vivekananda even the angels will have to come down again and again for salvation through a human body.

The educational ideals advocated by Vivekananda have been supported by most of the modern Western educationists. Education today is defined as the process of all-round development of the child. Such a development can take place only from within while the external environment provides

1. *Ibid.*, p. 101.
2. *Vivekananda, Complete Works*, Vol. I, p. 321.

occasion for such development. The teacher has to provide the environment so that the child may become aware of the treasure of knowledge lying buried in his mind. Modern psychologists point out that in every individual there are certain dormant powers, which have to be developed through education. The teacher's real job is to see that there should be no impediments in the child's path to self-development. He is like a gardener who prepares ground for the growth of his plants, protects them and nourishes them so that the plant may grow property. the teacher takes care of the child, provides him a suitable environment and looks after his proper growth. Thus, though education comes from within the teacher is an indispensable part of it. While the motivation comes from within the teacher activates it. He encourages the child to use his mind, body and sense organs. Thus, Vivekananda presented a positive system of education. He wrote, "Education is the manifestation of the perfection already in man. I look upon religion as the innermost core of education."[1] In his philosophy of education Vivekananda synthesised spiritual and material values. He felt that India needed a system of education based on the ancient Vedanta but at the same time worthy of making individual earn his livelihood so that the country may progress. He maintained that no profession is bad provided it is done with a sense of service and self-sacrifice. It is the absence of this dignity of labour, which is responsible for the degraded condition of this country. Long before M.K. Gandhi, Vivekananda pleaded for the worship of God in poor. He said, "So long as the millions lie in hunger and ignorance, I hold every man a traitor who having been educated at their expense pay not the least heed to them."[2] He asked young men to change the situation. He pleaded for universal, compulsory and free education. He asked the educator to reach every village and every hutment so that the country may awake from ignorance.

❑❑❑

1. *Ibid.,* Vol. IV, p. 358.
2. *Ibid.,* Vol. V, p. 45.

13

Sri Aurobindo

"Education to be complete must have five principal aspects relating to the true principal abilities of the human being: the physical, the vital, the mental, the psychic and the spiritual."

—Sri Aurobindo

After the war of independence in 1857, the seventh decade saw the birth of three great men in India: Vivekananda, Sri Aurobindo and M.K. Gandhi. Thus the birth of Sri Aurobindo marked an era of upheaval in national consciousness and its effort to reassert itself. A significant point about his date of birth was that in future India achieved freedom on the same date. Sri Aurobindo was born on 15th August 1872 at Kon Nagar village of the Hoogli District of West Bengal. His father Krishna Dhan Ghosh was a well-known civil surgeon who studied medical science in England and returned to India as a totally Western-oriented gentleman. His mother Mrs. Swarnlata Devi was a religious Hindu lady. Dr. Ghosh was convinced of the value of Western system of education. Therefore, sent his sons to an Irish Missionary School at Darjeeling. He went to England in 1879 and took his sons along with him. They were kept under the supervision of Mr. and Mrs. Drevet's in London their early education. In 1885, the Drevet's left England for Australia and Sri Aurobindo was admitted to St. Paul School of London.

At St. Paul London

The headmaster of St. Paul School, F.W. Walker gave specialised training in Greek language to Sri Aurobindo who progressed fast to higher classes. During the years 1884 to 1889 Sri Aurobindo achieved specialised knowledge in Greek and Latin languages and won several award. Besides, he also studied English and French literature. He also learnt Italian, German and Spanish languages. Thus he mastered half a dozen European Languages and through them acquired knowledge of European culture in original.

At Kings College, Cambridge

In 1890, Sri Aurobinod passed the last examination of St. Paul with merit and now joined King's College of Cambridge. Here he qualified in written examination of I.C.S. and stood XI in merit achieving highest marks in ancient languages. He, however, got himself disqualified in horse riding since he never aimed at the career of a bureaucrat. It was only due to the wish of his father that he appeared in I.C.S. examination. In Cambridge, he passed tripos in two years in first division and won awards in English literature.

Political Influence

Dr. Krishan Dhan Ghosh not only educated his three sons in Europe but he kept them scrupulously free from Indian influence. However, when he returned from England to India and passed some years here, his attitude towards British changed. Now he used to send cuttings to the British atrocities on Indians published in English paper *Begalee* in India. He also criticised British government in his letters. Thus, it was the father of Sri Aurobindo who for the first time attracted his attention to the Indian politics though he could not imagine that his son, brought up in Europe, will some day lead this country.

Patriotic Influence

In 1891, Indian Majlis was established in Cambridge. Sri Aurobindo was attached to this organisation and also acted as its Secretary. He participated in its discussions and used to deliver revolutionary lectures against the British government. Some more enthusiastic young Indians founded a secret organisation in

Cambridge named "The Lotus and Dagger." Sri Aurobindo and his two brothers all three joined this organisation. Each member of this organisation had to take a vow to fight for India's freedom and act to achieve this aim. Though this organisation could not achieve much, it played a significant role in achieving Sri Aurobindo's contact with the secret organisations in India. In his ideal of freedom Sri Aurobindo was also inspired by several European freedom movements and their leaders. He was particularly impressed by the national movement in Ireland and the biography of Mazzini. In 1891, when the Irish national leader Parlance died Sri Aurobindo wrote a poem in his memory. His poems during this period reflect an intense sentiment of patriotism. In 1896, three years after his return to India, he wrote a poem on Ireland, which showed deep impression of Irish national movement on his mind.

Return to India

In 1893, the occasion of Sri Aurobindo's return to his motherland arrived. At this time the late Maharaja of Baroda, Gaikvad Sayajirao was on tour of England. James Cotton told him that a brilliant Indian youth wanted a job in India. The Maharaja was always very careful in selection of his personnel. He called Sri Aurobindo for an interview and appointed him in the service of Baroda State. Thus in February 1893 Sri Aurobindo returned to his motherland after full 14 years of exile as the great Ramachandra returned to Ayodhya after 14 years of exile. While returning to his motherland Sri Aurobindo vowed for working for India's freedom. He served Baroda State till 1907 for thirteen years. In Baroda he first worked in Settlement department and then in Stamp and Revenue departments. He also seved in Baroda Secretariat. On the request of the Principal of Baroda College Sri Aurobindo was allowed to teach French there. Later on he was appointed Professor of English at Baroda College. Thus he joined Baroda College in 1900. He also served as Vice Principal of this college. Gradually his contact with Maharaja of Baroda decreased and his political activities increased. During the movement of partition of Bengal in 1905 he actively joined politics.

Indoligical Studies

After his return to India Sri Aurobindo devoted himself whole-heartedly to the study of Indian languages, history, culture and religion. He was already conversant with the Western contributions of these fields. Now he was in a position to conduct a comparative study of East and West. This was the background of the meeting of extremes in his thoughts. He was a master of English language and his poetry was acknowledged as being of a very high standard. He studied Bengali language and literature, and was very much impressed by the writings of Bankimchandra Chatterji and Madhusudan Datta.

Spiritual Advancement

Besides his advance in the fields of literature and politics, Sri Aurobindo was also progressing in another very important direction, the field of spiritualism. He has his first spiritual experience in 1893 when he alighted in Bombay from the ship *Carthage*. This experience was the feeling of infinite peace on putting his foot on the soil of the motherland after 14 years of exile in foreign land. In 1901 Sri Aurobindo had another spiritual experience in which he felt that some divine image came out of his own body to save him from a car accident. In 1903 he felt amidst Infinite while walking on Shankaracharya Hill at Srinagar in Kashmir. In his letter to his wife, written on 30 August 1905, he pointed out that he was fast progressing on the path of spirituality. He wrote that he wanted to have direct experience of God by any means. He said that if there is God, there must be some path to establish spiritual contact with Him. This was the aspiration, which led Sri Aurobindo to formulate the path of Integral Yoga later on. However, so far Sri Aurobindo did not receive any guidance from any one. In 1907 he met a Yogi Vishnu Bhaskar Lele during the Congress session at Surat. Before this he had a notable meeting with Swami Brahmanand in 1903.

Political Activities

Besides writing in *Indu Prakash,* Sri Aurobindo sent a young Bengali soldier of Baroda Army, Jateen Bannerjee to

Bengal to carry his revolutionary message and to establish secret organisation. Jateen organised the first secret organisation in Calcutta and established contact with other revolutionaries in Bengal. Later on Sri Aurobindo's younger brother Barindra Ghosh joined his organisation. Now they established youth organisations multiplied very fast. Sri Aurobindo was introduced to the revolutionaries of Bombay as member of West Bengal secret group of revolutionaries. Though this revolutionary organisation did not achieve much political success, Sri Aurobindo's political ideas were accepted everywhere. His political committee of five members included sister Nivedita, P. Mitra, Jateen Banerjee, C.R. Das and Surendra Nath Thakur, all illustrious persons.

In 1905 Sri Aurobindo arrived in Bengal. At this time, this political committee was organising the activities of revolutionaries. Along with the youth movements, Sri Aurobindo included Swadeshi and village industries in his political programme. On the occasion of partition of Bengal in 1905 Sri Aurobindo openly started political activities. Bengal was divided on 29 September 1905. On 12th March 1906 Barindra Ghosh, Sri Aurobindo's brother, published an English weekly named *Yugantara* which published Sri Aurobindo's writings. Sri Aurobindo participated in a political gathering at Barisal on 14th April 1906 where the police baton charged the public. On 6th August 1906 Bipin Chandar Pal started an English weekly *Bande Mataram* which was joined by Sri Aurobindo. During the middle of year 1909 Sri Aurobindo started has won famous English weekly *Karma Yogin*. Both *Bande Mataram* and *Karma Yogin* used to publish Sri Aurobindo's writings. These writings inspired the young and intellectual elite of not only Bengal but of the whole country and soon Sri Aurobindo was counted among the top national leaders. Thus, during the short span of five years between the years 1905 to 1910 Sri Aurobindo achieved the status of an all India political leader. The victory of the aggressive section of politicians as the Congress session in Surat in 1906 was particularly the acknowledgment of Sri Aurobindo's thoughts. After this session he made a tour of almost all the important cities of the country including Baroda, Bombay, Pune, Nasik and Amravati delivering political lectures. In 1907 he met the Maratha Yogi Vishnu Bhaskar Lele. This yogi helped Sri Aurobindo in the path of Spiritualism. He asked Sri Aurobindo to postponed his political programme for the time being in order to have some spiritual experiences. Sri Aurobindo postponed his political programme for three days and took to spiritual practices under the guidance of this Yogi. He attained some very important experience, which he described in his lectures later on. On 19th January 1908, while delivering a lecture to a vast public under the auspices of Bombay National Union, Sri Aurobindo felt that some overmental source inspired his speech. Gradually, his national thought was more and more inspired by religious and spiritual thinking. This influence was also explicit in his lectures in Calcutta in the year 1908.

Alipur Bomb Case

During this period terrorist activities were increasing in Bengal. The revolutionaries including B.B. Upadhyaya and Bhupendra Nath were imprisoned on the charge of his treason. The death of B.B. Upadhyaya in Campbell hospital triggered the bomb attack on the carriage of Muzzafarpur District Judge Kingsford on 10th April 1908 which killed the wife and daughter of Pringle Kennedy since Kingsford was not in the vehicle. During the enquiry of this case several persons were arrested including Barindra Kumar Ghosh, the younger brother of Sri Aurobindo. Sri Aurobindo was arrested on 4th May 1908. All these prisoners were kept in Alipur Jail, and charged under Alipur Conspiracy Case. Sri Aurobindo refused to be left on bail. After some months his case was transferred to session court on 19th August 1908. The British Government was determined to implicate Sri Aurobindo but the able pleading of C.R. Das led to his acquittal on 13th April 1909. During his stay in Alipur Jail Sri Aurobindo experienced the supramental force. He had some other important spiritual experiences as well. These experiences inspired him to progress on the path of spiritualism. After he was acquitted from the prison he never returned to politics. Now he published the fresh issue of *Karma Yogin* on 30th June 1909. Its last issue was published on 5th February 1910 after which Sri Aurobindo left for Chandra Nagar on the instruction of his inner voice after closing down *Karma Yogin*. On 4th April 1910 he reached Pondicherry out of the reach of the British Government. It was here that he solely devoted himself to the spiritual pursuit.

Life in Pondicherry

In Pondicherry Sri Aurobindo stayed at the residence of Shankar Chetty. Later on he shifted to his residence in White Town. His open latter to his countrymen published in *Karma Yogin* impelled the British Government to start a case against him but nothing could be done due to his political asylum at Pondicherry sanctioned by the French Government. During his stay at Pondicherry, Sri Aurobindo was offered the Presidentship of Indian National Congress at least twice, which he declined. Illustrious leaders including Lala Lajpat Rai, Devdas Gandhi and C.R. Das tried to persuade him to return to politics but he did not agree to their repeated requests, since now he was convinced that his mission is the search of that infinite force which may transform not only his country but the whole world.

Spiritual Writings

For the next four years Sri Aurobindo did not write any public essays. In 1914, he started a philosophico-spiritual monthly magazine named *Arya*. This magazine now published his spiritual essays which were later on compiled in his famous works entitled, *The Life Divine, The Synthesis of Yoga, Essays on Gita and Isopanishad,* etc. His poems composed during his stay in England and Baroda were also published in this magazine. The publication of *Arya* was however stopped in 1921.

Life in Sri Aurobindo Ashram

Gradually, spiritual aspirants from all over the world assembled around Sri Aurobindo and in 1926 was founded Sri Aurobindo Ashram with the explicit ideal of the descent of Infinite consciousness upon the earth. In this Ashram Sri Aurobindo ceaselessly advanced in his spiritual pursuit for the next 24 years. The Ashram soon became a laboratory for integral development of individual and society and the decent of supramental in the matter. For forty years till his death Sri Aurobindo made unprecedented contribution to the spiritual world and established as a great *Karma yogi* and spiritual leader. He was in close contact with the happenings all around the world through his correspondence with friends and spiritual aspirants everywhere. Everyday he devoted as many as seven hours to reply the letters received from all over the world. These letters were later on published in four volumes. The are treasure houses of Sri Aurobindo's views on politics, religion, ethics, philosophy, literature, art, in short every aspect of human life.

Works of Sri Aurobindo

In the tradition of ancient Indian philosophers Sri Aurobindo wrote commentaries on the Upanishads and the Bhagvad Gita. His *magnum opus, The Life Divine* was published in two volumes. His work entitled, *The Ideal of Human Unity* includes his analysis of international political issues. Another work, *The Human Cycle* discloses his Philosophy of History, Social Philosophy and the Philosophy of Culture. His great epic *Savitri* has occupied a very important place in English Literature. Sri Aurobindo wrote most of his essays in English Language. Most of them were published as series in the magazine *Arya* and later on compiled in the book form. A complete list of his works has been given at the end of this book.

On 5th December 1950 at 1.26 p.m. Sri Aurobindo entered *Mahasamadhi.* On 7th December, The Mother, Sri Aurobindo's life long companion in the spiritual path, declared that Sri Aurobindo will not leave the earth till his aim is achieved. His body did not show any sign of disintegration for full 111 hours after his death and the divine light continued to stay in the dead body during that period. The Siddhi day of November 1950 was the last public appearance of Sri Aurobindo. On 24th December,

The Mother gave the message that Sri Aurobindo was constantly guiding the Ashram activities after his death. On 24th April 1951, a vast congregation assembled to pay tributes to the *Mahayogin* on the seashore of Pondicherry under the presidentship of Dr. Shyama Prasad Mukherjee. It was on this occasion that an International University was founded to commemorate the memory of Sri Aurobindo. This International University was proposed to be the media of providing new light, new power and new life to humanity and transforming it into a new race.

OBJECTIVES OF EDUCATION

Defining the objectives of education Sri Aurobindo said, "It must be an education that for the individual will make its one central object the growth of the soul and its powers and possibilities, for the nation will keep first in view the preservation, strengthening and enrichment of the nation-soul and its dharma and raise both into powers of the life and ascending mind and soul of humanity. And at no time will it lose sight of man's highest object, the awakening and development of this spiritual being."[1]

Sri Aurobindo was not only one of the greatest philosopher and yogi of his time but also one of the greatest political leader, social reformer and educationist of his era. He was a great patriot whose first concern was always the good of motherland. Therefore, he presented a national system of education which may be adopted for the educational reconstruction in India and at the same time develop the Indians as world citizens and the forerunners of the advent of the supramental race upon earth. Sri Aurobindo's philosophy not only gives an important place to individual and nation but also to humanity. In these three principles, the higher determines the lower. Therefore, the national scheme of education will be not only from the point of view of the needs of the country but also from the standpoint of the needs of humanity. It is so since the highest principle governing the life of individual and nation is the humanity itself. It is as a human

---

1. **Sri Aurobindo, *Sri Aurobindo and The Mother on Education*, Part I, p.3.**

being first and last that the individual has to grow. It is as a member of a community of nations that a nations has to grow and develop. It is the forgetting of this central truth in the life of the individual and nation that has been the source of all evil and error. Again, Sri Aurobindo everywhere considers fulfilment of *Swadharma* as the law of life. Each individual in a nation has to fulfil his *Swadharma.* The purpose of education in a nation is to prepare the individual to serve their roles according to their status in society. Individual differences are the basis of modern system of education. Nature has bestowed different human beings with different capacities and powers. Therefore, the educationist has to develop in the child whatever has been already endowed to him by God. The child is, "A sould with a lean, a nature and capacities of his own, who must be helped to find them, to find himself, to grow into their maturity, into a fullness of physical and vital energy and utmost breadth, depth and height of his emotional, his intellectual and his spiritual being."[1] Thus, each human being is a self developing soul.[2] Parents and teachers have to help him in this development. In the words of N.C. Dowsett, the concept of education in Sri Aurobindo's philosophy is summarized thus, "The meaning of the word education is to reduce the inner, hidden, latent, dormant, potential secret within every human being, secret because it is not of the senses but of the inner truth of being and because it is that most unknown part of the being which has yet to evolve to its full stature."[3]

THE TRUE EDUCATION

Defining true education, Sri Aurobindo wrote, "There are three things which have to be taken into account in true and living education, the man, the individual in his commonness and in his uniqueness, the nation or people and universal humanity. It follows that alone will be true and living education which helps to bring

1. **Sri Aurobindo, *B.C.L., 1971* Volume 15, p. 605.**
2. ***Ibid., pp.* 27-28.**
3. **Dowsett, N.C., *Psychology for Future Education,* Aurobindo Ashram Pondicherry (1977), p. 9.**

out to full advantage, makes ready for the full purpose and scope of human life all that is in the individual man, and which at the same time helps him to enter into his right relation with the life, mind and soul of the people to which he belongs and with that great total life, mind and soul of humanity of which he himself is a unit and his people or nation a living, a separate and yet inseparable member."[1] Thus, the true education should take into account not only the individual but also the nation and the humanity. It has to prepare the mind and soul of the individual and also of the nation to serve humanity. It has to unfold the individual potentialities, uniqueness and commonness. At the same time it has to develop a right relation of the individual with the life, mind and soul of the community and humanity. In the words of Sri Aurobindo, the true national education is that, "Which helps to bring out to full advantage, makes ready for the full purpose and scope of human life all that is in the individual man and which at the same time, helps him to enter into right relation with the life, mind and soul of humanity of which he himself is a unit and his people or nation a living, a separate and yet inseparable member."[2]

Besides *Swadharma,* the role of a nation is determined by *Swabhava. Swadeshi* was the avowed principle in Sri Aurobindo's political philosophy. Each nation, according to him, has to grow and develop in tune with its peculiar *Swabhava* and *Swadharma.* This principle has been advocated by Indian thinkers since ancient times. Indian philosophy always considered everything as an instrument of spiritual growth. It may be called *spiritual instrumentalism* in contrast to the biological instrumentalism of John Dewey. Thus, the nation has to develop its mental, ethical and aesthetic being to make it a fit instrument for the growth of the soul. This is the highest *purusĥartha.* India, according to Sri Aurobindo, is a nation, which has to fulfil a spiritual role in the community of nations. Its ideal for the humanity also is spiritual.

1. *Sri Aurobindo and The Mother on Education, Part* **I, p. 1.**
2. *Sri* **Aurobindo,** ***B.C.L.,*** **1972, Volume 17, p. 198.**

Therefore, Sri Aurobindo has everywhere called for the spiritual growth of humanity.

Rational Education

This, however, does not mean that Sri Aurobindo finds no place for reason in education. In his philosophy everywhere Sri Aurobindo has supported reason like any staunch rationalist and lauded its role as the lawgiver to the irrational elements, the passions, the sensibilities and the sense organs. A true and living education also a rational education though it goes beyond reason for the spiritual growth of man. A rational education, according to Sri Aurobindo, includes the following three things :

1. To teach men how to observe and know rightly the facts on which they have to form a judgment.
2. To train them to think fruitfully and soundly.
3. To fit them to use their knowledge and their thought effectively for their own and the common good.[1]

Meeting of East and West

Brought up in the West Sri Aurobindo had the first had knowledge of the Western system of education. Like Vivekananda and Tagore he was also conversant with the advantages of European system of education. Though one of the greatest admirers of ancient Indian thoughts, Sri Aurobindo was a votary of the synthesis of whatever is good in East and West. This synthesis is visible everywhere in his thought. Therefore, while presenting a scheme for Indian education, he advocated synthesis of ancient Indian educational ideals alongwith the Western methods and techniques. As he said, "The first problem in a national system of education is to give an education as comprehensive as the European and more thorough, without the evils of strain and cramming. This can only be done by studying the instruments of knowledge and finding a system of teaching which shall be natural, easy and effective. It is only by

1. *Sri* **Auirobindo, *B.C.L.*, 1971, Vol. 15, p. 186.**

strengthening and sharpening these instruments of their utmost capacity that they can be made effective for the increased work which modern conditions require. The muscles of the mind must be thoroughly trained by simple and easy means, then, and not till then, great feast of intellectual strength can be required of them."[1]

Integral Education

True education, according to Sri Aurobindo, is not only spiritual but also rational, vital and physical. In other words, it is an integral education. This integral education has been explained by Sri Aurobindo's closest collaborator the Mother, in these words, "Education to be complete must have five principal aspects relating to the five principal activities of the human being : the physical, the vital, the mental, the psychic and the spiritual. Usually these phases of education succeed each other in a chronological order following the growth of the individual. This, however, does not mean that one should replace another but that all must continue, completing each other, till the end of life."[2] Sri Aurobindo's scheme of education is integral in two senses. Firstly, it is integral in the sense of including all the aspects of the individual being, physical, vital, mental, psychic and spiritual. Secondly, it is integral in the sense of being an education not only for the evolution of the individual alone but also of the nation and finally of the humanity. In his *Essays on Gita* Sri Aurobindo initially presented the concept of integral education as out bringing all the facts of an individual personality. The ultimate aim of education is the evolution of total humanity which includes the evolution of the nation which in its turn depends upon the evolution of the individual. In this scheme of evolution the principle of growth is unity in diverstiy. This unity again, maintains and helps the evolution of diversity. Thus each individual in nation and each nation in humanity has to develop a system of education according to its own *Swabhava* and fulfilling its *Swadharma.*

1. ***Sri Aurobindo and The Mother on Education,*** **Part I, p.7.**
2. ***Ibid.,*** **p.8.**

Supramental Education

The education again, is ultimately supramental education, that which leads to our evolution towards the supramental. This supramental evolution, however, will necessarily pass through and only after the evolution of the physical, the vital, the mental and the psychic. Physical education is the education of the body. It includes the order, discipline, plasticity and receptivity of the body. Its principal aspects are—

1. Control and discipline of functions,
2. A total, methodical and harmonious development of all the parts and movements of the body, and
3. Rectification of defects and deformities, if there are any.[1]

The vital education is indispensable, though difficult. It is so since the nature of vital has been often misunderstood. In the words of the Mother, the vital education involves two principal aspects, "The first is to develop and utilize the sense organs, the second is to become conscious and gradually master of one's character and in the end to achieve its transformation."[2] Thus vital education includes sense training and the development of character. This character again will be developed according to individual differences. It requires redirection and transformation of the instincts and emotions, drives and propensities. Describing the mental education the mother has laid down the following five phrases—

1. Development of the power of concentration, the capacity of attention.
2. Development of the capacities of expansion, wideness, complexity and richness.
3. Organisation of ideas around a central idea or a higher ideal or a supremely luminous idea that will serve as a guide in life.
4. Thought control, rejection of undesirable thoughts so that

---

1. *Ibid.*, p.10.
2. *Ibid.*, p.11.

one may, in the end, think only what one wants and when one wants.

5. Development of mental silence, perfect claim and a more and more total receptivity to inspirations coming from the higher regions of the being.

While the physical, vital and mental education are the means to develop the personality, the psychic education alone leads to the future evolution of man. Sri Aurobindo's system of education does not aim only at the adjustment and normal development of the human personality but its total growth and transformation. The idea of psychic education has not been developed in any existing philosophy of education. It is so since psychic element was never considered and understood by the Western educationists. In India also in spite of the importance of psychic element found in Yoga, its nature has been seldom understood. The core of the psychic education is the achievement of our identification with the psychic principles in us. This may be reached by psychological, religious or mechanical methods. Every one will have to find out the method best suitable to him and his aspiration. The psychic education requires sincere and steady aspiration, a persistent and dynamic will, concentration, revelation and experience. In the words of The Mother "Only one thing is absolutely indispensable : the will to discover and realise."[1] This is in fact the field of occult and yoga.

Thus the supramental education requires the above steps as a prelude to its realization. It is only after one gets through the physical, vital, mental and psychic education and realizes a certain transformation that one can enter into supramental education. To quote The Mother again, "Then will being also a new education which can be called the supramental education; it will, by its all-powerful action, work not only upon the consciousness of individual being, but upon the very substance of which they are built and upon the environment in which they live."[2] The idea of

1. *Ibid.*, p.14
2. *Ibid.*, p.16

supramental education like that of the psychic education is Aurobindo's significant contribution to the field of education. This is more important at the present juncture when most of the educationists are realising the need for an educational system aiming at man-making. According to Sri Aurobindo, humanity today has already reached what has been called by him a subjective stage. The future evolution has to be above the mental level. This will require a great insight and persistent efforts. The different types of education already discussed should not be given successively but simultaneously. The focus should be all the time on the inner growth. As the educand advances he should be taught to identify his real self and to find out the law of his being. The principles of this new type of education have been explained by Sri Aurobindo and the Mother in their different works.

AIMS OF EDUCATION

The aims of education in the educational philosophy of Sri Aurobindo are as follows—

1. Perfection—Sri Aurobindo was a perfectionist. He was never satisfied with partial remedies. It is hence that he left the political arena to pursue a more perfect method of realisation of perfection of human race. It is hence that he presents his integral yoga as a solution not only of the individual needs but also of the social and political problems facing nations and humanity. This perfectionism is the strength and this again is the weakness of Sri Aurobindo's philosophy of education. In tune with the Indian concept of human nature Sri Aurobindo considered the individual as, "A growing soul with a being, a nature and capacities of his own."[1] The aim of education therefore was to realise these capacities and grow, "into a fullness of physical and vital energy and utmost breadth, depth and height of his emotional, his intellectual and his spiritual being."[2]

2. Harmony—Hamony is the key to understand Sri Aurobindo's thought everywhere. Those who complain about the

1. **Sri Aurobindo, *B.C.L.*, 1970, Volume 13, pp. 499-500.**
2. **Sri Aurobindo, *B.C.L.*, 1971, Volume 13, pp. 605.**

difficulty in understanding his writing lack this inherent urge to harmony. On the other hand, those who seek harmony easily understand Sri Aurobindo's works. In his philosophy of education, as in his metaphysics, epistemology, political philosophy and social philosophy, Sri Aurobindo searches after the principle of harmony in the individual, community and humanity and aims at tis realization. He seeks to achieve harmony of the individual by the growth and evolution of his different aspects such as physical, vital, mental, mental and psychic, etc. For this he proposes a scheme of physical, vitial, moral, religious and spiritual education. He also seeks harmony of different individuals in a community. Compatibility and not uniformity is the law of collective harmony. The roles of the male and female, the different types of individuals in a community are not identical but diverse and therefore complementary. Thus Sri Aurobindo proposes an educational system in which details must be planned according to individual differences. This is particularly true about the women's education, education of backward classes and the education of below normal, abnormal and supernormal children.

3. Evolution—The edifice of Sri Aurobindo's philosophy is based upon his theory of evolution. It stands and falls with the truth of evolution. Evolution, however, has been felt and realised by almost all the thinkers of our age. Therefore, Sri Aurobindo aims at the evolution of the individual, nation and humanity through education. This evolution will be continued as spiral. It is hence that Sri Aurobindo aims at nothing less than supramental education. Evolution involves not only growth but also transformation, not only adjustment but a more intimate harmony. In the words of N.C. Dowsett, Sri Aurobindo's education aims, "To educate the true individual potential within each student, to help him to manifest that within him which is uniquely his, so he may find that as a perfection to be offered to life as his individual contribution to a collective perfection which is the evolving spirit of man and the true heritage to which he aspires."[1] This evolution

1. **Dowsett, N.C., *The psychology for Future Education,* Aurobindo Ashram Pondicherry (1977), p.13.**

can be achieved by man's opening and uniting with the universal divine. In other words this requires divine perfection.

4. Humanisation—Education, according to Sri Aurobindo, as according to Vivekananda, aims at man-making. The individual and the nation have to grow as members of one humanity. Sri Aurobindo's system of national education ultimately aims at evolution of humanity. Describing the aim of Sri Aurobindo's international university at Pondicherry The Mother declared, "It is in answer to this pressing need that Sri Aurobindo conceived the scheme of his international university, so that the elite of humanity may be made ready who would be able to work for the progressive unification of the race and who at the same time would be prepared to embody the new force descending upon earth to transform it."[1]

5. Harmony of the Individual and Collectivity—While most of the thinkers in social-political field have either laid emphasis upon the individual or the collectivity, Sri Aurobindo aims at realisation of harmony between individuals and also between nations. His scheme of education therefore is truly international. It is not only for India but also for the world. Explaining this ideas of Sri Aurobindo's scheme, The Mother said," For all world organisation, to be real and to be able to live, must be based upon mutual respect and understanding between nation and nation as well as between individual and individual. It is only in the collective order and organisation, in a collaboration based upon mutual goodwill that lies the possibility of man being lifted out of the painful chaos where he is now. It is with this aim and in this spirit that all human problems will be studied at the university centre; and their solution will be given in the light of the supramental knowledge which Sri Aurobindo has revealed in his writings."[2]

6. Building the Innate Powers—The central aim of education according to Sri Aurobindo is, "The building of the

---

1. *Ibid.*, pp.25-26
2. *Ibid.*, p. 28.

powers of the human mind and spirit—the evoking of knowledge and will and of the power to use knowledge, character, culture that at least if not more."[1] The child is born with certain innate powers of the body, the vital, the mind and the spirit. The aim of the school and the teacher is to develop these powers to their perfection. For this a programme of sense training, bodybuilding, character formation, development of logical and other mental faculties, religious education and finally a training in integral yoga is necessary. Moral development and aesthetic development should go side by side.

7. Cultivation of Values—The present crisis of man is due to the chaos of values. Old values have been challenged while new values have not firmly taken their place. In his social philosophy Sri Aurobindo has particularly discussed this problem.[2] The values to be cultivated should be physical, mental as well as spiritual. Character formation very much depends on value. The supreme value in Sri Aurobindo's thought is harmony. Other values are—spirituality, divinity, evolution, ascent, transformation, etc. All these must be cherished and developed. But the most important value required for all growth is sincerity. Once that is developed, the rest follows. Right emotions and *Sanskars, Swabhava* and nature are the foundation of Sri Aurobindo's scheme of education. Sri Aurobindo not only aims at moral status but also going beyond it, rising above virtue and vice. This is the supramental status aimed at both by the individual and collectivity in Sri Aurobindo's thought.

The Educational Model

While Sri Aurobindo outlined a national system of education, a model to realise his scheme was developed by The Mother in the form of Sri Aurobindo international university at Pondicherry.[3] It was developed as a new centre of education to

1. Sri Aurobindo, B.C.L., 1972, Volume, 17, p. 194.
2. Sharma, R.N., *Social Philosophy of Sri Aurobindo,* 1989, Vineet Publications, Meerut, Chapter I.
3. Sri Aurobindo, *B.C.L.,* 1972, Volume, 17.

experiment for the realisation of the aims outlined by Sri Aurobindo. The curriculum, The teaching methods, the system of education and all the other details were formed with this central aim. The fundamental principle underlying the model was freedom since freedom is the only essential spiritual principle working anywhere. As has been already pointed out, this ideal control of education not only aimed at revelation of Sri Aurobindo's aim in India but also in humanity. All the aims of education outlined earlier were practiced here. Children were admitted from a very early age. They gathered from all the parts of the country as well as from different countries in the world to make it a true representative of world cultures. The natural scenery, dress, games, sports, industries, food, art, etc., were developed on the principle of unity and diversity. An effort was made to realise a cultural synthesis. Students of different nations were placed at different places with their own groups so that while they may develop international culture, no rigid timetable, classes, curriculum, teaching method or system of evaluation and examination was insisted. This was left upon individual choice of the educand himself.

The idea was to give full freedom to the individual growth of the educand. The experiment fared very well but did not grow elsewhere due to obvious difficulties in such experiments. However, it is undoubtedly a model for a new system of education, which may be hoped to develop in India and also in the parts of the world.

THE SCHOOL

The ultimate ideal of the school is man-making. It prepares the educand to work first as a human being and then as a member of a nation and finally as an individual. The circles of moral responsibility and loyalties proceed from wider to narrower and not *vice versa*. The man has to develop first as a human being then as a citizen and finally as an individual. Most of the present confusion of values is due to an inversion of this order.

Sri Aurobindo believe in three ultimate principles, individuality, commonality and essentiality. These, in other words, are the educand, the society and the humanity. Integral evolution, according to him, must include evolution of all these three elements. This the individuality and commonality should develop together. This is the purpose of the school. The school should treat all children as equal and provide sufficient scope for the development of their individual variations without insisting upon similarities. In his lecture at Baroda College Sri Aurobindo observed that the colleges and universities should educate through their academic as well as social activities.[1] Thus the college should have its bearing upon the community around it.[2] The school cannot be isolated from society. It cannot give total education in isolation. Its teachings have to be practiced in the society outside it. The university merely gives some materials to the educand, which he may use.

In the integral school four types of rooms are required to carry on various activities.

1. Rooms of silence,
2. Rooms of collaboration,
3. Rooms of consultation,
4. Lecture room.[3]

Thus the school will develop different types of activities such as silence, collaboration, consultation and lectures. It will provide play, activity, discovery, innovation and finally development of the powers of the body, mind and spirit of the educand. In brief, the integral school will provide opportunities for integral development.

THE TEACHER

Like the ancient Indian system of education, Sri Aurobindo has assigned a very important place to the teacher. He has however

1. *Ibid.,* Volume III, p. 131.
2. *Ibid.,* p. 132
3. Joshi, Kirit, *Nav Chetana, Mothers* International School (1977), pp.5-7

not made him central as in the ancient Indian scheme. The central place, as in the Western systems of education, has been occupied by the educand. His philosophy of education, therefore, is paidocentric. However, the teacher remains the philosopher an the guide. The Guru does not have absolute authority. He aims at turning the disciple's eye towards the beacon lightly of his own Godhead. In fact, the real teacher is within the educand. He is the God. He is the ultimate guide and yet the teacher plays an important role in arousing the educand towards God within. He has not to impose his opinions or demand passive surrender from the educand. He has to create an atmosphere so that the educand may grow freely. Sri Aurobindo accepts the role of a gardener in the teacher as maintained by many Western educational philosophers. The teacher acts as an aid, a means and a channel. His relationship with the educand is very close. In the ancient Indian tradition, Sri Aurobindo emphasizes an inner relationship between the educator and the educand. For this the teacher should develop certain innate qualities.

Describing as to who is a teacher, The Mother has laid down the following qualification, "Teachers who do not possess a perfect calm, an unfailing endurance, an unshakeable quietness who are full of self-conceit reach nowhere."

One must be a saint and a hero to become a good teacher.

One must be a great *yogi* to become a good teacher.

One must have the perfect attitude in order to be able to exact from one's pupils a perfect attitude.

You cannot ask of a person what you do not do yourself. It is a rule.

You must then look within you at the difference between what is and what should be, and this difference will give you the mesure of your failure in the class.[1]

In brief, the teacher should be an integral *yogi*. He should be able to eliminate his ego, master his mind and develop an

1. ***Sri Aurobindo and The Mother on Education, Part II, pp. 4-5***

insight into human nature and to progress in impersonalisation. He should be absolutely disciplined and having an integrated personality. The most important thing in a teacher is not the knowledge but the attitude. An intellectual excellence is not sufficient without a development of other aspects of personality. The teacher should have the capacity to project himself to the educand so that he may have an understanding of the needs of the educand. The schools aim not only on the progress of the educand but also of the educator. In the words of the Mother, "The school must be an occasion of progress for the teacher as well as for the student. Each must have the freedom to develop himself freely. One never applies method well unless one has discovered it oneself"[1] In practice The central trait of the teacher is the inner calm. He should exercise influence not by scolding but by moral control. In the words of the Mother, "I must tell you that if a professor wants to be respected, he must be respectable."[2]

Personality Traits of the Teacher

In order to fulfil his role, the teacher should take it seriously and honestly. He should develop his personality more than the ordinary man so that he may be able to influence others. He should be a representative of the supreme knowledge, the supreme truth and the supreme law. Then alone his influence will work. The Mother has prescribed has prescribed the following personality traits for a true teacher :

1. Complete self-control not only to the extent of not showing any anger, but remaining absolutely quiet and undisturbed under all circumstances.
2. In the matter of self-confidence he must also have the sense of the relativity of his importance.

Above all, he must have the knowledge that the teacher himself must always progress if he wants his students to progress, must not remain satisfied either with what he is or with what he knows.

1. *Ibid.,* p. 7.
2. *Ibid.,* pp. 8-9

3. Must not have any sense of essential superiority over his student nor preference of attachment whatever for one or another.
4. Must know that all are equal spiritually and instead of mere tolerance must have a global comprehensions or understanding.
5. "The business of both parent and teacher is to enable and to help the child to educate himself, to develop his own intellectual, moral, aesthetic and practical capacities and to grow freely as an organic being, not to be kneaded and pressured into form like an inert plastic material."[1]

THE CURRICULUM

As has been already pointed out, the essential principle of Sri Aurobindo's philosophy of education is freedom. Unity is never demanded at the cost of diversity. On the other hand, diversity creates a rich unity. Therefore, no rigid scheme of curriculum has been prescribed. However, hints are scattered in Sri Aurobindo's works about different criteria of curriculum. The earliest permissible age for starting regular study according to Sri Aurobindo is seven or eight years. At this age the child is sufficiently grown up to take up regular study. The proper medium for early education of the child is the mother tongue. It is only after the mother tongue that the child can learn other languages. As has been already pointed out, the following criteria for planning curriculum are fond in Sri Aurobindo's writings :

1. Human Nature—The curriculum should aim at developing whatever is already given in seed form in the child. Education can only lead to the perfection of the instruments, which are already outside. In the words of The Mother, "Fundamentally the only thing you must do assiduously is to teach them to know themselves, and to choose their own destiny, the way they want to follow."[2]

1. *Ibid*., p. 8
2. *Ibid.*, p. 1.

2. Individual Differences—The curriculum should be planned according to individual differences. The mind has to be consulted in its own growth. The aim of the teacher is to help the growing soul in drawing out his best and to make it perfect for a noble use.[1]

3. From Near to the Far—Another principle governing the planning of curriculum is to proceed from near to the far, from that which is to that which shall be.[2]

4. Modern and Up-to-Date—Sri Aurobindo was not a reactionary or a conservative. He was a modern thinker with a love for modernity and up-to date knowledge. Therefore, he prescribed that the education must be up-to-date in form and substance and modern in life and spirit.[3]

5. Universal Knowledge—The curriculum should include whatever is universally true. That is the basis of all scientific knowledge and philosophy. Truth and knowledge are one and not confined to any country. Therefore according to Sri Aurobindo, education should be universal without any nationality or borders.[4]

6. Successive Teaching—Sri Aurobindo disagrees with some educationists who wish to introduce every subject simultaneously to the child. He prescribes that the subjects should be taught successively. New subjects should be introduced after the earlier are mastered. Thus few subjects should be taught at a time.

7. Co-curricular Activities—The school should provide not only academic but also co-curricular activities.

8. Five-fold Curriculum—As has been already pointed out, integral education is fivefold. It includes the physical, the vital, the mental, the psychic and the spiritual education. Therefore, the curriculum must be fivefold according to these five types of education. Of these the education of the mind involves the most

1. **Sri Aurobindo, *B.C.L.*, 1972 Volume 17, p. 205.**
2. ***Ibid***
3. ***Ibid.*, p. 194.**
4. ***Ibid.*, p. 193.**

detailed curriculum. It requires different curriculum for the development of the different powers of the mind such as observation, memory, judgment, comparison, contrast analogy, reasoning and imagination, etc. Sense training requires curriculum involving all the five senses.

9. Mutisidedness—Integral education is multisides. It aims at all-round growth. Therefore its curriculum involves music, poetry, art, painting and sculpture, besides the academic subjects. These are necessary for the aesthetic development of the child. These aim at contemplation and understanding of beauty and just arrangement of the tastes, habits and character of the educand. According to Sri Aurobindo, in contrast to many other educationists music, art and poetry purify, control, deepen and harmonize the movements of the soul.[1] In his work entitled *The National Value of Art*, Sri Aurobindo points out three uses of art. Firstly, it is purely aesthetic, secondly, it is intellectual and educative and thirdly, it is spiritual. The aesthetic development purifies conduct and disciplines the animal instincts and lower feeling of the heart. The artistic sense helps in the formation of morals and purification of the emotion.[2] Thus art has both intellectual and spiritual value. It is subtle and delicate and makes the mind subtle and delicate.[3]

10. Provision for the Genius—The curriculum must provide for the genius. According to Sri Aurobindo, "What we call genius is part of the development of the human range of being and its achievements especially in things of the mind and their will can carry us half way to the divine."[4] The curriculum should cater for the perfection of the different powers of the genius.

11. Moral and Religious Education—Curriculum for moral education should aim at refining the emotions and forming the proper habits and associations. Religious teaching like moral

---

1. ***Ibid.*, pp. 244-46.**
2. ***Ibid.*, pp. 24-42.**
3. ***Ibid.*, p. 245.**
4. ***Ibid.*, pp. 207-08.**

teaching does not involve so much of curriculum as teaching by example and provision of right atmosphere. In the words of Sri Aurobindo, "Whatever distinct teaching in any form of religion is imparted or not the essence of religion, to live for God. For humanity, for country, for others and for oneself must be made the ideal in every school."[1]

Thus the aim of the curriculum according to Sri Aurobindo, is the actualization of the potentialities of the educand. The material is the basis and spiritual is the summit of education. The curriculum gradually becomes more and more abstract leading to the realization of higher experiences. Same curriculum may be followed by male and female. The schools may be co-educational. Sufficient emphasis should be laid upon aesthetic, moral and religious teaching. The curriculum should not be fixed but flexible and evolutionary. A variety of choice and opportunities must be prescribed for maintaining the freedom of growth. The integral curriculum should find a due place for every subject and every discipline.

TENTATIVE EDUCATIONAL PLAN

Norman C. Dowsett has presented the following tentative educational plan developed by International Centre of Education, Pondicherry, based upon educational philosophy of Sri Aurobindo.[2]

1. The Play School (1-3 years)

   Provision of love, security, wonder, discovery and adventure.

2. Pre-School discipline of the physical mind (3-5 years)

   (a) order

   (b) activities, physical exercises and games.

3. Prime-School of fulfillment of the vital mind (5-7½ yrs.)

---

1. *Ibid.*, p. 212.
2. Dowsett, N.C., *Psychology for Future Education,* Aurobindo Ashram, Pondicherry (1977), pp. 218-29.

(a) body awareness—discipline of the physical mind to continue.

(b) Fulfillment of vital energies—The vital should be fulfilled through art, drawing, painting, sculpture, dance, drama, music, etc.

4. High school of the freedom of the mental mind I phase (7½ – 10½ years) use of the instruments of knowledge.

5. High school of the freedom of the mental mind II phase (10½ – 14½ years) integration of the progressive series of creative energies.

6. Graduation school of psychic education (14-17 years) : appreciation of individuality, progressive understanding of his inner potential and his contribution to the group, society, nation and the world.

7. College of spiritual education (17-21 years) : spiritual realisation, integration of all that has been achieved.

THE IDEAL CHILD

Sri Aurobindo's system of education is paidocentric. It aims at the creation of ideal children. The ideal children are absolutely sincere and constantly progressive. They are forbidden fighting anywhere. The are always truthful. The Mother has given the following description of an ideal child.[1]

1. **Good-Tempered**—He does not become angry when things seem to go against him or decisions are not in his favour.

2. **Game**—Whatever he does it to the best of his capacity and keeps on doing in the face of almost certain failure. He always thinks straight.

3. **Truthful**—He never fears to say the truth whatever may be the consequences.

4. **Patient**—He does not get disheartened if he has to wait a long time to see the results of his effort.

---

1. *Sri Aurobindo and The Mother on Education,* **Part II pp. 28-29.**

5. Enduring—He never slackens his effort however long it has to last.

6. Poised—He keeps equanimity in success as well as in failure.

7. Courageous—He always goes on fighting for the final victory though he may meet with many defeats.

8. Cheerful—He knows how to smile and keep a happy heart in all circumstances.

9. Modest—He does not become conceited over his success, neither does he feel himself superior to his comrades.

10. Generous—He appreciates the merits of others and is always ready to help another to succeed.

11. Courteous—On the field he does not jeer at errors, he does not cheer at the opponent's defeat; he treats them as guest, not enemies. In school he is considerate to the authorities, the fellow students, and the teachers. In life he is respectful to others; he treats them as he would be treated.

12. Obedient—On the field he observes the regulations. In life he respects the rules which help to promote harmony.

13. Fair—On the field he competes in a clean, hard-fought but friendly way; he helps an injured opponent. In school he does not waste his time or that of the teachers. He is always honest. In life he sees impartially both sides of a question.

Thus Sri Aurobindo's integral education gives highest place to the children. They are considered as divine force, the leaders of the future gnostic race on the earth. All the hopes for man's future lie upon the proper development of the younger generation. There is no gap between the teacher, the Guru and the children. Integral education considers the inner relationship and rapport as the first condition of all education. It is in this spirit that The Mother said to the children of the Ashram, "My children, we are united towards the same goal and the same accomplishment will give you. The divine Force is with you, feel its presence more and more and be very careful never to betray it. Fee, wish, act, that you may be new beings for the realisation of a new world and for this my blessings shall be always with you."[1]

Thus the children are highly respected. The job of the teacher is not utilitarian or for earning his bread but for man-making. It is in the spirit of offering of one's action to God that the teachers can create the spirit of sacrifice in the children. Sri Aurobindo's integral education is based upon faith in human nature. As against the explanation of human nature offered by most of the Western thinkers including Hobbes, Sri Aurobindo, like many other religious savants, considers man as divine. It was in this spirit that the Mother said to the children of the Ashram, "Be courageous, enduring, vigilant; above all be sincere, with perfect honesty. Then you will be face all difficulties. And victory will be yours."[2]

TEACHING METHODS

Thus the teaching methods in integral education of Sri Aurobindo are based on the one hand on faith in the inner goodness and evolutionary nature of the educand and on the other hand on the psychological principles involved in teaching. Sri Aurobindo's explanations and suggestions are everywhere psychological. Without going into the details he has always kept his eye focussed on the tendencies working within him. Therefore his suggestions are very valuabvle.[3]

TEACHING CHILDREN

Sri Aurobindo and The Mother gave particular attention to the methods of teaching children. In this connection the following suggestions are offered :

1. The teachers should have sufficient documentation of what they know. They should be able to answer all questions.
2. They should have at least the knowledge if not the

1. *Ibid.*, part III, p. 22.
2. *Ibid.*, p. 23.
3. *Ibid.*, pp. 19-21.

experience of true intellectual and intuitive attitude. This knowledge can be attained through mental silence.

3. He is best teacher who has the capacity and not only knowledge of the different field of evolution.
4. Thus the professors must be sincere in discipline and experience. They should not be propagandists.
5. To start with, "The children, as soon as they have the capacity to think (it begins at 7 years but towards 14 years it is very clear) should be given small indications at 7 and a complete explanation at 14, of how to do it, and that it is the unique method to enter inter into relation with the profounds, that all the rest is a mental approximation, more or less inapt of something that can be known directly."[1]

Teaching Very Small Children

About the teaching of very small children, The Mother has laid down the following principles for the teacher :[2]

Never to deceive oneself.

Never to be angry.

Always to be understanding.

Never try to impose on them.

Never scold but always try to understand. With Rousseau Sri Aurobindo, believes that the child is naturally good but gradually corrupted by bad environment. In an adverse environment the child looses all contact with the self in him. Therefore, The Mother has insisted that the most necessary thing to be taught to the child is to follow the inner psychic consciousness. As she said, "That is why I insist on that and I say that from the very earliest age children must be taught that there is a reality within themselves, within the earth, within the universe and that he himself, the earth and universe, exist only as a function

1. *Ibid.*, p. 20.
2. *Ibid.*, p. 21.

of this truth and if it did not exist, he would not last, even the short time he lasts and that everything would dissolve as soon as it is created."[1]

This, however, does not require philosophical explanations. The child is not prepared for mental understanding of the self. He should be made to realise the inner consciousness. His education, therefore, should be by projects and playway methods. The child responds to the psychic vibrations. He is most impressed by affection and feelings. Therefore, integral education rules out all harsh treatment, scolding or being angry towards the children. One must have sufficient patience with them. The habits for cleanliness and hygiene should start very early. This however, does not require creating fear of illness in the child. The Mother has warned, "Fear is the worst incentive to education and the surest way of attraction what is feared."[2] This warning is timely not only for early education but for secondary and university education in our country.

How to Teach

Sri Aurobindo, in his exposition of teaching methods, keeps his eye focused on the truth alone. He is neither prejudiced in favour nor against the ancient Indian teaching methods or the Western ways of teaching. As he said, "The past hangs about our necks will all its prejudices and errors and will not leave us; it enters into our most radical attempts to return to the guidance of the all-wise Mother. We must have the courage to take up clearer knowledge and apply it fearlessly in the interests of posterity."[3]

Successive Teaching

Accepting that every child has multiple tendencies and abilities requiring teaching of various subjects, Sri Aurobindo favours successive teaching as against simultaneous introduction of so many subjects in early education. Among the different

1. *Ibid.*, p. 23.
2. *Ibid.*, p. 26.
3. *Ibid.*, p. 11.

subjects to be taught to the child, the basic subjects should be introduced first so that a sound foundation for education is made. As Sri Aurobindo points out, "The old system was to teach one or two subjects well and thoroughly and then proceed to others and certainly it was a more rational system than the modern. If it did not impart so much varied information, it built up a deeper, nobler and more real culture."[1] Thus different subjects should be studied one by one. The same principle is applicable to the teaching of textbooks. Each chapter should be studied thoroughly and in succession. In the words of the Mother, "One should leave a chapter when it has been fully grasped then only take up the next one and so on. If a chapter is finished, it is finished; and if it is not finished it is not finsihed"[2] The child's education should start at the age of 7 or 8 for, according to Sri Aurobindo, "That is the earliest permissible age for the commencement of any regular kind of study."[3] At this age the child is capable of concentration and interest. Therefore, the first thing to be created in the child is interest in the subject.

Education Through Political Experience

Thus, like all other modern educators, Sri Aurobindo pleads for introduction of different subjects to the child through practical experience. First of all he should acquire mastery of the mother tongue as the medium of the education, because that is the required sound basis for regular instruction. Elaborating the needs of practical foundation of child's education, Sri Aurobindo gives valuable suggestions for the teaching of different subjects appealing to the imagination, the dramatic faculty, love for the narrative, hero worship, urge to enquiry and other natural characteristics of the child. To quote his advice, "Almost every child has an imagination, an instinct for words, a dramatic faculty, a wealth of idea and fancy. These should be interested in the literature and history of the nation. Instead of stupid and dry

---

1. **Sri Aurobindo, *B.C.L., 1972,* Volume 17, p. 213.**
3. ***Sri Aurobindo and The Mother on Education,* Part II, p. 17.**
3. ***Ibid.***

spelling and reading books, looked on as a dreary and ungrateful task, he should be introduced by rapidly progressive stages to the most interest parts of his own literature and the life around him and behind him, and they should be put before him in such away as to attract and appeal to the qualities of which I have spoken. All other study at this period should be devoted to the perfection of the mental functions and the moral character. A foundation should be laid at this time for the study of history, science, philosophy, but not in an obtrusive and formal manner. Every child is a lover of interesting narrative, a hero-worshipper and a patriot. Appeal to these qualities in him and through them let him master without knowing it the living and human parts of his nation's history. Every child is an inquirer, an investigator, analyzer a merciless anatomist. Appeal to those qualities in him and let him acquire without knowing it, the necessary fundamental knowledge of the scientist. Every child has an insatiable intellectual curiosity and turn for metaphysical inquiry. Use it to draw him on slowly to an understanding of the world and himself. Every child has the gift of imitation and a touch of imaginative power. Use it to give him the ground work of the faculty of the artist."[1]

Three Principles of Teaching

Now, before trying to understand methods of teaching of different instruments of the educand one should remember the following three principles of teaching laid down by Sri Aurobindo:

1. The first principle is that nothing can be taught.
2. The second principle is that the mind should be constantly consulted in its growth.
3. The third principle is to work from the near to the far, from that which is to that which shall be.[2]

Integral Teaching

Integral teaching involves training of all the aspects of the

1. *Ibid.*, pp. 11-12.
2. Sri Aurobindo, *B.C.L.*, 1972, Volume, 17, p. 204.

educand's mind and personality. Starting with sense training it develops the memory and judgment, the observation and comparison, analogy, reasoning, imagination, language, grammar and meaning of the logical faculty, etc. All these characteristics are present in every child. In the words of Sri Aurobindo, "Every child is an inquirer, an investigator analyzer, a merciless anatomist."[1] The first thing to do is to arouse the curiosity, imagination and natural interest of the child so that he may spontaneously enquire, understand and learn. As Sri Aurobindo advises the teachers, "The first work is to interest the child in life, work and knowledge, to develop his instruments of knowledge with the utmost thoroughness, to give him mastery of the medium he must use. Afterwards the rapidity with which he will learn will make up for any delay in taking up regular studies and it will be found that ...he will learn many things thoroughly well."[2]

Observation

Sense training starts with observation. The child has a natural urge to observe the nature around. It is hence that most of the educationists have advised that early education should start with child's observation of nature under the guidance of the teacher. Explaining this method of teaching Sri Aurobindo said, "We may take the instance of a flower. Instead of looking casually at it and getting a casual impression of scent, form and colour, he should be encouraged to know the flower to fix in his mind the exact shade, the precise intensity of he scent, the beauty of curve and design in the form. His touch should assure itself of the texture and its peculiarities. Next the flower shoul be taken to pieces and its structure examined with the same carefulness of observation. All this should be done not as a task, but as an object by skillfully arranged questions suited to the learner which will draw him on to observe and investigate one thing after the other until he has almost unconsciously mastered the whole."[3]

---

1. *Ibid.*, p. 215.
2. *Ibid.*
3. *Sri Aurobindo and The Mother on Education*, Part II, p. 13.

The observation is not confined to the flowers and leaves. The child will also learn by the observation of stars, earth, stones, insects, animals and things made by human beings. The example of observation given above is particularly useful in the teaching of botany. To quote Sri Aurobindo, "The observation and comparison of flowers, leaves, plants, trees will lay the foundations of botanical knowledge without loading the mind with names and that dry set acquisition of information which is the beginning of cramming and detested by the healthy human mind when it is fresh from nature and unspoiled by unnatural habits."[1] Elaborating further use of observation method of teaching other subjects, Sri Aurobindo said, "In the same way by the observation of the stars, astronomy, by the observation of earth, stones, etc. geology, by the observation of insects and animals, entomology and zoology may be founded. A little later chemistry may be started by interesting observation of experiments without any formal teaching or heaping on the mind of formulas and book knowledge."[2]

Training of Memory and Judgment

As in the case of sense training so also in the case of training of the mind Sri Aurobindo wants to make them spontaneous and unconscious. He is against all mechanical, burdensome and unintelligent way of memory training. He is against any use of rote memory. Memory training should involve nothing of similarities and differences in things observed. According to Sri Aurobindo, "A similar but different flower should be put in the hands and he should be encouraged to note it with the same care, but with the avowed object of noting the similarities and differences. By this practice daily repeated the memory will naturally be trained."[3] This in turn will train the faculty of judgment. To quote Sri Aurobindo again, "At every step the boy will have to decide what is the right idea, measurement, appreciation of colour, sound,

---

1. ***Ibid.*, p. 14.**
2. ***Ibid.***
3. ***Ibid.*, p. 14.**

scent, etc., and what is the wrong. Often the judgements and distinctions made will have to be exceedingly subtle and delicate. At first many errors will be made, but the learner should be taught to trust his judgment without being attached to its results. It will be found that the judgement will soon begin to respond to the calls made on it, clear itself of all errors and begin to judge correctly and minutely. The best way is to accustom the boy to compare his judgements with those of others, When he is wrong, it should at first be pointed out to him how far he was right and why he went wrong; afterwards he should be encouraged to note these things for himself. Every time he is right, his attention should be prominently and encouragingly called to it so that he may get confidence."[1] The training of memory and judgement is the basis of every scientific teaching. In the opinion of Sri Aurobindo, "There is no scientific subject the perfect and natural mastery of which cannot be prepared in early childhood by this training of the faculties to observe, compare, remember and judge various classes."[2] Judgement gives the ability to choose between right and wrong. It is therefore a prelude to every decision about values.

TRAINING OF LOGICAL FACULTY

Training of judgement very much depends upon the training of logical faculty. According to Sri Aurobindo, training of logical reasoning requires the following three elements:[3]

1. The correctness of the facts,
2. The completeness as well the accuracy of the data,
3. The elimination of other possible or impossible conclusions from the same facts.

The young child should be trained to take interest in drawing influences from the facts. For this purpose he should proceed, "From the example to the rule and from the accumulating harmony

1. *Ibid.*, p. 15.
2. Sri Aurobindo, *B.C.L.*, 1972, Volume XVII, p. 223.
3. *Ibid.*, p. 226.

of rules to the formal science of the subject."[1] The reasoning should proceed from concrete to abstract, since this is the law of training of mental faculties, the sound should be acknowledged before the sense. Explaining his principle in this connection Sri Aurobindo has remarked, "The true knowledge takes its base on things, and only when it has mastered the thing, proceeds to formalize its information."[2]

Training of Imagination

Several subjects including literature, particularly, require a training of imagination. This is the first requirement of any excellence in any creative art. As Sri Aurobindo has given an important place to art and literature in his plan of education, he insists upon the child's training in imagination. According to him, "This is a most important and indispensable instrument."[3] For the training of imagination Sri Aurobindo recommends, "It may be divided into three functions, the forming of metal images, the power of creating thoughts, images and imitations or new combinations of existing thoughts and images, the appreciation of the soul in things, beauty, charm, greatness, hidden suggestiveness, the emotion and spiritual life that pervades the world."[4]

Training of Language

Explaining his principle for training of language, Sri Aurobindo finds out that first the child should know the things and then the ideas. He laments that most of the dealings with language show an absence of fine sense of words. He suggests, "The mind should be accustomed first to notice the word thoroughly, its form, sound and sense; then to compare the form with other similar forms in the points of similarity and difference, thus forming the foundation of the grammatical sense; then to distinguish between

---

1. *Ibid.*, p. 226-27.
2. *Sri Aurobindo and The Mother on Education*, Part II, p. 17.
3. *Ibid.*
4. *Ibid.*

the fine shades of sense of similar words and the formation and rhythm of different sentences, thus forming the foundation of the literary and the syntactical faculties."[1] All this should be done informally. One should avoid set rules of teaching and memorizing. Sri Aurobido is everywhere against mechanical processes. The teaching should first arouse the interest of the child and then depend upon spontaneous use of his abilities. The child should be allowed absolute freedom in his progress.

Free Progress System

The followers of Sri Aurobindo have developed a free progress system of education, whose salient features are as follows:[2]

1. The structure is oriented towards individual needs, interests and abilities.
2. The aspiration, experience of freedom, self-education and experimentation relating inner needs with the curricular provisions, discovering the higher lines of life and the art to encompass.
3. Each student is free to study any subject he chooses at any given time under a sympathetic guidance.
4. Promotion of individual endeavour.
5. Weekly announcement of time-table and lectures to be delivered.
6. Promotion of discussion between teachers and taught and between taught and taught.
7. Projects are announced in each subject and the students select according to their choice.

No Set Distinction

In his system of education, Sri Aurobindo does not make any distinction on the basis of sex. The education for man and woman should be similar in all respect. Clarifying this rejection of sex

---

1. *Ibid.*
2. Joshi Kirit, *Nev Chetna,* Mother International School, New Delhi (1977), pp. 5-7.

distinctions in education, The Mother said, "What we claim is this, that in similar conditions, with the same and the same possibilities, there is no reason to make a categorical distinction, final and imperative between what we call men and women. For us human beings are the expression of a single soul.[1] In his interpretation of his Indian social system Sri Aurobindo laid emphasis upon equality of sexes. He lamented that later on the women were subjected to men leading to degeneration of society. He proposes that the women should be everywhere treated as equals to men. He is against Indian psychological dictum that male and female should avoid each other's company. He, on the other hand, maintains, "There is no impossibility of friendship between man and woman pure of this element (sex), such friendships can exist and have always existed. All that is needed is that the lower vital should not look in it through the back door or be permitted to enter."[2] Therefore, no distinctions are made between boys and girls in Mother's International School or Sri Aurobindo International University at Pondicherry. The most unique feature of the education at these two institutions is the prescription of physical exercises both for boys and girls. Clarifying this policy the Mother said, "In all cases, as well as for boys as for girls, the exercises must be graded according to the strength and capacity of each one. If a weak student tries at once to do hard and heavy exercises must be graded according to the strength and capacity of each one. If a weak student tries at once to do hard and heavy exercises, he may suffer for his foolishness. But with a wise and progressive training girls as well as boys can participate in all kinds of sports, increase their strength and health."[3] According to Sri Aurobindo both men and women are equally capable to evolve toward perfection to reach gnostic age.

DISCIPLINE AND FREEDOM

The Mother has rightly said, "No big creation is possible

1. *Sri Aurobindo and The Mother on Women,* 1978 p. 17.
2. Sri Aurobindo, *B.C.L.,* 1970, Volume 23, p. 817.
3. *On Women,* 1978, p. 58.

without discipline."[1] Defining discipline in terms of the highest principle Sri Aurobindo maintained that it is "to act according to a standard of truth or a rule or law of action or in obedience to a superior authority or the highest principle discovered by the reason or intelligent will."[2] Thus discipline is a controlled life. The physical, the vital and the mental sources are guide by spirituality. It is against unbridled indulgence in fancies, impulses and desires. It is obedience of the inner sense. Partly, it is also obedience of authority.

Kinds of Discipline

Discipline, according to Sri Aurobindo, is : Individual discipline, Group discipline and finally Discipline towards the Divine. These distinctions have been made on the basis of the authority functioning in imposition of discipline. Individual discipline is imposed by the individual himself. Group discipline is imposed by the group or the majority or the leader in it. Discipline towards the Divine means, rigorous perusal of the dictates of the Divine. However, these three types of discipline are essentially the same since underlying the individual, group and the universe there is only one Divine principle. Sri Aurobindo maintains that the three aspects of reality, *viz.*, individuality, commonality and essentiality are in fact one.

Disciplinary Measures

The best way to impose discipline according to Sri Aurobindo is the atmosphere and the example by the teacher. The following measures have been recommended by Sri Aurobindo and The Mother to inculcate discipline among the students :

1. Generally speaking, the discipline should start at the age of twelve.
2. The most important measure is the example of the teacher. The Teacher should be punctual, properly dressed, calm,

---

1. ***Sri Aurobindo and The Mother on Education,*** **part II, p. 26.**
2. **Sri Aurobindo *B.C.L., 1970,* Volume 23, p. 862.**

methodical, orderly, sympathetic and courteous. He should himself present high examples of sincerity, honesty straightforwardness, courage, disinterestedness, unselfishness, patience, endurance, perseverance, peace and self-control. He should first of all train his own emotions and morals. He should have a respect of the child. Nothing should be imposed from outside but suggested by examples. Examples are the best for the personal guidance and to exercise influence upon the educands. In the words of The Mother, "It is through example that education becomes effective. To say good words, give wise advice to a child has very little effect, if one does not show by one's living example the truth of what one teaches."[1]

The vibrations between the teacher and the taught should be favourable, there should be no use of force in discipline. According to The Mother, before the age of seven years the child is not conscious of himself and does not know why and how to do things. During this period he should be trained to acquire traits of a human being. From the age of seven years to fourteen years of age, the child should be taught to choose what he wishes to be. At 14, he should be clear at what he wants to do. After 14 years of age he should be left independent to pursue his course. He may be only advised now and then.

There can be no definite rules for the guidance of the students in the process of discipline. Sri Aurobindo recommends emphasis upon individual difference without any hammering of the child. He believes that, "Every one has in him something divine, sometimes his own, a chance of perfection and strength in however small a sphere which God offers him to take or refuse. The task is to find it, develop it and use it."[2]

Finally, discipline is ultimately spiritual. This requires psychic realisation. Sri Aurobindo suggests the following two

1. ***Sri Aurobindo and The Mother on Education,* part II, p. 27.**
2. **Sri Aurobindo, *B.C.L.*, 1972, Volume 17, p. 204.**

ways for converting mental seeking into living spiritual experience."[1]

1. The concentration of the consciousness within especially in the main centres—in the heart (the cardiac centre in the middle of the chest) and the head.
2. To accord the nature—physical, vital and mental with the inner realisation so that one may not be divided into two discordant parts.

Among the several ways to accord the nature with the inner realisation, the following two have been particularly emphasised by Sri Aurobindo:

1. To offer all the activities to the divine and call for the inner guidance—the inward soul is being opened, the psychic being comes for help, gradually the imperfections are being removed and the physical consciousness is being reshaped.
2. To stand back detached from the movements of the physical, vital and mental being—becoming aware of the inner opening of body, life and mind in the psychic entity.

Discipline and Freedom

From the above discussion, it is clear that according to Sri Aurobindo, freedom is the real discipline. This however, is only spiritual freedom. In the realm of Spirit there is no chasm between discipline and freedom. Each one has to grow and expand according to his own principle. The inner voice in every educand is in fact the divine principle in him. Thus realistation of freedom is God realisation. As order is the prelude to liberty, similarly discipline is a precondition for realisation of freedom.

Code of Conduct

This, however, does not mean that there is no code of conduct at The Mother's International School or at Sri Aurobindo's International University. As the principal guide of

76. *Ibid.*, Volume 23, pp. 517-19.

both these institutions The Mother has laid down code of conduct for the educands. She is against any outward limitation of the child's liberty but she insists that once the choice for joining the above mentioned institutions has been made, there is no turning aside. She is against any use of compulsion or obligation. She however insists upon taking judgement and following them. She advise the edcands to arrive at rational decisions and to follow them. She maintains that the class discipline must be followed. In her own words, "But if a student has decided to follow a class, it is an absolutely elementary discipline for him to follow it, he must go to the class regularly and behave decently there: otherwise he is quite unfit to go to school."[1] She was against any illusions about the abilities of the educands. She warned, "Do not mistake liberty for licence and freedom for bad manners. The thought must be pure and the aspiration ardent."[2] She laid down the following code of behaviour for the students :

1. The good manners should be always observed.
2. Everyone should always speak the truth.
3. Truth in speech demands truth in acts too.
4. It is forbidden for children to fight at school, in the street, in the playground and at home. "Always and everywhere it is forbidden for children to fought among themselves, for each time one gives blow to someone, it is to one's own soul that one gives it."[3]
5. The child should always remember:

   The necessity of an absolute sincerity.

   The certitude of Truth's final victory.

   The possibility of constant progress with the will to achieve.[4]

---

1. *Sri Aurobindo and The Mother on Education,* **Part III p. 20.**
2. *Ibid.*, p. 72.
3. *Ibid.*
4. *Sri Aurobindo and The Mother on Education,* **Part III, p. 22.**

EVALUATION AND EXAMINATION

Rejecting the so-called mental test, the Mother said, "I find tests an obsolete and ineffective way of knowing if the students are intelligent, willing and attentive. A silly, mechanical mind can very well answer a test if the memory is good and these are certainly not the qualities required for a man of the future."[1] She not only rejects the mental test but also suggests alternatives. "To know if a student is good, needs, if the tests are abolished, a little more inner contact and psychological knowledge for the teacher. But our teachers are expected to do yoga, so this ought not to be difficult for them."[2]

Spontaneous Evaluation

In two words, the method of evaluation in Sri Aurobindo's system of education, may be called spontaneous evaluation. This depends upon the inner contact, keen observation and impartial outlook of the evaluator. The tests of progress are not the essay type examination. In the words of Sri Aurobindo, "We must direct our school and university examinations to the testing of these active faculties and not of the memory."[3] Criticising the prevalent system of education conducted by the British in India, Sri Aurobindo pointed out that in it the students do not achieve the real purpose of education. He was against education only for earning livelihood. According to him the students are, "To learn in order to know, to study in order to have the knowledge of the secrets of nature and of life, to educate oneself in order to increase one's consciousness, to discipline oneself in order to be master of oneself, to overcome one's weakness, one's incapacity and ignorance, to prepare oneself in order to progress in life towards a goal that is nobler and vaster, more generous and more true...."[4]

To meet the above purpose, Sri Aurobindo's International Centre of Education, Pondicherry, has evolved "Free Progress

1. *Ibid.,* part II, p. 30.
2. *Ibid.,* p. 31.
3. *Ibid.*
4. *Ibid.*

System," based upon subjective evaluation by the teacher. Progress records ware to be filled by the students while the teacher has to note their comments. Clarifying this system of evaluation, The Mother told the teachers,

"At the end of the year you will give notes to the students, not based on written test-papers, but on their behaviour, their concentration their regularity, their promptness to understand and their openness of intelligence."[1]

Our discussion of the philosophy of education, as given by Sri Aurobindo, clearly points out that this is a new experiment in education. Its philosophical foundations and psychological credibility is sound. Its success, however, requires a large band of devoted, sincere and spiritual teachers, prepared to carry on the burden of education against all odds. So long as such a band is not available it is just an experiment.

❑❑❑

1. *Ibid.*

14

Mohandas Karam Chand Gandhi

"By education I mean an all round drawing out of the best in child and man, body, mind and spirit" **—M.K. Gandhi**

Mohandas Karamchand Gandhi was born on Oct. 2, 1869 at Porbander in Kathiawar. His father was a Diwan (Prime Minister) at Porbander and Rajkot. His mother was a religious lady. He was married at the age of 12. In 1888, he passed his matriculation examination and was sent to London to qualify for the bar. Before Leaving India at the age 19, he made a promise to his mother that he would avoid meat, wine and women.

After qualifying himself (for the bar, her began to practice at Rajkot and from there he shifted to Bombay. During his stay in England, he became interested in 'Bhagwad Gita" and was also influenced by Arnold's *"The light of Asia"* i.e. poem about Buddha. During his stay at Bombay, he came in contact with Raj Chandra Raujibhai and learnt his first lessons of non violence and truth etc. He practiced law but did not get much success due to his adherene to principles.

In 1893, Gandhi had to leave for South Africa to conduct the case of a Gujarati Muslim merchant. He was deeply moved by the hard conditions under which his countrymen had to live. He was unable to tolerate injustice which they were getting. His opportunity came in 1906 when the Asiatic Registration Act was passed. He protested against it and put into practice his weapon of Satyagraha. He led a struggle which later on bacame a cause of down fall of British Empire. He had to suffer hard-ship and imprison men there but he got success in his aim there.

Having won his laurels in South Africa, Gandhi came to India in 1914. Uptil now he did not oppose British rule in India. In 1915, he said, "I have found that it is possible for me to be governed least under the British Empire. Hence my loyalty to British Empire.... But passing of Rowlatt Bills in teeth of opposition by the people forced him to change his view and came to conclusion that the British Rule in India was Satanic." In India, he chose Gopal Krishna Gokhale as his political guru. But he was also influenced by Tilak. Thus he learnt. Indian diplomacy and was acquainted also with the British diplomacy.

The period of 1914 to 1947 was the most glorious phase of Gandhiji's activities. In 1918, he wrote to Victory, "I would make India offer all her able bodied persons as a sacrifice to the Empire at this critical moment; and I know that India by this very act, would become the most favoured partner and racial distinction, would become a thing of the past. But Gandhi's hopes were shattered on the sharp rocks of reality. In August 1920 he wrote, "Events that have happened during the past months have confirmed me in the opinion that the Imperial Government have acted in the khilifat matter in (or omit) an unscrupulous immoral and unjust manner....(and estranged me completely from the present Government and have disabled me from rendering as I have hitherto whole heartedly rendered my total co-operation"). He further added, "In European countries condonation of such grievous wrongs as the Khilafat and the Punjab would have resulted, in a bloody revolution by the people. They would have resisted at all costs national emasculation. Half of India is too weak to offer violent resistance and the other half is unwilling to do so, I have therefore decided to suggest the remedy of non-cooperation...."

Gandhiji started his non-violent, non co-operation movement with great hopes but his dream of swarajya did not materialize. From 1920, when he got his resolution passed at Calcutta, Gandhi era begins. Now Mahatma Gandhi became unquestioned leader of India who lead her to freedom. In 1922, there took place serious rioting at Chaurichaura near Gorakhpur in U.P. Gandhi stopped further activities as movement became violent.

There was a split within the Congress on the question of Council entry, Swarajya party lead by Moti Lal Nehru and C.R. Dass favoured Congress entry in the legislatures and fighting the government from within also. But the scheme of Swarajist failed because in the words of Zakaria, "They desired to eat the cake as well as to save it."

From then onwards Mahatma Gandhi became the unchallenged leader. He dominated the entire polities of the country. In 1931, he went to attend Round Table Conference, but came empty handed. In 1931, he started Civil Disobedience Movement, a greater success than the movement of 1921. It ended with Gandhi Irwin Pact which was victory for Indian National Congress. In 1942, India witnessed Quit India Movement under the leadership of Mahatma Gandhi. India won her independence on 14 August 1947 under the leadership of Mahatma Gandhi. Although neither the Prime Minister of India nor the President of Congress, his was the last word on every point. He worded whole heartedly for Harijan uplift and for the cause of downtrodden peasants and workers and for woman uplift. He also championed the cause of handwoven Khadi to provide employment to weavers. He turned resolution making Congress into a mass movement body and created a situation which forced Britishers to quit so some scholars think without his leadership attaining of Swaraj would have been difficult.

On Jan. 30, 1948 Gandhi was shot dead. It was a great blow, not only to India, but to the whole world. In his book "*Mahatma Gandhi-The Meaning of his Death*," Dr. Stanley Jones writes "if Mahatma Gandhi had been privileged to choose the issue on which he could have died, he could not have chosen a better issue.

It exactly sums up his life....No human being ever summed up more perfectly in his death the things for which he lived in his life." He expressed his feelings in following words, "I never saw Gandhi. I do not know his language. I never set foot in his country and yet I feel the same sorrow as if had lost some one near and dear. The whole world has been plunged into mourning by the death of this extra ordinary man." He now belongs to ages. He was the greatest man since Buddha that India has ever produced. According to Sheriden, "Gandhi and Lenin gave immortal ideas to the world." According to Dr. Homes, "World has to decide whether it desires Atom Bomb or non violence of Mahatma Gandhi and it is the decision of life and death....Gandhiji proved that the spiritual power is more powerful than the physical force."

Gandhiji was not a philosopher but a Karmyogi. It is often remarked that there is no ism like Gandhism. He observed in 1936, in his book, *My Experiments with Truth*, "There is no such thing as Gandhism and I do not want to leave any sect after me. I do not claim to have originated any new principle and doctrine. I have simply tried in my own way to apply the central truths to our daily life and problems.... You will not call it Gandhism; there is not ism about it."

INFLUENCES ON GANDHIJI

Man is the creature of circumstances as well as the moulder of the circumstances. Hi thougths are moulded by the environment and various influences. As such we may trace out the sources which moulded the political thoughts of Gandhiji. The Gita influenced his most. He himself wrote, "Where doubts surround me, when disappointments stare me in the face, and I see not one ray of light on the horizon, I turn to the Bhagwat Gita and find a verse to comfort me, and I immediately begin to smile in the midst of overwhelming sorrow. My life has been full of external tragedies and if they have not left any visible effect on me, I owe to the teachings of Bhagwat Gita."

Jain monk Becharji Swami and Buddhism also had its influence on Gandhiji. John Ruskin's book "*Unto His Last*" and its teaching, the life of labour as the life worth living, profoundly influenced him. Thoreau's Essays on "*Civil Disobedience*" which he read in prison in 1908 in South Africa also influenced him. Tolestory also influenced Mahatma Gandhi. His book, "*The Kingdom of God is Within You*" had a profound influence on Gandhiji. Gandhi wrote that "Tolstoy is one of the three moderners who have exerted the greatest spiritual influence on my life." Rajchandra, a distinguished social reformer of Bombay, also exercised a lot of influence on him. Inspite of these influences, he was a Karmyogi, a practical idealist and his philosophy grew out of his own experiences and experiments with truth and non-violence.

AIMS AND IDEALS OF EDUCATION

1. Drawing Out the Best—Elaborating his views about the aims of education, Gandhihi has said, "By education I mean an all round drawing out of the best in child and man, body, mind and spirit. Literacy is not the end of education, not even the beginnings. It is one of the means whereby, man and woman can be educated. Literacy in itself is no education."

2. Livelihood—Gandhi was highly critical of the education policy implemented by British government. In his opinion, the aim of education is self-dependence, and education must enable every girl and boy to develop the ability to depend upon himself or hereself. The ability to earn one's livelihood is part of this independence or self-reliance. As he himself put it, "This education ought to be for them a kind of insurance against unemployment." That is why Gandhiji placed so much emphasis upon industrial training in his own plan for basic education which was intended to acquaint the child with real life. He wanted the educator to become the means of producing ideal citizens. Seeing the endemic poverty of the nation, he suggested that education in India should be based on industrial training and the development of manual skill and handicrafts.

3. Character Formation—Like Rousseau, Gandhiji also believed in paidocentric education, that is, education which centres around the child. He impressed upon people that the cultural aspect of education was far more important than its literary aspect, because it is through the cultural aspect that the child learns conduct and ideas and develops his character and ideals. As he puts it, "True education is that which draws out and stimulates the spiritual, intellectual and physical faculties of the children." Hence, the aim of education is the complete development of the child, its physical, mental and spiritual aspects. For him character formation was more important than literacy. He was once asked what his education would aim at after country won its independence. He answered without hesitation that it would be designed to develop the character of the people. And, in character, Gandhiji addressed the importance of thought, word and deed, nonviolence and truth. He, like many before him, felt that abstinence was an essential weapon for the educand. He was a supporter of the ancient Indian ideals of education. He, in fact, felt that the words educand and Brahamchari should be treated as synonymous. And for him, abstinence meant a persistent effort to reach God in the least possible time.

4. Complete Development—It is clear from the foregoing account that Gandhiji viewed education from a comprehensive or broadminded standpoint. Any education that develops only one aspect of a child's personality can be dubbed narrow and one-sided. And it is just such an education which has been the bane of our culture. Education must aim at developing the child's personality instead of limiting itself to providing the child with bits and pieces of information. Not only must education guide the individual towards self-knowledge, it must instil in him all those qualities which go to the making up of a good and responsible citizen. Gandhiji has made a distinction between the immediate and long term aims of education suggesting that such aims, as getting certificates of merits or degrees or obtaining education for livelihood, should be considered the immediate aims. But the final aim of education can only be self-knowledge. Thus, Gandhiji states that education must make the individual to live and earn his daily bread, to be the means of his sustenance. As he himself puts, it, "I value individual freedom, but you must not forget that man is essentially a social being. He has risen to his present status by learning to adjust his individuality to the requirements of social progress." His faith in religion is at the base of his liberal attitude to education. Realisation of good is, in fact, the end or the goal of all human activity and service to humanity its finest means. It is only natural that such a faith should lead him to stress the social objectives of education more than the personal or individual ones.

5. Synthesis of Individual and Social Aims—In this way Gandhi synthesized the individual and social aims of education. He did not restrict education to the achievement of any one single aim. He looked to the process of education from various perspective. Therefore, he assigned different aims of education at different times, so much so that sometimes they liked mutually contradictory and even self-defeating. A closer examination of all these statements of Gandhi, however, shows that these aims of education are complementary to each other.

6. All Round Growth—In the history of education, different educationists have defined the ideals of education in different ways. Most educationists have, however, felt that the aim of education is intergral development of human personality. Such was also the ideal of education formulated by Gandhi. Like Vivekananda, Gandhi maintained that character formation and manual skill were equally important. On the one hand, he wanted the child to earn while he learns. On the other hand, he also wanted the child to develop his character. According to him, the criterion of an individual's cultural development is not the width of his knowledge but his inner growth. Culture according to him, is not an adjunct of the mind but a characteristic of the soul. The aim of education is the development of such a culture. Gandhi's plan of education laid stress upon all types of education, physical, mental, moral, aesthetic and religious.

7. Self Reliance—As has been already pointed out, Gandhi aimed at self-reliance through education, Therefore, he visualised a craft-centred education. Explaining his scheme of Basic education as an insurance against unemployment in India, Gandhi said, "The child at the age of 14, that is, after finishing a seven year course should be discharged as an earning unit. Even now the poor peoples, children automatically lend a helping hand to their parents, the feeling at the back of their minds being what shall they give me to eat, if I do not work with them? That is an education in itself. Even so the State takes charge of the child at seven and returns it to the family as an earning unit. You impart education and simultaneously cut at the root of unemployment." Recommending this scheme of education in the report on national education the Kothari Commission declared, "We recommend that work experience should be introduced as an integral part of all education general or vocational. We define work-experience as participation in productive work in school, in the home, in a workshop, on a farm, in a factory or in any other productive situation."

8. Democratic Ideals—Like his contemporary Indian educationists, Gandhi aimed at the evolution of democratic ideals through education. His basic plan of education amply demonstrates this fact. He aimed at an education for ideal citizenship. Education, according to him, should make children ideal members of a democratic society. The school, according to Gandhi, is itself a small democratic society in which such democratic values are imparted to the children as wide outlook, tolerance and good neighbourhood. In the miniature society of the school, the child learns the virtues of sympathy, service, love, brotherhood, equality and liberty, etc. These qualities are transferred from one generation to another through education. The welfare of the individual and the nation are complementary to each other. Therefore, if the country has to progress, the future generation should develop the virtues of democratic citizenship. As Gandhi said, "A nation cannot advance without the units of which it is composed advancing, and conversely, no individual can advance without the nation of which it is a part also advancing."

9. Character Building—All knowledge is useless without a good character. In his speeches to the students at various institutions, Gandhi laid emphasis upon the moral and spiritual aims of education. Emphasizing the moral aim of education Gandhi said, "The end of all knowledge must be the building up of character." Character building is the moral ideal of education. According to Gandhi that is most important in a man's life. His ideals in this connection were as much in agreement with the ancient Indian thinkers as with contemporary Western thinkers like Emeson, Riskin, etc., Gandhi very much admired the Indian Gurukula system of education and the Ideal of Brahmacharya according to ancient Indian ideal education aims at liberation. This was also the aim of Gujarat Vidyapeeth established by Gandhi in 1929. Gandhi, however, defined liberation in a very wide sense, including political, social and economic liberation of all the members of society. Real freedom is spiritual freedom. To attain this freedom is the task of education. Again, education equally aims at intellectually, economic and political uplift, though its chief aim is moral and spiritual. Condeming the wide spread indiscipline among the students, Gandhi asked them to follow the Ideal of Brahmacharya.

10. God Realisation—According to Indian philosophy, the ultimate end of all knowledge is God realisation. This God realisation which again, is the meaning of which self-realisation has been considered to be the ideal of education by most of the education philosophers in East and West. Agreeing with this line of thinking, Gandhi maintained that a student should live a life of Sanyasi. God realisation and self-realisation are mutually complementary, the one leads to the other. This spiritual ideal of education must achieve something more than one objective. That is why he ascribed to it many different aims. At times a superficial study of these aims may give the impression that they are mutually contradictory or self-defeating, but a deeper examination will show that they complement each other.

Even a cursory glancing through the history of education will show abundantly that different educationists have ascribed different aims to education. For some it is training for livelihood and sustenance, for others it is self-realization, for yet others the individual aims take precedence over the social objectives of education while some educationists favour the social aspects. Most educationists, however have felt that education must strive for human perfection. Cultural development is another aim that has been ascribed to education. Idealists emphasis the idealistic aspect more than the realistic while naturalists and realists stress the realistic forms of education. Gandhiji's philosophy of education aims at harmo nizing all these controdictory veiewpoints. His Wardha plan of education placed great stress upon training in self-reliance, because he felt that the highest criterion of an educational system was its ability in putting an end to unemployment. For him both character formation and manual skill were important. Education should also be accompanied by earning money, and that is why he felt that the educator's salary should be paid out of goods produced by the educands. He believed that character building was as important as. If not more than, collecting information.

11. Cultural Development—The criterion of an individual's cultural development is not the extent of his knowledge but the qualities he manifests. In the cultural aspect of education, he emphasis upon the behaviour and thinking of educands. Culture, according to him, is not an adjunct of the mind but a quality of the soul and cultural development an important objective of education. Education is the means to the child's physical, mental and spiritual development. His plan of education gave importance to physical, moral, aesthetic and religious education along with the teaching of mathematics and literary skills. In addition to this he stressed that handwriting should be neat and clean.

M.K. Gandhi fell that the present educational system is not suitable for social and cultural aspects of life. Accordingly he pointed out, "For that which should be remembered is this. The greatest visible evil of the present educational method, in it self evidence of deeper defects, is that it has broken up the continuity of our existence. All sound education is meant to fit one generation to take up the burden of the previous and to keep up the life of the community without breach or disaster....if at any stage one generation gets completely out of touch with the efforts of its predecessors or in any case gets ashamed of itself or its culture, is lost."[1]

It is, thus obvious that Gandhi's aim of preservation of cultural heritage and the development of it for the sake of posterity is one of the most important function of education.

It can be observed that through various aims of education laid down by Gandhiji, he wanted to strike a balance between the ideals of social service and individual development. It was his conviction that individuality develops only in a social atmosphere where it can feed on common interests and common activities. He insisted that individuality shall have freescope, within the common life, to grow in its own way and that it shall not be warped from its ideal bent by forces "heavy as frost and deep almost as life."[2] He, therefore, suggested that we should transform our schools into communities where individuality is not damped down, but developed through social contacts and social service.

MEANS OF EDUCATION

Since Gandhi was of the firm conviction that literacy in itself is not education, he held, "I would therefore, begin the child's education by teaching it a useful handicraft and enabling it to produce from the moment it begins its training....I hold that the highest development of the mind and the soul is possible under such a system of education."[3] However, The handicraft taught should be not merely mechanically, but scientifically such that the child becomes aware of the why and wherefore of every process.

Gandhiji further stated that useful manual labour, is the means **par excellence** for developing the intellect. A balanced

1. Ibid, p. 27
2. Patel, M.S., Educational Philosophy of Mahatma Gandhi, Navjeevan Publishing House, Ahmeadbad, 1958, p. 56.
3. Harijan, July 31, 1937, p. 197

intellect, according to Gandhi, presupposes a harmonious growth of body, mind and soul. In Gandhi's own words, "An intellect that is developed through the medium of socially useful labour will be an instrument for service and will not easily be led astray or fall into devious paths."[1]

In order to acquire the essential modicum of social and civic training Gandhiji suggested various means which would enable the child to adjust himself intelligently and actively to his social environment. For this he put forth an activity curriculum, with a plan to transform the schools into places of work and experimentation. In this curriculum he included (a) Basic Craft (b) Mother-tongue, (c) Mathematics, (d) Social studies, (e) General science, and (f) Music.

About Mathematics, he was of the opinion that "the teaching of Mathematics is not to be confined merely to the facts and operation of number....Measurements of quantities and values in these connections would supply amply opportunity for the development of the reasoning capacities of the pupils."[2] About the utility of Music, Gandhiji wrote, "Music means rhythm, order. Its effect is electrical. It immediately soothes....If I had any influence with volunteer boy scounts and *Seva Samiti* organisations, I would make compulsory a proper singing, in company, of national songs."[3] Gandhi thought that modulation of the voice is as necessary as the training of the hand. He, therefore, held, "Physical drill, handicrafts, drawing and music should go hand in hand to draw the best out of the boys and girls and create in them a real interest in their tuition.[4]

Methods of Teaching

In Gandhi an system of education the methods of teaching are considered more relevant and suitable than the contents, to

---

1. Harijan, **September 8, 1946, p. 306**
2. **Hindustani Talimi Sangh (ed)** Educational Reconstruction **Sevagram, 1947, p. 129.**
3. **Bose Nirmal Kumar,** Selections from Gandhi op. cit. **p. 274**
4. Ibid **p. 274-75**

realise the aims of education proposed by Gandhiji. Gandhi believed that in order to train the whole man, his body, mind and spirit, education should be craft-centred. In his opinion a system of education in which craft is the centre can lead to the highest development of the whole man, provided the craft chosen is manual and productive. Gandhi held that it is to be starting point of the other subjects as well, "a meeting point of both physical and social environment represented by such subjects as General Science, Social studies and creative and expressional arts."[1] Gandhiji admits that craft-centred education lays emphasis on such important principles of teaching as provision of useful experiences and activity as well as correlation of subjects.

Gandhiji also suggested that children should be taught the art of drawing before learning how to write. In an infant school, drawing should from a part of practically every subject.

The Role of Teacher

The role of the teacher is very significant in Gandhi an educational philosophy. He expected that the teachers would make attractive and intelligible, what to the pupils may at first appear repulsive and uninteresting. He further said, "It is the duty of the teacher to teach his pupils, discrimination....The best way to do this is for the teachers rigorously to practice these virtues in their own person. Their very association with the pupils whether on the play-ground or in the class-room will then give them (pupils) a fine training in these fundamental virtues."[2]

This means that in the opinion of Gandhiji, a teacher who is himself a stranger to self-restraint could never teach his pupils the value of self-restraint. Similarly, the teachers who themselves do not believe in non-violence or truth or non-cooperation cannot impart to their students the spirit of any of these moral principles, Gandhi was very vocal in this respect because he disliked the principle of drinking wine and preaching water simultaneously. He

1. **Dhiman O.P.,** Op. Cit. **p. 170**
2. Ibid, **p. 171**

said, "I have found that pupils imbibe more from the teachers' own lives than they do from the books they read to them, or the lectures they deliver to them with their lips....Woe to the teacher who teaches one thing with his lips and carries another in his breast."[1] Gandhi, therefore, asks the teachers to cultivate their hearts and establish a heart-contact with the students. He should fashion their hearts rather than their brains. That shall be the best means of education.

Gandhi believed that discipline is an important aspect of a sound system of education. He held that education without discipline is like a boat without a rudder. He said, "It is discipline and restraint that separates us from the brute. If we will be men walking with our heads erect, and not walking on all fours, let us understand and put ourselves under voluntary discipline and restraints."[2]

It was the dream of Gandhiji that the narrowness and bigotry which have for long poisoned the relationship between the people of different faiths and cultures, should end. He held, "Nothing can be farther from my thought than that we should become exclusive or erect barriers. But I do respectfully contend that an appreciation of other cultures can fitly follow never precede an appreciation and assimilation of our own."[3] It is possible that a generation brought up free from the virus of bigotry might be in a position to touch a higher level of culture than its forefathers ever achieved.

Medium of Instruction

Gandhi loved his mother-tongue so much that he would cling to it as to his mother's breast. He knew very well the evils of the foreign medium and held that it deprived the students of their birth-right if they received education through a language other than their mother-tongue. He said, "I find daily proof of the

1. Ibid, **p. 172**
2. Ibid, **p. 173**
3. **Bose Nirmal Kumar,** Op. cit. **p. 254**

increasing and continuing wrong being done to the millions by our false de-Indianising education."[1] According to Gandhi, instruction through a foreign medium was a national tragedy of first importance. That is why he encourged education through the vernaculars. He said, "The medium of instruction should be altered at once and at any cost....I would prefer temporary chaos in higher education to the criminal waste that is daily accumulating."[2] Gandhiji was aware of the problem that we never master the English language and with some exception it has not been possible for us to do so. Speaking about the wastage in learning to express in foreign language, Gandhi points out, "Just consider for one moment what an unequal race our lads have to run with every English lad....every Indian youth, because he reached his knowledge through the English language, lost at least six precious years of life."[3]

Thus, Gandhi was convinced that much time and labour of nation can be saved if learning is imparted through mother-tongue.[4] He therefore advocated for providing the rightful place to the vernaculars in education. He said, "I have no doubt, whatsoever that if those who have the education of the youth in their hands, will but make up their minds, they will discover that the mother-tongue is as natural for the development of man's mind as mother's milk is for the development of the infant's body."[5] He, therefore, regarded it as a sin against the mother-land to inflict upon her children a tongue other than their mother's for their mental development.[6] Thus, according to Gandhi, mother-tongue of the child should be the medium of instruction at all stages of education.

1. **Prabhu R.K. & Rao U.R.**, op. cit. **p. 382**
2. Harijan, **July 9, 1938, pp. 177-78**
3. **Gandhi M.K.**, Towards New Education **op. cit. p. 47**
4. **Mani R.S.**, Op, cit **p. 99**
5. **Gandhi M.K.** Medium of Instruction, **edited by Sailesh Kumar Bandopadhyay, Navjeevan Publishing House Ahmedabad 1954, p. 8**
6. Ibid, **p. 8-9.**

This does not, however, mean that Gandhi altoghter ignores the place of English. The very columns of the ***Harijan*** in which he expressed his wonderful ideas in beautiful English are sufficient evidence of his love for English. He makes his stand clear and states, "English is a language of international commerce, it is the language of diplomacy and it contains many a rich literary treasure, it gives us an introduction to Western thought and culture. For a few of us, therefore, a knowledge of English is necessary."[1]. Although he desired that, "the highest development of the Indian mind must be possible without a knowledge of English."[2] Yet he was also very much aware of the practical utility of English. It was his considered opinion that "English has put a severe strain upon the Indian students' nervous energy and made of us imitators."[3] But still he advocated for its retention. He said, "English is today admittedly the world language. I would therefore accord it a place as a second, optional language, not in the school, but in the University course. That can only be for the select few, not for the million."[4] This show that Gandhi was not a blind opponent of English. He held, "I love English tongue in its own place but I am its inveterate opponent, if it usurps a place which does not belong to it."[5] Making his position very clear on the issue of learning English, Gandhi made a categorical assertion that : "I would have our young men and women with literary taste to learn as much of English and other world-languages as they like, and then expect them to give the benefit of their learning to India and to the world like a Bose, a Ray or the Poet himself (meaning Poet Tagore). But I would not have a single Indian to forget, neglect or be ashamed of his mother tongue...."[6] This shows that Gandhi wanted India to flourish in her own climate, scenery and literature and for that the medium of instruction suggested by Gandhi was mother-tongue of the child.

1. **Gandhi M.K.** To the Students, Op. cit. p. 53.
2. Young India, **February 2, 1921, p. 34.**
3. Ibid, **April 27, 1921 p. 130**
4. Harijan, **August 25, 1946, p. 284**
5. **Gandhi M.K.,** Towards New Education, op. cit. **p. 65-66**
6. **Bose Nirmal Kumar,** op. cit. **p. 267.**

BASIC EDUCATION

The new scheme of education which Gandhi launched in 1937 and advocated widely in India was named Basic National Education or the Wardha Scheme.[1] This was the scheme which he had tested for over forty years in actual practice in small groups on the children in the Phoenix Settlement and on Tolstoy Farm. In 1937, the All India National Educational Conference was held in Wardha which unanimously approved Gandhiji's idea and appointed a committee of the leading educationalists with Dr. Zakir Husain as its Chairman to give shape to this plan of new education. The report of this committee came to be known as Basic National Education.[2]

The conference adopted a few resolutions which have become the formulative postulates of Basic education viz.

1. That is the opinion of the conference, free and compulsory education be provided for seven years of a nation-wide scale.
2. That the medium of instruction be the mother-tongue.
3. That the process of education throughout this period should centre round some form of manual and productive work, and that all the other abilities to be developed or training to be given should as far as possible, be integrally related to the central handicraft chosen with due regard to the environment of the child.
4. That it is expected that this system of education will be gradually able to cover the remuneration of the teachers.[3]

A planned syllabus on the basis of the above fundamentals was prepared later. It is evident from the first proposition of the scheme of Basic education that Gandhiji wanted education to be free and compulsory for all boys and girls below the age of

1. **Mani R.S.**, op. cit. **p. 77**
2. **Biswas A, & Aggarwal J.C.**, op. cit. **p. 129**
3. **Gandhi M.K.**, Basic Education, **Navjeevan Publishing House Ahmedabad, 1955, p. 26**

fourteen. Gandhi's aim was to achieve the target of universal minimum education for maximum possible Indians. Here the foundation was to be laid for the future of the child and of the country. Gandhi was definite that "between the boy who has passed the matriculation under the purely literary education introduced by the Britishers, and the boy who has gone through basic education, the latter will give a better account of himself because his faculties have been developed. He would not feel helpless when he goes to college as matriculates often do."[1]

The basic idea of Gandhian scheme was that education should be imparted through some craft or productive work which should provide the nucleus of all the other instructions provided in the school. Explaining his case, Gandhi said, "In my scheme of things, the hand will handle tools before it draws or traces the writing. The eyes will read the pictures of letters and words as they will know other things in life....the whole training will be natural, responsive and therefore the quickest and the cheapest in the land."[2] He further pointed out that, "his idea was not merely to teach a particular profession or occupation to the children, but to develop the full man through teaching that occupation."[3] The observations that Zakir Husain Committee made in this connection are very apt : "Modern educational thought is practically unanimous in commending the idea of educating children through some suitable form of productive work. This method is considered to be the most effective approach to the problem of providing an integral all-sided education."[4]

This vocational training is closely linked with the concept of free and compulsory education : In Gandhi's own words, "I am a firm believer in the principle of the free and compulsory primary

1. Ibid., **p. 95**
2. **Tendulkar, D.G.,** Mahatma : Life of Mohandas Karamchand Gandhi **Publication Division, Govt., of India New Delhi, 1969, Vol. IV, p. 186.**
3. Ibid, **p. 200**
4. **Hindustani Talimi Sangh (ed)** Educational Reconstruction, **Sevagram, Wardha, 1950, p. 92.**

education in India. I also hold that we shall realise this only by teaching the children a useful vocation and utilising it as a means for cultivating their mental, physical and spiritual faculties. Let no one consider these economic calculations in connexion with education as sordid or out of place."[1] There are many advantages of making crafts the centre of education, which have been listed by the Zakir Husain Committee, "Psychologically, it is desirable because it relieves the child from the tyranny of a purely academic and theoretical instruction against which its active nature is always making a healthy protest."[2] From social point of view, as the report goes on, "the introduction of such practically productive work in education, to be participated in by all the children of the nation will tend to break down the existing barriers of the prejudice between manual and intellectual workers, harmful alike for both."[3]

"Considered economically, the scheme, if carried out intelligently and efficiently, will increase the productive capacity of our workers and will also enable them to utilise their leisure advantageously."[4]

However, it is still more important from strictly educational point of view. The Committee holds, "Greater concreteness and reality can be given to the knowledge acquired by children by making some significant craft the basis of education. Knowledge will thus become related to life and its various aspects will be correlated with one another."[5]

In Gandhi's opinion, education was to be based essentially on rural occupations and the child was to be trained to be a producer. Thus his scheme of education was to be purposive and organically connected with and centred round the child's social

---

1. **Bose Nirmal Kumar,** op, cit., **p. 258.**
2. **Hindustani Talimi Sangh** op. cit. **p. 93.**
3. Ibid.
3. Ibid. **p. 93.**
5. Ibid. **p. 93-94.**

and cultural environment. Gandhiji pointed out, "We have to make them true representative of our culture, of our civilisation, of the true genius of our nation. We cannot do so unless we give them a course of self-supporting primary education."[1] It was the main aim of basic education to teach handicraft not merely for production work but for developing the intellect of the pupils.[2] Gandhi therefore, suggested, "The old idea was to add a handicraft to the ordinary curriculum of education followed in school. To me that seems a fatal mistake. The teacher must learn the craft and correlate his knowledge with the craft, so that they will give all the knowledge to their pupil through the medium of the particular craft they choose."3 This means that Gandhi wanted to teach through hand-work, all the subjects like History, Geography, Arithmatic, Science, Language, Painting etc.[4] It is evident that a knowledge of handicraft is not limited to the mere craft, but it includes a knowledge of its science.

Gandhi has also laid due emphasis on the self-supporting aspect of Basic education. He was keen on finding the expenses of a teacher through the product of the manual labour of his pupils because, "he was convinced that there was no other way to carry education to crores of our children."[5] He approached the problem with the confidence that every school can be made self-supporting, provided the State would take over the manufactures of these schools. He pointed out, "My *Nai Talim* is not dependent on money. The running expenses of this education should come from the educational process itself. Whatever the criticism may be, I know that the only education is that which is self-supporting."[6]

The primary education thus conceived is bound to be self-supporting even though for the first or even the second year's

1. **Gandhi M.K.,** Basic Education, **op. cit. p. 30.**
2. Ibid. **p. 44**
3. Ibid, **p. 90-91.**
4. **Tendulkar D.G.,** op, cit. **Vol. IV, pp. 186-87.**
5. Ibid, **p. 192.**
6. Harijan, **March 2, 1947, p. 48.**

course it may not be wholly so. Gandhi made his idea clear and said, "When I used the word self-supporting, I did not mean that all the capital expenditure would be defrayed from it, but at least the salary of the teacher would be found out of the proceeds of the articles made by our pupils."[1] Thus, the economic aspect of basic system of education becomes self-evident.

The self-supporting aspect of the scheme may be interpreted in two ways viz., education that will help one to be self-supporting in later life and the education which is in itself self-supporting. He maintained that, "for the all round development of boys and girls, all training should be given, as far as possible, through a profit yielding vocation."[2] This will prove a kind of insurance against unemployment. However, Gandhi was not fanatic about it. Laying down that self-sufficiency is not a prior condition, but it is the acid test, Gandhi held, "If such education is given, the direct result will be that it will be self-supporting. But the test of success is not its self-supporting character but that the whole man has been drawn out through the teaching of the handicraft in a scientific manner....The self-supporting part should be a logical corollary of the fact that the pupil has learnt the use of everyone of his faculties."[3]

It becomes evident that through Basic Education, the children will be taught the dignity of labour and learn to regard it as an integral part and a means of their intellectual growth. They would also realise that, as Gandhi held, it is, "patriotic to pay for their training through their labour."[4]

One of the important provision incorporated in the provisions of Basic Education, was that the education must be imparted through the mother-tongue. It not only gives a sense of national pride, but makes our education really meaningful. Gandhi

1. **Gandhi M.K.,** Basic Education, op cit. **p. 10.**
2. Ibid, **p. 22.**
3. Ibid, **p. 64.**
4. Ibid, **p. 44.**

pointed out, "Our language is the reflection of ourselves, and if you tell me that our languages are too poor to express the best thought, then I say that the sooner we are wiped out of existence the better for us."[1] To get rid of the defeatist mentality that we cannot do without English, Gandhi suggested, "I hold it be as necessary for the urban child as for the rural to have the foundation of his development laid on the solid rock of the mother tongue."[2] At another place he re-iterated the same thing and said, "If you can but make up your minds to free the children from the incubus of learning their subject in a foreign tongue....the educational puzzle is solved."[3] In the light of the views expressed by Gandhiji from time to time, Zakir Husain Committee, made certain important observations. It pointed out, "The proper teaching of the mother-tongue is the foundation of all education. Without the capacity to speak effectively and to read and to write correctly and lucidly, no one can develop precision of though or clarity of ideas."[4]

As a means of introducing the child to the rich heritage of his people's idea, it can be made a valuable means of social education whilst also instilling right ethical and moral values.[5]

Gandhi temperamentally was a religious man and therefore it was natural that he wanted the children also to know about the highest values of Truth and Reighteousness. But he was not in favour of bigotry or fundamentalist approach. It was on this consideration that the, "religious instruction in the sense of denominational religious have been deliberately omitted" from his scheme."[6] He however, pleaded, "A curriculum of religious instruction should include a study of the tenets of faiths other than one's own. For this purpose, the students should be trained to cultivate the habit of understanding and appreciating the doctrines

1. **Gandhi M.K.** Medium of Instruction **op, cit. p. 12.**
2. **Gandhi M.K.** Basic Education, op. cit. **p. 99.**
3. Ibid, **p. 4.**
4. **Hindustani Talimi Sangh (ed)** op. cit. **p. 99.**
5. **Mani R.S.** op. cit. **p. 86.**
6. **Gandhi M.K.,** Towards New Education op. cit. **p. 85.**

of various great religions of the world in a spirit of reverence and broadminded tolerance."[1]

Gandhi was of the opinion that if this is done properly, it would give them a spiritual assurance and a better appreciation of their own religion.

This type of education, as Gandhi conceived, becomes in fact, coextensive with life itself. It is evident from this that the ultimate objective behind Basic Education was not only a balanced and harmonious individual life, but also a harmonious society and just social order as well.

EDUCATION OF BACKWARD CLASSES

The basic principles of education of Gandhi's conception are the same for all sections of society. Gandhi knew that two things are fundamental to the problems of the backwards; these are poverty and social segregation. Gandhi began by making these two the pivots of the education of Backward section of the society. He held that the, "law of Varna prescribes that a person should, for his living, follow the lawful occupation of his forefathers. I hold this to be a universal law governing the human family. Hinduism rendered a great service to mankind by the discovery of and conscious obedience to this law."[2] At some stage this law suffered corruption and the canker of superiority and inferiority entered which vitiated it. In fact there was no one superior to any other in this scheme. Gandhi said, "All occupations are equal and honourable in so far as they are not in conflict with morals, private or public."[3] In this scheme a scavanger has the same social status as a Brahman. Thus, education should be planned in this way as every one may be taught to sincerely discharge his social obligation, Gandhi points out, "Was it not Max Muller who said

1. Ibid, **p. 46.**
2. **Gandhi M.K.,** In Search of the Supreme **(copliled by B.B. Kher) vol. III, Navjeevan Publishing House, Ahmedabad, 1962, p. 134.**
3. Young India, **November 17, 27, p. 384.**

that it was in Hinduism more than in any other religion that life was no more and no less than duty."[1]

The term other 'backward class' is of very recent origin. In Gandhi's time, the repressed classes were called 'Harijan', which was the name of Gandhiji's coining.[2] Gandhi started a powerful social movement for the uplift of this down-trodden section and declared with great confidence that 'the service rendered to suppressed humanity by reformers, will be a substantial contribution to human progress and will be its own reward. It will certainly find honourable mention in God's eternal book of life."[3] This means that giving education to this backward section of society shall be a sacred mission.

Gandhi was also fully aware of the prevalent disparities in society. He knew that in traditional society, all the *varnas* did not have equal facilities in the field of education. It is well known that, Brahmins had absolute right to learning and scholarship and it was their privilege to perform *yajnas* and other religious rites. "Shidras alone were not allowed to the rite of initiation and the study of the *Vedas*."[4] A cry for justice was raised by Gandhiji against these atrocious wrongs heaped upon the helpless men and women of their own faith.[5] Gandhi admitted that a *shudra* has every right to knowledge but he did not agree that after getting education and acquiring knowledge a *'shudra'* should go in search for a job other than ordained for him.[6] He, however, suggested to the oppressed people that, "You must have the right to worship in any temple in which members of other castes are admitted. You must have

1. **Gandhi M.K.** In search of The Supreme Vol. III **p. 135.**
2. Harijan, **February 11, 1933, p. 7**
3. Ibid, **June 15, 34, p. 140.**
4. **Hasan, Z,** Gandhiji and the Harijans, **Shree Publishing House, New Delhi, 1986, p. 3.**
5. **Tendulkar D.G.,** Gandhiji : His Life and Work, **Karnatak Publishing House, Bombay, 1949, p. 355.**
6. **Hasan, Z.,** op. cit. **p. 32.**

admission to schools alongwith the children of other castes without any distinction."[1] This was, in fact, his plan of the removal of untouchability.

Gandhiji saw that almost all the backward classes were illiterate and deprived of all the fruits of learning and education, "The caste Hindus," as Gandhi observed, "have deprived them of the fundamental necessities of life; of the facilities of education and health, by dint of which they could manifest their potentialities and save their lives."[2] Gandhi was also aware that since schools and colleges were run by caste Hindus, no Head Master or teacher would admit a Harijan child as it displeased caste people. He observed that Ambedkar, when a school child, had to stand outside the class room and was, then, allowed to sit on his own mat in a corner well segregated from his high-caste classmates.[3] He was not in favour of any sort of segregation in his scheme of Basic education. He however, suggested that only teachers endowed with missionary spirit could work among the children of backward classes and Harijans, who were so dirty that no school teacher would admit them to his class.[4] The first thing therefore, was how to make these children look like school going children. Gandhi wrote, "Preliminary training should consist in teaching these children manners, good speech and good conduct; how he sits; how he dresses...."[5]

Gandhi himself had experimented on these lines and this is the true Gandhian approach to the problem.

Gandhiji was not much in favour of high technical or academic education for Harijans as he favoured that people should take to their parental profession. But he was also fully aware that education was the potent instrument for exorcising the demon of

1. Young India, **January 22, 1925.**
2. **Pal Jaladhar,** The Moral Philosophy of Gandhi, **Gyan Publishing House New Delhi, 1998, p. 259.**
3. **Hasan, Z.,** op. cit. **p. 47.**
4. Harijan, **March 4, 1933.**
5. Ibid, **May 18, p. 35.**

untouchability. When Mr. David presented a scheme of educating selected Harijans, he alone approved of it and noted that such a scheme would produce important and sustained results. It would create a large number of lawyers, teachers, doctors etc., from among Harijans and the existence of a considerable number of such persons would be of material help in raising the social status of the depressed classes. Gandhi admired Dr. Ambedkar and said, "He is equal in intelligence and ability to the tallest among us."[1] However, he desired that *Harijan Sevak Sangha* should encourage the academical side by side with the industrial education.[2]

CRITICAL EVALUATION

The Gandhian theory of education has two notable aspects i.e. total education of man and total education of the people. His principles and values of basic education have a great relevance in present day context to tackle the serious menaces to Indian democracy. Transformation of children into model citizens is the goal of education and it is in this context that his **Nai Talim** may be called his most precious gift to the nation. John Dewey remarked "Gandhiji's system of education is, I am sure one step ahead of all the other systems and is full of immense potentialities."[3]

Gandhi, like Swami Vivekanand, believed in man-making education. This man-making or integral personality-making education, as prof. Dashrath Singh puts it,[4] is a value-education and hence it gives us new meaning though very old as they are rooted in our cultural heritage, Through his Basic education Gandhi revived the ancient value-orientation, giving a new impetus to action and experimentation which he derived from

---

1. Harijan, **July 6, 1934.**
2. Young India **June 22, 1921.**
3. **(Quoted) Kirti Singh M.,** Philosophical Import of Gandhism **South Asia Publications, Delhi, 1994. p. 206.**
4. **Singh Dashrath, Value and Value Education: A Gandhian perspective" in Mishra Anil Dutta (ed)** Gandhian Approach to Contemporary Problems, **Mittal Publications, New Delhi, 1996, p. 344.**

science as well as his own experiences. Gandhi educated people for the sustainable all-round development.

Gandhi's concept of education involves the making of education self-supporting, so that the student may be trained to become an earning unit after the completion of his studies. Like the concept of bread-labour, Gandhi also seems to have assimilated this concept of education from John Ruskin, who wrote, "Education does not mean teaching people what they do not know. It means teaching them to behave as they do not behave. It means training them into the perfect excercise and kingly continual of their bodies and the souls."[1] Gandhi also defined education as "drawing out of the best in the child and man-body, mind and soul." This system can lead to the establishment of an egalitarian society, and remove the class dimention of Indian education pattern. Dr. Prem Kripal holds, "Between the class education and the mass education we have favoured the children of the well to do families. Between those who can afford full time-education and the working population, India has exercised the choice in favour of the priviledged ones."[2] It is in this context that there is a need of fundamental change in the total education system in India and as Prof. Anil Mishra suggests, it must be replaced, by taking Gandhian nation of education so that the goal of Swaraj can be fulfilled, not in theory, but in practice.[3]

In cultural synthesis, there is no intellectual disagreement among the great modern Indian thinkers. Gandhi was one of those great leaders of contemporary period, who had the capacity for synthesis. He expounded his ideal of the project of Gujarat Vidyapith, which according to him would build up a new culture rooted in the past and enrich itself from the new experiences taking place in the west.[4] Expressing this idea of systhesis of East and

1. **Ruskin John (Quoted) Mishra Anil Dutta,** op. cit. **p. 333.**
2. **Prem Kripal, "How to Plan Education of the Future" in** Yojna **Vol. 33, No. 14-15, August 1989, Govt. of India New Delhi. p. 82.**
3. **Mishra Anil Dutta,** op. cit. **p. 334.**
4. **Kirti singh M.,** Philosophical Import of Gandhism **op. cit. p. 203.**

West Gandhi said, "I do not want my house to be walled in on all sides and my windows to be stuffed. I want the cultures of all lends to be blown about my house as freely as possible. But I refuse to be blown off my feet by any."[1]

Gandhi inherited the Indian traditions from his mother and his family environment. Accordingly, he favoured the realisation of God or Truth i.e. self-realisation as the ultimate aim of education. He was quite convinced that India would never be godless. Children must receive some education of religion. But he was also aware that the task of religious education was really stupendous. He therefore, gave wider connotation to the concept of 'religion' and thereby made religious education very broad-based to suit the modern mind. He said, "To me religion means Truth and Ahimsa or Truth alone because Truth includes Ahimsa....Therefore anything that promotes the practice of these virtues is a means for imparting religious education."[2] In fact, Gandhi was of the view that true education should result not in the material power, but in spiritual force, for which children should be taught the fundamental virtues of truth, love, justice and non-violence.[3] Despite being a votary of religion, his views on religious matters are characterised by catholicity and broad-mindedness. He declared, "By religion, I do not mean formal religion or customary religion, but that religion which underlies all religions."[4] This approach, is obviously, the result of his deep understanding of the western liberal thought and of other religions. However, he was firmly of the belief that religious instruction of its youth must be held as necessary as secular instruction.[5] In the schools under his Wardha scheme fundamental principles common to all religions were taught to the children and according

1. **Bose Nirmal Kumar,** op. cit. **p. 267.**
2. **Gandhi M.K.,** Towards New Education op. cit. **p. 45.**
3. **Tendulker D.G.,** Mahatma : Life of Mohandas Karam Chand Gandhi **op. cit. Vol. III, p. 359-360.**
4. **Prabhu R.K. & Rao U.R.,** The Mind of Mahatma Gandhi op. cit. **p. 85.**
5. **Mani R.S.,** op. cit. **p. 119.**

to Gandhi, these should be regarded as adequate religious instruction.[1]

The rise of humanism in West and his own idea of establishing a socialist order made Gandhi to think to take education to the masses. He was critical of inordinately expensive education and said, "When it is difficult for millions even to make the two ends meets, when millions are dying of starvation, it is monstrous to think of giving our relatives a costly education."[2] He further went on to say, "We have only touched fringe of an ocean of children. The vast mass of them remain without education."[3] It was because their parents cannot give them highly expensive education. It is in this context, that Gandhi's Basic Education Scheme, if properly implemented, fulfills the needs of modern India. In his scheme every child will have full opportunity for the balance and harmonious development of all his faculties and will acquire the capacity for self-reliance in every aspect of clean, healthy and cultured life, together with an understanding of the social and moral implication of such a life.[4]

❑❑❑

1. Ibid, **p. 122.**
2. **Gandhi M.K.,** To the Students, op. cit. **p. 75.**
3. Ibid., **p. 65-66.**
4. **Hindustani Talimi Sangh,** op. cit. **p. 3.**

15

Rabindranath Tagore

"The fundamental purpose of education is not merely to enrich ourselves through the fullness of knowledge, but also to establish the bond of love and friendship between man and man." —***Rabindranath Tagore***

Born in 1861 in a rich family in which Upanishads were highly valued. Rabindranath himself could not get high education. In 1893 he raised a voice against the passing of Sedition Act. In 1918 he became the Noble Prize winner due to his *Gitanjali* and was subsequently given the title of Knight. In 1919 he gave up the title as a protest against the high-handedness and cruelties of British Government in Jallianwala Bagh. In 1941 he died but till his last he continued to work and write.

Born and brought up as an aristocrat and a lover of beauty, Rabindranath Tagore became conscious of his higher mission of bringing men closer to each other. With eyes fixed on the future of mankind, he explored political, social and religious areas of human relationship. His philosophy of man is largely based on perception: "In the vessel of man's affecting I taste His divine nectar."[1] He voiced the ancient wisdom of India.

CONTEMPORARY CIRCUMSTANCES

In his speech in China in 1924, Tagore is reported to have pointed out that at the time he was born, three distinct movements

1. **Tagore, *Arogya*, p. 29.**

had met in the life of his country. The first was the religio-intellectual movement led by Rammohan Roy which restored confidence in Indians about their religion and culture. The second was the literary movement whose greatest representative was Bankim Chandra Chatterjee. The third was the national movement for the political, economic and social relief of the country. For twenty-three years of his early youth, Tagore wrote poetry and looked at life as a visionary inspired by his father Maharishi Devandranath Tagore. In 1883, Tagore published his poem, "The Awakening of the Waterfall", which marked his entry into the wide world. The "Waterfall" suggested the life-force and symbolished the enlargement of the individual's and his entry into the universal life of humanity.

Influence of Upanishads

With the onset of the twentieth century Tagore's ideas turned from the praise and contemplation of beauty to that the Lord of life. Under the influence of the liberal tradition of his family and the philosophy of the Upanishads, he developed a positive view of life and love of humanity. He carried India's message of love and universal brotherhood to all parts of the world and thus tried to bring East and West together on the pure and lofty platform of human relationship. He abhorred all conflicts between man and man, between nation and nation. He could easily understand the demands of the new age and warned. "From now onward any nation which takes an isolated view of its own country will run counter to the spirit of the New Age, and know no peace. From now onward the anxiety that each country has for its own safety must embrace the welfare of the world."[1]

Influence of Buddhism

Rabindranath was deeply influenced by the humanist tradition of the Buddha, and the Buddhist way of life appealed to

1. **W. Norman Brown, "Some Ethical Concepts for the Modern World from Hindu and Indian Buddhist Tradition." (Article in Centenary Volume of Rabindranath Tagore), Delhi, Sahitya Academy, 1961, p. 395.**

him most. Tagore stressed that man must come out of the shell of his individual self in order to enter into the larger self of humanity. So long as he remained confined within the walls of his individuality, his selfishness, his own material longings, joys and sorrows, he could not realise the universal man, neither could he get relief form the misery of the world. Tagore said, "To live in perfect goodness is to realise one's life in the infinite. This is the most comprehensive view of life, which we can have by our inherent power of the moral vision of the wholeness of life. And the teaching of Buddha is to cultivate this moral power to the highest extent, know that our field of activities is not found to the plane of our narrow self."[1]

Influence of Medieval Indian Spiritualism

Rabindranath was deeply influenced by the medieval Indian religious and social philosphy. In the spirit of the medieval saints and poets he talked of the divinity of Man. Like Rajjab, a poet-saint of medieval India, he considered man as God-man (*Nara-narayana*). Like Ravidas, another saint, he called man Divine Man (*Narhari*), Like Chandidas, he said that the truth of man was the highest truth. All this proves that Tagore perceived humanity as an objective truth.

Influence of Kabir

Kabir's attempt to reconcile Mohammedan mysticism with the tradition theology of Brahmanism in the interest of harmony left an abiding impression on Tagore. Kabir's direct apprehension of God as the supreme object, of love as a comrade, which finds passionate expression in his poems, captivated Tagore's imagination and coloured his religious outlook. Tagore translated one hundred poems of Kabir into English. He may be considered as the most sympathetic interpreter of Kabir's vision and thought.

Like Kabir, Rabindranath considered the universe as the

---

1. **Tagore, *Sadhana*, London, Macmillan and Co., 1954, p. 57.**

manifestation of God. This finds expression in his poetry, especially in *Gitanjali.* For example, at one place he wrote :

Thou art the sky, and thou art
The nest as well.[1]

This idea of divine manifestation in Kabir's poems[2] was interpreted by Tagore in the light of his own belief in the reality of both God and Nature Kabir's large-heartedness, his love for all mankind irrespective of caste, creed and sex, his relentless campaign against all kinds of dogmas and superstitions of Hinduism, and lastly, his attitude towards life in the word largely moulded Tagore's philosophy of life.

Product of Composite Culture

Rabindranath Tagore has been aptly described as a product of a composite culture. The best of Indian culture was preserved in the traditions of his family. At the same time it also borrowed liberally the virtues of the European culture. Early in his youth, Tagore was influenced by humanism of the West, especially love of freedom and the large hearted radicalism of the British people. He accepted the Western definition humanism that man was the dominant and ultimate reality. If there is a God, He must be interpreted in human terms. Rejecting the traditionalism and orthodoxy of Hinduism, Tagore adapted to the spirituality of Western humanism.

Humanism

Tagore felt that it was only on the basis of humanism that the wide gulf between the East and the West could be bridged, a synthetic culture could be evolved. His imagination was roused and the desire of creating a new civilization from the synthesis of East and West began very early in his life, and throughout his life he worked for the fulfillment of his noble ideal. Tagore carried

1. **Tagore, *Gitanjali*-67, London, Macmillan and Co., 1953 (English).**
2. **Kabir, *Tu surat main nihat—Kabir's poems*, Calcutta, Macmillan and Co., 1929, LXXVI, 1929.**

the humanistic message of India and the nationalism of the East for the universal brotherhood, peace and prosperity of all mankind irrespective of nationality, religion and colour.

Cosmopolitanism

Appreciating the variety of cultures of the different nations, their development in different ways, Tagore considered it essential that all nations meet at a point of benefit to each other. "It is best for the commerce of the spirit that people differently situated should bring their different products into the market of humanity each of which is complementary and necessary to the other."[1] As a realist, Tagore was of the opinion the differences were essential for the smooth and harmonious development of humanity. Such differences should only create a desire for greater understanding of each other's point of view and each other's merits. In 1917 Tagore said, "The monsoon clouds generated on the banks of the Nile fertilize the far distant shores of the Ganges—ideas may have to cross from the East to the Western shores to find a welcome in men's hearts and fulfil their promise. East is East and West is West—God forbid that it should be otherwise, but the twain must meet in unity, peace and mutual understanding."[2] Thus Tagore was better fitted than anybody else to call for a real appraisal of the spirit of East and West and their reconciliation.

Rationalism and Humanitarianism

As a rationalist and humanitarian in his attitude towards the whole problem of East and West relationship Rabindranath was disgusted by the artificial divisions in men on the basis of castes and creeds and rebuked Indians for being dogmatic and superstitious. He was pained by the materialistic basis of Western civilization. He wanted a compromise between Western science and Indian spiritualism in order to guide the human race, in order to evolve a common culture and uniform ethical standards. He was aware that the mechanical character of occidental civilisation had

---

1. Tagore, *Sadhana,* London, Macmillan and Co., 1954, p. 12.
2. Tagore, *Lectures on Nationalism,* Macmillan and Co., London, 1917.

turned human beings into mere slaves, killed their freedom and initiative, to act in a natural way. But he also discovered that there was an organised effort in the West toward physical and intellectual perfection. Tagore wanted it to come forward with its science and culture to the aid of the weak and helpless nations. Thus, could it justify itself in the eyes of humanity.

Opposition to Colonialism

At times he was disturbed with the attitude of the British imperialists in their exploitation of the various Asian colonies must know that red tape can never be a common human bond; that official sealing-wax can never provide means of mutual attachment."[1] On the occasion of his eighteenth birthday at Shantiniketan, Tagore said, "It is no longer possible for us to retain any respect for that mockery of civilisation which believes in ruling by force and has no faith in freedom at all."[2]

East and West

Distinguishing the attitude of the East and the West, Tagore pointed out that the West did not believe that the universe had a soul, it only believed in the soul of man. On the other hand the whole mental contribution of the East to mankind is filled with the idea of universal soul. Both must co-operate with each other, give each other whatever they can offer in order to fulfil their aspirations. No one can deny the scientific achievements of the West. At the same time India could supply a corrective to the misuse of science through her contribution to religion and philosophy. The unity between East and West would mean the unity of spiritual and scientific knowledge.

Vishwa-Bharti : Ideal of One World.

Rabindranath wanted to realise the ideal of one world on the basis of intellectual co-operation between the East and the West. In order to provide a common platform to the men of different

1. Tagore, *Creative Unity,* London, Macmillan and Co., 1926, p. 109.
2. Sasadhar Sinha, *Social Thinking of Rabindranath Tagore,* p. 143, N. Delhi, Asia Publishing House, 1962.

cultures, Tagore planned to establish an international university. The synthesis of the East and West, as for their relligious and cultural values, he thought could help in realising lasting peace and happiness for mankind. The idea of such a university included the thought of a conference of East and West, a common fellowship of learning and common spiritual striving for the unity of the human race. Tagore said, "Being strongly impressed with the need and responsibility, which every individual must realise according to his power, I have formed the nucleus of an international university in India as one of the best means of promoting mutual understanding between the East and West."[1] Thus, Vishwa-Bharti became the centre of world culture to promote goodwill among people of different nations and religions. The ultimate aim before Tagore was to promote international amity and understanding and fulfil the highest mission of the present age, the unification of mankind. The motto he selected for his university is '*yatra visvam bhavti ekanidam*'—where the universe becomes a single nest.

Tagore knew that in spite of efforts from various directions the East and West were not showing any real sign of meeting. He felt that, "the reason is because the West has not sent out its humanity to meet the man in the East, but only its machine."[2] The political civilization which has sprung up from Europe has overrun the weak nations of the world. Instead of helping the weak nations in their progress, it has gone everywhere with hungry jaws and bloody teeth.

With his strongest faith in man, Tagore, could never accept the idea of non-cooperation with the West. He always advised his countrymen to have a wide outlook and meet vice with good, hatred with love. At the same time, he considered it essential for the East to learn from the West with an open mind. The true greatness of the West consisted in its spirit of service devoted to the welfare of man.

---

1. **Tagore, *Creative Unity,* London, Macmillan and Co., 1926, pp. 172-73.**
2. ***Ibid.,* p. 109, 1926.**

A few weeks before his death Tagore wrote, "I had one time believed that the springs of civilization would issue out of the heat of Europe. But today when I am about to quit the world, the faith has gone bankrupt altogether."[1] Tagore advised all nations to take up the responsibility in future to build a new society devoid of hatred and selfishness. He was of the view that only a humanitarian approach could resolve mutual conflict. In the words of Dr. S. Radhakrishnan, "Rabindranath puts forward a plea for mankind by advocating the ideal of a family of nations to which every member will bring his unique gift. This ideal of international unity and national independence will break down barriers of nations and make for sweet harmon."[2]

NEO-VEDANTA

Rabindranath Tagore imbibed Vedantic orientation from his early childhood. The family had a mixed environment. He was very much impressed by his father, "The Maharishi." Upanishads too appealed to him most. He was a lover of nature from the very beginning. The seclusion of the child made a positive contribution towards drawing him more and more to nature. It made him think for long about the secrets of nature. The young mind would think not only over the creation but the creator also.

Upanishad's impact on Tagore's mind is evident from his lines: "To me the verses of the Upanishads and the teachings of Buddha have ever been things of the spirit, and therefore endowed with boundless vital growth; and I have used them, both in my own life and in my preachings as being instinct with individual meaning for me, as for others, and awaiting for their confirmation, my own special testimony, which must have its value because of its individuality."[3]

---

1. **Tagore, *Towards Universal Man,* p. 356. Bombay, Asia Publishing Hosue, 1962.**
2. **S. Radhakrishnan, *Philosophy of Rabindranath Tagore,* p. 285. London, Macmillan and Co., 1918.**
3. **Tagore, R.N., *Sadhana,* Preface. D. VIII**

RELIGIOUS BACKGROUND

Tagore thought and worked in Indian tradition. His entire thought is based on personal observation or 'Anubhava'. He was a visionary who reached conclusions by deducting generalities from observation. This method of his holds good for his religion also. He admits "my religion is poet's religion; all that I feel about it is from vision and not from knowledge. I frankly say that I cannot satisfactorily answer your question about evil, or what happens after death. And yet I am sure that there have been some moments when my soul has touched the infinite and has become intensely conscious of it through the illuminations of joy."[1]

For Tagore religion is an effort of man to attain the ultimate truth. He says, "It consists in the endeavour of man to cultivate and express those qualities which are in him. If those qualities were absolutely natural in individual, religion could have no purpose."[2]

For Tagore religion is a means to higher values in man. "Man in his religion cultivates the vision of a being who exceeds him in truth and with whom also he has his kinship. These religions differ in details and often in their moral significance, but they have a common tendency. In them men seek their own supreme value in some personality, anthropomorphic in character. The mind which is abnormally scientific, stops at this; but it should know that religion is not essentially cosmic or even abstract; it finds itself, when it touches the Brahman in man; otherwise it has no justification to exist."[3]

Tagore has assigned a definite constructive purpose to religion. He opines "Religion has its function in reconciling the contradiction by subordinating the brute nature to what we consider as the truth of man.......Religion concentrates itself on humanity, which illumines our reason, inspires our wisdom, stimulates our love, claims our intelligent service."[4]

---

1. **Soarej, Anthony, *Lectures and Addresses of Rabindranath*, pp. 16-17.**
2. **Tagore, R.N., *The Religion of Man*, p. 144.**
3. ***Ibid.*, p. 63.**
4. ***Ibid.*, p. 144.**

Opposed to Ritualism

In order to translate their preaching into action religious leaders develop some organisation. Tagore feared that with the coming up of the organisation the natural growth of the religion is hampered. He points out, "Where religion has to make way for religious organisation it is like the river being dominated by its sandbed; the current stagnates and its higher aspects become desertlike."[1]

The ritualistic aspect of religion presupposes some deity or set of deities, places of worship, rituals and dogmas. This aspect is as essential as the ideational one. Tagore is opposed to this aspect of religion. He maintained that unintelligible rituals and dogmas are at best only cohesive principles that hold together individuals of a particular community marking them off from individuals of other groups. Rabindranath has no sympathy for these. Man tends to separate one individual from another, or one group from another, tends in effect to deny the humanity of man and is as such anti-religious, unless, of course, religion is something totally divorced from the essential spirit in man, *viz.*, reason, morality and love. This, in a netshell, is Rabindranath's reaction against rituals and dogmas."[2]

Opposed to Orthodoxy

Due to his humanistic orientation towards religion Tagore was opposed to fanaticism. He opines that "orthodoxy is not necessarily narrow-mindedness. What matters seriously is whether these orthodoxy people are fanatics or not. Fanaticism is definitely anti-religious, and when Rabindranath condemns unintelligible rituals and dogmas, this is only because the line between fanaticism and orthodoxy is very thin."[3]

Opposed to Idolatry

As a result of this rational outlook towards religion,

1. *Modern Review*, p. 325.
2. Bhattacharya, K., *Homage from Vishwa Bharti* (1962), p. 32.
3. *Ibid.*, p. 33.

Rabindranath opposed Idolatry. "Rabindranath is against Idolatry, not so much because idolators circumscribe God but primarily because they hypostatise a person or entity what is really a living function; and he would equally speak against those who, even knowing that he is a functional unity, yet pesonify him. If God is a person, He is every dynamic, ever dissolving Himself, as the indwelling spirit of all individuals."[1]

Votary of Golden Mean

Tagore always believed in the theory of golden mean. He was a synthesizer and as such "he had never been an orthodox puritan and had no sympathy for the iconoclasts of his time, and yet he never shook hands with the orthodox."[2]

Unity of Mankind

The main end of religion for Rabindranath was the unity of mankind. He believed that this unity could come through spirituality alone. Though Tagore had great faith in the spirituality of the East yet he did not contribute to the opinion that it was the monopoly of the East. He was convinced that the material advancement of the West could not occur in the absence of spirituality.

Tagore's God lives at humble places in the company of humble people.

"Here is thy footstool and there rest thy feet where live the poorest, and lowliest and lost....My heart can never find its way where thou keepest company with the companionless among the poorest, and the lowliest and the lost."[3]

The God is there "Where the tiller is tilling the hard ground and where the path maker is breaking the stones, He is with them in sun and shower, and His garment is covered with dust. Put off thy holy mantle and even like Him come down on the dusty soil."[4]

---

1. *Ibid.*, p. 42.
2. *Ibid.*, p. 44.
3. Tagore, R.N., *Gitanjali,* Song 10.
4. *Ibid.*, Song 11.

PHILOSOPHICAL BACKGROUND

Philosophy is in a certain sense based upon interpretation of history, since history is not merely an anthology of the deeds of some individuals but a record of the pace of humanity in its various stages and directions, it gives a peep into the future of man. Tagore was a keen student of history. This is explicit form his article "Itihas Katha". Written in 1905 this article is an important document about Tagore's interpretation of history. He laid emphasis upon the importance of knowledge of history. He said, "If you think closely, we shall see that the greatest disparity in knowledge between the education and uneducated in our country lies in the knowledge of history..... It is a most lamentable ignorance for man not to know what man has done or can do in this world."[1]

History acquaints people with their country. It is the record of the glory and weaknesses of the race. Therefore, the historians owe a great responsibility towards the people. Indian history so far, however, has been rather royal biography. Therefore. Tagore pleaded for re-writing of Indian history. Explaining his idea of history he said, "History is the manifestation of the dialectical process, of the play of opposing forces and the attempt to establish a balance between them, Indian history presents a clear picture of this historical dialectics and the attempt to strike a balance, which should be duly stressed by historians."[2]

He also criticized teaching of history in India, which was mainly based upon cramming of instances. He, on the other hand, emphasized critical examination and authenticity. In the words of H.B. Mukherjee, "Tagore attached considerable importance to the collection of original and authentic historical material by the students from direct sources through 'region study' and independent researches as also excursions and tours to places of historical interest in order to have a vivid and realistic impression

1. ***Rabindra Rachnawali,* Vol. XII, Vishwa Bharti, 1939-48, p. 520.**
2. ***The Vishwa Bharti Ideal, Vishwa Bharti, Natesan,* pp. 13-14.**

of the historical significance of the places visited and the objects see at first hand."[1]

Interpretation of Indian History

In the world of Tagore, "Man's history is the history of his journey to the unknown in the quest of the realisation of his immortal self—of his soul. Through the rise and fall of empires, through the building up of gigantic piles of wealth and the ruthless scattering of them upon the dust; through the creation of vast bodies of symbols that give shape to his drama and aspirations, and the casting of them away like the playthings of an outworn infancy, through the forgoing of his magic keys with which to unlock the mysteries of creation, and through his throwing away of this labour of ages to go back to his worship and work afresh in some new form! Yes : through it all man is marching from epoch towards the fullest realisation of his soul, the soul which is greater than the things man accumulates, the deeds he accomplishes, the themes he builds, the soul whose onward course is never checked by death or dissolution."[2]

Indian history is a record of the stages, progress the ideals of Indian people. It records the social life and spiritual attainments of India. According to Tagore Indian history however needs to be re-written. It has been a process of constant adjustment between different sections of people. Explaining the goal of history Tagore pointed out, "Neither the colourless vagueness of cosmopolitanism, nor the fierce self-idolatoly of national worship, is the goal of history. And India has been trying to accomplish her task through social regulation of differences on the one hand, and the spiritual recognition of unity on the other. She has made grave errors in setting up the boundary walls to rigidly between races, in perpetuating in her classifications the results of inferiority, often she has crippled her children's minds and narrowed their lives in

---

1. **Mukherje, H.B., *Education for Fulness,* Asia Publishing House, 1965, p. 401.**
2. **Tagore, R.N., *A Message,* p. 78.**

order to fit them into her social forms, but for centuries new experiments have been made and adjustments carried out."[1]

In his analysis of Indian history Tagore found the keynote in the principle of the unity in diversity. This has been supported by other historians as well. Even the *Mahabharata* and the *Ramayana* mainly portray attempts at synthesis and adjustment between good and evil, different classes, various races and ideologies. In his pamphlet entitled, *A Vision of India's History,* Tagore showed a deep insight into the processes of Indian history when he said, "The history of India has been the history of the struggle between the constructive spirit of the machine, which seeks the decadence of order and conformity is social organisation, and the creative spirit of man, which seeks freedom and love for its self-expression. We have to watch and see that the latter is still living in India; and also whether the former offers its service and hospitability to life, through which its system can be vitalized."[2]

Thus, Tagore maintained that the history of India is a history of social evolution. In his interpretation of the two great epics the *Ramayana* and the *Mahabharate,* Tagore has shown them as records of two great social revolutions. *Mahabharata* and *Ramayana* both depict the conflict between Aryans and the Dravidians and finally a synthesis between the two. In his interpretation and explanation of both these epics Tagore has laid special emphasis on their spiritual nature. He has taken special pains to explain the mythology found in these epics. He has accepted Rama and Krishna as Avataras, who came on the earth for some special purposes. According to Tagore both the epics depict cultural assimilation between Aryans and Dravidians. In his opinion Indian culture is a product of cross-fertilisation between these two great cultures. To quota his words, "Dravidians might not be introspective or metaphysical, but they were artists, and they could sing, design and construct. The transcendental

---

1. Tagore, R.N., *Nationalism,* Macmillan, London, 1960 p. 5.

2. Tagore, R.N. *A Vision of India's History,* Vishwa Bhatri, 1960 p. 90.

thought of the Aryans by its marriage with the emotional and creative art of the Dravidians gave birth to an offspring which was neither fully Aryan, nor Dravidian, but Hindu."[1] Besides these two cultures, India has been the scene of synthesis of several other cultures of the people who invaded the country from the West. Tagore was against dividing Indian history into periods based upon the rule of particular people of the country such as Moghal period and Pathan period etc. This, according to him, is an unwarranted division of a continued history of the country. About the Moghal and Pathan periods he points out that they were invaders and not part of the nation. Therefore, their rule should not be particularly emphasized. Similarly, British rule in India was a great misfortune and therefore it should not be emphasized in the teaching of history. As compared to earlier invaders the Britishers had some novelty which was realised by Tagore though he did not mince words in condemning the rule of British people over India. Thus, according to Tagore, Indian history was yet to be written in its true spirit. In his own words, "The real history of India was yet to be written by Indian writers, who were in a better position to undertake the task from a more accurate perspective than foreign writers nursed in different historical traditions. Though the Indian historians are likely to interpret Indian history from a viewpoint entirely opposed to foreign historians, and to be equally blameworthy for partisanship and lack of dispassionate historical objectivity, the two opposite extremes would help a third party to approach the task with considerable impartiality and objectivity."[2]

IDEAL OF PROGRESS

Interpretation of history very much depends upon the ideal of progress. Progress is interpreted in terms of movement towards a goal. Different thinkers have laid emphasis upon different goals of life, thereby presenting different concepts of progress. Tagore's ideal of progress is religion-oriented. The ideal of man, according to him, is perfection. This requires spiritual progress. For the

---

1. *Ibid.*, p. 31.
2. Tagore, R.N., *Itihas Katha*, p. 118.

attainment of this aim man has to conquer the weaknesses of his flesh. The real progress, however, is not only the progress of the individual, it is the progress of the Nation and ultimately of the Humanity.

According to Radhakrishnan, "To him progress and reform consist in conserving the ancient ideas and building upon them. Preserving the soul of the Indian style, we may adopt whatever is good and noble in the West."[1] Thus, Tagore synthesised the Eastern and Western concepts of progress. Progress, according to him, lies in harmony. Harmony has been the central principle of Indian culture. Disharmony, on the other hand, is detrimental to progress. In Indian society the agricultural pattern has to be synthesised with the industrial order. Science has to be harmonized with the spirituality. The knowledge of the West should be synthesised with the wisdom of the East. It is accepted that India is more spiritual while West is more material. A solution for their ideal progress requires a synthesis of both. Criticizing he materialistic ideal of progress Tagore said, "What is called progress is the progress in mechanical contrivances; it is in fact an indefinite extension of our physical limbs and organs, which owing to the enormous material advantage that it brings to us, has tempted the modern man away from his inner realm of spiritual values."[2]

Thus, Tagore wanted a synthesis of spiritual and material values for real progress of mankind. This is very explicit in his ideas concerning Indian society and its problems and remedies, which we will now discuss in sequence.

EDUCATION AS SELF-REALISATION

Rabindranath Tagore believed that the aim of education is self-realisation. He was poet and a saint, who had through his imagination and insight, realised the universal soul in himself and

1. **Radhakrishnan S., *The Philosophy of Rabindranath Tagore*, Macmillan, London, 1919, p. 197.**
2. **Tagore, R.N. *Boundless Sky, Vishwa Bharti*, 1964, p. 297.**

in nature. He believed that this realisation was the goal of education. Because the universal soul is the root of our own soul, man's aim in life is to reach that universal soul of which all human beings are parts. The evolution of nature is consciously or unconsciously driving us towards this universal soul, a process which can assisted by education. Even if it is not assisted the progress towards the universal soul will continue, but then individuals will be deprived of self-realisation. It is thus evident that Rabindranath's educational philosophy is an adjunct of his general philosophy of life. In fact, he did not find any dichotomy between thought, life and philosophy. Besides, he believed that every human being is one who has potentialities of progressing towards the Super human being, the universal soul. His conception of the universal soul bore clear imprint of Gita and Upanishadic philosophies. Although Rabindranath was clearly aware of the ideas of Western thinkers on education, he based his own ideas on the ancient Indian thought. Indian tradition believes that man's soul and the universal soul are one, and that self-realisation amounts to realisation of integration with God.

Principles of Self-Education

Self-education is based on self-realisation, and the process of self-realisation is as permanent as that of education. What is most important in this is that the educand must have faith in himself and in the universal self, underlying his own individual soul. All those actions which provide a natural sense of satisfaction and contentment will promote the educative process. The contentment is the reaction of the soul, and hence not the same as mere satisfaction and pleasure. In following Rabindranath's concept of self-education, the educand had to follow the three following principles :

1. Independence—Rabindranath believed in complete freedom of every kind for the educand—freedom of intellect, decision, heart, knowledge, action and worship. But in order to attain this freedom the educand had to practice equanimity, harmony and balance. Through this practice the educand can learn to distinguish between the true and the false, the natural and the artificial, the relevant and the irrelevant, permanent and temporary, universal and individual, liberal and narrow, etc. Consequently, after making this distinction the educand can bring about a harmony and synthesis in the true, natural, relevant, permanent and real elements that he has acquired. Once he educand has acquired this ability he can turn to self-guidance, for which he is now competent. He can himself distinguish between the elements likely to impede his progress and those, which may help him. Rabindranath interprets independence as normalcy or the fact of being natural. In other words, when intelligence, feeling and determination are naturally distributed, it can be said to be a state of freedom. This independence is not to be confused with the absence of control, because it is self-control, it implies acting according to one's own rational impulse. Once this level of freedom has been achieved, there is no danger of the individual straying from his path, because his senses, intelligence, emotional feelings and all other powers are directed by his ego.

2. Perfection—The second active principle underlying self-education is that of perfection. Perfection here implies that the educand must try to develop every aspect of his personality and all the abilities and powers with which he has been endowed by Nature. Hence, the aim of education is not merely passing examinations, acquiring degrees and certificates of merit and ultimately achieving economic self-sufficiency through pursuing some profession. The sole aim of education is development of the child's personality, which is possible only when every aspect of the personality is given equal importance, when no part of the personality is neglected and no part is exclusively stressed.

3. Universality—Development of the individual remains imperfect and incomplete until he acquires an abiding faith in the universal soul, a part of which exists inside himself. And for this, it is necessary to identify one's own soul with the universal soul. Thus, education exists not in simple development but it inheres in literally a rebirth in which the individual rises above the limitations of his individual personality and loses this individuality in the universality of the universal soul. One can search for this universal soul not only within oneself, but in every element of Nature and of one's environment. This search is assisted by knowledge, worship and action. Once this realisation of the universal soul is achieved, it becomes easier to progress further.

It is evident from the foregoing account that the aim of Rabindranath's pattern of education is independence, perfection and universality. In the process of education, the educator creates an environment in which the child's personality undergoes a free, perfect and unrestricted development.

AIMS OF EDUCATION

According to Rabindranath, the aim of education is self-realisation. He is a poet and a saint who through his imagination and insight, realized the univeral soul within himself and in Nature. According to him this realisation by every one is the goal of education. Self-realisation, according to Rabindranath, means the realisation of the universal soul in one's self. Man's aim of life is to achieve this status. It is a process which cannot be realised without education. In the absence of education the individual will be deprived of self-realisation. Rabindranath does not find any dichotomy between thought and life, philosophy and education. He believes that every one is potentially divine and every one can realise his potentiality. His philosophy is very much influenced by the 'Gita' and the 'Upanishads'. He is, however, well aware of the educational ideas prevalent in the west. Therefore, like Vivekananda, he synthesizes the ancient Vedanitic traditions with the modern Western scientific attitude in formulating the goal of education.

1. Integral Development—During the aim of education, Rabindranath says, "The fundamental purpose of education is not merely to enrich ourselves through the fullness of knowledge, but also to establish the bond of love and friendship between man and man."[1] This is the humanistic aim of education in Tagore's

1. *Bhartiya Vishva Vidyalaya Adarsa, Siksha* **(1342) B.S. Ed., p. 270.**

philosophy. His approach to ultimate reality is integral. He believe in an inner harmony between man and Nature and God. In man, again, the physical, the mental and the spiritual aspects are equally important and internally related. Therefore, like Sri Aurobindo, Rabindranath believes in a multisided education with physical, intellectual, moral and religious aims.

2. Physical Development—Like Vivekananda, Rabindranath condemned the prevalent system of education, which partially exercise the intellect only to the entire neglect of the body. According to Rabindranath, "Education of the body in the real sense, does not exist in play and exercise but in applying the body systematically to some useful work."[1] Thus, one of the aims of education according to Rabindranath, is physical development. It is hence that he so much emphasizes games in school education. Pointing out the value of physical activities in the child's education he says, "Even if they learnt nothing, they would have had ample time for play, climbing trees, diving into ponds, plucking and tearing flowers, perpetrating thousand and one mischiefs on Mother Nature, they would have obtained the nourishment of the body, happiness of mind and the satisfaction of the natural impulses of childhood."[2] Thus physical fitness in the first cardinal principle in the child's development. This is realised through his intimate contact with Nature. As a poet Tagore very well realises the life giving values of Nature's contact with man. About the child's contact with the Nature he says, "I speak in very moderate terms : Seven years – till then let child has nothign to do with clothes and shame. Till then let Nature alone conduct the indispensable education of the savage."[3] This is particularly important for the educational institutions in our society. Almost all contemporary Indian philosophers of education, including Gandhiji Vivekananda, Dayananda and Sri Aurobindo, besides Tagore, lay emphasis upon the importance of setting educational

---

1. **Tagore, R.N. *Alochana,* July 1925.**
2. ***Shiksha* (1342), p. 2.**
3. ***Ibid.*, p. 84.**

institutions in natural environment so that the educand may learn by their touch with Nature.

3. Mental Development—Besides the physical aim of education, Tagore equally lays emphasis upon the mental aim of education. Like Vivekananda, he is critical of the prevalent system of education, which laid sole emphasis upon bookish learning. Presenting this attitude he says, "We touch the world not with our mind, but with our books. This is deplorable. Intellectualism takes us away from Nature and creates a gulf between man and man."[1] To quote Rabindranath, "We know the people of books, not those of the world, the former are interesting to us, but the lattertiresome."[2] In fact, the intellectual aim of education, according to Rabindranath, is the development of the intellectual faculties which should be developed through education. These are: the power of thinking and the power of imagination. Both these are necessary for real manhood. Rabindranath criticises the prevalent system of education, which puts too much stress on memory and two little on imagination and thinking. He suggests, "Ever since childhood, instead of putting all the burden on the memory, the power of thinking and the power of imagination should also be given opportunities for free exercise."[3]

4. Harmony with Environment—In the end, the aim of education according to Rabindranath is the harmony of the educand with the environment. The educand should know his environment and create harmony with it. To quote Rabindranath, "True education consists in knowing the use of any useful material that has been collected, to know its real nature and to build along with life a real shelter for life."[4] This is particularly true about the rural education. Education should facilitate the educand's assimilation of his national culture. Through education, the educand should imbibe his cultural heritage and should be able to

1. *Ibid.*, p. 90.
2. *Ibid.*, p. 91.
3. *Siksar Herpher*, p. 8.
4. *Ibid.*

use it in his inter-action with the environment. Explaining this aim of education, Rabindranath says, "If we believe that the chief aim of education in India is to be initiated into this unique pursuit of India, then we must constantly remember that neither the education of the senses, nor the education of the intellect, but the education of the feeling receive the place of honour in our schools.... Our true education is possible only in the forest, through intimate contact with Nature and purifying austere pursuits.

5. Earning Livelihood—Thus, about the aim of education, Tagore's approach is realistic. He, however, does not favour the utilitarian aim of education. This is his objection against the imposition of British system of education upon India. He says, "Knowledge has two departments: one pure knowledge, the other utilitarian knowledge. Whatever is worth knowing is knowledge. It should be known equally be men and women, not for practical utility, but for the sake of knowing....The desire to know is the law of human nature."[1] But Rabindranath does not ignore the earning of livelihood aim of education. He appreciates the practical bias in Western system of education. Though he does not want to make education an instrument for earning bread alone but he admits that bread earning is a necessary part of any sound goal of education. Therefore, he says, "From the very beginning, such education should be imparted to them (village folks) that they may know well what welfare mass means and may become practically efficient in all respects for earning their livelihood."[2] While he is critical of the British system of education which wanted to create clerks out of the Indian educated people, he emphasised that the real aim of education is to develop men and women who may be able to fulfil the needs of the country. In his own words, "One of the main aims of education is to prepare the individual for the services of the country."[3]

1. *Shiksha* (1342), p. 145.
2. *Shiksha* (1351), Vol. I, p. 151.
3. *Swadhin Shiksha*, p. 522.
4. *Rabindra Rachnawali*, Vol. XII, p. 517.

6. Multisided Aim—The above discussion concerning the means of education according to Rabindranath, make it clear that his is a multisided attack on this problem. He is against any one sided aim of education. He is humanist. A humanistic aim of education requires a multisided approach.

CONTRIBUTION TO EDUCATION

1. Education for Human Re-generation—Thus Rabindranath's philosophy of education aims at developing a system of education for human re-generation. Man is in the centre of all his thinking, his philosophy, religion, literature, poetry, social activities and educational programmes. He is a humanist in the real sense of the term, not a naturalistic humanist but at integral humanist in the Indian tradition. He is not rationalist but believes in something higher than reasons in man. He does not think science along to be capable of delivering the human goods but wants to synthesise it with Vedanta. He is a nationalist and at the same time an internationalist. To him the ultimate God is the universal man and only aim of all the man's activities was the realisation of this God. Human regeneration is the sole aim and only ideal. His educational system is a means to achieve this aim. He, therefore, bases his educational system on essential human virtues such as freedom, purity, sympathy, perfection and world brotherhood.

2. Corrective to Prevalent Defects—Like other contemporary Indian thinkers of his time Tagore objected to the prevalent system of education due to its origination in a foreign country. He protested against emphasis on foreign language resulting in the alienation of the educated people from the general society. He tried to build up educational centres where these defects may be removed. He deliberated on different problems of Indian society particularly that of the rural people and tried to remove them through education. His educational system was a synthesis of East and West, Ancient and Modern, Science and Vedanta. It is hence that man like Jawaharlal Nehru considered Vishwa-Bharti as the true representative of India.

❑❑❑

16

Dr. Sarvepalli Radhakrishnan

"The real aim of education is to help man to know the inner values." **—S. Radhakrishnan**

Born on the 5th September 1888 at Tiruttani, South India, Dr. Sarvepalli Radhadrishnan received his education at Madras Christian College. He joined as Assistant Professor of Philosophy, Presidency College, Madras, in 1911, was appointed Professor of Philosophy in 1916 and worked there till 1917. He was appointed University Professor or Philosophy, Mysore University, in 1918 and served it till 1921. He was appointed King George V. Professor of Philosophy at the Calcutta University in 1921 and worked there in this position till 1939. He was appointed upon Lecturer in comparative Religion, at Manchestor College., Oxford, in 1926 and again in 1929-30. He was appointed Haskell Lecturer in Comparative Religion. University of Chicago and Hibbert Lecturer in 1929. He was appointed Honorary Fellow of All Souls College Oxford in 1930. He worked as Vice-Chancellor of Andhra University in Waltair from 1931-36 and Vice-Chancellor of Banaras Hindu University from 1939 to 1948.

Dr. Radhakrishnan was Member, International Committee on Intellectual Co-operation 1931-39; Member, International League of Nations, Geneva 1931-39; Fellow, Royal Asiatic Society, Bengal. He was honoured as Knight in 1931. He was a member and Leader of Indian Delegation of UNESCO in 1946, 1947, 1948, 1949, 1959. He was elected Chairman of the Executive Board, UNESCO in 1948.

He was Chairman of University Education Commission (1948), Government of India. He was appointed Indian Ambassador Extraordinary and Minister Plenipotentiary to Soviet Russia during the period of 1949-52. He was elected as Vice-President of Indian Republic in 1952 and again in 1957. He also held the position of Chancellor of Delhi University. He was also the Chairman, Indian P.E.N. And Vice-President, International P.E.N. He went on a two months' goodwill tour of European countries, namely Belgium, Poland, Czechoslovakia, The Soviet Union, Hungary and Bulgaria and African countries, namely, East and Central Africa in June-July 1956. He visited Singapore. Indonesia, Japan and China on a goodwill tour in September-October 1956. He went on a three-week tour of Indo-China States, China, Mongolia and Hongkong in September 1957. He attended East West Philosophers' Conference in Honolulu (Hawaii Islands) and also visited U.S.A. In July 1959, he attended the P.E.N. Congress in Germany. He went on a goodwill tour of England and Scandinavia in January and February 1960. He attended the UNESCO Conference at Paris in November 1960. He acted as President of India in June-July 1960. He was elected Hony. Fellow of the British Academy on July 11, 1962.

Dr. Radhakrishnan was given a large number of National and International honours as Knight (1931), F.R.S.L., M.A., D. Litt. (Hon.), LL.D., D.C.L., Litt.D., F.B.A., Bharat Ratna, 1954, German pour Le merite (1955), Master of Wisdom (Mongolia, 1957), Goethe Plaquette (1959). He became the President of Indian Republic in May 1962.

Dr. Sarvepalli Radhakrishnan fulfills the dream of a 'a philosopher king' of ancient Greek Philosopher Plate. He is regarded as one of the greatest contemporary philosophers. He has rendered a great service to the cause of philosophy and right thinking. He realised that in the war-weary and confusion-stricken world only a wholesome thought and philosophy could restore a happy, intellectual and emotional harmony, which would served as an edifice for an adequate political, economic and cultural regeneration of mankind.

Dr. Radhakrishnan was a versatile genius who rendered service not only as a philosopher but also as an intellectual reformer and and a clear farsighted statesman. His service to Philosophy has been recognised equally by the West and the East. He succeeded happily in evolving a mean between the oriental and the occidental thinking. He synthesised the different currents of light and fused them into a lighthouse bound to guide humanity along the path that leads to the ultimate truth and salvation.

In Dr. Radhakrishnan, wisdom and power went together. The world knows him as a Philosopher, statesman, world teacher and cultural Ambassador. Indian nation was enriched in having him as its President. He served India in a most dignified way and was very popularly known as Philosopher-Statesman.

A rare example of combination of philosophy and politics Dr. Radhakrishnan was imbibed in himself all the humanistic trends of ancient Indian philosophy and culture. This rich cultural heritage of Vedas and the Upanishads and scholarship of East and West was visible throughout his life as a teacher, Professor, Ambassador and the President of the Indian Republic. He was the true cultural Ambassador of our nation who brought before the world the ideals for which India stood. He brought the East and the West closer in thought by interpreting the one to the other. He pushed the old ancient ideal of one world and of World-Government to establish world peace. His thought clearly shows his leaning towards humanism.

A proverb goes "Some men are born great, some achieve greatness and greatness is thrust upon some." Dr. Radhakrishnan comes under all these three categories. He had inborn qualities of greatness; he achieved greatness by virtue of his ambitions, hardwork and friendly attitude towards every one; situations and circumstances in India and the world have also made him great.

Pt. Madan Mohan Malaviya, the founder of the Banaras Hindu University, has great insight and quality of assessing individuals. He picked up Dr. S. Radhakrishnan and appointed him the Vice-Chancellor of the Banaras Hindu University. Under his Vice Chancellorship, the University earned an enviable status in the world of learning and attracted a large number of students from foreign countries.

Impressed by the scholarship and qualities of head and heart and political insight of Dr. Radhakrishnan, Jawahar Lal Nehru picked him up first for the post of Ambassador to U.S.S.R., then Vice-President and ultimately President of India.

Mahatma Gandhi recommended him for some dignified position in the Government. Rabindra Nath Tagore admired his scholarly achievements and learning. Dr. Archie. J.Bahm says, "Dr. S. Radhakrishnan's name is better known than that of Shankara or even Sri Aurobindo. He is better known than any other Indian except Gautam, Gandhi, Nehru and perhaps Tagore. His command to Western philosophy makes western philosophers respect him quite apart from his other achievements. His ability to speak to them in a language, which is closer to their own way of thinking." He further adds, "The profundity of interest in Philosophy in India is the cause of envy of philosophers in all other countries. And success of Radhakrishnan not only in teaching philosophy but in rising in personal stature to a position of practical political prominence gives many American philosophers further cause of worry."

WORKS OF DR. RADHAKRISHNAN

Dr. Radhakrishnan achieved international recognition for his writings on religion and philosophy. His striking eloquence and admirable memory for quotations, references and recognition of persons was unusual. He was the first Indian to hold a Chair at Oxford, a teacher in five Indian Universities and Vice Chancellor of two Indian universities, namely, Andhra University and the Banaras Hindu University. Chairman of the First University Education Commission, his election to the British Academy was a recognition of his services to the cause of learning in many counties.

One of the most renowned publishers George Allen & Unwin of London published almost all works of Dr. Radhakrishnan distributed them throughout English speaking world. He wrote about thirty books on Philosophy, Religion and Culture. Some of his very well recognised books include. *Philosophy of Rabindra Nath Tagore, Reign of Religion in Contemporary Philosophy, Indian Philosophy, two volumes, The Hindu View of Life, An Idealist View of Life, East and West in Religion, Kalki or the Future of Civilisation, The Religion We Need, Gatuama the Buddha, Eastern Religions and Western Thought, India and China, Religion and Society, Education, Politics and War, Bhagwadgita, Dhammapda, The Principal Upanishads, Recovery of Faith, East and West—Some Reflections and Brahma Sutra.* Besides a large number of books, he delivered hundreds of addresses-Convocation addresses, Inauguration Speeches and various speeches on different occasions.

His book on *Indian Philosophy* published in two volumes found a place in the courses of all the universities of the world where Indian Philosophy was being taught. His works, especially translations and commentaries of the Vedanta Texts, attracted English speaking readers having interest in the Indian Philosophy. His writings brought awareness of Indian thought to the English readers all over the world.

METAPHYSICAL BACKGROUND

Radhakrishnan has acclaimed ancient Vedanta philosophy as the basis of his philosophical ideas. He is a neo-Vedantic and the Vedanta philosophy is characteristically monistic, idealistic and integral. The integral spirit is characteristic of not only the philosophical thinking of S. Radhakrishnan but also of his multisided life involving not only religious and philosophical activity but also intense activity in social, educational and political fields.

Radhakrishnan was an idealist philosopher. He was an advocate of ancient Indian Vedanta philosophy. This is very much clear from his works *The Hindu View of Life, Brahmasutra, An Idealist View of Life* etc. He defined philosophy as a combination of reflection and intuition.[1] According to hin the aim of philosophy is to search that synthesis which may include all the aspects of creation. Philosophy, according to him, "is an attempt to human being to know the problems of creation and the nature of ultimate reality."[2] In epistemology Radhakrishnan admitted value of both reason and faith, logic and experience. He admitted the value of perceptual, conceptual and intuitive knowledge in education. According to him intuitive knowledge is that highest knowledge.[3] It is an integral experience. He admitted mystic experience as a part of intuitive experience.[4] Total experience is gained by total self and it is much higher than any other experience gained by any part of man's being.[5] Creative insight has an important place in total knowledge. Radhakrishnan however, is nowhere an anti-intellectualist like Bergson or Bradley. He was not a mystic in the final analysis. His philosophy has been rightly interpreted as integral experience. Integral experience finds place for every other type of experience in it.

PSYCHOLOGICAL BACKGROUND

Human personality, according to Radhakrishnan, is not determined by physical environment, economic or otherwise. So far as physical changes are concerned they may be generally determined by the environment but the human will be free to decide to win or loose. The real human freedom is the freedom

1. **Radhakrishnan, S., *An Idealist View of life* (London), George Allen & Unwin (1947), pp. 15-16.**
2. **Radhakrishnan, S., *The Philosophy of Rabindranath Tagore* (Baroda), Good Companions (1961), p.101.**
3. **Radhakrishnan, S., *The Bhagwadgita,* p. 67.**
4. **Radhakrishnan, S., *An Idealist View of Life,* p. 153.**
5. ***Ibid.,* p. 147.**
6. **Arapura, J.G., *Radhakrishnan and Integral Experience,* Bombay: Asia Publishing House (1961), p. 33.**

of will. This has been granted to man. In the tradition of ancient Indian thinkers Radhakrishnan had admitted the principle of *Karma.* According to this principle our present is determined by our past and the future depends upon the present. In the words of S. Radhakrishnan, "*Karma* or relationship with the past does not mean that man cannot do anything freely but free action is involved in it."[1] The law of *Karma* is not fatalism. According to it, "An individual will gain according to the use of his energy. The world will respond to the individual *Jivatma's* demand. The nature will reply the insistent call of the man."[2] Thus, like Karl Marx, Radhakrishnan believed that man can change the world. On the basis of his will he can make his future. The principle of Nature are the principles of justice. In Nature and in human world, everywhere one universal divine law functions. Therefore, the law of *Karma* is not an external but an internal determinant of human life.

In the line of evolution, man is distinguished by self-consciousness, which is not found either in plants or in animals. Therefore, the mental processes cannot be interpreted in terms of physical changes. The physical movements do not explain total behaviour. Modern psychology takes a one-sided view of man while presenting behaviouristic interpretation. Behaviourism has only historical value. Man's behaviour cannot be explained by stimulus-response formula. An organism is not merely a sum total of parts. Its parts are internally related. Consciousness does not come out of matter, it is a new creation. Again, self-consciousness is not a biological phenomena. It should not be explained in physiological or biological terms. With the evolution of self-consciousness Nature evolves to a new level of existence. The self-conscious man is rational. Self-realisation is the aim of life. This self is the Spirit. In the words of S. Radhakrishnan, "Spirit is life, not thing, power not status, real in itself and through itself

1. **Radhakrishnan, S., *The Hindu View of Life* (Londan), George Allen & Unwin (1961), p. 256.**
2. ***Ibid.***

and cannot be compared to any substance subjective or objective"[1] The spirit expresses as itself, God and the world. Thus human nature is essentially spiritual. Spiritual also means natural because nature is as much an expression of Spirit as the self. Human life is not only natural but also divine since its essential nature is spirit. The world is a gradual evolution towards spirit. In this evolution man is at the apex. This evolution is both emergent as well as continuous. What is not cannot happen, whatever is, it develops. This metaphysical hypothesis is very important in the philosophy of education. The child will develop only that which is potential in it. What is not implicit cannot be explicit. However, every level of evolution expresses new elements. The characteristics of spirit are seen in creativity, change, system and progress. These are the characteristic of every field of life and so of education. Education aims at complete expressions of the inherent spirit in man.

MYSTICISM

It appears that Radhakrishnan's philosophy is mysticism so far as the concept of spirit is concerned. In his book *An Idealist View of Life,* Radhakrishnan has called spirit total Brahman. Brahman precedes creation. Identifying God and creator Radhakrishnan said, "They are the different forms of seeing the same ultimate reality."[2] Thus like Sri Aurobindo, Radhakrishnan believes the world to be the expression of God. This metaphysical proposition lays down the spiritual goal of education and certifies its possibility. In fact, Radhakrishnan has synthesised idealism and realism, mysticism and pragmatism in his philosophy. He welcomes all sorts of experience to arrive at some general principles. As he said, "We should weave different parts of experience in a total pattern. We should keep our general ideas connected so that different experiences may be explained."[3]

---

1. **Muirhead and Radhakrishnan, (Ed.) *Contemporary Indian Philosophy* (London), George Allen & Unwin (1956), 2nd Ed., p. 492.**
2. **Radhakrishnan, S., *Recovery of Faith,* pp. 89-99.**
3. **Schilpp, P.A., *The Philosophy of Sarvepalli Radhakrishnan,* The Tudor Publishing House (1952), p. 27.**

In spite of being a votary of science Radhakrishnan is not a determinist of environmentalist. This fact is of capital importance in his explanations of human nature. Science proves that every effect has a cause but it does not definitely prove the cause of every effect. As David Hume has rightly pointed out, the principle of causation in the field of science is a mere probability. So far as physical incidents are concerned, they are determined by natural laws but man has been provided freedom of choice in life. He is not free to choose his cards but he is free to play, win or loose, as he likes. This freedom of winning or loosing is given to man.

SPIRIT : THE ULTIMATE REALITY

Radhakrishnan interprets the world as the play and evolution of spirit. Matter, life, mind are the manifestations of the spirit in the world. Spirit is not a substance but life itself. In the words of Radhakrishnan "It is the basis and background of our being, the university that cannot be reduced to this or that formula."[1] The self, God and Absolute are all names of the one universal spirit in different aspects. Thus the most characteristic feature of the spirit is its integrality. It leaves nothing out of its ken, it integrates all, it permeates everything. In order to know it we must look to life from all sides, gross as well as refined, higher as well as lower, primitive as well as civilised. It is so since, "Spirit is life not thing, power not status, real in itself and through itself and cannot be compared to any substance subjective or objective."[2]

The dominant theme in the metaphysics of Radhkrishnan is the presence of one universal spirit as the inner essence of all being and becoming. Spirit has been acclaimed as the Reality in the ancient Upanishads and the works of all the idealist thinking in the world. Therefore, it is not an original idea of Radhakrishnan. However, he has made original contribution by connecting the idea of spirit with the findings of modern science. The greatest merit of his philosophy is that it is an interpretation of the real

1. **Radhakrishnan, S.,** ***An Idealist View of Life,*** **p. 205.**
2. **Muirhead and Radhakrishnan, (Ed.)** ***Contemporary Indian Philosophy,*** **Londan, George Allen and Unwin, 1956, 2nd Ed., p. 492**

world and real life. He does not confine philosophy to realisation of truth like the ancient Indian seers, but applies it to actual problems of his time. Therefore all his ideas revolve around science, intuition and religion. He does not accept dialectical materialism or any materialism for that matter. He is mystic so far as the reply to the ultimate why is concerned. He admit that spirit is the basis and background of all reality, a universal substance, which cannot be explained by this or that formula.[1] The three elements of metaphysics—the self, the God and the world—are the different expressions of one universal spirit. This universal Spirit has been variously called God and Absolute, Ishwar and Brahman. In man Spirit expresses in a limited field. In God it expresses in a universal from. In Absolute in involves not only the present manifestations but also the immense future possibilities.

UNIVERSITY EDUCATION COMMISION

Terms of Reference

As the Chairman of University Education Commission Radhakrishnan had an occasion to examine different aspects of Indian education in details. The terms of reference of this commission of enquiry were as follows—

1. The aims and objects of university education and research in India.
2. The changes considered necessary and desirable in the constitution, control, functions and jurisdiction of universities in India and their relations with Government, Central and Provincial.
3. The Finance of universities.
4. The maintenance of the highest standards of teaching and examination in the universities and colleges under their control.
5. The course of study in the universities with special reference to the maintenance of a sound balance between

1. **Radhakrishnan, S.,*An Idealistic View of Life*, p. 205.**

the Humanities and Sciences and between Pure Science and Technological Training and the duration of such courses.

6. The standards of admission to university courses of study with reference to the desirability of an independent university entrance examination and the avoidance of unfair discrimination, which militates against Fundamental Right 23(2).
7. The medium of instruction in the universities.
8. The provision for advanced study in Indian culture, history, literatures, languages, philosophy and fine arts.
9. The need for more universities on a regional or other basis.
10. The organisation of advanced research in all branches of knowledge in the universities and institutes of higher research a well co-ordinated fashion avoiding waste of effort and resources.
11. Religious instruction in the universities.
12. The special problems of the Banaras Hindu University, the Aligarh Muslim University, the Delhi University and other institutions of an all-India character.
13. The qualifications, conditions of service, salaries, privileges and functions of teachers and the encouragement of original research by teachers.
14. The discipline of students, hostels and the organisation of tutorial work and any other matter which is germane to a complete and comprehensive enquiry into all aspects of university education and advanced research in India.

DEFECTS OF PRESENT SYSTEM OF EDUCATION

The commission pointed to the following grave defects in the present system of education.

1. In comparison to the universities in West the standard of people in Indian Universities is very low. This is particularly due to the lower standard of education on intermediate stage.

2. The condition of teachers in Indian universities is far from being satisfactory. Their salary is inadequate and the working conditions are far from satisfactory. Therefore able persons are not coming forward to take up the career of teaching.
3. The curriculum is not sufficiently diversified and integrated.
4. There are not sufficient vocational, engineering and technological institutions in the country.
5. National and regional languages have not been given sufficient opportunities to develop.
6. The examination system is far from being objective. It is full of grave defects.
7. The administration system does not find place for all the sections of society concerned with education.
8. The government is not providing sufficient economic support to the institutions of higher education.
9. As the universities are functioning property they are not fulfilling the important purpose of creating new generation of leaders in democracy.
10. Women education has not been extended sufficiently.
11. Rural education, necessary in a country like India, has been neglected.
12. Religious education has been generally sectarian, which is not consistent in a secular state.

AIMS AND OBJECTIVES OF EDUCATION

Dr. Radhakrishnan recommended the following aims of education for higher education in India :

1. To teach that life has a meaning.
2. To awaken the innate ability to live the life of soul by developing wisdom.
3. To acquaint with the social philosophy, which should govern all our institutions — educational as well as economic and political.

4. To train for democracy.
5. To train for self-development.
6. To develop certain values like fearlessness of mind, strength of conscience and integrity of purpose.
7. To acquaint with cultural heritage for its regeneration.
8. To enable to know that education is a life-long process.
9. To develop understanding of the present as well as of the past.
10. To impart vocational and professional training.

Self-Development

Criticising the present system of education Radhakrishnan said, "Our education has not freed us from intellectual bondage. It stimulates the mind without satisfying it."[1] Freedom, according to Radhakrishnan, is the goal of education. He lamented that the present system of education does not grow free thinking among students. The student does not know what is higher thinking. He does not develop any creativity. Our institutions are preparing human machines not developed human beings. The true education should aim at developing a total human personality, a free mind, a multisided growth, a creative aptitude and a spiritual evolution. The aim of life according to Radhakrishnan is to train the mind. As he said, "The real aim of education is to help man to know the inner essence."[2] Physical success and material progress is not the aim of education. True education does not aim at any diploma or degree. It is self-development. In the words of Radhakrishnan, "The real aim of education is this that the character of man may become rhythmic and his soul creative."[3] The primary aim of education from beginning to end is to attain knowledge. This knowledge however, cannot be achieved only through books. The

---

1. **Radhakrishnan, S., *Kalki* (Ludhiana: Kalyani Publishers, 1974), Sixth Ed., p. 37.**
2. **Radhakrishnan, S., *The Concept of Man* (London: George Allen & Unwin, 1960), p. 246.**
3. **Frankena, W.K. (Ed.) *Philosophy of Education*, p. 54.**

books cannot transform human personality. This transformation is the real aim of education. Transformation is the real aim of education. Transformation can be achieved only by putting knowledge in practice. Transforation is necessary for the realisation of human freedom. According to Radhakrishnan, "The freedom of human soul is the most valuable."[1] Therefore education should aim at realisation of this freedom. This freedom again is the basis of character formation.

Man-Making

According to almost all contemporary Indian philosophers of education, education is a process of man-making. Man-making means character formation. As Radhakrishnan rightly pointed out, "The fate of a nation depends upon character. A country whose people have low character can never become great. When we want to build a great nation, we should educate more and more young men and women in such a way that they may have strength of character."[2] In a moral character, Radhakrishnan placed world fraternity as the highest virtue. His aim of education is humanist and internationalist.

Self-Expression

Education aims at teaching self-expression. This is possible only through the mastery of language. In the end no education is complete without the development of institution. The ancient Indian Upanishads identify intuition with wisdom and education. Intuition however, cannot be achieved by the study of books alone. It requires guidance by the ability test. Therefore, Radhakrishnan insisted upon the appointment of able teachers particularly in the institutions of higher learning.

MEANS OF EDUCATION

Practical Training

Radhakrishnan strongly favoured modern means of

1. **Radhakrishnan, S., *Speeches and Writings,* Vol. II, p. 267.**
2. ***Ibid.,* p. 259.**

education. He laid down the standards of teaching at various levels of education in the report of commission headed by him. He maintained that students of different professions should be given practical training as far as possible. Elaborating this principle, the university education commission under him made the following recommendation :

1. Agriculture—The study of agriculture in primary, secondary and higher education be given high priority in national economic planning. So far as is feasible, agricultural education be given a rural setting.

2. Commerce—A commerce student should be given opportunities for practical work in three or four different kinds of firms.

3. Education—The course be remodelled and more time given to school practice and more weight to practice in assessing the student's performances.

4. Engineering and Technology—The number of engineering schools of different grades be increased particularly for training of grades 4 and 5 (foremen, craftsmen, craftsmen, overseers, etc)

In establishing new engineering colleges or institutes there should be fresh, critical inquiry as to the types of engineering service needed in India. Uncritical reposition and imitation of existing institutions here and abroad should be avoided.

5. Law—A three-year degree course be offered in special legal subjects. Students pursuing degree course in law shall not be permitted to carry other degree courses simultaneously except in a few instances where advanced students have proved their interest and are studying related subjects in law and some other fields.

6. Medicine—The maximum number of admission to a medical college be 100, provided the staff and equipment for that number are available.

TYPES OF EDUCATION

The means of education will be further clarified by a review of Radhakrishnan's views about various types of education. These are as follows :

1. Moral Education—Like Vivekananda, Sri Aurobindo and M.K. Gandhi, Radhakrishnan wanted to make moral education a compulsory part of education at primary and secondary levels. Without it the educational institutions cannot fulfil their objective of education the youth of the country. Moral character has been given the most important place in Indian culture. Moral education is the education of will. It starts in the family. In the school the educand learns moral norms in the limitation of the conduct of the teachers. The moral education clarifies the goal of life without which no meaningful life is possible. The greatness of a country cannot be measured by its progress in physical civilisation but by its moral and spiritual advancement. Therefore , whatever is done for the achievement of vocational goal, education cannot be complete without moral instruction. This has become even more important in the face of the fact that morality is the only reliable instrument for saving the world from the catastrophe of a future world war. The seeds of morality will be sown in educational institution. Therefore, Radhakrishnan advised that society ought to be based on proper foundation. Economically prosperous man is not a perfect human being. A perfect being requires bliss and beauty of the soul, which should be full of love and faith and endeavours for rejuvenating humanity.[1]

2. Religious Education—Along with other contemporary Indian Neo-Vedanta philosophers of education, Radhakrishnan supports religious education. Religious education for him, however, is not the instruction of a particular religion. It is a means for developing spiritual intuition because, "The aim of religion is spiritual and not merely a change in metaphysical ideal."[2]

---

1. **Radhakrishnan, S., *My Search for Truth* (Shivlal Agrawal), p. 20.**
2. **Radhakrishnan, S., *Recovery of Faith*, p. 158.**

Religious education is a means for propagation of the ideal of world brotherhood. According to Radhakrishnan, the modern substitutes of religion such as communism cannot fulfil any useful purpose. Real religion is spiritual religion. Therefore religious education will provide freedom and spiritual progress to the educand. It is not contrary to the education of science but complimentary to it. India can progress in science in spite of its religious character. From this viewpoint Radhakrishnan is not prepared to accept secularism as meaning aversion to religion. According to him the only secularism worth the name means that every individual has full liberty to follow his religion. Radhakrishnan himself gives highest importance to *The Bhagwadgita* but does not derogate the importance of the scriptures of other religion. About *The Bhagwadgita* he wrote, "*Bhagwadgita* has everything, rational, moral and spiritual, and answer to every question of human progress and its perfection."[22] Such a book may be the basis of religious education. However, religious education is in fact spiritual education. It is a means while spiritual education is the end. The University Education Commission, under the Chairmanship of Radhakrishnan, made the following recommendations about religious education :

(a) All educational institutions should start work with a few minutes for silent meditation.

(b) In the first year lives of the great religious leaders like Gautama the Buddha, Confucius, Zoroaster, Socrates, Jesus, Samkara, Ramanuja, Madhva, Mohammad, Kabir, Nanak, Gandhi be taught.

(c) In the second year some selections of a universal character from the scriptures of the world be studied.

(d) In the third year, the central problems of the philosophy of religion be considered.

3. Primary Education—Radhakrishnan praised M.K. Gandhi's scheme of basic education as a pattern for primary education in India. He said, "This education establishes contact of the student with everyday life. It explains the importance of physical education. The body is the means of the expression of human soul, therefore, physical education must be properly given."[1] He recommends teaching of both humanities and science subjects alongwith languages on the primary level.

4. Secondary Education—Radhakrishnan has considered secondary education as a next step continuous with the primary education. Therefore, on secondary stage also, the student should be provided a multisided curriculum including science, humanities and languages, The curriculum should be modified according to the needs of the country because the primary aim of education is to meet the needs of the nation and to create national unity. National unity may be created by teaching of history. Teaching of mathematics is necessary as it is on the primary stage as well. Agricultural and industrial art and crafts should be taught so that the students may be capable of earning their livelihood. In India few people go to the institutions of higher education due to poverty and other causes. Therefore, presuming that most of the students will drop out after the secondary stage, they should be taught something of everything and also some useful craft to enable them to earn their livelihood.

5. University Education—The most significant contribution made by Radhakrishnan to Indian education had been in the area of higher education. This contribution was made through the University Education Commission report. According to this report the objectives of the universities were as follows :

(a) To seek and cultivate new knowledge, to engage vigorously and fearlessly in the pursuit of truth, and to interpret old knowledge and benefits in the light of new needs and discoveries.

(b) To provide the right kind of leadership in all walks of life, to identify gifted youth and help them develop their potential to the full by cultivating physical fitness,

1. **Radhakrishnan, S.,** ***Speeches and Writings,*** **Vol. II, p. 175.**

developing the powers of the mind and cultivating right interests, attitudes and moral intellectual values.

(c) To provide society with competent men and women trained in agriculture, arts, medicine, science and technology and various other professions, who will also be cultivated individuals, imbued with a sense of social purpose.

(d) To drive to promote equally and social justice and to reduce social and cultural differences through diffusion of education.

(e) To foster in the teacher and students, and through them in society generally, the attitude and values needed for developing the good life in individual and society.

(f) To provide part-time and correspondence courses and extension programmes of various kinds so as to provide varied educational facilities for a widening clientele.

(g) To undertake carefully worked out programmes for school improvement.

PROBLEMS OF HIGHER EDUCATION

Radhakrishnan recommended selective admissions for institutions of higher education. He particularly laid emphasis upon research as the main aim of the universities. He favoured university autonomy in the selection of students, the appointment and promotions of teachers, the determination of syllabi, the methods of teaching and areas of research. He recommended establishment of an Inter University Board and the University Grants Commission. He recommended the establishment of at least one agricultural university in every state. He pointed out the need of reform in major universities. He analysed the problems of development of Higher Education in India. According to him the most important problems of higher education are—

1. Role of the university system,
2. Improvement of standards,
3. Restructuring of courses,

4. Postgraduate education and research,
5. Diversification of courses,
6. Decentralisation,
7. Autonomous colleges,
8. Academic freedom,
9. Medium of instruction,
10. Extension services,
11. Student discipline,
12. Role of UGC.

Recommendations

Analysing all these problems Radhakrishnan made important recommendations. Among these recommendations, the most important, from the point of view of philosophy of education, are the recommendations concerning the role of university system in a nation. These recommendations sum up the aims and ideals of education according to Radhakrishnan. Therefore it is necessary to enumerate these recommendations. They are as follows—

1. To inculcate and promote basics human values and the capacity to choose between alternative value systems;
2. To preserve and foster our great cultural traditions and blend them with essential elements from other cultures and peoples;
3. To enrich the Indian languages and promote their use as important means of communication, national development and unity;
4. To promote a rational outlook and scientific temper;
5. To promote the development of the total personality of the students and inculcate in them a commitment to society through involvement in national service programme.
6. To act as an objective critic of society and assist in the formulation of national objectives and programmes for their realisation;
7. To promote commitment to the pursuit of excellence;

8. To promote the development of science and technology and of an indigenous capability to apply it effectively with special emphasis on national problems; and above all.
9. To contribute to the improvement of the entire educational system so as to subserve the community.

MEDIUM OF EDUCATION

Value of Mother Tongue

Almost all the contemporary Indian philosophers of education have recommended mother tongue as the proper medium of education. Along with Sri Aurobindo and R.N. Tagore, Radhakrishnan raised his voice against making English the medium of instruction in India. Its biggest disadvantage is the formation of a class of educated persons, which is cut off from the ordinary national at least from linguistic point of view. Such educated persons do not represent Indian culture since they imbibed Western culture through the medium of English literature. The most natural medium of instruction for a child is his mother tongue. In India this credit should be given to regional languages.

Limitation of English Medium

In spite of having an extraordinary master over English language, Radhakrishnan maintained, "It can never be seriously through that English may ever become *lingua franca* of India."[1] Pointing out the reason for it, he said that the Indians can never create great literature or original writings through English language. Psychological researches have approved that bilingualism is an impediment in the child's mental growth. It kills originality and creates confusion. Therefore, according to Radhakrishnan, a serious disadvantage of bi-lingualism in our education has resulted in the absence of originality.

Value of Sanskrit

Along with regional languages Radhakrishnan also laid emphasis upon the study of Sanskrit since it is the repository of

1. **Radhakrishnan, S., *The Philosophy of Rabindranath Tagore* (Baroda: Good Companions, 1961), p. 128.**

Indian culture. It is the language of Indian scriptures and lays down Indian philosophy of life. It is the medium through which the unity of nation may be preserved. Along with regional language and Sanskrit.

Hindi a National Language

Radhakrishnan has accepted Hindi as an all India language. He accepts the three-language formula in which the child is taught the mother tongue, the national language Hindi and the international language English. However, Radhakrishnan was against forcibly imposing Hindi on the people of South India. According to him, every state should make efforts for the growth of regional languages along with national language. Even on the question of script he admitted the rights of regional languages. He pointed out that Devanagari script should not be forcibly imposed upon others. The function of a language is to create bridges not to create gulfs. The University Education Commission, under the chairmanship of Radhakrishnan recommended that the regional languages should be adopted as media of education at the university sage in phased programme spread over ten years. At the earlier stage of the undergraduate course, the bulk of the instruction may be given through the regional language while at the postgraduate stage, it may be in English. The teaching of important European languages other than English should be stressed, in particular the study of Russian, on larger scale.

TEACHING METHODS

Value of Teacher

Radhakrishnan finds a place in the galaxy of great Indian teachers. Therefore his views about teaching methods are not only theoretical principles but based upon actual experience of decades of teaching in Indian and Western universities. In his philosophy of education the teacher has been given a very honourable place in keeping with the ancient Indian philosophy of education. He recommends absolute freedom to the teachers in universities to follow such methods of teaching which they may deem fit for their purpose. According to Radhakrishnan, "The type of education, which we may give to our youth, depends on the fact that what type of teachers we get."[1] The teachers should have devotion to teaching besides their knowledge and scholarships. In ancient India the teacher was given highest status in the field of education and also in society since his life was as high as his ability. Most of the problems of the present system of education are due to failures of some teachers. In order to develop character in the educand the educator should himself develop his own character. According to Radhakrishnan, "The teachers have a special place in the formation of the mind and heart of our youth."[2] The teachers should have self control and humanist standpoint. Great teachers in India have always preserved its culture, though many of them also travelled far and wide to know about other culture.[3] Thus the teacher should be inquisitive. He should take interest in expansion of knowledge. As the Chairman of the University Education Commission Dr. Radhakrishnan insisted upon recruiting suitable teachers on various levels of education. The university teachers have the dual responsibility of character formation and research guidance. Therefore, while selecting them it is not only the scholarship but also their enthusiasm in character formation of the students, which must be considered.

Teacher-Taught Relationship

Proper teaching methods require proper teacher-taught ratio. Therefore Radhakrishnan recommended that overcrowding at universities and colleges should be avoided. According to him the maximum number in the Arts and Science faculties of teaching universities should be 3,000 and in affiliated college 1,500. He recommended a minimum of 180 working days in a year exclusive of examination days. He was in favour of selective admissions to higher institutions. Along with reform of teaching method he suggested measures for student discipline. The teachers and

1. **Radhakrishnan, S., *Speeches and Writings,* Vol. II, p. 259.**
2. **Radhakrishnan, S., *op. cit.,* p. 202.**
3. ***Ibid.,* p. 204.References**

students should carry out their part of the responsibility through intensive efforts to improve standards and the whole academic community should strive to serve society, through sustained, dedicated work, and commitment to pursuit of knowledge, excellence and national development. A nation-wide effort should be organised to achieve a simultaneous breakthrough on the social as well as educational fronts.

EDUCATION FOR DIFFERENT SECTIONS OF SOCIETY

It is a common knowledge that in contemporary Indian society all the sections were not given equal opportunities for education. The backward classes did not get sufficient opportunity even for acquiring primary education for their children. The women education started only during the British period and even then the first girl to aspire for the graduation of Calcutta University had to seek special permission for it. As a teacher and as a Vice-Chancellor Radhakrishnan was very much conscious of this inequality. Therefore, he made particular reference to the education of those sections of society, which have not been given sufficient opportunity. As the Chairman of the University Education Commission he made particular reference to women's education in the country. He pointed out that women students in general should be helped to secure their normal places in a normal society, both as citizens and as women, and to prepare for it. College programmes should be so designed that it will be possible for them to do so. The standards of courtesy and social responsibility should be emphasised in co-educational institutions.

In India it is a common knowledge that so many parents cannot send their wards for higher education due to economic difficulties. Referring to these sections of society, Radhakrishnan recommended enabling talented but economically weaker students to pursue their studies on a whole time basis by ensuring to them the full cost of their education, through appropriate bursaries, for which funds may be raised from public and private bodies.

CONTRIBUTION TO INDIAN EDUCATION

University Education Commission

Among contemporary Indian philosophers of education Radhakrishnan had the longest and the most intimate experience of both college and university education, Indian and Western. Therefore, it is natural that his philosophy of education is most pragmatic. As the Chairman of the University Education Commission was instrumental in planning the present higher education in India. Many of his recommendations have to be still worked out such as the idea of autonomous colleges. His recommendations were thorough and multisided and based upon solid philosophical foundations. They were guided by a basic integral approach avoiding all one sidedness.

Sound Foundation of Education

Radhakrishnan's philosophy of education is based upon sound psychological and sociological foundations. He has rightly considered every aspect of human personality to be valuable for development. He aimed at the building up of integral spiritual human beings through education. In the tradition of ancient Indian philosophy of education he defined education as a process of character formation. Among values he laid emphasis upon democratic values and therefore asked for inculcation of liberty, equality and fraternity both among teachers and students.

Integral Approach

Radhakrishnan's approach to aims and ideals, means, curriculum, school administration etc. show an integral approach. He gave place to every subject in syllabi of education at different stages.

17

Manabendra Nath Roy

"New humanism expresses a new viewpoint toward the problem of education, which suggests that given opportunity every human being has the capacity to develop his abilities to an ultimate extant."

—M.N. Roy

Born in West Bengal in 1886, M.N. Roy joined Bengal Revolutionary Movement in his teens. He develop deep into the philosophy of Karl Marx and rubbed shoulders with some of the greatest Marxists of contemporary history. He founded the Communist Party in Mexico in 1918. He remained a member of the presidium and secretariat of the Communist International. He also remained in-charge, training and organisation of Asiatic communists in Eastern University in Moscow. For some time he was Chief Adviser of the Communist Party of China. In 1928, he developed serious differences with communist International and returned to India.

Lenin described M.N. Roy as "the symbol of revolution in the East." In view of the existing conditions in the world, the future of humanity appeared to be gloomy. But Roy made a call to all loves of peace and human values not to develop feelings of helplessness but to fight with unity and determination for human freedom. In this personality and idea, Roy combined the value of freedom with firmness of commitment. With a remarkable open-mindedness and capacity to absorb new ideas Roy tried to learn from the record of human experiences.

Among the modern Indian thinkers, Manabendra Nath Roy was more a philosopher than a mass leader. He was, essentially, one of the greatest thinkers of the twentieth century and truly a citizen of the world. His philosophy may be described as a mid-twentieth century version of the Renaissance modified and enriched by the experience of the intervening centuries. He was least concerned about himself and most of his life suffered due to on honest and straightforward approach to different national and international problems. His chief concern was to realise freedom for himself and for others.

INFLUENCES

Roy was a born revolutionary. His revolutionary career started when he was hardly 14 years of age. On him was the most significant influence of Marxian philosophy, which he studied very thoroughly and which remained virtually the basis of his subsequent ideology thought he differed from it in detail. In addition to this he was inspired by social and political leaders of Indian life. He was educated in the national schools and as such the movements started by Swami Ram Tirth and Swami Vivekananda reminding Indians of their supremacy and past cultural glory very much influenced him. Similarly, Roy was inspired by those national leaders who worked through the forum of Indian National Congress and devoted themselves to this national struggle. Great on him, was the influence of Bankim Chandra Chatterji who wrote his famous *Ananda Math.* Then we find that Roy was absolutely dissatisfied with the methods through, which the Britishers tried to exploit the Indians and denied individual right and liberties. From his very early age the growing poverty of India was an eye-sore for him and freedom, both national and individual, was the only solution to the problem. He was very much influenced by the revolutionaries who devoted themselves thoroughly in undoing the evils of partition of Bengal and were determined to revoke the action. He found that Swadeshi and boycott programmes were active and a realistic approach to Indian political problems. On the international field the victory of Japan over mighty Russia in 1905 was a great moulding and motivating factor on him. He gained confidence that colonial subjects in Asia, including India, could also win their freedom if they had determination and proper organisation.

WORKS

Roy wrote sufficient to leave back his political philosophy. Some of his significant works are :

1. *India in Transition;*
2. *Revolution and Counter-Revolution in China;*
3. *Our Differences;*
4. *Materialism;*
5. *Science and Philosophy;*
6. *On the Congress Constitution;*
7. *People's Plan;*
8. *National Government People's Government;*
9. *Reason, Romanticism and Revolution.*

In addition to this Roy contributed very many articles in various papers and was responsible for establishing his own journals through which he tried to propagate his ideas and philosophy.

M.N. Roy was sufficiently under the influence of Communism and basically adhered to that philosophy though he differed from Marx in details. As the time passed his faith in individual freedom increased and he also came to the conclusion that Communism provided to solution to individual liberty. He developed his own philosophy, which he called Radical Humanism and for which he wanted everyone to have an independent nature and character.

PHILOSOPHICAL BACKGROUND

Human Nature

According to M.N. Roy, individual was an end in itself and every other organisation in the society was simply means to an end. He pleaded that everything was below individual freedom, which should not be subordinated to anything else. He was not ready to subordinate individual freedom even to religion or morality or to any hotter supernatural power. He believed that man had always been struggling for freedom and his joining the civil state and society was only on the condition that his freedom would be protected. In his opinion it was an evolutionary process and history was a witness that man always struggled to preserve his freedom. It at any stage there was threat to his freedom man faced that very boldly and tried to preserve that. He went on saying that those institutions and organizations, which had been set up to safeguard individual freedom often have tried to master him and that was quite unhealthy. In his opinion, state was primarily brought into being unhealthy. In his opinion, state was primary brought into being to check all impediments and hindrances which checked the growth of man but today the state was trying to subordinate individuals and wanted to become an end in itself instead of being means to an end. Similarly religion had become the master of man's mind and tried to check individual freedom though gradually its grip was weakening.

According to M.N. Roy by nature man loves freedom. With regard to human nature he was rather close to Rousseau who said that man was born free and everywhere he was in chains. In his opinion man was governed by the same principle as physical sciences and in fact there was no basic difference between the two. He, however, distinguished between the two on the basis of rationalism. In his philosophy man was rational and as such above all other living beings. Rationalism was the most essential and basic standard of human development. He also believed that as against man in the physical beings there was no option of making choice. In his own words, *"It is the reason in man, which harmonizes the people of human will with the law governess of physical universe."*

Contemporary Moral Crisis

In twentieth century most of the philosophers of history in East and West drew attention to the moral crisis in human society and warned of the danger. This danger was clearly seen in the 2nd World War, which occurred in spite of all the attempts of the League of Nations. Thoughtful persons everywhere realised that the development of atomic power has led humanity to a stage where even its existence is at stake. From Sri Aurobindo to Sorokin, the philosophers of history pointed out that human race is passing through a critical stage whose problems require an urgent solution. Thus, the consciousness of crisis was almost universal. However, different thinkers analysed its causes differently and suggested different remedies. As has been already pointed out, Sri Aurobindo considered the rational dualism as the main cause of the present crisis and advised to evolve to supranational level. Admitting the crisis, M.N. Roy explained it differently. In contrast to Sri Aurobindo, the present crisis according to him, is not due to rationality but because of its absence. Therefore, the solution of the crisis is not to rise above reason but to be rational. This solution has been supported by most of the contemporary Western social thinkers including Bertrand Rusell and Karl Marx. According to Roy, our present crisis is moral in nature and due to crisis of values. The civilised human society today is moral in nature and due to crisis of values. The civilised human society today faces unprecedented social problems. Just as Buddhism in India criticised traditional religion and presented a scientific attitude, which was later on overshadowed by the *Mayavada* of Samkara, similarly the rational consciousness started due to progress of science in twentieth century was soon overpowered by Neo-mysticism characteristic of so many contemporary social theories. This Neo-mysticism had led to man's forgetting of his real nature, the nature of the physical world and man's status in cosmos. According to Roy the contemporary crisis is due to the confusion of intellectual methods. The sensitive persons may feel this crisis everywhere. Though most of the people want liberty one nowhere witnesses real freedom. Though most of the people want peace yet the clouds of wars are hovering everywhere. At this juncture, "What is needed is a restatement of Materialism so as to recognise explicitly the decisive importance of the dynamics of ideas in all the processes of human evolution—historical, social, political and cultural."[1]

M.N. Roy analysed the present crisis and tried to unravel its reasons. His analysis is based upon reason and experience of the entire human race. He pointed out defects and inadequacies of ancient Indian solutions of the present difficulties.[2] According to the old philosophy, it is not potent enough to save us in the present crisis. The crisis itself exhibits the facts the traditional social, political and economic thinking is nor more capable to guide us. All these interpretations were dualistic, unscientific and traditional, confined to some specialists. Therefore, Roy concluded that, "Philosophy can answer this question only in the light of scientific knowledge."[3]

Pointing out the failures of past philosophies M.N. Roy arrived at what he calls Radical Humanism, which, according to him, is only solution of the present day difficulties being faced by human society. This avowed social system including epistemology. metaphysicas and exiology. The epistemological and the metaphysical background of M.N. Roy's social thought should be understood in order to understand in more fully.

Epistemological Foundations

M.N. Roy calls his theory of knowledge of scientific. He starts with a critical evaluation of the traditional empiricist and rationalist theories of knowledge in the west and concludes like Immanual Kant, "Knowledge is possible because there is a causal connection between mind and matter."[4] Ideas, according to him, are representative of realities only if they are based upon experience. Thus, knowledge is the result of perception. "We know things, not ideas."[5] The validity of any idea may be

1. **Roy, M.N. *Reason, Romanticism and Revolution,* Vol. 1, Renaissance Publishers Ltd., Cal., 1952, p.11.**
2. **Roy. M.N., *Politics, Power and Parties,* Renaissance Publishers Ltd., Cal., 1960, p. 6.**
3. ***Ibid.***
4. ***Ibid.***
5. ***Ibid.***

examined by putting it to practical test. The epistemology of the British empiricist philosophers is a one-sided theory. Further, the ideas must change according to the knowledge of the world. Roy distinguishes between things and objects and concludes, "Ideas correspond not with things, but with objects."[1]

Radical Humanism

Thus, according to Roy, as according to the Greek philosopher Protagoras man is measure of all things. He agrees with Karl Marx that the individual is the basic unit of human society. Therefore, he aims at the foundation of a corporate society of free individuals. Distinguishing this humanism from other brands of humanism, Roy has called it scientific humanism, new humanism or radical humanism. His humanism is different by being radical. This radicalism however, is different from the earlier Western radicalism, which was collectivist. Radical humanism of M.N. Roy is individualist. According to Roy, "Radical Humanism says nothing new when it demands that man must be the measure of everything. Protagoras made the declaration more than 2500 years age. Yet, mankind seems to have forgotten its soul. The same liberating principle was repeated by Karl Marx, who is today honoured as the prophet of proletarian dictatorship, the advocates of which fanatically demand sacrifice of the individual at the alter of an imaginary collective ego."[2] Suggesting a new constitution for free India Roy declared that in it political power will directly belong to the public, which will include every adult individual. He accepted the contribution of M.K. Gandhi to Indian politics though he very much differed from Gnadhian though. Explaining his philosophical and scientific attitude concerning other social theories Roy laid down, "I am not a blind follower of anybody. I do not take anything for granted. Before I accept any doctrine, I submit it to a critical analysis, which is to test the consistency of its internal logic. If I find it self-contradictory, I have no hesitation in rejecting it however exalted may be the authority. But in the

1. *Ibid.*
2. **Roy, M.N.** Radical Humanism, **Eastern Economic Pamphelets, No. 14, pp. 5**

process of the analytical examination, the behaviour of certain persons, or a certain doctrine may reveal certain positive features, which must be retained and admired even when the claims of the person and the doctrine as whole, are to be rejected."[1]

As has been already pointed out, Radical humanism gives special status to science. The philosophy of Roy however, may be called integral. Laying down the principle twenty-one of radical humanism, Roy said, "Radicalism integrates science into social organisation and reconciles individuality with collective life; it gives to freedom a moral intellectual as well as a social content; it offers a comprehensive theory of social progress in which both the dialectics of economic determinism and dynamics of ideas find their due recognition; and it deduces from the same a method and a programme of social revolution in our time."[2] Against Marxism, Roy rejects economic determinism and dictatorship through he accepts materialism.

The foundation of the educational philosophy of M.N. Roy are rooted in Radical Humanism. Radical humanism is neither materialism nor idealism but a scientific philosophy insisting upon the freedom of the individual. The function of philosophy, according to M.N.Roy, "is to explain existence as a whole."[3] Distinguishing between the function of philosophy and science Roy said. "The function of science is to describe; that of philosophy is to explain. Therefore, philosophy is called the science of sciences."[4] Thus philosophy, according to Roy, should be based upon scientific foundation. According to him, "Modern scientific philosophy is decidedly opposed to any idealist doctrine."[5] Again, it is against mysticism. "Mysticism results from

---

1. **Roy, M.N., *Men I Met,* Lalwani publishing House, Delhi, 1968, p.p. 26-27.**
2. **Roy, M.N., *New Humanism,* p. 59.**
3. **Roy, M.N., *Science and Philosophy* (Calcutta : Renaissance Publishers, 1947), p. 31.**
4. ***Ibid.***
5. ***Ibid.* p. 34**

ignorance," said M.N. Roy. It implies an admission of defeat. Roy is against all brands of mysticism, metaphysical, logical or spiritual. According to him, "General laws of science have philosophical validity."[1] Science gradually explains philosophical problems. Scientific knowledge is the result of scientific method. These methods utilize experience and reason. Scientific investigation, according to Roy, "must placed ontology before epistemology."[2] In the world view of M.N. Roy being and becoming both are important. "Becoming is the essence of being."[3] The world, according to Roy is dynamic. Therefore it is becoming, change and evolution. Criticising absolute idealism, Roy said, "Absolute idealism is a double-edged sword. It throws matter out of the front-door only to let it in by the back-door."[4] Noumenon as well as phenomenon are projections of our consciousness. Consciousness is the soul of reality. Roy has condemned subjective approach to reality.

Materialistic Monism

The metaphysical theory of the educational philosophy of M.N. Roy may be called materialistic monism or monistic naturalism. While according the forme, matter is the only ultimate reality, according to later the ultimate reality is Nature. Thus the philosophy of M.N. Roy is monistic. As has been already pointed out, Roy considered dualism to be the greatest difficulty faced by the philosophers. On his part he presents a philosophical view which involves the latest findings of physical and social sciences. The values, according to Roy, cannot be derived from the facts. They are self-evident and no less objective than facts. The ultimate reality is Nature or Matter. From matter has gradually evolved life and from animal life has evolved man. Therefore, man according to Roy, is biological. The humanist ethics is evolutionary.

---

1. *Ibid.* p. 37
2. *Ibid.* p. 45
3. *Ibid.* p. 47
4. Roy, M.N., *New Humanism* (Calcutta : Renaissance Publishers Pvt. Ltd., 1961). p. 51.

AIMS OF EDUCATION

To Establish Humanist System

The aim of live is to live. Struggle for existence is the basic drive in organism. Thus Roy believes in Darwinian theory of evolution. The highest value in the human world is liberty. Our aim is to establish a social system, which finds maximum freedom for the individual. Value cannot exist apart form man. Knowledge, truth, liberty are meaningful only in human context.

Quest for Freedom and Search for Truth

Thus the worldview of M.N. Roy is man-centred. Man has the central position in cosmos. According to the rule 1 of Radical humanism, "Man is the archetype of society, co-operative social relationships contribute to develop individual potentialities. But the development of the individual is the measure of social progress."[1] Explaining social progress Roy laid down the second principle "Quest for freedom and search for truth constitute the basic urge of human progress."[2] Making liberty of man the basic search in progress Roy said, "The purpose of all rational human endeavour, individual as well as collective, is attainment of freedom, in ever increasing measure."[3]

The peculiar trait of man is his rationality. Man can make the world better with the help of science. Thought and environment interact. Real revolution requires full freedom of the individual. Therefore, Roy reject the economic interpretation of history advanced by Karl Marx. Man according to him, is not an economic being but a moral being. Intellectual and spiritual life are conditioned by instinct of reason. According to Roy, "The residue of humanness, therefore, is the biological heritage of reason. To put the same thing differently, human nature is not to believe, but to struggle for freedom and search for truth, the latter

---

1. *Ibid.*
2. *Ibid.* p.p. 51-52
3. Roy, M.N., *Reason, Romanticism and Revolution,* Vol. I, p. 23.

aspect manifesting itself in *homo sapiens*."[1] Morality is not directly derived from religion. Even the savage has a strong sense of good and bad. The quest for freedom distinguishes man from animals. Truth is a matter of human experience. Man's struggle for freedom is guided by his knowledge of nature. According to Roy, "The search for truth, therefore, is intimately associated with the quest of freedom as the essence of human nature."[2] This is the fundamental principle in the educational philosophy of M.N. Roy.

Manifestation of Unmanifested Capacities

According to Roy there can be no other purpose of life than living. Thus human life aims at expression of human processes. Since human society is constituted by human being therefore its purpose is to serve the purposes of individuals. Thus human life itself is the aim of human collectivity. Since man has evolved out of the animal therefore the purpose of human life may be initially interpreted in biological terms. Struggle for existence is the first purpose of human beings. The human society makes the individual well versed in this study. The human reason contributes for the efficiency in this struggle for existence.

The aim of education is to manifest the unmanifested capacities of human individuals inherited as a biological organism. The reason has developed in the struggle for survival and the powers of judgement have evolved. This evolution has further led man to the moral level. The capacity of judgement is the basis of ethics and all moral values. Thus the struggle for survival together with conscious and rational efforts become the urge for liberty. The struggle for survival is waged in an environment. Efficiency in it requires all the instruments of struggle. The society is the outcome of man's urge to liberty since without it the individual alone could not face natural calamities. He needed the co-operation of others for hunting, agriculture and many other pursuits. It is hence that individuals combined to form society. Thus the only aim of society is to help the individual. Any social organisation, which is an

---

1. *Ibid.*, p. 32.
2. *Ibid.*, pp. 51-52.

impediment to the free growth of the individual, frustrates the very purpose for which it has been created. Therefore there is hardly any contradiction in social organisation and liberty of the individual. In fact there is hardly any problem in the relationship of the individual and collectivity. This problem is the result of the false notion that the collectivity is above the individual or that it has any purpose different from the purpose of its constituents. If it is understood that the collectivity has no purpose apart from the purpose of the individual the controversy never arises.

Individual Welfare

The above mentioned principle may be used for the interpretation of the aim of education. The first and foremost need of man is to maintain physical existence. But, gradually as the society became more and more complex, the intellectual, moral and spiritual needs manifested. Man is the representative of society and requires social relationships for the development of individual capacities. The individual development is the criterion of social development since the individual is prior to collectivity. The moral traits like liberty, progress, welfare etc., are first achieved by the individuals. In the end any welfare is ultimately individual welfare. There is no separate welfare of the collectivity. In the words of Roy, "Collective well-being is a function of the well-being of individuals."[1]

Meaning of Liberty

Explaining liberty as the aim of education Roy said, "The purpose of all rational human endeavour, individual as well as collective, is attainment of freedom in ever increasing measure. Freedom is progressive disappearance of all restrictions on the unfolding of the potentialities of individuals, as human beings, and not as cogs in the wheels of a mechanised social organism."[2] According to the third principle of democracy the freedom of the individual is the only aim of the collectivity of the state. As has

1. **Roy, M.N., *Radical Humanism*, p. 17.**
2. ***Ibid.***

been already pointed out, reason is the fundamental characteristic of human nature. A long with reason man has been endowed with emotions. The human will is the most potent element in human society. It is the determinant of human history. Marxist economic interpretation of history is born out of dualism. It is true that history is a determined process but the factors determining it are not one but many, of which human will is an important factor. Therefore, according to the third principle of radical humanism the only purpose of the collectivity and the state is the liberty of the individual. It is clear that man's freedom is the highest moral standard according to radical humanist ethics. In the words of M.N. Roy, "The axiology of Radical Humanism deduces all values from the supreme value of life, because the urge for freedom is the essence of human existence."[1] In the process of evolution, according to Roy, moral values have evolved out of the animal traits. Radical humanist ethics does not require any religious or trans-mundance basis. In the words of Roy, "To be moral, one needs only to be human; it is not necessary to go in search of divine or mystic-metaphysical sanction. Humanist morality is evolutionary."[2]

Need Based Values

Humanist educational values have evolved out of human needs. Besides liberty Roy refers to other values. To quote his own word, "The hierarchy of humanist axiology, thus, is freedom, Knowledge, truth. They are no autonomous; they are interrelated, logically as well as ontologically."[3] Thus liberty and goodness are intimately related. So are related knowledge and virtue. Reminding the ancient Greek Socratic ethics Roy said, "Therefore, freedom cannot be attained by immoral means, nor can an enlightened man be a liar."[4]

1. *Ibid.*
2. *Ibid.*
3. Roy M.N., *New Humanism* (Calcutta : Renaissance Publishers, 1961), p. 53.
4. Roy, M.N., *Politics. Power and Parties,* p. 72.

Value of Reason

Reason, according to Roy is the basic trait of human being. This reason is he determinant of history as well as economics. Revolution according to Roy requires economic reorganisation for the provision of maximum liberty to everyone. To quote his words, "For creating a new world of freedom, revolution must go beyond an economic re-organisation of society. Freedom does not necessarily follow from the capture of political power in the name of the oppressed and exploited classes and abolition of private property in the means of production."[1] Again, a moral order will result from a rationally organised society, because, viewed in the context of his rise out of the background of a harmonious physical Universe, man is essentially rational and therefore moral. Education fulfills the rational desire for harmonious and mutually beneficial social relations.

MEANS OF EDUCATION

Encouragement of Reason

In his work, *Politics, Power and Parties,* M.N. Roy has elaborated his educational thought. Like : Plate he insists that no ideal republic can be established in the absence of educated persons. According to him so long as the individuals are unable to distinguish between right and wrong no good society can be established. In other words, an ideal society is constituted by rational men and women. This rationality is a characteristic found everywhere. According to Roy it is scientific knowledge that every human being possesses reason and rational thought, a characteristic of intelligence, a trait of human nature.[2] Therefore what is required is to encourage reason in man. This is possible only through education. According to Roy those who want to put democracy in practice should feel that democracy is impossible without education.[3]

---

1. *Ibid.*, p. 58.
2. *Ibid.*
3. *Ibid.*, p. 59.

Freedom from Compulsions

Here education does not mean literacy nor compulsory primary education. Roy is against any compulsion in education because compulsion is against liberty. Criticising the prevalent system of education, Roy pointed out that what is required is a different type of education. An education, which seeks to maintain the *status quo,* is not suitable for making the community conscious of its inherent powers. Education should help men and women to think rationally and to decide themselves, about the problems to be solved. Roy lamented that no government provides such an education. Almost all the government in the world aim at creating mental slavery through education. The state governed education, teaches the masses to sing songs of patriotism to salute the national flag, to study the history edited by government, and to work collectively to achieve success of the state. Therefore, the demand of the state-governed education is suicidal in backward and underdeveloped countries. No national education provided by government in any country is the true democratic education.

TYPES OF EDUCATION

Education of Citizenship

In his radical social thought Roy has considered education the foundation for democracy since it is only through it that rational individual may be created. Clarifying the aim of his new system of education Roy pointed out that believing in the modern scientific knowledge that man is basically rational; we will attempt to arouse rationality of all the citizens. This is the aim of education.[31] Once this process of education is started, other steps may be taken for the establishment of democracy because every such steps requires rational judgement. According to M.N. Roy education of the citizens and the gradual building up of a political organization from below is the only guarantee against the dangers of party system.[2] Further clarifying this guarantee Roy pointed out that scientific education will make people self-dependent, rational

1. *Ibid.,* p. 85.
2. *Ibid.,* p. 101.

and distinctive and therefore they will not be further hypnotized for any evil purpose. It will give birth to a new institutional organisation, which will be a guarantee against exploitation by an individual or a group of individuals.[1]

Political Education

Thus the expansion of education will make the citizen oppose all sorts of exploitation by an individual or a group. In the present situation victory in elections is not the proof of a party of being democratic since most of the voters are uneducated and cannot oppose the political party in power. It is only through education that the public will rise to oppose any immoral or inadequate political party and may not allow it to come in power again. Thus humanist politics is ultimately base upon education.

Education of Freedom

Explaining his democratic new educational system Roy pointed out that as a precondition of democracy education is not primary education nor is it traditional higher or scientific education. It is the process of raising the intellectual and cultural level of the mass.[2] Therefore, so long as the moral and cultural level of the people does not rise, the aim of education is not realised. The education provided in so-called parliamentary democracies is not the education of freedom but an education of slavery. These states provide compulsory free primary education to create citizens supporting the state and not free individuals. According to M.N. Roy, new humanism expresses a new viewpoint toward the problems of education, which suggests that given opportunity every human being has the capacity to develop his abilities to an ultimate extent.[3] According to new humanism it is not in the interest of the government or the state to curb the citizen's freedom to grow their capacities because ultimately a welfare state aims at making its citizens more and more free. The aim of education is not merely to provide three R's but to create

1. *Ibid.*
2. *Ibid.*, p. 118.
3. *Ibid.*, p. 119.

among the people a consciousness towards humanity, coconsciousness towards its right to be human beings and consciousness of its excellence and dignity. The purpose of education is to help them in utilising their reason in this thinking.[1] It is only such an education, which may create true democracy not only in a nation but in the whole world. This educational system however, as has been already pointed out, will be run not by the government but by the public itself.

EDUCATION FOR DIFFERENT SECTIONS OF SOCIETY

According to M.N. Roy the basic difficulty with the present society is the suppression of individual freedom. Social justice requires that all individuals must be free and equal. Roy is not satisfied by merely establishing political democracy. He pleads for economic social democracy. The essential conditions of success of democracy according to him is the creation of free individuals. This can be done by means of education. This education must be equally available to all the sections of society. Roy condemns the ancient Indian distinction between male and female, Brahmin and Shudra regarding the facility of education, his spiritualism is anti-traditionalism. Therefore he strongly condemns any distinction between different sections of society based upon political, Economic or social considerations. The aims and ideals of education can be achieved only be realisation of human values and the establishment of a humanist society. The sole aim of the state is to help in the achievement of this aim. Therefore, the state must arrange for the education of different sections of society. This requires additional help to backward sections since they are lagging behind other sections of society. During Roy's time sufficient facility of education was not available to females and backward classes in India. Along with most of his contemporary Indian philosophers of education Roy raised his voice against this inequality. The credit of the vast expansion of education among these sections of Indian society goes as much to Roy as to other contemporary Indian philosophers of education.

❑❑❑

1. *Ibid.*, p. 121.

GREATEST WORKS OF GREAT EDUCATIONISTS

Plato	The Republic
Aristotle	Politics
Ignatius Loyola	Constitutions
John Amos Comenius	The Great Didactic
John Locke	Some Thoughts concerning Education.
J.H. Pertalozzi	How Gertnide Teaches Her Children
Jean Jacques Rousseau	Emile
John Friedrich Herbert	Minor Pedagogical Works
Friedrich August Froebel	The Education of Man
Maria Montessori	The Advanced Mantessori Method
John Dewey	Democracy and Education
Vivekananda	Complete works Vols I, II, III, IV and V
Sri Aurbindo	A system of National Education
M.K. Gandhi	Basic Education
R. N. Tagore	Shiksha
S. Radhakrishnan	Education, Politics and War
M. N. Roy	Politics, Power and Parties